A PHILOSOPHY OF THE CHRISTIAN RELIGION

A PHILOSOPHY OF THE CHRISTIAN RELIGION

NANCEY MURPHY

WESTMINSTER
JOHN KNOX PRESS
LOUISVILLE · KENTUCKY

First published in Great Britain in 2018
as *A Philosophy of the Christian Religion for the Twenty-First Century*
by Society for Promoting Christian Knowledge
36 Causton Street
London SW1P 4ST
www.spck.org.uk

Published in the United States of America in 2018 by
Westminster John Knox Press
100 Witherspoon Street
Louisville, KY 40202

18 19 20 21 22 23 24 25 26 27—10 9 8 7 6 5 4 3 2 1

The author and publisher have made every effort to ensure that the external website and email addresses included in this book are correct and up to date at the time of going to press. The author and publisher are not responsible for the content, quality, or continuing accessibility of the sites.

Scripture quotations marked nrsv are from the New Revised Standard Version of the Bible, copyright © 1989 by the Division of Christian Education of the National Council of the Churches of Christ in the USA. Used by permission. All rights reserved.

Quotations marked rsv are from the Revised Standard Version of the Bible, copyright © 1946, 1952 and 1971 by the Division of Christian Education of the National Council of the Churches of Christ in the USA. Used by permission. All rights reserved.

Cover design by Allison Taylor

Library of Congress Cataloging-in-Publication Data

Names: Murphy, Nancey C., author.
Title: A philosophy of the Christian religion / Nancey Murphy.
Description: Louisville, KY : Westminster John Knox Press, 2018. | Originally published: London : Society for Promoting Christian Knowledge, 2018. | Includes bibliographical references and index. |
Identifiers: LCCN 2018038196 (print) | LCCN 2018039357 (ebook) | ISBN 9781611649284 (ebk.) | ISBN 9780664263287 (pbk. : alk. paper)
Subjects: LCSH: Christian philosophy. | Christianity--Philosophy.
Classification: LCC BR100 (ebook) | LCC BR100 .M8155 2018 (print) | DDC 230.01--dc23
LC record available at https://lccn.loc.gov/2018038196

To my late husband, James Wm. McClendon, Jr.
And to so many who have taught me so much:
Warren S. Brown
George F. R. Ellis
Paul K. Feyerabend
Alasdair MacIntyre
Robert John Russell

Contents

Part II
CRISES IN MODERN CHRISTIANITY

Contents

Contents

Figures

Preface

Prefaces seem to serve a variety of purposes; this one is to express gratitude to the many people who helped to bring this book into being.

First are my students: most professors know that one can teach the same material either to a sullen and resistant class or to one whose students are predominantly interested and excited to learn. Nearly all of my classes in my twenty-five years at Fuller Seminary were of the second sort. These students' enthusiasm has always brought out the best in me.

I thank Dr. Philip Law, Publishing Director at SPCK. I do not believe that it is possible to write a text on religion in general, and I do not have a gift for explaining philosophical concepts to undergraduates. Instead, he offered me a chance to write largely for Christian seminarians—the level at which I had (largely) been teaching. I realized that this was an opportunity to sum up the work I had been doing and to bring it up to date.

I also thank Dr. Robert Ratcliff, Executive Editor at Westminster John Knox Press, for publishing the US version of the book. Robert has been a friend for many years whom I met when he was assisting my husband, James McClendon, in finishing his books during the last years of his life.

Dr. Rima Devereux, Project/Commissioning Editor, has provided advice and quick and patient answers to numerous questions.

I cannot give enough thanks to theology PhD student Viktor Toth. Our collaboration began with his offering, as an experienced graphic artist, to provide professional renderings of the figures. This led to productive discussions about the character of the drawings based on his knowledge of the tradition. There were many smaller helps as well, as after I had spent two hours trying to make my new software do things, he would fix the problem in two seconds. Finally, he likes to make indices. After doing so many myself (inexpertly), I hope he will teach me his more efficient procedure.

There is a group of women who deserve my thanks. These have helped me raise my son, Andre Fedán, especially Gloria, whose name Andre pronounced "Lola." A series of lovely women have helped care for my home, giving me an extra day to write, especially Kimiko, Lydia, and Irma. They have been not only professional helpers but also friends over the years.

All of you have made this book a possibility. To you all, thank you!

Nancey Murphy
Altadena, CA

Abbreviations

Camb. Dict.	*The Cambridge Dictionary of Philosophy*, 2nd edition, ed. Robert Audi (Cambridge: Cambridge University Press, 2007); references in text are to 1st edition (1995).
Macmillan	*The Encyclopedia of Philosophy*, 8 vols., ed. Paul Edwards (London and New York: Macmillan, 1967); references in text are from 1972 reprint, two vols. per book.
Oxford Companion	*The Oxford Companion to Christian Thought*, ed. Adrian Hastings et al. (Oxford: Oxford University Press, 2000).
Routledge	*Routledge Encyclopedia of Philosophy*, 10 vols., ed. Edward Craig (London: Routledge, 1998).
Stanford	*Stanford Encyclopedia of Philosophy*, ed. Edward N. Zalta. Available at https://plato.stanford.edu/.

Introduction

The title of this book, *A Philosophy of the Christian Religion for the Twenty-First Century*,[1] is meant to signal two things: First, that there are good reasons, now, for recognizing the impossibility of writing a single book about religion in general. Second, that there have been some significant changes in philosophical conceptions over time. These can make problems that may, on the surface, appear to have been the same over centuries turn out, in fact, to be quite different in our own day.

Previously, and even in many cases today, typical texts in philosophy of religion begin with definitions of religion, of philosophy, and of philosophy of religion. However, an important change has occurred in the study of religion. There have been attempts beginning two centuries ago to provide a definition of religion. The question has been asked: What are the essential features that all religions share, and that distinguish them from other aspects of culture? And if scholars disagree about these essential features, how could they go about settling their disagreements? So, more recently, the quest has been abandoned because these questions have been debated by great scholars for generations and no satisfactory conclusions have been reached.

Philosopher Ludwig Wittgenstein (1889–1951) has provided a helpful way of understanding many of our important concepts: they apply not to sets of things that all have the same essential features, but rather to sets of things that resemble one another in the way members of families usually do. He calls the latter *family* concepts, and this is quite relevant to the problem of defining religion. As David Stewart (b.1938) writes:

> Many religious traditions are thoroughly bound up with cultic and ritual practice, but others are not. Some religions are tied to a priesthood, but this is not true of all. Divine revelation plays an important role in some traditions, but the relative importance of revelation in contrast to what can be known by reason alone is itself often a matter of disagreement.[2]

In any case, because this text is intended primarily to address a Christian audience, no definition of religion in general would need to be provided. We can notice the close family resemblances between Christianity and its nearest kin (Judaism and Islam) and more sketchy resemblances to those more distant.

---

[1] Title of the original UK edition.
[2] David Stewart, *Exploring the Philosophy of Religion*, 5th ed. (Upper Saddle River, NJ: Prentice-Hall, 2001), 1.

1

But can we then provide an account of the essence of Christianity itself? This also has been tried (particularly since the nineteenth century) and is now judged to have failed. Students pursuing a seminary or divinity degree may note that it is in fact the task of the entire curriculum to attempt to answer this question, and denominational differences may provide interestingly different answers.

A second feature of the title of this book is to do justice to one of the major developments of the entire modern period; this has been the gradual recognition in various disciplines of the historical conditioning of knowledge. This is not just to say the obvious—that each discipline has a history; it is rather to make the deeper (and I think more interesting) claim that there has been a succession of worldviews and that each worldview has traded in concepts that do not always translate precisely into the concepts of the others.[3]

I was privileged to be studying philosophy of science at the University of California at Berkeley in the 1970s, when Thomas Kuhn's (1922–96) book, *The Structure of Scientific Revolutions,* was a central focus of attention.[4] He claimed that scientific textbooks were misleading because they represented the history of science as a gradual accumulation of facts and development of theories. In contrast, Kuhn pointed out that there have been radical breaks in the history of science, after which the same terms may be used, but they reflect a radically new conception of the nature of reality. For example, we translate the Latin *materia* as "matter," but in the Aristotelian–Thomist system it stands for omnipresent neutral stuff, and the important questions had to do with how different qualities were imposed on it to form different bodies or substances. In early modern physics, "matter" instead referred to tiny particles whose characteristics (especially motions) produced the observable features of bodies.

Kuhn told his students when reading scientific texts from the past, especially the long-respected ones, to

> look first for the apparent absurdities in the text and ask yourself how a sensible person could have written them. When you find an answer . . . then you may find that more central passages, ones you previously thought you understood, have changed their meaning.[5]

---

[3] This text has the limitation of considering the development of Christianity in the West, and it would take a number of books to survey the developments in other parts of the world, where, again, conceptual incongruity is to be expected.

[4] Thomas S. Kuhn, *The Structure of Scientific Revolutions,* 2nd enlarged ed. (Chicago: University of Chicago Press, [1962] 1970).

[5] Thomas S. Kuhn, *The Essential Tension: Selected Studies in Scientific Tradition and Change* (Chicago and London: University of Chicago Press, 1977), xii.

And so it becomes possible to recognize that other authors are working with different conceptions of the nature of reality and knowledge. This, itself, was a radical shift during the 1970s in our concept of scientific knowledge.

After Berkeley, I went to the Graduate Theological Union for a second doctorate, one in theology.[6] Scientists, of course, are supposed to be the intellectual ground-breakers, with theologians clinging to the past. So I was surprised and delighted to find that historical consciousness had begun in biblical studies and history of doctrine already in the second half of the eighteenth century. Scholars had become increasingly aware of "apparent absurdities" in Scripture and had asked how "a sensible person could have written them." Theologian Hans Frei (1922–88) says of some interpreters that neither of two options seemed palatable: that the biblical authors "had carefully hidden their actual intentions . . . or they hadn't even realized what they were writing about." Thus, they concluded that to do the authors justice,

> they must be understood from within their own cultural context, and not that of modernity. The understanding appropriate to the authors and their writing is therefore historical, in a relatively new sense of the word. Rather than inquiring simply into what had taken place (though this was also involved), "historical understanding" sought to understand how the ancient writers had experienced and thought, in their own distinctive, culturally or historically conditioned consciousness.[7]

The gradual change reflecting the recognition of different worldviews and histories can be glimpsed simply by looking at the titles of textbooks. Thus, in 1963 John Hick (1922–2012) began his text in philosophy of religion as follows: "Many of the problems of philosophy are of such broad relevance to human concerns . . . that they are, in one form or another, *perennially* present,"[8] and in 1970 Ninian Smart (1927–2001) called his text **The** *Philosophy of Religion.*[9] Earlier texts (and some standard ones still today) cover closely overlapping lists of topics: the nature of God; arguments for the existence of God; religious experience; faith and reason; the problem of evil; divine action or miracles; life after death; religious language; religious pluralism; the relation of God to morality. A number of texts are anthologies—collections of readings addressing some or all of these topics—and

---

[6] Notice that in this text I talk about myself. In recent years, this would not have been acceptable in scholarly work. In fact, we used all sorts of awkward grammar to avoid ever using the word "I": "This dissertation argues that . . ." This homely fact about academic style in itself reflects the rejection of the ahistoricism of modern thought.

[7] Hans W. Frei, *The Eclipse of Biblical Narrative: A Study in Eighteenth and Nineteenth Century Hermeneutics* (New Haven, CT and London: Yale University Press, 1974), 63.

[8] John Hick, *Philosophy of Religion* (Englewood Cliffs, NJ: Prentice-Hall, 1963), 1. (My italics.)

[9] Ninian Smart, *The Philosophy of Religion* (New York: Oxford University Press, 1970). (My boldface type.)

often including in the same sections readings from Plato (427–347 BC) to the present.

However, it is now becoming more widely recognized that philosophy of religion is not a single discipline, reaching back to ancient times, and dealing largely with perennial problems arising from any or all religions. Rather, there are particular problems, arising in various time periods, from reflections on particular religions. This is represented in titles such as Paula Sue Anderson's (1955–2017) text, *A Feminist Philosophy of Religion*,[10] and David Cheetham (b.1969) and Rolfe King's (b.1959) *Contemporary Practice and Method in the Philosophy of Religion: New Essays*, which aims to engage individually a variety of religious traditions as well as a variety of philosophical perspectives.[11] (The title of the present book, of course, is wildly optimistic in that it suggests that what I write today could still be a definitive contribution to the field for an entire century!)

One of the last disciplines to recognize significant conceptual changes in its subject matter has been philosophy, and as with all intellectual changes, the recognition has not been instantaneous. Contemporary philosopher Alasdair MacIntyre (b.1929) writes:

> Philosophers have often been prepared to acknowledge this historical character in respect of scientific theories; but they have usually wanted to exempt their own thinking from the same historicity . . . [T]he history of epistemology . . . is usually written as though . . . it were not a narrative.[12]

MacIntyre attributes his ability to recognize different conceptual schemes in philosophy, first, to his having grown up in a Gaelic oral culture while being educated in the Scottish school system. Second, at university he studied classics and puzzled over the problem of rendering Greek philosophy into either English or Gaelic. "I had my first inklings that different languages as used by different societies may embody different and rival conceptual schemes, and that translation from one such language to another . . . may not always be possible."[13]

The point of the foregoing is that, during the past generation, philosophers of religion have begun to recognize that problems in different eras that are apparently

---

[10] Pamela Sue Anderson, *A Feminist Philosophy of Religion* (Oxford: Blackwell, 1998). (My boldface.)

[11] David Cheetham and Rolfe King, eds., *Contemporary Practice and Method in the Philosophy of Religion: New Essays* (London: Continuum, 2008).

[12] Alasdair C. MacIntyre, "Epistemological Crises, Dramatic Narrative, and the Philosophy of Science," *Monist* 60, no. 4 (October 1977): 453–72; reprinted in Gary Gutting, ed., *Paradigms and Revolutions: Applications and Appraisals of Thomas Kuhn's Philosophy of Science* (Notre Dame, IN: University of Notre Dame Press, 1980), 54–74; and in Stanley Hauerwas and L. Gregory Jones, eds., *Why Narrative: Readings in Narrative Theology* (Grand Rapids, MI: Eerdmans, 1989), 138–57 (141). Quotations are from the latter.

[13] Alasdair MacIntyre, "Nietzsche or Aristotle?" an interview with Giovanna Boradori in Boradori, ed., *The American Philosopher* (Chicago and London: Chicago University Press, 1994), 137–52 (141).

the same, when examined more closely in their contexts, may actually be quite different. A significant example is what has in the past been called *the* problem of free will. A careful look shows that there are actually a variety of problems that have fallen under this heading: Ancient Greek dramatists explored the role of fate. In the early Christian era, two problems arose: First, if God had predestined some humans to be saved, is this reconcilable with anyone's freely choosing to obey the will of God? The second problem is whether human freedom is reconcilable with divine foreknowledge. This topic is still hotly debated. Yet another problem, prominent in the behaviorist era, was the question of social or other environmental determinism. Today, challenges are taken to come from particular sciences: physics, genetics, or neurobiology.

Thus, readers will not be surprised to discover that the very nature of philosophy is up for debate. There are still philosophers in the Anglo-American tradition who would describe themselves as analytic philosophers, and believe that by analyzing the concepts that are essential to philosophy (*knowledge, truth, causation* . . .) they are capable of providing timeless insights into the nature of reality by means of non-empirical investigations. Jeffrey Stout (b.1950) suggests that a better term, in place of "conceptual analysis," would be "conceptual archaeology," the investigation of what such concepts entail in particular times and places.[14]

Two accounts of the nature of philosophy that attract me come from dueling philosophers in Britain. Both argued for different alternatives to the supposition that philosophy deals with perennial problems. Wittgenstein attempted to show that all philosophical problems arise from confusions about the workings of language, and should not be solved, but rather dissolved—that is, shown to be the consequences of a confusion. This text will follow his lead in some respects. However, a better model comes from Karl Popper (1902–94), who argued that to do philosophy (rather than to report on its history) is to be engaged in attempts to solve problems. Genuine philosophical problems, he claimed, are always rooted in urgent questions arising outside of philosophy, in mathematics, cosmology, politics, social life. Popper was particularly interested in those arising from science, but he recognized that some arise as well from religion.[15]

This text will focus primarily on the problems that have arisen within Christianity, beginning in the modern period—a few of which can be dissolved in Wittgensteinian fashion. In other cases, I report here on the current status of attempted solutions. The first problem may have arisen already in the minds of readers. If all knowledge (including Christian theology) is historically conditioned,

---

[14] Jeffrey Stout, *The Flight from Authority: Religion, Morality, and the Quest for Autonomy* (Notre Dame, IN: University of Notre Dame Press, 1981), 2, 8, 15.

[15] Karl R. Popper, "The Nature of Philosophical Problems and Their Roots in Science," *British Journal for the Philosophy of Science* 3 (1952): 124–56.

then does this not entail relativism, and in turn, that there is no truth? So we begin with the question of knowledge and its history. Thus, Part I sketches "a history of reason," and considers the various ways in which this history has related to the developing Christian Tradition. It ends with what I argue is the best account developed so far of the nature of human rationality. This account will be used to structure the remainder of the text, as well as to provide a means for evaluating responses to other recent and contemporary problems confronting Christian scholars. An important goal of Part I will be to argue that the fact of historical change in knowledge does not entail that there is no knowledge at all.

As we shall see in Part I, philosophy has become less of a self-sufficient discipline (all about everything) and more of a second-order discipline that investigates problems in first-order disciplines such as science, history, logic, and, especially for our interests, religion and Christian theology. Thus, while I hope that this book attracts students of all levels, it will be most meaningful for those who already have some grasp of the *content* of the Christian Tradition itself, since I shall be reflecting on intellectual problems that have already "Popped" up (cf. Popper) in the minds of Christian students and scholars.

This last sentence above is important: many students have little or no background in philosophy and face a philosophy of religion (or philosophical theology) course with trepidation. However, from my years of teaching in a seminary, I know that nearly all of my students have already been *doing* philosophy of religion, but usually without recognizing it; they have been striving to think through questions and intellectual problems with which their Christian faith confronts them. My hope is to have captured many of these problems in this text: Is it rational to be a Christian? Can Christianity be reconciled with science? What are humans, and what happens to them after death (including those who are not Christian)? How can a good God be reconciled with so much evil and suffering? See the Contents and the Overview of Part II of the text for a more detailed map of the territory to be covered.

Part I

A BRIEF HISTORY OF REASON

Overview of Part I: A brief history of reason

A frequent topic covered in philosophy of religion is "faith and reason." It constitutes a chapter in some texts; in others, it could be considered the main topic of the book. Yet it is too slippery to be considered to be a single, "perennial" problem. One prominent version has been the relation between the Christian belief system and other worldviews of the times. In Colossians, Christians are warned to make sure "that no one takes you captive through philosophy and empty deceit, according to human tradition, according to the elemental spirits of the universe, and not according to Christ" (Col. 2.8 NRSV). And indeed, the development of theology in the first centuries of the church involved careful reflection on various philosophies and competing religions of the time. Neoplatonism (to be described below) came largely to be seen as an ally, the dualistic Gnostic religious movements as enemies.

Another important version of the issue is the question of the extent to which patterns of reasoning whose sources lie outside of Christianity could *or should* be used in support of Christian claims. Here again, "faith" refers to the content of the Christian belief system. There has been significant debate about the extent to which Paul used conventional argument forms developed by ancient philosophers. In the late Middle Ages, Thomas Aquinas (1225–74) showed that Aristotelian reasoning could be used to argue for the truth of certain parts of theology, later called natural theology, but maintained that much of it depended on revelation. As accounts of the nature of reasoning have developed from the Middle Ages up to the present, scholars have continued to debate the relevance and value of new developments for showing the rationality of the Christian worldview.

In the modern era, a third version of the problem of faith and reason emerged. Due to the Reformation emphasis on "faith alone," the act of believing (of *having* faith) has come to be contrasted, for some, with accepting claims on the basis of evidence, or of reason more broadly understood. Thus, the question has arisen of whether it is necessary or even appropriate to test Christian beliefs against external standards of rationality.

Diogenes Allen (1932–2013) writes that the "two main sources of Christian theology are the Bible and Hellenic culture, especially Greek philosophy."[1] Looking at the history of Christianity over time, we might say, very roughly, that during the ancient period Christian theology came to be more and more influenced by Greek philosophies, so that by the beginning of the Middle Ages (which I shall date somewhat arbitrarily with the death of Augustine in 430) the two streams

---

[1] Diogenes Allen, *Philosophy for Understanding Theology* (Atlanta: John Knox Press, 1985), 1.

of thought had become inextricable. Again, speaking roughly, the beginning of the modern era (in the seventeenth century) marked the beginning of the separation of Christianity from an increasingly secular worldview—what I shall call a competing "Naturalist Tradition." Therefore, it is tempting to represent the history of thought in the West by an hourglass-shaped figure, with the Hebraic and Greek strands gradually converging, and then, in modern times, philosophy and the empirical sciences branching off (Figure 1).

However, a better image for the development of Christian thought in relation to the reasoning of the times might be a tree, with various roots tangling together and flowing to a single trunk, and farther along, with various branches, and then more streams of thought branching off again (Figure 2). The simpler hourglass shape correctly represents the fact that philosophy and theology simply cannot be understood apart from one another in the medieval period. Yet the Hebraic strand is itself complex, and by the time of Jesus it had incorporated a variety of

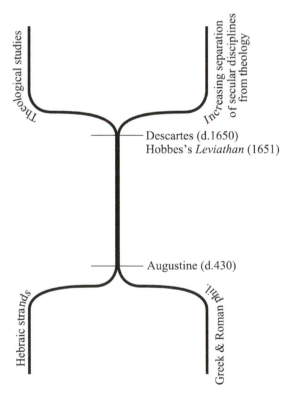

Figure 1 A simplistic "hourglass" figure to represent the merging of ancient and medieval Christianity with philosophy (by 430) and the beginning of the split between theology and secular thought in modernity (c.1630 with the publication of Galileo's *Dialogues*)

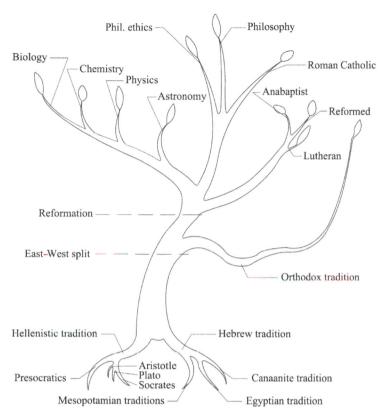

Figure 2 A more realistic "tree" figure to represent the large number of "roots" of the Medieval Synthesis, and its many branches, religious, scientific, and philosophical

influences. Thanks to source criticism, it is possible to determine earlier and later points of view in the Old Testament (OT); and by comparison with the writings of other cultures of the times, to discern their influences in the texts. To a more limited extent, New Testament (NT) authors can be seen to represent different viewpoints.

There had already been influences of Greek philosophy on Hebraic thought by Jesus' day. The fact that NT authors used the Greek translation of the Hebrew Bible, the Septuagint (thought to have been completed around 250 BC), is important in that the Greek *vocabulary* introduced conceptual changes wherever there were no exact equivalents to the Hebrew terms.[2] There have been arguments about whether parts of the NT, such as the Gospel of John and Paul's letters, were

---

[2] An important example of this will be seen in Chapter 9, on the development of the concept of an immortal soul and its later rejection.

influenced by Greek philosophy; the current consensus appears to be that they were. The intentional adoption of Greek and Roman philosophies for the purposes of apologetics and the development of theology was well underway by the end of the second century.

Chapter 1 will provide a sketchy history of the flowing together of streams of thought in the ancient and medieval periods, only bringing out some of the more interesting twists and turns in the interactions between theology and philosophy. Our primary examples will be Platonic influences in Augustine's theories of knowledge and truth, and Thomas's reconciliation of the Augustinian theological tradition with newly available works by Aristotle. As with the biblical tradition, Platonic thought is particularly difficult to understand without some knowledge of the earlier streams flowing into it.

Chapter 2 will recount some of the ways in which the demise of Thomas's synthesis created problems for understanding the rational status of and appropriate methods for theology, while Chapter 3 traces further developments in philosophical accounts of reasoning, along with their consequences for philosophy of religion.

Chapter 4 ends Part I, offering an account of what I judge to be the best understanding of the nature of human reasoning described to date—that of Alasdair MacIntyre. This chapter is something of a high point of the text, as it will be the understanding of rationality that informs the rest of the book.

1

Ancient and medieval ways of knowing the divine

1 Introduction

The purpose of this chapter, as noted in the Overview, is to consider ways in which earlier Christian teaching interacted with reason, understood both in the sense of methods of reasoning and in the sense of bodies of thought created by using those methods. We focus here on four figures. The two philosophers who had the greatest impact on Christian thought in the ancient and medieval periods were Plato and his student Aristotle (384–322 BC). The two theologians who did the most to systematize theology and to reconcile their theology with the philosophies of their day were Augustine (AD 354–430), whose influences were largely Platonic, and Thomas Aquinas, who reconciled the Augustinian theological tradition with the works of Aristotle.

This chapter is not intended as historical exposition for its own sake, but rather to set the stage for later discussions by, first, illuminating Augustine's peculiar (in the eyes of many contemporary readers) understanding of truth. While this theory of truth itself may not be well known, the association of truth with God still haunts Christian thought. Second, we shall need an account of Thomas's synthesis of Aristotelian and Christian thought (the complete replacement of which occupied the whole of the modern period). In the process, we shall see that philosophical concepts such as *reality*, *reason*, and *truth*, which have so often been thought to be universal and unvarying, do need to be understood in their historical contexts.

To many contemporary readers, Plato's thinking will be unintelligible, not in the sense that the English translations are unreadable (Plato wrote beautifully, in dialogue form), but rather in the sense that one cannot imagine *why* he would think what he did. So section 2 will begin with some of the history of Greek thought preceding Plato—some of the tributaries that flowed into this powerful stream of thought, which has been influential from his day to our own.

The study of Plato and his background will set the stage for an account of Augustine's theory of knowledge. But after Augustine we will backtrack historically to consider Aristotle's work, focusing as narrowly as possible on his understanding of rationality. This is appropriate for the purposes of the present chapter because Aristotle's influence became significant primarily in the late Middle Ages.

The interesting twists in this story will be, first, the way Augustine's theology led him to revise Plato's theory of knowledge, and, second, the way in which Augustine's Platonized theory of knowledge and truth governed Thomas's appropriation of Aristotelian rationality.

2 Before Plato

One problem in writing intellectual history is that wherever one begins, it is difficult to understand the thought of the era in question without knowing what came before. This is particularly true of Plato. I offer here not the usual attempt at "broad brush-strokes," but rather a few *narrow* strokes that have done the most to make Plato's thinking intelligible to me, and that, I hope, will do so for my readers. The earlier strand will be an account of the shift that occurred from the archaic Greek thought of the Homeric era (beginning ninth or eighth centuries) to that of the Presocratic philosophers (seventh through fifth centuries). The other will be to trace the influences of one Presocratic, Pythagoras (*c.*570–*c.*500), on Plato and his followers.

2.1 From much knowing to true knowledge

Here I follow philosopher of science Paul Feyerabend (1924–94) in his reconstruction of archaic Greek thought.[1] Our interest will be in the different understandings of knowledge before and after the shift to the Presocratics, but we need to begin with an account of the surprisingly different *objects* that make up each of these worlds.

Feyerabend argues that objects for inhabitants of the archaic world are "paratactic aggregates."[2] Here an entity, for example a human being, is simply the sum of its parts, with each part given equal importance: head, trunk, arms, legs. Archaic Greek, in fact, had no word for the whole—there is no single word for "body." Likewise, the word for "soul" refers to an aggregate of "mental" events, not initiated by an autonomous I, but coming from the outside—including from the gods.[3]

Feyerabend's evidence for objects as paratactic aggregates comes primarily from his study of the forms of the Homeric poetry and the "frontal" art style (which the Greeks shared with a number of other ancient cultures). In both drawing and writing, representation depends on making verbal or visual lists of stylized parts added together, whether these be parts of things or parts of actions. For example,

---

[1] Paul K. Feyerabend, *Against Method* (London: New Left Books, 1975). Note that later editions include revisions, so pagination is different.

[2] Feyerabend, *Against Method*, 233.

[3] Feyerabend, *Against Method*, 243.

in a scene showing a kid being eaten by a lion, "the lion looks ferocious, the kid looks peaceful, and the act of swallowing is simply *tacked on* to the presentation of what a lion *is* and what a kid *is*."[4]

Closely related to this conception of the make-up of reality is the concept of knowledge that lasted up through the writings of Thales (*c.*625–*c.*547 BC). Knowledge was not thought of in terms of depth of understanding, but only in terms of more or less quantity. Quantity of knowledge comes simply from exposure to many parts of the world; there is no essence to be grasped behind appearances. In fact, there are no appearances of things in this world; there are simply the things themselves. It is exactly at this point that the contrast between archaic and later Greek thought can best be apprehended. The new cosmology distinguished between much knowing and true knowledge. True knowledge is not of the world of appearances, but rather of the true world that "lies behind" appearances and is dimly reflected in them. Objects now are imperceptible essences underlying a multitude of appearances.

Feyerabend does not provide an account of what drove the change to a worldview allowing for a distinction between appearance and reality; however, Alasdair MacIntyre spells out in detail the collapse of the archaic worldview as represented in the failure of its moral language. For the archaic Greeks (as well as for other "heroic" societies), every individual has a given role and status in a highly determinate system of roles and statuses, particularly the household and the kinship group. There simply is no way of raising the question of whether one ought to fulfill the duties associated with one's roles; to be virtuous *is* to fulfill these roles in an excellent manner.[5]

The cultural factors calling this understanding of morality into question were undoubtedly many, but the tragic plays of Sophocles (*c.*496–406) epitomize a central problem: in the more complex social orders that had emerged by that time, plural systems of roles and obligations make conflicting claims on one's behavior. For example, when Antigone's brother is killed as a traitor she is forced to choose between the family obligation of burying him and the obligation to obey the king's order not to bury traitors. Only now can the question arise, and it must arise, as to which is her *true* duty.

2.2 The Presocratic philosophers

The point of the preceding subsection has been to convey some sense of how the idea of knowledge shifted from that of a collection of things known to that of pursuit of some reality *behind* observations that would make sense of them all—organizing and especially prioritizing them. This was the quest of the Presocratic philosophers, whose lives span the seventh through the fifth centuries BC. We know

---

[4] Feyerabend, *Against Method*, 233.
[5] Alasdair MacIntyre, *After Virtue: A Study in Moral Theory*, 2nd enlarged ed. (Notre Dame, IN: University of Notre Dame Press, [1981] 1984), 122–3.

of over a dozen of these, beginning with Thales (*c.*625–547) and ending with Democritus (*c.*460–360). These early philosophers spoke dialects of Greek; they would have been familiar with the poetry of Homer; and would have been brought up to worship the Greek gods. These were not philosophers in the modern sense; they were also early scientists, and several of them were religious leaders.

Wallace Matson (1921–2012) attributes the beginning of this movement and its lasting importance to the Ionians (Thales and Anaximander) having been unique among the peoples of the world in emancipating themselves from myth- ological explanations.[6] However, rejection of the gods of Greek mythology is not a rejection of religion *per se*. And even if the whims of the gods are no longer taken to explain natural phenomena, this does not provide guidance for the *kind* of explanation to be used in their place.

In general, the Presocratics followed two different strategies: One approach, which seems intuitively plausible, is to ask what is the (physical) substance under- lying the various kinds of things encountered in the world. This was the approach taken by Thales, Anaximander, and Anaximenes; and later carried on by Aristotle in his postulation of "prime matter." Another was Democritus' claim that all things are made of atoms—the theory that became the starting point for modern physics. The second approach to understanding nature was through mathematics. We turn now to this line of thought, whose most influential representative was Pythagoras.

2.3 Pythagoreanism

Pythagoras was born on the island of Samos, off the coast of current-day Turkey. He apparently traveled widely, largely in search of religious enlightenment, but is credited with bringing Egyptian and Persian mathematics to Greece. He founded a school in southern Italy and initiated a movement that lasted for centuries. No writings of his survive, but his many followers preserved his teachings and elabo- rated upon them significantly. Thus, when I write of Pythagoras I may be includ- ing ideas that were not his but attributed to him later.[7]

Pythagoras believed that mathematics was the key to all knowledge; numerical relationships (ratios) were the archetypes of all physical forms. The universe itself was a great musical instrument resounding with divine mathematical harmonies.[8]

---

[6] Wallace I. Matson, *A New History of Philosophy*, 2 vols. (San Diego: Harcourt Brace Jovanovich, 1987), 1:17. There is a second, enlarged edition (Wadsworth: Belmont, CA, 2000); however I have used Matson's first edition so many times that I shall continue to use its pagination.

[7] All historical knowledge is to a greater or lesser extent uncertain. I shall dispense in what follows with qualifications such as "It is said that . . ." unless there are different positions on historical facts or interpretations that matter for our purposes in this text, or when the controversies are so significant that students of history simply need to know about them.

[8] Margaret Wertheim, *Pythagoras' Trousers: God, Physics, and the Gender Wars* (New York: Times Books, 1995), 10. The title of the book reflects the fact that Pythagoras chose to wear the trousers of Persian style rather than the typical long robes of the Greeks.

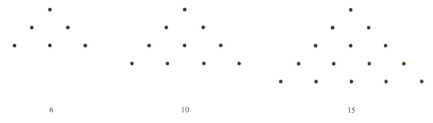

6	10	15

Figure 3 Shapes composed of dots to represent numbers 6, 10, and 15

Figure 4 The shape of dots representing the twins in the constellation Gemini

He replaced the Greek gods with immaterial number gods, who dwelt in a heavenly realm.

Margaret Wertheim (b.1958) has provided insights into how Pythagoras could have come to hold these peculiar ideas.[9] He recognized that numbers could be associated with shapes. For example, 6, 10, and 15 were called triangular numbers because six, ten, or fifteen dots could be arranged into equilateral triangles (Figure 3). Wertheim writes: "Pythagoras reasoned that if numbers had forms, then perhaps, reciprocally, all forms could be associated with numbers ... A simple example of associating a number of dots with a complex form could be seen in the constellations of the stars."[10] (Figure 4)

The association of numerical ratios with music came from the recognition that harmonies were produced in accordance with the ratios of the lengths of strings on

---

[9] It would be more precise to say that students of humanities will find them peculiar, since such intuitions are common among mathematicians and theoretical physicists.

[10] Wertheim, *Pythagoras*, 26–7.

instruments. The association of numbers with divinity is a bit more obscure, but the reasoning may go something like this: All physical things are subject to change and especially to decomposition. A common theme among ancient writers was to contrast the corruptible world with the eternal and incorruptible. Pythagoras recognized that whereas any group of, say, four things in nature would disintegrate, the number 4 itself could not. He therefore assigned these immortal "entities" to a realm transcending the physical world, for even the (supposedly) eternal heavenly bodies changed positions. Note that in contrast to contemporary use, in ancient and medieval thought "reality" admits of degrees. Whatever was highest in the hierarchy of beings must be entirely unchanging, as were the numbers, and whatever are the highest beings are also divine.

The Pythagoreans believed that moral concepts must also be associated with numbers. For example, 4 was the number of justice because, being the product of two equal numbers, it signified balance. They also believed that the human soul was associated with the great numerical pattern of the universe, and was reincarnated every 216 years, this number being associated with cyclical patterns.[11]

One student of Pythagoreanism needs to be mentioned. Parmenides (*c.*515 to after 450) rejected much of Pythagorean teaching and developed a philosophy of his own, set in verse, and represented as the product of divine revelation. He says that it is proper to learn everything: on the one hand, "well rounded truth," and on the other, "mortal beliefs in which there is no true assurance."[12] We see here an extremely important development in the ancient concept of reason, one which will last until the modern period—the sharp distinction between *episteme* (knowledge in the true sense of the word) and *doxa* (mere belief or opinion).

With these (somewhat) reasonable connections of ideas in mind, we now turn to Plato.

3 Plato

Plato was born in Athens in 428 or 427 and died 80 years later. His aristocratic birth resulted in his being concerned early on with politics. Two crucial events in his life were, first, the execution by the government in 399 of his friend and teacher Socrates (b.469). The second was his invitation in 387 to Syracuse, the dominant Greek city in Sicily, to meet there with the tyrant Dionysius II (*c.*397–*c.*345). Although the relationship soon became acrimonious, the trip was important because he had the opportunity to meet there with followers of Pythagoras. After returning from Syracuse, Plato established his famous Academy, which was intended to form future statesmen. The students participated in common worship

---

[11] Wertheim, *Pythagoras*, 27.
[12] Matson, *A New History*, 1:29.

and studied mathematics, astronomy and other physical sciences, music, and philosophy.

Plato's attempts to educate political leaders provided at least one of his motives for philosophical enquiry—they needed to know what a city should *really* be like, what the *true* good of political organization is. This quest led to the development of his theory of Forms or Ideas, to be explained below.[13]

Plato's dialogues are classified according to four periods in his life: early, transition, mature, and old age. In the early period, he largely reported and elaborated on Socrates' thought. These dialogues are primarily focused on the question of true virtue, which, as I noted above, was one of the problems precipitating the collapse of the Homeric cosmology. Plato uses the term *eidos* (idea) in this period, for example, in the *Euthyphro*, where Socrates asks Euthyphro to "explain the general idea which makes all pious things to be pious." Translators do not capitalize "idea" here because it is not yet a technical philosophical term. The early dialogues call into question common notions of virtue but do not end with positive answers.

The dialogues of the transition period were composed after Plato's return from Syracuse. Phillip Cary (b.1958) states that in the *Meno* "Socrates does a new, un-Socratic, Platonic thing": "he embarks on an inquiry that arrives in the end at the right answer."[14] "Socrates," by means of clever questioning, gets Meno's slave boy to produce an answer to a problem in geometry that he was not supposed to know. The question, then, is *how* the boy knew it, and Plato's conclusion is that somehow he already had the knowledge *within* him, in his soul, and only needed to be led to remember it. In the *Meno*, the explanation of how he came to have the knowledge in the first place is not satisfactory, but we see a likely Pythagorean influence: the soul learned what it knows in a past life. Yet this answer results in a regress: how did he learn it *then*?

It is not until the *Phaedrus* that Plato has an answer and, along with it, his doctrine of the Forms. Before any souls fell into the body they "kept company with the gods in heaven, contemplating eternal Forms that lay outside the very bounds of the universe."[15] In its state before the Fall, the soul knows the Forms by intellectual vision with the "eyes" of the soul. The ability to recollect this knowledge in the embodied state requires the kind of dialectical reasoning exemplified in the dialogues and also moral purification to counter the tendency to attend to the world of the senses, where lower appetites are satisfied.

Plato's metaphor of intellectual vision was central to Western conceptions of knowledge for a millennium and a half, but to us today it is quite foreign. I believe

---

[13] It is conventional to capitalize these terms to indicate that they are being used in a technical sense rather than that of current English.

[14] Phillip Cary, *Augustine's Invention of the Inner Self: The Legacy of a Christian Platonist* (Oxford: Oxford University Press, 2000), 15.

[15] Cary, *Augustine's Invention*, 16–17.

that our best insight (note the metaphor) comes from keeping the role of mathematics in mind (another metaphor). Recall that Plato's doctrine of recollection begins with the slave boy's ability to do geometry. The boy's performance does reflect experiences we have all had, beginning as children. For example, we can "see" that $2 \times 3 = 6$ by making two rows of three dots each.

In a variety of ways, Plato indicates a "mathematization" of his concept of Form. In a late dialogue, the *Timaeus*, we find the Pythagorean emphasis on numerical ratios. Here Plato offers the "likely story" or myth of a divine craftsman who creates the physical universe in accordance with the hierarchy of the Forms by investing "pre-existing matter with every form of life and intelligence by the application of harmonious mathematical ratios."[16] We get another hint of a Pythagorean influence in remarks by Aristotle. Frederick Copleston (1907–94) writes that "Aristotle used to relate how those who came to hear Plato's lectures on the Good, were often astonished to hear nothing but arithmetic and astronomy, and of the limit and the One."[17] For Pythagoreans the numbers began with 2, so our number 1 would then be the lower limit to the numbers. Note that if numbers are represented by *patterns* of dots, the smallest would be a set of two.

We can get another glimpse of what Plato was thinking in calling Forms ratios by noting another influence in this thought, that of atomists such as Democritus. In the *Timaeus*, he claimed that the atoms comprising physical reality, in their variety, were all composed in turn of triangles, and the relations of the triangles' sides could be expressed in terms of numerical ratios.[18] To see how Plato could have wed this notion of harmonious mathematical ratios to his earlier discussion of the virtues, we need only consider that Pythagoras had already linked numbers to moral concepts.

Note that while we still think that progress in mathematics, both on the part of those developing it in the first place and in learning it for ourselves, involves sometimes startling and exciting insights, in the modern period mathematics (and formal logic) have come to be sharply distinguished from other kinds of knowledge. But prior to making distinctions between the sort of knowledge that constitutes a formal, deductive system, on the one hand, and ethics and empirical science on the other, it would not have been unreasonable to believe that all knowledge (*episteme*) could be attained simply by intense concentration leading to immediate and obviously true insights.

Aristotle's remark relating the Good with the One points to a central aspect of Plato's thought. He claimed that the Forms were organized hierarchically, with the

---

[16] Malcolm Schofield, "Plato," *Routledge*, 7:399–421 (401).

[17] Frederick Copleston, SJ, *A History of Philosophy*, 9 vols. (Westminster, MD: Newman Press, 1946–74; reprint ed., Garden City, NY: Image Books, 1962–89), 1:131. References are to the reprint.

[18] Karl Popper, "The Nature of Philosophical Problems and their Roots in Science," *British Journal for the Philosophy of Science* 3 (1952): 124–56 (§5).

Good at the apex. The Good cannot be described directly, but in two ways its role is linked metaphorically to the sun. The sun gives being to earthly things, as in causing plants to grow. It also provides the light that enables the eyes of the body to see. Thus, the Good gives being to the other Forms, and it also provides the "light" for the eyes of the soul. I find Copleston's account of the relation between the Good and the One most persuasive. His explanation is that "Plato is clearly working towards the conception of the Absolute, the absolutely Perfect and exemplary Pattern of all things, the ultimate ontological Principle."[19]

Note that we have here a complete reversal of the Archaic Greek conception of knowledge as the acquisition by experience of as many details about the world as possible. Perceptual "knowledge" is *doxa* because that which is known is changeable, and the sense organs upon which it is dependent are also changeable. Furthermore, Plato has completed the quest begun by the Presocratics to find the *one* organizing principle behind the chaos of appearances.

Plato's influence has waxed and waned through all subsequent history, but for our purposes the most significant of his followers are the Neoplatonists of the early centuries of the Christian era.

4 Neoplatonism

Neoplatonism has been described as "the finest flowering of ancient Greek thought, from the third to the sixth or seventh century AD. It was not just a philosophy but the higher education system of its age."[20] The Neoplatonists were influenced by both Plato and Pythagoras, but also by Aristotle and the Stoics (flourishing from about 300 BC to about AD 180; indebted to Socrates and Plato; concerned with the nature of reality and ethics). The best known of the Neoplatonists in the Latin West, and the ones who most influenced Augustine, were Plotinus (AD 205–70) and Porphyry (*c.*232–*c.*304). Porphyry is noted for having organized Plotinus's writings and created from his work "a coherent system, intensely religious and otherworldly."[21]

Plotinus was born in Egypt and studied with the philosopher Ammonius Saccas in Alexandria. He later moved to Rome to teach philosophy, and his voluminous writings covered ethics and aesthetics, physics and cosmology, psychology, metaphysics, logic, and epistemology. He is best known for his development of Plato's concept of Ultimate Reality, accepting Plato's identification of the Good with the One. The One is the highest good, being above all composite entities. It

---

[19] Copleston, *History*, 1:176.

[20] Lucas Siorvanes, "Neoplatonism," in *Routledge*, 6:798–803.

[21] Peter Brown, *Augustine of Hippo: A Biography* (Berkeley and Los Angeles: University of California Press, 1967), 91.

eternally emanates Mind, which is a unified composite of all of the Forms. From Mind emanates Soul, whose higher part contemplates the Forms, but whose lower part is turned away toward the material world. Divine Soul differentiates into pieces, which, embodied, constitute human souls. The relations among the three divine hypostases are hierarchical, in accord with the common Greek theme of the unchanging (and indivisible) as being of a higher level of reality than the changing (i.e., decomposable) physical beings. However, the relations are also expressed in terms of spheres: the One is an indivisible point at the center, Mind and Soul radiate outward.

The highest part of the human soul (*nous*) is divine not only because of its origin in Soul, but also because of its ability while still in the body to contemplate the Forms. In doing so it is identical to the Forms, and if identical to the Forms, then also identical to Mind itself.

The notion that the knower is somehow identical to what is known is a thesis taken from Aristotle,[22] and we shall consider it below. However, we may get a sense of how such a thesis, strange to us today, could be accepted from Wallace Matson's explanation: "the relational statement that '*A* knows *B*' requires an underlying identity of *A* and *B*; if they were entirely distinct the sort of fusion involved in knowing could not take place."[23] That is, the knower and known must be of the same nature. Notice that this assumption depends on not clearly distinguishing between saying that *A* is *identical* with *B* (as in the case of I myself now being the same person as I was earlier) versus *A* is *like* *B* (as in the case of "identical" twins).

For Plotinus, the good life was pursuit of the reunion of souls with Soul, which was to be accomplished by turning one's attention away from the sensible world and the related demands of the body, and by dialectical reasoning—a process of thinking intended to recognize unifying principles above a variety of related ideas, and thus contemplating the truths of the intelligible world of the Forms. Plotinus coined a metaphor that will be extremely important for Augustine and for all later Western thought. If the highest part of the soul is also its central part, then pursuit of knowledge, and indeed of God, involved turning "inward." This is a metaphor, of course, in that its only literal meaning is to turn one's *attention* away from that which is, literally, outside of oneself.

Neoplatonism was developed in Alexandria as an alternative to Christianity, with Pythagoras presented as a rational alternative to Christ. Thus, it is ironic that it was the means by which Augustine came to adopt so much of Plato's philosophy into his theology.

---

[22] Cary, *Augustine's Invention*, 19.
[23] Matson, *New History*, 1:177.

Another (sad) irony worth mentioning, since women so far have played no part in this account, is as follows: There was one woman among the Neoplatonists, Hypatia of Alexandria (AD *c.*355–415), also a follower of Pythagoras. She contributed to mathematical and astronomical texts, and also designed some important scientific instruments.[24] She was the most eminent woman philosopher of antiquity. The irony, given the influence Neoplatonism was to have in Christianity, was that she was beaten to death (in 415) by a fanatical mob of Christians. She is remembered today in that there is a publication, *Hypatia: A Journal of Feminist Philosophy.*

5 Augustine

Augustine was born in present-day Algeria (an especially good reminder of the multiracial origin of Christianity). He first rejected his mother's Christianity in favor of Manichaeism, a religio-philosophical system that explained evil by postulating a second, evil deity. After moving to Milan, where he came to know Christian Platonists, including Bishop Ambrose (*c.*340–97), he converted to Christianity and began a long life of scholarship. He was soon ordained, then promoted to bishop of Hippo in his native North Africa.

Augustine had available in Latin only a few texts of Plato and Aristotle, so his knowledge of the Platonic tradition was through the Neoplatonists, and here primarily Plotinus. He perceived the quest of the Platonists as a pursuit parallel to his own quest for truth, and in both cases this was a quest for God. My focus in this section will be on how Augustine justified his identification of God and truth, and what it meant for his understanding of human rationality and its relation to faith. First, though, I describe ways in which his Christian convictions required corrections of Plotinus's thought.

Augustine accepted and appreciated Plotinus's location of the Forms in the mind of God, but of course it was the Christian God rather than Plotinus's first emanation, Mind (and in his Trinitarian theology he rejected the concept of emanation entirely). For Plotinus, the Forms were active in producing the material world, but for Augustine, of course, God alone creates and the ideas in his mind are merely exemplars.

Augustine rejected the divinity of the human soul, along with its pre-existence. This meant rejecting the Plotinian view that human minds could know the Forms directly, as God does, as well as Plato's account of knowledge as recollection. He speaks a great deal about memory (*memoria*), but for him memory is nearly synonymous with mind or intellect.

---

[24] Wertheim, *Pythagoras*, 35–6.

He rejected the Platonic account of the Fall as the soul "falling" from the transcendent realm into the material body.[25] Because of the doctrine of creation, the body could not be counted as evil. Yet the body occupies a negative place in Augustine's theory of knowledge. As did the Platonists, he believed the soul to comprise three hierarchically ordered parts, from the will to the intellect, to the appetitive part; the soul and body are hierarchically ordered as well. So moral transformation in the form of turning away from the pursuit of bodily pleasures to pursuit of the activities of the intellect is necessary for the acquisition of knowledge.

Despite all of these modifications, Augustine took over from Plotinus the view that knowledge of God comes from turning inward to one's own soul. But because the soul is not divine, knowledge of God cannot be read off from the nature and content of the soul. As Cary states, "Augustine's inward turn requires a double movement: first *in* then *up*."[26] The upward turn reflects the conception of the hierarchical conception of reality: God is *above* all creatures, including the soul. Cary says:

> In the interval between the turning in and looking up one finds oneself in a new place, never before conceived: an inner space proper to the soul, different from the intellectual world in the Mind of God. The soul becomes, as it were, its own dimension—a whole realm of being waiting to be entered and explored.[27]

Note the peculiarity of this metaphorical complex: it is not just that my soul is inside my body, it is that I, the *real* I, am somehow *inside* of my soul, which is inside my body. The result was the introduction, in Augustine's *Confessions*, of the idea of memory as a capacious inner chamber, in which are found "innumerable images of all kinds . . . whatever we think about . . . all the skills acquired through the liberal arts . . . the principles of the laws of numbers . . ." and most important of all, God.[28] The justification for expecting God to be present in the soul came from Christian teaching on Christ's presence in the heart of the believer. Augustine identified Christ as the eternal Wisdom that the philosophers sought, but without their knowing of Wisdom's earthly life.

Augustine accepted Plotinus's conclusion that to know God is to know the Forms. But due to the Fall and to the mere creaturely status of the soul, the intellect cannot engage automatically in direct contemplation of the Forms. Therefore,

---

[25] The notion that the evil and suffering in the world must be the result of a catastrophic Fall in the past was widespread in the ancient Mediterranean world.

[26] Cary, *Augustine's Invention*, 39.

[27] Cary, *Augustine's Invention*, 39.

[28] Augustine, *Confessions*, tr. Henry Chadwick ([397–400] Oxford: Oxford University Press, 1991), Book 10, *passim*.

Augustine returned to Plato's metaphor of illumination. God, by grace, illumines the soul so that when one seeks knowledge of eternal things, such knowledge is possible.

Augustine also accepted Plotinus's identification of knowledge with that which is known, and this provides the rationale for his (to us) peculiar use of the word "truth." If vision of the Forms is *true* knowledge, then the Forms themselves are said to be true. This same identification of knower and known results in calling God himself the Truth, and Christians even today are willing to accept this usage in theology (if not in other discourse) because of Jesus' statement that he is the way, the truth, and the life.

Another use of "truth" for Augustine was with regard to the physical world. Alasdair MacIntyre writes that to "progress in understanding the world of creation as it truly is is to move away from the initial judgments of everyday life . . . toward the formation of a mind whose judgments conform to what things are." So far this does not sound strange to contemporary ears, but he goes on to say: "And the truth of things lies in their conformity to the exemplars."[29] So God is Truth *par excellence*; the human mind can have true knowledge of the truth of the Forms; human judgments can be true of physical things insofar as such judgments conform to the truth of those physical things; and the truth of things is in their conformity to the Forms.

While Augustine's very elaborate theory of truth is difficult for us today even to understand, nonetheless in some Christian circles there is still an association between God and *The* Truth, such that philosophical discussions of less exalted theories of truth tend to suggest that the whole of theology is being called into question—even the very existence of God.

However much the philosophical assumptions behind Augustine's conception of truth may have changed for us today, it was fundamental for the succeeding years of Western Christian thought. Cary sums it up this way: for Augustine "there is nothing in the world more fundamental than the soul's ability to see intellectual truths, for this is none other than the soul's ability to see God, who is 'immutable Truth which contains all that is immutably true.'"[30]

There is one further aspect of Augustine's account of reason that will be central to Christian thought right up to the beginning of the modern era. We have already seen that the fallen intellect is unable to perceive truth apart from divine illumination. In addition, the fallen will does not, without assistance, move toward the good that is the truth. The Fall came about by an act of disobedience that was a manifestation of pride. Thus, the first step toward learning is acquisition of the

---

[29] Alasdair MacIntyre, *Three Rival Versions of Moral Enquiry: Encyclopaedia, Genealogy, and Tradition* (Notre Dame, IN: University of Notre Dame Press, 1990), 84.

[30] Cary, *Augustine's Invention*, 19; quoting Augustine, *De Libero Arbitrio*, 3 vols. (387–9, 391, 395), 2:33.

virtue of humility, such that one is willing to submit to the authority of a teacher—human teachers and their interpretations of sacred texts. Faith in authority must precede rational understanding.[31]

Here we have a more specific statement of the relation of faith and reason, with which we began this Part of the text. Faith in the sense of personal trust is a prerequisite for beginning the quest for knowledge. Faith in the sense of belief in the authorities' interpretations of the texts (*opinio*) allows one to read the texts correctly and in the process to be personally transformed by the texts. As this transformation proceeds, one is enabled to pursue the Truth within, and this, at last, constitutes true knowledge (*scientia*).

6 Aristotle

We now turn back seven centuries to consider Aristotle's understanding of reason. Aristotle (384–322 BC) was born in Ionia and sent at the age of 17 to Plato's Academy, where he stayed until Plato's death in 347. After that he moved several times, finally founding his own school, the Lyceum, in Athens. An important influence on his philosophy was a stay on the island of Lesbos, where he engaged in zoological investigations. This study is significant for this reason: For understanding Plato, it is helpful to keep in mind that his general account of knowledge was based on extending to other areas the characteristics of mathematical knowledge. In Aristotle's case, he is best understood as extending his theory of biological science to other areas of knowledge.

Matson shows that there is an important distinction among philosophers as to whether they start first with the epistemological question of how we know, and then use their answers to determine their positions on what there is; or they start with what there is, in order to explain how it is that we can have knowledge. While Augustine is the source of most "inside-out" philosophy in the West, Aristotle is of the "outside-in" type, so we begin here with his theory of the nature of reality.

Aristotle accepted various Platonic theses at various times, but commentators divide as to whether the Platonic emphases came first and then were progressively rejected, or whether he began with emphases of his own and became increasingly Platonic. A definitive answer is not possible here because it is not possible to date all of his writings. I lean toward a less Platonic view than some scholars simply because so many of his writings are concerned with the material world, something with which a true Platonist should not waste time. Thus, when I distinguished above between two general directions taken by the Presocratics in their quest for explanations of phenomena (between those seeking mathematical insights and

---

[31] MacIntyre, *Rival Versions*, 84.

those seeking material explanations), I put Aristotle in the latter group, pursuing the question of what everything is made of.

Aristotle's answer, which remained basic to science until the early modern revolution in physics, was matter and form—thus his theory is called hylomorphism—in Greek, literally "matter-formism." Aristotle does use Plato's term "Form," along with his notion that the Forms account for the particular characteristics of classes of things. However, for Aristotle they are not entities in a transcendent realm that material things resemble; they are immanent and active in that which they form.

No contemporary concept is commensurable[32] with Aristotle's concept of Form. I believe that the best way to convey its meaning is by means of a description of what the Forms do, and the best account I have found is that of T. H. Irwin (b.1947):

> The role of the form in determining the persistence of an organism results from its role as the source of unity. For form, including the organism's vital functions, makes a heap of material constituents into a single organism (*Metaphysics* VII 16). A collection of flesh and bones constitutes a single living organism in so far as it has the form of a man or a horse; the vital functions of the single organism are the final cause of the movements of the different parts. The organism remains in being through changes of matter, as long as it retains its formal, functional properties. Since the structure, behaviour and persistence of the organism must be understood by reference to its form, the form is irreducible to matter; the organism, defined by its form, must be treated as a subject in its own right, not simply as a heap of matter.[33]

If we think of biology today, we can see why Aristotle theorized that there must be more than matter to account for the variety of organisms in the world—for what makes them living in contrast to the inorganic materials that constitute them, and why they develop and behave in goal-directed ways. There must *be something* that accounts for all of this, and Aristotle adapted Plato's concept of Form for this purpose.

Aristotle's concept of matter is a radical alternative to the atomism both of his day and of early modern physics. If we ask whether some bit of material is in principle infinitely divisible, the atomist answer is that it is not: *atom* in Greek means uncuttable. The atomist answer to why different things are different is then in terms of the characteristics and arrangements of the atoms. In contrast, Aristotle accepted his precursors' theory of the four elements of earth, air, fire, and water. But these basic materials take their characteristics from the Forms of earth,

---

[32] See Chapter 4 for an explanation of commensurability and incommensurability.
[33] T. H. Irwin, "Aristotle," in *Routledge*, 1:414–35 (422).

air, and so forth. The Form of the element earth gives this basic material its characteristic properties and behavior; for example, earth pursues its natural motion downward, in contrast to that of fire, which is upwards.

In Aristotle's hierarchy of beings, the four elements are at the bottom. In various proportions they compose increasingly more *en-formed* beings. For example, blood might be formed of water and earth; earth and blood might become flesh. Organisms are hierarchically ordered according to the increasingly varied and complex powers they exhibit. So the hierarchy is one of increasing dominance of Form relative to matter. There is a topmost being in the hierarchy, pure Form, which is Aristotle's God, the Unmoved Mover. The lowest level of the hierarchy, in contrast *would* then be pure matter—prime matter—but it does not exist; it is rather a postulate of his explanatory system.

A particularly interesting segment of the hierarchy is living things, from simple to complex plants, from simple to complex nonhuman animals, and finally humans. The Forms of living things are called souls, and the human soul comprises all of the powers of the nutritive (plant) and sensitive (animal) souls, but adds reason as well.

This is by no means an adequate account of Aristotle's theories of metaphysics, physics, and biology, but I believe that it is enough to explain his theory of knowledge. The different sensory organs are constituted by different materials that are capable of being en-formed by different aspects of the Forms of the things perceived. Perceptual knowledge is *absorption* of the same Forms that constitute the essential make-up of the world.[34] I mentioned in describing Plotinus's account of the identity of the knower with the known that he was following Aristotle here. So this is one sense in which knower and known are related: they are both determined by the same Forms. In the modern period, we shall see, the problem of perception became one of explaining how accurate sense perception could be possible, but for Aristotle and his followers, it is difficult to explain how perceptual *error* is possible.

A mental capacity that humans share with animals is translated as the "common sense." This is the ability to take the deliverances of the various senses and recognize that they are properties of a single entity. However, to know what that entity *is* requires grasping the Form that several similar particulars share. For example, study of a variety of horses allows for a reasoning process something like induction to extract the essential features (not just appearance but typical powers and behaviors, such as the ability to run) from the accidental variations (such as color). This capacity of *nous* (mind or intellect) is what distinguishes humans from the higher animals; it involves formation of

---

[34] Theo C. Meyering, *Historical Roots of Cognitive Science: The Rise of a Cognitive Theory of Perception from Antiquity to the Nineteenth Century* (Dordrecht: Kluwer Academic Publishers, 1989), 11, 14–15.

universal concepts and the ability to make true judgments such as "horses give birth to colts."

Much of Aristotle's contribution to the medieval worldview, and even to current knowledge, consisted in his creation of disciplines of study and recognizing that different disciplines require different methods. For example, he began the categorization of biological genera and species. By considering progressively higher instances and classifications of things, one grasps the most abstract, unifying principles of the relevant science. The highest principles of all are the concepts of matter and Form, the correlative concepts of causation, the distinction between what is actual versus merely potential, and so forth. The goal of any science is thus to progress up the hierarchy of being to the first principles from which the phenomena can be deduced. For example, the universal concepts of Form and matter explain both how vision is possible (one can see a horse because the Form of horseness en-forms the eyes) and how reproduction is possible (mating transmits the Form of horseness from the stallion to the mare; the mare provides the matter).

So here Aristotle has an account of how the mind comes to grasp abstract universal ideas (Forms) that contrasts with the Platonic metaphors of recollection and direct intellectual vision. It will be important for our account of Thomas's project to note that while Aristotle needs a concept of God (the Unmoved Mover) to explain his cosmology (in particular, the movements of the stars and planets), Aristotle does *not* need God in his theory of knowledge.

Aristotle's writings were reconciled as far as possible with Plato's by the Neoplatonists, and thereby had a measure of influence on Christian writers such as Augustine. However, little use was made of his own writings by theologians until the late Middle Ages. The reasons for this were many: scarcity of his texts in the Latin West, decrease in knowledge of Greek among Latin-speaking scholars, and a Platonic de-emphasis on knowledge of the physical world. After the fall of the Roman empire, many books in Europe were lost or destroyed, so that only two of Aristotle's writings were known: the *Categories* and *On Interpretation*.

However, by the tenth century, Greek writings were beginning to accumulate in Europe, and theologians proceeded to attempt to reconcile them with Scripture, as had already been done by Augustine and others with Plato's *Timaeus*. Yet this work involved scattered samplings of texts, and the reconciliations proceeded piecemeal. It was only in the twelfth century that all of the texts we have of Aristotle's became available: texts plundered from Constantinople by crusaders, and those brought to Europe by Muslim scholars such as Averroës (Ibn Rushd; 1126–98), Aristotle's most competent commentator in Cordoba. The brilliance, scope, and coherence of this system dazzled European scholars, some of whom judged it a gift from God. Others perceived it as a threat. Thomas Aquinas perceived both the threat and the promise.

7 Thomas Aquinas

Thomas was born near Naples, the son of the Count of Aquino. He began studies at the age of six and arrived at the University of Paris at age twenty, where he did much of his work. There he encountered Albert the Great (1200–80), an enthusiastic Aristotelian absorbed in furthering Aristotelian studies in biology.

I first explain the threatening aspect of the Aristotelian system and Thomas's solution. I end with a brief indication of the scope of the worldview that he (and his followers) developed in their synthesis of the Christian theological tradition with the Aristotelian corpus.

7.1 Aristotelian threats

There were easily recognized contradictions between Aristotle's writings and the Christian Tradition. For example, Aristotle taught that the world was eternal, while the Christian doctrine of creation seemed to require a temporal beginning. Nonetheless, at the University of Paris in Thomas's day most of his works were required readings in the liberal arts (grammar, rhetoric, logic, arithmetic, geometry, music, and astronomy). What to say of their truth? The followers of Averroës could only say that Aristotelian theses in conflict with theology were merely the conclusions of philosophy. Thus, philosophy concludes that the universe is eternal, but in truth it is temporally finite. This is an obviously unsatisfactory solution, but what Thomas realized was that the very existence of Aristotle's system undermined the whole of the Augustinian conception of knowledge.

Cary states that for Augustine, true knowledge of God cannot be found in texts, but only by means of an inner vision.[35] Nonetheless, through the Middle Ages, to do theology was in fact to study and attempt to reconcile texts. However, these were not merely theological treatises, since for Augustine and his followers the natural world, as God's creation and revelation, was itself a text. So scholarship up to Thomas's day involved reconciling of authorities, both theological and others—sometimes "bowdlerizing" philosophical texts when they did not fit with theology.[36]

The Augustinian thesis that, due to the Fall, the pursuit of knowledge first needs to be directed by authority creates a crucial inconsistency in the Augustinian conception of knowledge, in that those lacking God's salvation and illumination should not be able to acquire abstract knowledge. That is, pagans and infidels might have beliefs (*opinio*) about the sensory world, but they should not be able to construct a science (*scientia*) that gives a systematic account of reality. MacIntyre

---

[35] Cary, *Augustine's Invention*, 40–1.

[36] N. Max Wildiers, *The Theologian and His Universe: Theology and Cosmology from the Middle Ages to the Present* (New York: Seabury Press, 1982), 15.

states that all Augustinians were necessarily committed to "one central negative thesis about all actually or potentially rival positions: that no substantive rationality, independent of faith, will be able to provide an adequate vindication of its claims."[37] So if the Aristotelian system is (even largely) true, its very existence falsifies the Augustinian. If the Augustinian system is true, then it predicts that the Aristotelian system *must* be false.

Here lay the true threat of the Aristotelian system. While it included an account of God, there was no role for God in Aristotle's theory of knowledge—no need for divine illumination. In contrast to the Platonic–Augustinian requirement of turning away from the world of the senses, Aristotle's system begins with sensory knowledge. The intellect is not deprived of its powers by sin, but rather actualizes its potential, pursues its natural *telos*, in progressing toward the truth. The mind possesses truth insofar as it is "adequate" to that which it knows.

Here again we have (for us) a foreign concept of truth. The mind's adequacy to what it knows is not, as in modern thought, the possession of some sort of *representation* of the object, but it is a state of being en-formed by the same Forms that themselves constitute the things known.

7.2 Aristotle's gifts

A full account of Thomas's solution can only be sketched here. Thomas accepted Aristotle's position that reason is capable of producing a system that consists of a hierarchical ordering of the sciences, with knowledge of the Unmoved Mover as its highest principle. Thomas extended Aristotle's account: the First Mover is also the eternal and necessary first *cause* of all else. This unified hierarchical system can be seen as a prologue to Christian theology: Christian knowledge of God is required to complete it.

Thomas accepted Augustine's account of the relation of particulars to exemplars in the mind of God, thus explaining the source of the (Aristotelian) Forms that reason extracts from sense perception and then organizes under first principles. He also accepted, of course, the Christian doctrine of revelation, whose teachings are the object of faith (a category different from mere opinion because it is held with assurance). True knowledge, as for Augustine, is by vision, the Beatific Vision, occasionally glimpsed in this life, but reserved in its entirety for the next, when God will be known directly and all things known in their proper relation to God.

So there is a proper domain of reason: the sciences, including metaphysical principles such as causation, matter, and Form. There is a proper domain of faith: sacred doctrine, whose content reason can neither prove nor disprove. But there is also a region of overlap: knowledge that can be arrived at by both revelation and

---

[37] MacIntyre, *Rival Versions*, 101.

reason. This overlap incorporates the sciences as an integral part of the Christian theological tradition and in turn reinterprets science by means of a theological understanding of its very possibility.

In Thomas's work, first rejected by the church, but later canonized and extended by his followers, we have a theology that unites cosmology, physics, biology, psychology, ethics, politics, ecclesiology, epistemology into a single, mutually reinforcing system. When we appreciate this unification of knowledge, ethics, and social–ecclesial structure it will give us a better appreciation of the radical nature of the scientific revolution at the beginning of the modern period.

8 Retrospect and prospect

Is it rational to believe in God? Can Christian beliefs about God be justified? Is theological (or religious) knowledge of a different and more obscure sort than knowledge of other subjects? This chapter is written in a contemporary context in which religion is being called radically into question. The very idea of religious *knowledge* is considered nonsense by many. Among those who think religions can make cognitive claims, many believe that no better justification can be given for one religion over another.

This chapter has shown how far our current situation is from that of the ancient and medieval worlds. For Augustine, God was the Truth, and human knowledge could only be considered true in a derivative sense. For Thomas, knowledge of God was the ultimate principle toward which all enquiry was (consciously or unconsciously) directed and that in light of which all other knowledge needed to be understood. Yet the theories of knowledge involved in these claims are not only different from ours but strange enough to us so as to be nearly unintelligible. The historical variability of concepts of *knowledge, truth,* even *rationality* demonstrated here may itself feed the relativism so common in our culture.

However, a certain degree of relativization of the concept of *reason* has been one of the purposes of this chapter. I will argue in what follows that the shifting perception of theology from that of queen of the sciences and primary exemplar of rationality to its questionable status in our era may not reflect a more enlightened recognition of what is wrong with Christian theology, but rather reflects defects in modern conceptions of rationality and knowledge.

In the next two chapters, I trace radical shifts in understandings of the nature of reason, along with the negative consequences of many of these for understanding theological knowledge. In Chapter 4, I argue that it is only now that we have an account of human rationality sophisticated enough to make the question of the rationality of Christian belief a reasonable question.

2

Modern epistemology and the possibility of theology

1 Introduction

The *possibility* of theology? It must be possible—just think how many books of it there are in the library! The central purpose of this chapter is to present the intellectual developments that have had significant consequences for theology (and secondarily for religious belief more generally) in the modern era. While early modern writers were almost without exception Christian believers, their writings produced a new intellectual world in which justification of Christian belief has proved to be difficult indeed. Historian Claude Welch (1922–2009) began his history of nineteenth-century Protestant theology as follows:

> At the beginning of the nineteenth century the theological problem was, simply, "how is theology possible?" This was a question of both rationale and method, and included, at least implicitly, the question of whether theology is possible at all. Of course, this had been a question in every age, but now it emerged with new strength and in a special configuration provided by the eighteenth century. The theologies of orthodoxy were still present, but fundamentally they were fighting rearguard actions as they retreated steadily before the force of Enlightenment into the backwaters of intellectual and cultural isolation.[1]

René Descartes (1594–1650) is called the father of modern philosophy, and philosophers date the origin of the modern period with the year of his death. It may not be too much of an exaggeration to say that the methodological problems Christian theologians and apologists were to face for the next 300 years can all be traced to the epistemological setting in which he worked, and particularly to the responses he made to that setting.

I described in Chapter 1 how smoothly theological method had been integrated with the ancient and medieval epistemological categories of *scientia* and *opinio* (or "probable knowledge"). While theology has the status of *scientia* only in the mind of God, studying and reconciling the authorities allowed nonetheless

---

[1] Claude Welch, *Protestant Thought in the Nineteenth Century*, 2 vols. (New Haven, CT and London: Yale University Press, 1972, 1985), 1:59.

for human knowledge of Christian doctrine. As in Chapter 1, I do not present a history of philosophy here, but rather pick out elements that shed light on the question of the rationality of Christian thought. I shall argue that whereas the particulars of Descartes's theory of knowledge were rather quickly abandoned, he introduced into Western philosophy two *metaphors* that guided (and bedeviled) epistemology for the next 300 years. One is the foundationalist metaphor—the image of knowledge systems as buildings requiring solid foundations. The other is a distorted version of Augustine's image of entering into his own mind or soul[2] in pursuit of knowledge—what I labeled in Chapter 1 as inside-out epistemology.

In section 2, I mention some of the intellectual changes that prepared the way for Descartes. In sections 4.1 and 4.2, I describe the lasting hold of the metaphors he introduced. Section 4.3 recounts the shift in the meaning of "probable knowledge" from that of ancient and medieval *approbation* by authorities to the modern sense of knowledge based on the weight of evidence. Section 4.4 presents John Locke (1632–1704) as something of a transitional figure between Descartes and later views of science (in the modern sense) with the purpose of showing how susceptible his apologetic moves were to demolition (the building metaphor again!) by David Hume's (1711–76) skeptical arguments.

In section 5, I trace the influences of Descartes's two metaphors in the development of modern theology. Among the effects, I argue, has been the sharp differentiation between liberal and conservative Protestant theologies. This chapter will also begin a critique of both foundationalism and inside-out epistemology, but the misleading nature of these images will become clearest when alternatives are described in Chapters 3 and 4.

I hope that by the end of this chapter it will be clear how theology could come to be seen by so many in late modernity to have failed to measure up to the demands of reason.

2 Before modernity

Despite philosophers' specifying a precise date for the beginning of modernity, no change in worldview can happen so suddenly. A number of significant developments had already begun the transition.

The Medieval Synthesis was a worldview in which theology reigned as the queen of the sciences; the hierarchically ordered sciences were taken to reflect the hierarchical ordering of the cosmos itself; and the cosmic order justified the ecclesiastical and political ordering of society. The most noticeable change outside

---

[2] "Mind" and "soul" are nearly synonymous for Descartes and have only become distinct in recent generations as "soul" took on religious connotations while "mind" did not.

of the academy was, of course, the disruption of the old order of empire and church by the Reformation, resulting in (and being fueled by) the rise of nation-states. An important change in historians' assessment of these developments is a recognition of the strong political motives in what have so long been called the wars of religion. This change calls into question one overly simple account of the origins of modernity: the story has long been told in terms of the essentially violent nature of religion resulting in such devastation in Europe that religion was abandoned by many and otherwise subjugated to state powers. This curtailment of the influence of (superstitious) religion then allowed for the rise of science.

In fact, science as we know it (empirical science) had been on the rise concurrently with the conflicts spawned by the Reformation (and other disruptions of the medieval feudal system). To speak of the "Copernican revolution" gives more credit to Nicolaus Copernicus (1473–1543) than he deserves, since his heliocentric model of the cosmos was not the first; it did not arouse much of a stir when it was published in 1543; and it was not scientifically supportable until it was modified by others, particularly Johannes Kepler (1571–1630). The significance of heliocentrism was not its conflict with scriptural proof texts for the immobility of the Earth—a real but trivial conflict.[3] It was rather that Aristotelian physics required the Earth to be the center of the universe: the falling of material bodies was explained in terms of the element earth seeking its natural position. So Aristotle's theory of motion was most directly in need of replacement, but for many this meant that his entire hylomorphic metaphysics, in which Forms account for *all* natural changes, needed replacing. Of the many proposals offered in Descartes's day (including Descartes's own), the one that came to shape modern physics was Pierre Gassendi's (1592–1631) revival of ancient Epicurean atomism.

I see the rejection of the very concept of *Form* as the linchpin in the collapse of the Medieval Synthesis, in that forms played a role in all branches of knowledge from biology to cosmology and theology, in the theory of sense perception, and the epistemological ideal of a unified hierarchy of sciences. The existence of forms had already been called into question by William of Ockham (*c.*1285–*c.*1349) and others on the grounds that God's creation of the forms would thereby limit God's freedom. The alternative theory of how we can have general concepts such as *horse* and *white* is called nominalism: we perceive similarities and give the same name (*nomen*) to similar things.

The epistemological consequence of this movement was to diminish confidence in human reason: if there are no forms for reason to grasp, and if God has no fixed ideas/forms regularizing his creative acts, then *scientia*, as Thomas understood it, would be impossible, and a replacement seemed to be essential.

---

[3] For Galileo's role, see Chapter 8.

Recall the ancient Greek distinction between *episteme* (true knowledge) and *doxa* (belief or opinion). Augustine had heightened the importance of *opinio* or "probable knowledge," that is, knowledge with the *approbation* of the authorities, because the fallen intellect is not willing or able to pursue *scientia* without relying on authoritative teachers and texts. Thomas preserved the Augustinian ideal of *scientia*, but in practice theology and all other scholarship (apart from mathematics) fell short of the ideal and was largely a matter of reconciling authoritative texts.

We now come to a more realistic assessment of the epistemological significance of the Reformation. With the divisions within the church, there came the problem of *too many authorities*—the problem of knowing which authorities to trust. Many Renaissance thinkers were content to live with a moderate skepticism about the great truths. However, the ghastly destruction wrought by the Thirty Years' War (1618–48) and the English Civil War (1642–8) made it evident to philosophers in Descartes's day (1596–1650) that some form of reasoning, available to thinkers across theological dividing lines, was necessary in order to find a common way forward, particularly in ethics and politics. So a significant feature of modernity is that it begins with the rejection of tradition in all forms, but particularly theological tradition, and sets out to find some (new) basis for certainty, based on the powers of human reason alone.

3 René Descartes

Descartes was born in France and sent at age ten to the Collège Royale de La Flèche, a Jesuit school. The core of the curriculum was Aristotelian logic, metaphysics, physics, and ethics. He wrote later that as soon as he left school he rejected much of what he had been taught; he set out on a career as a military engineer. Soon, however, he was tempted to a life of scholarship when he learned of attempts to combine new currents in science, particularly atomism, with mathematics. Although he is now classified as a philosopher, he made significant contributions to mathematics (relating algebra and geometry), developed his own version of mechanistic physics, and wrote on topics as varied as music, physiology, optics, and heliocentric astronomy.

While much of Descartes's "scientific"[4] writings can be described in terms of what he rejected of the Aristotelian–Thomist system (cosmology, physics, and particularly Aristotle's hylomorphic metaphysics), one feature that he maintained was the view that all of knowledge needed to form one coherent system—with the exception of revealed theology. He did not live long enough to complete his system, and his science has not stood the test of time. Thus, it is fair in the end that

---

[4] The quotation marks are a reminder that these subjects were still considered part of natural philosophy.

he be remembered for his contributions to the narrower, modern discipline of philosophy, and particularly to the subdiscipline of epistemology.

Our current conception of "probable" knowledge, based on the preponderance of evidence, was not yet developed in Descartes's day, so for him the only remaining category of knowledge was *scientia*, but *scientia* itself needed to be reinvented. His epistemology is indeed revolutionary, but this is despite his acceptance of so much of the tradition he thought himself to be abandoning. The unified structure of knowledge was to begin with indubitable first principles (from Thomas), and these were to be found by (Augustinian) intellectual vision of the contents of his own (Augustinian) soul. From these first principles the rest of the structure could be built by demonstrative reasoning.

Some have argued that Descartes's foundationalism is also taken from Augustine, but what is different is the expectation that one could renounce all previous knowledge and begin from scratch. This is where his building metaphor has had such power. Descartes describes the occasion when this image first struck him. Kept indoors by a cold spell in a small town in Germany, he divided his attention between contemplation, on the one hand, of the architecture that he could observe from his window and, on the other, of the ideas in his mind, which he could "observe" by means of introspection. He wrote:

> We never tear down all the houses in a city just to rebuild them in a different way and to make the streets more beautiful; but we do see that individual owners often have theirs torn down and rebuilt, and even that they may be forced to do so when the building is crumbling with age, or when the foundation is not firm and it is in danger of collapsing. By this example I was convinced that . . . as far as the opinions which I had been receiving since my birth were concerned, I could not do better than to reject them completely for once in my lifetime, and to resume them afterwards, or perhaps accept better ones in their place, when I had determined how they fitted into a rational scheme.[5]

To execute his demolition project, he engaged in his famous method of doubt. He devised several arguments as to why sense perception could not be trusted. He even imagined that he could be deceived by an omnipotent God into mistakenly believing mathematical truths. When all else is gone, he finds that there is one thing he cannot doubt, the fact of his doubting itself. And if doubt (a form of thought), then a thinker—in Latin, *Cogito ergo sum*.

Then, in typical Augustinian fashion, he examines other contents (ideas) in his mind, and judges that those that are clear and distinct must be true. He has two

---

[5] "Discourse on Method," in *Discourse on Method* and *Meditations*, tr. Laurence J. Laffleur ([1637] reprint Indianapolis: Bobbs-Merrill, 1960), 11–12.

arguments for the existence of God, each dependent on clear and distinct ideas. Furthermore, because he sees clearly and distinctly that goodness is an essential part of the idea of God, God must not have created him to be regularly deceived by his senses. This justification for the pursuit of empirical knowledge then serves as the foundation first for physics and then for the rest of knowledge. We shall see below how the quest for adequate foundations has shaped modern theology.

Despite Descartes's Augustinian heritage, there are striking differences. Augustine's primary purpose in turning inward was to find God, and as a consequence of finding him he is enabled to glimpse truth by participation in the divine Ideas. But when Descartes turns inward, he encounters a mere idea (in the modern sense of a representation) of God, yet by the power of his own reasoning he is able to conclude that God actually exists. God is important in his epistemology, but merely because his goodness licenses Descartes to trust his own thinking and perception. As Daniel Garber (b.1949) puts it: "The project then is to build the entire world from the thinking self. It is important that it is not just the mind that is the foundation, but *my* mind."[6]

There is a tremendous irony here: Descartes was attempting to refute the moderate skepticism of his age by showing individuals the way to certainty, but in fact he set up for his followers a 300-year struggle with radical skepticism.

4 After Descartes

Three significant features have characterized modern epistemology: the inward turn, individualism, and the quest for foundations. These, in turn, have had a tremendous effect on modern theology.

4.1 Modern inwardness and individualism

Phillip Cary explains the skeptical consequences of the modern inward turn in terms of two differences from Augustine's. The first is that in the Augustinian spiritual tradition one has a choice of whether or not to enter into oneself, but for moderns "the real I" is never found anywhere else. Cary says: "One of the consequences of the Western secularization of reason is that the privacy of the inner self comes to be seen not as a tragedy attendant upon the Fall, but as something essential and inevitable, as if it were the very nature of the human mind to be an inner room that no one else can enter."[7]

The second change is that while Augustine's roomy chamber is actually more like a courtyard—"it is open to the light of the Sun above"—the modern version

---

[6] Daniel Garber, "Descartes, René," *Routledge*, 3:1–19 (8).
[7] Phillip Cary, *Augustine's Invention of the Inner Self: The Legacy of a Christian Platonist* (Oxford: Oxford University Press, 2000), 123.

has a roof.[8] This change can be explained in part by the changed role of God in Descartes's epistemology, mentioned above—God is no longer the Platonic source of illumination.[9]

Cary claims that it was the English philosopher John Locke who elaborated this image most vividly. The mind, for Locke, is a *camera obscura* with no openings to the world except the senses. Locke wrote:

> These alone, as far as I can discover, are the windows by which light is let into this *dark room*. For, methinks, the Understanding is not much unlike a closet wholly shut from light, with only some little openings left, to let in external visible resemblances or ideas of things without.[10]

Cary concludes:

> Not only is each of us locked in our own separate little closet for as long as we live, but we don't even get to look out the window! We never actually see the world outside, but only its image projected on the inner wall of our private dark room. Hence all we are really certain of is what is inside our own minds. This thought has haunted a good deal of modern philosophy, especially in English-speaking countries.[11]

A consequence of the inward turn in philosophy, then, has been the constant threat of skepticism. If all one knows directly are the ideas in one's own mind, then one can always (or *must* always) raise the question of whether the mental ideas accurately represent external reality—or if indeed there is an external reality at all. Thus, typical modern accounts of knowledge involve two parts: first, an investigation of mental contents; second, an argument of some sort to justify the claim that the mental contents give accurate knowledge of what is outside the mind. Some philosophers have placed confidence in such arguments; others have concluded that the problems of the external world and of other minds (the problem of solipsism) are insoluble.

4.2 Foundationalism

Descartes was set on finding *certain* knowledge because nothing else for him counted as knowledge—medieval probable knowledge was based on the authority

---

[8] Cary, *Augustine's Invention*, 123.
[9] I believe that the shift to atomism in physics also played a role: the new physics made it appear that all knowledge from the "outside world" needed to be transmitted by particles striking the sensory surfaces, from which coded information could be sent "inward" to the brain and thence to the mind. It was not unreasonable to worry about the reliability of this transmission process.
[10] John Locke, *An Essay concerning Human Understanding* (1689), bk. II, ch. XI, §17.
[11] Cary, *Augustine's Invention*, 123.

of texts and, as noted, the problem now was to determine which texts *were* authoritative.

So far, I have spoken of foundationalism as a metaphor, but we are now able to put it in terms of a philosophical theory about knowledge. When we seek to justify a belief, we do so by relating it to (basing it upon, deriving it from) other beliefs. If these other beliefs are called into question, then they too must be justified. Foundationalists insist that this chain of justifications must stop somewhere; it must not be circular or constitute an infinite regress. Thus, the regress must end in a "foundation" of beliefs of a sort that are not themselves called into question. Yet, as we shall see below, as soon as plain old empirical facts are recognized as the foundation for science the requirement of unchallengeability is given up. The scientific facts are less questionable than the theories they support, but not indubitable. In addition, for any kind of empirical knowledge, there can be no indubitable means of construction. Thus, the particulars of foundationalist theories, in different times and different disciplines, all vary. So we need a criterion by which to judge whether a thinker is a foundationalist or not. The criteria I suggest are two: first, the assumption that knowledge systems must include a class of beliefs that are somehow resistant to challenge and, second, the assumption that all reasoning within the system proceeds in one direction only—from that set of special, unchallenged beliefs to others, but not the reverse.

Eventually, "science," the English cognate of *scientia*, came to be applied to empirical knowledge, even though, technically, scientific claims lack the certitude that Descartes sought and are never more than highly probable (in the new sense of the word). Certitude is now taken to be found only in mathematics and formal logic. But the end of the quest for *certitude* about matters of existence was not the end of a quest for *foundations* of knowledge.

4.3 The new probable knowledge

I mentioned above that Descartes saw no alternative to an attempt to reinvent medieval *scientia* because he had no other concept of knowledge available to him—our modern sense of empirical knowledge, based on the weight of evidence, only became respectable after Descartes's death (1650).

The transformation happened more or less this way: According to Augustine and many who followed him, God authored two books: the Bible and the Book of Nature. If nature is indeed a book and God its author, just as he is the author of the Bible, then events in nature, like linguistic expressions, are signs. To study them is to decipher God's meaning. Here natural observations do play a part in the determination of belief, but they do so only because they are a kind of *testimony* and therefore fit into the epistemic categories relating to authority. But soon the testimony of nature came to have a new kind of status.

Scholars connected with an abbey at Port Royal in France published a very influential book titled *Logic, or the Art of Thinking* (1662). The authors incorporated the frequency calculations that Blaise Pascal (1623–62) had developed, based on games of chance, in order to create a "rule for the proper use of reason in determining when to accept human authority." This involved, among other things, judging the acceptability of an authority's pronouncement on a given matter on the basis of frequency of past reliability. Here we see our modern sense of probability intertwined with the medieval sense. Furthermore, if nature itself has testimony to give, then the testimony of a witness may be compared with the testimony nature has given in the past. Thus, one may distinguish between internal and external facts pertaining to a witness's testimony to the occurrence of an event: External facts have to do with the witness's personal characteristics; for example, witnesses are believable if they are known to value the truth, and if they have much to lose or would be subject to disgrace if the report turned out to be false. Internal facts have to do with the character of the event itself, that is, with the known frequency of events of that sort. Given the problem of many authorities, the task increasingly had become one of deciding which authorities could be believed, and the new sense of probability—of resorting to internal evidence— gradually came to predominate, making external evidence, the testimony of witnesses, count as evidence only at second remove. The transition from authority to internal evidence was complete.[12]

We have seen that Descartes's epistemological innovations were motivated by a quest for certitude, and this was for two interrelated reasons. Descartes died before *Logic* was published, and apart from demonstrative (that is truth certifying) reasoning there was no other known way to secure agreements and settle the theological disputes that had torn Europe apart. His Augustinian heritage led him to "discover" his foundationalist metaphor.[13] His Augustinian heritage also made it natural (if not inevitable) that he would turn to the contents of his own mind/ soul for indubitable foundations.

There was in fact a direct connection between Descartes's work and that of the Port Royal logicians: much of their *Logic* was intended as a defense of his system. Given their affinities, if Descartes had lived long enough to participate in the discussions at Port Royal, the history of both philosophy and theology might have gone quite differently.

---

[12] See Jeffrey Stout, *The Flight from Authority: Religion, Morality, and the Quest for Autonomy* (Notre Dame, IN: University of Notre Dame Press, 1981), 54–61. For an abbreviated account of Stout's thesis, yet more detailed than the one above, see Nancey Murphy, *Theology in the Age of Scientific Reasoning* (Ithaca, NY and London: Cornell University Press, 1990), 3–9.

[13] I put "discover" in scare quotes because of the irony of finding it so natural to think in terms of the tradition he believed himself to be disowning.

4.4 John Locke

Locke provides an interesting intermediate case between Descartes and later modern epistemology and philosophy of science. He distinguished three kinds of knowledge: There was empirical science, founded on ideas from sensory experience. There was also a kind of indubitable knowledge, similar to Descartes's, based on "relations of ideas" and constructed by means of demonstrative reasoning; geometry is one instance of this, and another is Locke's argument for the existence of God.[14] A third kind of knowledge was based on revelation—that is, on God's "extraordinary way of communication." In *The Reasonableness of Christianity* (1695), Locke presented his conclusions regarding the theological doctrines that could be supported by Scripture: the Messiahship of Jesus was essential, but most other doctrines (such as the Trinity and predestination) he judged unfounded.

So we may imagine the epistemological scene as envisioned by Locke to include the edifice of science, a separate structure of theology founded upon Scripture, and additional deductive structures founded upon "the relations of ideas." But the theological structure is not entirely independent of the deductive argument for the existence of God: God's existence makes the whole idea of revelation intelligible so, pursuing the architectural imagery, we might say that these two structures are connected by an arch or buttress (Figure 5).

The problem Locke faced, and one that has plagued scriptural foundationalists ever since, is how to know that *this* book, the Christian Bible, is in fact the expected revelation. The very fact that this question can be asked creates problems for a *foundationalist* use of Scripture—it undermines it. Conservative apologetics from Locke's day to the present have attempted to shore up the basement. Locke argued that miracles served as outward signs to convince "the holy men of old" that God

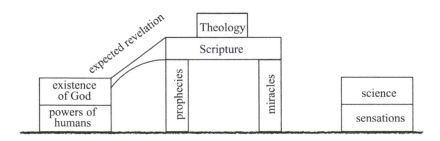

Figure 5 John Locke's foundationalist structure of knowledge: A peculiar set of buildings for three types of knowledge, with a "flying buttress" representing the argument that the existence of God supports the belief that the Christian Scriptures are indeed the expected revelation of God

---

[14] Locke, *Human Understanding*, bk. IV, ch. X.

was indeed the author of their purported revelations.[15] Another typical argument is that the fulfillment of scriptural prophecies shows the Bible to contain knowledge that only God could have revealed.

Locke's theories of knowledge took over from Descartes not only the foundationalist model, but also, as we have seen, Descartes's inside-out epistemology. Although he was willing to take sensory knowledge as foundational for science, what he meant by sensory knowledge were the "visible resemblances or ideas of things" that were let in through the "little openings" of the senses. I noted above that modern philosophers have had varying degrees of confidence in the extent to which ideas in the mind provide knowledge of what is "outside." Scottish philosopher David Hume has been one of the greatest skeptics.

4.5 David Hume

According to Wallace Matson, "Hume drew the logical conclusions from the initial premise of the Cartesian philosophy. That premise, the *Cogito*, requires philosophy to be inside-out. What alone we are sure of, what therefore we have to begin with, is our immediate knowledge of our own mental states."[16] The arguments used by Hume's predecessors to justify the transition from mental states to external reality all rely on the principle that all things, including our ideas, must have a cause. "Hume is the first to subject this allegedly self-evident truth to critical scrutiny. Causality he finds to be not a necessity of logic but a human habit of expecting things to go on as usual."[17] So, for example, to believe that the nature of things causes one billiard ball striking another to make it move is not indicative of a fact of nature—it is merely a human belief.

There are several ways to respond to Hume's critique of our purported knowledge of the external world. One is to ignore it, since we obviously do have such knowledge. A second response is to take it as a critique of the Cartesian starting point; another Scottish philosopher, Thomas Reid (1710–96), took this route. A third response was German philosopher Immanuel Kant's (1724–1804) monumental philosophical system. We return to Kant and Reid below.

What Hume may be best remembered for today in the secular philosophical world is his devastating critique of Lockean-style apologetics. One point of attack was to rebut arguments for the existence of God. The second was to dispute the use of miracles and fulfilled prophecies in arguments for the revelatory status of Scripture. Hume had a number of lively arguments against establishing the existence of Christianity's God on the basis of the apparent design of the universe,

---

[15] Locke, *Human Understanding*, bk. IV, ch. IX, §14.
[16] Wallace I. Matson, *A New History of Philosophy*, 2 vols. (San Diego: Harcourt Brace Jovanovich, 1987), 2:352.
[17] Matson, *New History*, 2:352.

pointing out that a variety of other explanations of the origin of the world were possible. The critical one, though, was based on his critique of the concept of causation. If we have no justification for imputation of causal connections in the world of ordinary experience, then all the less are we justified in inferring from the order of the universe that it was *caused* by a benevolent and intelligent deity. (We consider this and other arguments for God's existence in Chapter 4.)

Hume argues not that miracles are impossible (his skepticism does not allow for such a definitive conclusion). Rather, he argues that we could never be justified in believing strongly enough in a miracle so as to use it as a foundation for religious belief. He defines a miracle as a violation of the laws of nature. This puts any claim to have witnessed a miracle in competition with our knowledge of the regularities of nature and in a position *far* less credible than testimonies that agree with experiential knowledge. (Note the lingering association of the concept of experiential knowledge with the testimony of witnesses.) He disposes of the argument from fulfilled prophecies more quickly. If a prophecy was indeed knowledge of the future, then it would be a miracle, and the same argument against it would apply.

This account of early modern philosophy sets us up to examine theological responses, and, I hope, to appreciate how difficult modern epistemology has made the problem of theological methodology.[18]

5 Reasoning in modern theology

The two responses to Hume, mentioned above, by Thomas Reid and Immanuel Kant have played significant roles in the development of modern theology. Reid is representative of arguments that have informed conservative theologies, both fundamentalist and evangelical. Kant was the inspiration for Friedrich Schleiermacher (1768–1834), called the father of modern liberal theology. We shall see that the modern quest for foundations led conservative and liberal theologians down two different roads: One, as with Locke, took Scripture as foundational. The liberal turn employs experience—not "experience" in the ordinary sense, but in the peculiar modern inward sense.

5.1 Thomas Reid and scriptural foundationalism

Thomas Reid was founder of the school of Scottish common-sense realism. His writings and those of his followers had wide influence in both Britain and the USA in the eighteenth and nineteenth centuries, and in both theology and philosophy.

---

[18] What I have not mentioned here, and what has presented a (nearly) invisible challenge to theology, was Hume's contribution to the naturalization of historical methodology, as a challenge to the "prophetic-providential" structuring of history, from ancient through early modern historiography. See Chapter 5, section 4.1 below, and especially Donald W. Livingston, *Hume's Philosophy of Common Life* (Chicago and London: University of Chicago Press, 1984), ch. 8.

Although Reid's popularity at the time cut across liberal–conservative divides, his lasting influence comes to us today through the Princeton School of theology, whose works spanned the century from Archibald Alexander's (1772–1831) *Evidences of the Authenticity, Inspiration, and Canonical Authority of Holy Scriptures* (1836) to J. Gresham Machen's (1881–1937) *Christianity and Liberalism* (1923). These works established a conception of theological epistemology that continues to influence conservative theologians today.

Reid was explicitly foundationalist in his epistemology, but he broke no new ground here. He is best known for his critique of inside-out epistemology. His attack on what he called the theory of ideas was motivated by reading Hume. He saw no flaws in Hume's reasoning, so if his reasoning led to such absurdities as our inability to justify any claims about the world around us, there must be something wrong with his premises. To identify the error, he deployed a linguistic argument. In ordinary talk about knowledge, all languages make a threefold distinction among the process of perceiving, the mind doing the perceiving, and the object perceived. None has a word for a fourth entity, the "idea"; this is a philosophical invention. Reid rejected the philosophical invention because it contradicted the common-sense principle that the things that we directly perceive by our senses do exist and are what we perceive them to be.

This critique of the nonstandard way in which philosophers are apt to use language, and thereby create insoluble philosophical problems, is an early example of the approach to philosophy associated with Ludwig Wittgenstein (see Introduction). By bringing language back to its use in ordinary life, we can see that the problem dissolves. As Roderick Chisholm (1916–99) puts it, Reid's "'principles of common sense' are the intuitive truths that all sane people accept *when they are not doing philosophy*."[19]

Reid's contribution to scriptural foundationalism was to shore up the Princeton theologians' confidence in our innate ability to perceive facts—facts of all sorts—and to know reality directly. Based on Augustine's metaphor of the two books, Charles Hodge (1797–1878) argued for a theological epistemology parallel to Reid's scientific epistemology. Just as Reid predicated confidence in the testimony of the senses on the trustworthiness of God, so Hodge predicated confidence in the testimony of the Scriptures on their status as the word of God. Archibald Alexander Hodge (1823–86) later replied to the introduction of historical-critical study of the Bible by asserting that just as the truth about nature was accessible by means of an ordinary looking and seeing, similarly the facts of the Bible were accessible to a disciplined but ordinary process of reading and understanding.

The two-books metaphor led Princeton theologians to apply to theology current theories of scientific reasoning. They made use of the inductivist view of scientific

---

[19] Roderick M. Chisholm, "Commonsensism," *Routledge*, 2:453–5 (454). My italics.

method, whose most significant early proponent was Francis Bacon (1561–1626). According to inductivists, scientific reasoning involves the formation of general principles on the basis of observable facts. Charles Hodge wrote that the Bible "is to the theologian what nature is to the man of science. It is his store-house of facts; and his method of ascertaining what the Bible teaches, is the same as that which the natural philosopher adopts to ascertain what nature teaches." The task of the theologian is to "ascertain, collect, and combine all the facts which God has revealed concerning himself and our relation to Him."[20]

Early conservative theologians vary in their accounts of the means of construction from Scripture to theology. They tended to speak rather indiscriminately of induction, of deduction, and of theology as mere organization of the facts of Scripture. But in all cases, the assumed direction of reasoning is what the foundationalist theory would lead us to expect: from the scriptural foundation to the higher levels of doctrine and theology; never from doctrine to the truth or meaning of the texts.

Among contemporary conservatives, we find more nuanced accounts of the foundational role of Scripture in theology. Donald Bloesch (1928–2010), professor of theology at Dubuque Theological Seminary, was explicitly foundationalist in his understanding of the justification of theological claims:

> As evangelical Christians we can and must speak of *foundations* of the faith. These are not, however, a priori principles or self-evident truths but the mighty deeds of God in the history of biblical Israel, the significance of which is veiled to us until our inner eyes are opened by the working of the Spirit.[21]

So, in contrast to the view of theologians such as A. A. Hodge, it is not the words of Scripture themselves that undergird theology, but rather the acts of God that are recorded therein. Bloesch would like to be able to say that the Scriptures are *inerrant*, but he believes the term has been co-opted by "a rationalistic, empiricistic mentality that reduces faith to facticity." Instead, he speaks of the abiding truthfulness and normativeness of the biblical witness. "What makes the Bible significant is not that it contains self-evident truth—truth that is universally recognizable— but that it conveys particular truth that is at the same time self-authenticating."[22]

So we see here a softening of the original foundationalist demand for *universally* accessible truth based on *indubitable* foundations. Yet despite the hesitancy regarding inerrancy (and the absolute certitude such a doctrine provides), it is still the case that the authority of Scripture is *unchallengeable*. There is no other norm

---

[20] Charles Hodge, *Systematic Theology*, 3 vols. ([1871] New York: Scribner's Sons, 1891), 1:11.
[21] Donald G. Bloesch, *Holy Scripture: Revelation, Inspiration and Interpretation* (Downers Grove, IL: InterVarsity Press, 1994), 20; his italics.
[22] Bloesch, *Holy Scripture*, 27–8.

by which it can be called into question, neither religious experience, nor church teaching, nor culture.[23]

5.2 Inside-out epistemology and liberal theology

I began this chapter with a quotation from Welch's *Protestant Thought in the Nineteenth Century*, stating that the question was whether and how theology was possible. Why this was a pressing problem at this particular time, he sums up as follows: "The historical reliability, apologetic value, and even moral authority of the Scriptures had come under heavy attack, and the possibility (or even the desirability) of revelation was in doubt. With Hume and Kant, natural theology also reached the end of the line."[24]

Developments in biblical criticism will be addressed briefly in Chapter 5, and we have already seen Hume's arguments, so here we look only at the role of Immanuel Kant in shaping liberal theology. Kant's work is voluminous and notoriously difficult to interpret, so all I claim to present here is a sketch. Kant had three goals relevant for our purposes: (1) to save Newtonian science from Hume's skepticism; (2) to save human freedom from (deterministic) Newtonian science; and (3) to save religion from both Newtonian determinism and Humean skepticism.

To accomplish the first of these goals, Kant distinguished between the *content* of our experience (colors, noises, and so forth) and the *form* of experience.[25] Its form consists in the fact that sensations are necessarily perceived as belonging to individual objects, extended in space, in temporal sequences, and in causal relations to one another. For an analogy, think of the difference between seeing only the pixels on a TV screen and seeing three-dimensional objects moving in temporal sequences. The forms of experience, he argued, are imposed on experience by the human mind. Newtonian science pertains to the forms of experience only, not the content; it describes physical bodies causing one another to move in time and space. Thus, so long as the structures of the mind were unchanging (and Kant never imagined otherwise) Newtonian science was safe from revision or refutation.

However, this assurance came at a cost: Things-as-they-appear-to-us, that is, the world of "formed" experience, he called "phenomena." Things-as-they-are-in-themselves he called "noumena." The reasoning capacity, theoretical reason, that allows us to know phenomena can never go beyond, to know noumena. We cannot even say that there are noumenal *objects* that *cause* our phenomenal experiences, since object-hood (substance) and causality are phenomenal categories only and

---

[23] See Bloesch, *Essentials of Evangelical Theology, Volume 1: God, Authority, and Salvation* (San Francisco: Harper and Row, 1978), ch. 4.

[24] Welch, *Protestant Thought*, 1:59.

[25] Note that, as with so many philosophical terms, "form" for Kant has essentially nothing to do with "Form" in Aristotle and his followers' philosophies.

cannot legitimately be applied to noumena or to relations between noumena and phenomena. Notice that this move actually supports Hume's critique of arguments for God being the *cause* of the universe. However, it preserves human freedom from Newtonian determinism, since human selves are noumenal (because not perceptible) and thus not subject to physical (phenomenal) causation.

We have seen that one of Kant's objectives was to save religion; the reader may be thinking at this point that with friends like Kant, religion needs no enemies. Nonetheless, he saw his work as a service to true religion. True religion, he believed, had nothing to do with speculative theology and metaphysics, but rather with the moral life. In his *Critique of Pure Reason*, he was denying knowledge of God (knowledge of the sort available to theoretical reason) to make room for faith. His positive approach was to argue that God's existence (as well as human freedom and immortality) could be known by means of "practical reason," since they are necessary postulates for making sense of the *moral* world. Moral obligation is known directly by intuition, not from experience of the world.[26]

So Kant's distinction between phenomena and noumena set up a correlative distinction between spheres of thought: theoretical reasoning (science and a limited sort of philosophy) and practical reasoning (ethics and a limited form of theology). From these two, he distinguished a third kind of judgment, those of aesthetics. These judgments rest on feeling, yet they claim universal validity. In all three cases, justification is inside-out: from the forms and categories in the mind, from inner conviction of moral duty, and from one's immediate inner delight in the presence of beauty.

These features of Kant's philosophy provide essential background for understanding the contribution Schleiermacher made in his famous book, *On Religion: Speeches to its Cultured Despisers* (1799). In the introduction to the 1958 edition, Rudolf Otto (1869–1937) provides the more immediate cultural background. Otto describes culture at the beginning of the nineteenth century as an "incomparably rich fabric of the burgeoning intellectual life of modern times." Schleiermacher wrote at a high point of "the germination and the blossoming of modern intellectual life"—poetry and literature, science and philosophy. In contrast to these developments, religion seemed to be a thing of the past, of interest only to the old-fashioned and "uncultured."[27]

Otto says that no matter what one's attitudes are toward Schleiermacher's account of religion and theological methods, "one is time and again enthralled

---

[26] Here a significant disagreement needs to be mentioned. Many philosophers take Kant to be saying only that the *presupposition* of God's existence is needed for making sense of the moral order; others take him to be making an argument for the actual existence of God.

[27] Rudolf Otto, "Introduction," in Friedrich Schleiermacher, *On Religion: Speeches to its Cultured Despisers*, tr. John Oman ([1799] New York: Harper and Row, 1958), vii–viii. Parenthetical references in what follows will be to this edition.

by his original and daring attempt to lead an age weary with and alien to religion back to its very mainsprings; and to reweave religion, threatened with oblivion," into the cultural life of his times (vii). I, too, have been enthralled by Schleiermacher's *Speeches*. What struck me the first time was how shockingly different his account of religion was from my own. What strikes me as I read it again for the purposes of this book is the way his intellectual journey fit perfectly into the developments of modern philosophy described so far in this chapter. I will use an unusual number of quotations here to provide a taste of Schleiermacher's classic Romantic prose and intersperse comments regarding his philosophical context.

Otto recounts that while in seminary Schleiermacher underwent a severe crisis of faith and described in a letter to his father that he began "to examine the faith of his fathers and to cleanse his heart of the debris of former ages" (xiii–xiv). After that, he embarked on the study of philosophy. Note the similarities to Descartes's rejection of the opinions he had been taught. As did Descartes, he turned to his inner resources. Schleiermacher wrote: "As a man I speak to you of the sacred secrets of mankind according to my views—of what was in me as with youthful enthusiasm I sought the unknown, of what since then I have thought and experienced, of the innermost springs of my being . . ." (3). His purpose was to describe the true essence of religion, and to distinguish it from that with which it had been confused. Among Kant's three spheres of culture (knowing, doing, and feeling), he planted religion firmly in the sphere of feeling. It is not to be confused with either doctrinal systems or moral codes. "If you have only given attention to these dogmas and opinions, therefore, you do not yet know religion itself, and what you despise is not it" (15). "In order to make quite clear to you what is the original and characteristic possession of religion, it resigns at once, all claims on anything that belongs either to science or morality" (35).

Schleiermacher struggled throughout his career to come to an adequate expression of the nature of the feeling that is the essence of religion, but then he did not expect any outward expression to do justice to something so far beyond normal human speech. Two passages in the *Speeches* are particularly illuminating:

> Why [in seeking the true nature of religion] do you not regard the religious life itself, and first those pious exaltations of the mind in which all other known activities are set aside or almost suppressed, and the whole soul is dissolved in the immediate feeling of the Infinite and Eternal? (16)

> The contemplation of the pious is the immediate consciousness of the universal existence of all finite things, in and through the Infinite, and of all temporal things in and through the Eternal. Religion is to seek this and find it in all that lives and moves, in all growth and change, in all doing and suffering. It is to have life and to know life in immediate feeling. (36)

49

Welch concludes that the beginning of modern liberal theology is marked by the subjective turn, a "Copernican revolution," that places the human subject at the center of religion:

> In the work of [Friedrich] Schleiermacher and [Samuel Taylor] Coleridge particularly [1772–1834] . . . we see a decisive Socratic turn to the self, to an understanding of religious truth that may rightly be called "existentialist." Theology now had to start from, to articulate, and to interpret a subjective view of the religious object . . . Consciousness of the truth was peculiarly one with self-consciousness.[28]

Schleiermacher's achievement in the systematic theology of his later years was to show that all *legitimate* doctrines were derivable from this inner experience. Regarding Christian beliefs, he states: "There is an inner experience to which they may all be traced; they rest upon a given, and apart from this they could not have arisen by deduction or synthesis from universally recognized propositions."[29] But doctrines are not derivable in a logical sense; rather in the sense that they were apt or adequate *expressions* of that core experience. So, for example, the source of the doctrine of creation is the awareness not only of our own dependence upon God, but of the absolute dependence of everything else as well. The doctrines of sin and grace express our experience of the waxing and waning of our God-consciousness. The divinity of Christ consists in his uninterrupted and perfect God-consciousness.

It is not technically correct to say that Schleiermacher took religious awareness as a *foundation* for theology, since foundationalism is a theory of knowledge and Schleiermacher distinguishes religious discourse from knowledge. Nonetheless, there are interesting foundationalist-like features of his approach to theology. Recall the two criteria I set out earlier: First, the foundation has to be unchallengeable (or as nearly so as possible). For Schleiermacher's purposes this means that the religious awareness must be universal and unmediated. It is universal in the sense that, while it is colored differently in different cultures, and for Christians, especially, by the influence of Jesus, it is the common source of *all* religions. It is unmediated in the sense that it is not dependent upon inference or interpretation. It is the true source or origin of religion, not a product of anything prior. To put it in foundationalist terms, there is no deeper foundation.

The second criterion for foundationalist epistemology is one-way reasoning. This requirement is satisfied in Schleiermacher's system in that doctrine is to be evaluated in light of experience, never the reverse. So God-consciousness is the

---

[28] Welch, *Protestant Thought*, 1:59–60.
[29] Friedrich Schleiermacher, *The Christian Faith*, ed. H. R. Mackintosh and J. S. Steward ([1821–2] Edinburgh: T. & T. Clark, 1960), 67.

"given" for all religion; first-order religious language (prayer, preaching, etc.), as well as doctrine and theology, are all built up from this experience. Liberal theologians since Schleiermacher have followed him in taking human religious experience or awareness as a universal feature of human life, and in supposing that this religious self-consciousness was to be the starting point for theology.

If inside-out approaches always invite the criticism that they have not adequately assured that the inner reflects the outer, we should not be surprised that already in 1841 Ludwig Feuerbach (1804–72) had charged that the idea of God is nothing more than an idea.[30] Feuerbach's theory of religion might be summarized as follows. The possibility of religion lies in consciousness, in the possibility of an inner life. The basis of religion is found in feelings or emotions and in wishes. "Man believes in gods because he seeks help from them. What he is not himself but wishes to be, he projects into the being of the gods in order that he may get it back from them."[31]

To put it in terms of our discussion of Descartes, whereas Descartes believed that only a real, objective God external to the believer was capable of producing the idea of God, Feuerbach argues that humans are quite capable of producing such an idea simply by summing up their own highest aspirations. So the argument from inner idea to external God fails. This led the mid-twentieth-century neo-orthodox theologian, Karl Barth (1886–1968), to conclude that a starting point for theology like Schleiermacher's will lead inevitably to a skeptical conclusion like Feuerbach's.[32]

5.3 Distinct types of theology

It is not uncommon to note that modern American Protestantism (but I think not British) is bifurcated into conservative and liberal strands. In this section I have "blamed" modern foundationalist epistemology for offering two, and apparently only two, possibilities for developing theological methodologies. However, the differences go beyond methods. In earlier writings, I have developed two ideal types to which liberal and conservative theologians tend to conform.[33]

In addition to the differences in theological foundations, the two types are distinguished by different theories of language. We have seen that Schleiermacher developed an expressivist theory of religious language—expressive of human religious awareness. Conservatives hold a "propositionalist" theory of language

---

[30] Ludwig Feuerbach, *Das Wesen des Christentums*, tr. George Eliot (i.e. Marian Evans) as *The Essence of Christianity* ([1841] Amherst, NY: Prometheus Books, 1989).

[31] Welch, *Protestant Thought*, 2:173.

[32] Karl Barth, *Church Dogmatics*, 14 vols. (Edinburgh: T. & T. Clark, 1936–69), I/2:288–91.

[33] An ideal type is a construction that abstracts and summarizes the common features of complex phenomena. See my *Beyond Liberalism and Foundationalism: How Modern and Postmodern Philosophy Set the Theological Agenda* (Valley Forge, PA: Trinity Press International, 1996), 6–7, 61.

that comes closer to the mainstream of modern philosophy of language: ordinary language is representative of (physical) realities; theological language is representative of theological realities. Historical theologian George Lindbeck (b.1923) thus characterizes the conservative and liberal types as cognitive-propositionalist and experiential-expressivist respectively.

I argue that the differences between these two types are due to a deeper issue (and one to which I devote Chapter 6): theories of divine action. Kant's and his followers' respect for the Newtonian closed causal order of nature led them to reject miracles and special providence, and to argue that God only works *immanently* in and through natural and historical processes. Conservative theologians, while not denying God's immanence, argued that God, as author of the laws of nature, can and does *intervene* in history, performing special revelatory actions.

These two types of theology are not mere collections of positions (Figure 6). For the conservatives, God's intervention is the source of divine revelation and therefore provides Scripture's credential as the epistemological foundation of theology, and scriptural and theological language can then be taken to describe objective realities. For the liberals, God only acts immanently within the whole and does not directly impart knowledge of religious realities. Thus, this knowledge must arise within human consciousness in accordance with natural means—by perception of the divine dimension within or under surface realities. The theological task is to express these experiences in religious language (Figure 7).

Have we reached a point in history when it is fair to say that both of these theological strategies face insuperable obstacles? The problem for the conservatives is the question of how one can know, with the requisite certitude, that the Christian Bible is, in fact, the revealed word of God. Conservative theologians

	Liberal	*Conservative*
Knowledge	experiential foundationalism (inside-out)	scriptural foundationalism (outside-in)
Language	expressivism	propositionalism
Relationship with science	incommensurability	commensurability
Divine action	immanentism	interventionism

Figure 6 A table representing the contrasting views of liberal and conservative theologians on epistemology, philosophy of language, relations with science, and divine action

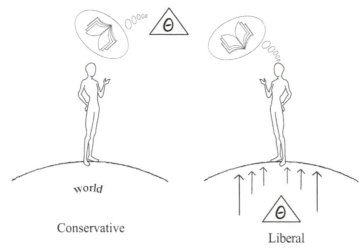

world

Conservative

Liberal

Figure 7 A representation of conservative versus liberal accounts of the action of God in revelation

provide arguments, but none of them is strong enough to serve as the *foundation* for a system of religion. The liberal use of experience in theology seems to lack sufficiently strong justifications for the claim that the experiences are experiences *of God*, and not merely symbolic expressions of humankind's highest aspirations or basic life attitudes.

6 Retrospect and prospect

Recall that the purpose of Part I of this text is to survey the development of relations between "faith and reason," and that I am employing this vague terminology intentionally. At the beginning of this chapter and again in the previous section, I have taken "faith" to refer to Christian theology—the academic study of Christian doctrines. In the historical narrative I have presented, "reason" has come to represent what is currently meant by "philosophy."

However, to end the chapter here would fail to do justice to the complex geography of current engagements between Christianity and modern developments in philosophy. So I shall sketch here an account of how philosophy has changed over the past three centuries, and then I shall be able to indicate the broader academic territory to be addressed in Chapter 3 (as, e.g., p. 12).

For Descartes, as for the ancients and medievals, philosophy was still all about everything: his system included what we now call epistemology; philosophy of religion (his arguments for God's existence); but also natural philosophy, now called natural science, and so on. I noted in the Overview of Part I that in the modern period we see the gradual separation, from the Medieval Synthesis, of all of the separate empirical disciplines we know today: cosmology, physics, biology, psychology, the social sciences. Kant made the distinction between science and philosophy official, and ruled God out of science.

A significant feature of modern thought has been the development of (new) philosophical approaches to ethics and politics, not dependent on theological tradition. But aside from this, with the subject matter of practically everything else gradually taken over by the sciences, one may well ask what was left for philosophers to do? Descartes's epistemology provided the central answer for most of the modern period: philosophy's job is to examine and evaluate the foundations of the various branches of knowledge. In this way, epistemology came to be "first philosophy"—the starting point for other subdisciplines.[34] Already in Kant's work philosophy is no longer a body of knowledge (metaphysics) but a second-order discipline that rules on the legitimacy of philosophical, scientific, ethical, and religious claims. In due course, we have come to have philosophy *of* science, of history, of logic, of mathematics.

An important shift across philosophy generally came in the mid twentieth century: "the linguistic turn."[35] Here philosophy of language became the central starting point for philosophical enquiry. There were two reasons for the shift. First, philosophers from Descartes on had taken ideas—mental contents—to be the starting point for epistemology. The besetting problem was how to know that ideas adequately represent reality. But the very idea of an idea was never clear. The German philosopher Gottlob Frege (1848–1925) is credited with ridding philosophy of "psychologism." That is, the three-way relation of language representing ideas, and ideas in turn representing the world could be replaced with the more manageable question of whether and how language represents the world. The second motive for the linguistic turn is related; it was the recognition that questions such as "What is knowledge?" could be clarified by asking what the word "knowledge" means and what are the criteria for its proper employment.

Thus, the methods of Anglo-American philosophy in the twentieth century became linguistic analysis or conceptual analysis.[36] Concepts for Kant were mental structures, but they are now understood linguistically: the concept of *knowledge*

---

[34] See esp. Richard Rorty, *Philosophy and the Mirror of Nature* (Princeton: Princeton University Press, 1979).

[35] See Richard Rorty, ed., *The Linguistic Turn: Recent Essays in Philosophical Method* (Chicago and London: University of Chicago Press, 1967).

[36] Note that "Anglo-American" is a conventional designation, having nothing to do with race or ethnicity, but distinguishing it from another *style* of philosophy, called Continental, although each approach has proponents in various geographical regions. The history of the separation is too complex to go into here, but a rough characterization might be that the Continentals follow in the lineage from Kant, G. W. F. Hegel, and beyond, while Anglo-American philosophy grew out of movements (such as the Vienna Circle) that were strictly opposed to Hegelianism.

is that which the English word "knowledge" and its cognates in other languages have in common.

The rationale for analytic philosophy is the recognition that statements about the world involve both empirical and conceptual content. For example, "John knows that the Earth is 4.5 billion years old" is true both because of the way the world is and because of the meanings of "Earth," "year," and—of particular interest to the philosopher—what "know" means. What is it for anyone to know some proposition, *p*? A long-standing answer analyzes the concept of *knowledge* as follows: (1) *p* is true; (2) person *x* believes that *p*; and (3) *x* is justified in believing that *p*. Next, what are the analyses of *truth, belief,* and *justification*?

If it is assumed that such basic concepts are universal and timeless, then philosophy yields universally valid knowledge that is immune from empirical falsification. We shall see in Chapter 3 that this conception of the nature of philosophy is being called into question. Nonetheless, it features prominently in current philosophy of religion.

An important development in theology in the modern period was the distinction, already seen in Schleiermacher's work, between first- and second-order religious language. First-order religious language is that of the Christian community in prayer, confession of faith, worship. For Schleiermacher, theology was second-order reflection on the legitimacy of doctrines, the first-order teachings of the church. There are a variety of views today of the proper relation between theologians' language and ordinary Christians' expressions of their beliefs.

So the limits of this chapter include its concentration on the rationality of second-order, theological claims. However, it is a feature of most contemporary philosophy of religion that it focuses almost exclusively on the rationality of first-order claims of individual religious believers.

The hope of the Enlightenment in general, and of analytic philosophy as well, was to have universal knowledge, and so it has been common to distinguish two disciplines, philosophy of religion and philosophical theology. These consider many of the same topics, but it was presumed that the philosopher works from an objective point of view, while the philosophical theologian is committed to a particular tradition. Current developments have blurred this distinction, but nonetheless there are relatively distinct academic communities, both concerned with "faith and reason." A third discipline, apologetics, has drawn on resources from both philosophers and theologians.

In the next chapter, we need to see what contemporary philosophers of religion are saying, and to see where the disciplines of philosophy of religion and philosophical theology may be going in the future.

3

Faith in late modern reasoning

1 Introduction

In Chapter 1, we dashed through 25 centuries of development, from the Homeric age (ninth or eighth century BC) to the beginnings of modernity (c.1600). In Chapter 2, we covered developments up to the end of the nineteenth century, with some scant attention to the twentieth. In this chapter, we consider developments in philosophy, including philosophy of religion, from the 1920s to the present.

I ended Chapter 2 by noting two of the chapter's deficits. First, it considers "faith" primarily in terms of theology—what I have called second-order discourse—but not the beliefs of the ordinary believer. Second, I noted that two relatively distinct communities of scholars have developed—philosophical theologians and philosophers of religion—and that I had not given adequate attention to the latter. Because current philosophers of religion tend to focus on first-order beliefs and language, giving attention to their work in this chapter will thereby remedy the first of the previous chapter's deficits as well as the second.

Section 2 will describe three principal positions in recent philosophy of religion. The debates among their proponents are interesting, but they may be interminable: there is something right about each, but the criticisms of each also have merit. This will also be an appropriate place to consider critiques of what I have been calling "inside-out" philosophy. In section 3, I return to the topic of epistemology and trace the accumulation of problems facing foundationalist theories of knowledge. I then describe (in section 4) their replacements, beginning around 1950. This change in the philosophical world is good news for theology and for religious belief more generally, because it is the inadequacy of the modern epistemological theories, not of Christianity itself, that made justification of belief so difficult for 300 years, as I show by noting briefly some of the uses of holist epistemology in theology. I end this chapter with an account of the new challenge that holist epistemology has created for religious belief (and theology): a new and more virulent form of religious relativism.

Chapter 4, the final chapter in Part I of this text, describes the most ambitious and, I argue, most adequate account of rationality, that of Alasdair MacIntyre. I intend to show how his account both addresses the problem of relativism and also incorporates the best of the three prominent recent positions in philosophy of religion, while explaining the weaknesses of each. Then I consider what MacIntyre's work entails for the various types of arguments for God's existence (a topic to which much more space is usually given in philosophy of religion texts) and explain why they fail to be convincing in our current intellectual world. I end with an alternative, MacIntyrean, account of what it would now look like to make a case for the rationality of Christian belief.

2 The shape of current philosophy of religion

Of all the topics that have been investigated by philosophers of religion, the one that has received the most attention in the modern period is what I am loosely calling faith and reason. Evaluation of arguments for the existence of God forms a large part of many texts, and this is a subtopic within that of faith and reason.

I mentioned in the Overview to this Part that one faith-and-reason issue is the question of whether religious belief *needs* to be rational or not, and if so, what would count as showing its rationality. This is where some of the most recent work in the philosophy of religion is focused. I consider three positions, called evidentialism, Reformed epistemology, and "Wittgensteinian fideism."[1]

2.1 Evidentialism

Evidentialism is the thesis that belief in God does indeed need to be supported by adequate evidence.

In Chapter 2 (section 4.3), I noted the change in meaning of "probable knowledge" in the early modern period, from belief approved by authorities to belief supported by the preponderance of evidence. I noted that this latter sense of the term was not available to René Descartes, but soon afterwards it came to influence discussions of the rationality of Christian belief. John Locke was concerned about the proliferation of radical religious sects in his day and argued that it is a misuse of our God-given faculties, and therefore a sin, to believe anything without sufficient evidence. So evidentialism has been common throughout most of modern thought. Over the years, the proportion of thinkers who have judged some form of religious belief to be adequately supported has gradually diminished, while the number arguing explicitly that it does not has increased. David Hume's arguments, published both before and after his death in 1776, have been highly influential. He argued that in addition to positive evidence, such as goodness and order in nature, one needed to give equal attention to the negative, such as the evil and disorder.

W. K. Clifford (1845–79) is credited with invention of the term "evidentialism" in "The Ethics of Belief" (1879), where he claimed that there is an intellectual

---

[1] Two books are particularly helpful overviews of debates: Antony Flew and Alasdair MacIntyre, eds., *New Essays in Philosophical Theology* (London: SCM Press, 1955); and Alvin Plantinga and Nicholas Wolterstorff, eds., *Faith and Rationality: Reason and Belief in God* (Notre Dame, IN: University of Notre Dame Press, 1983).

and moral duty not to believe in God without a sufficient argument. More recent religious skeptics are Antony Flew (1923–2010), J. L. Mackie (1917–81), and Kai Nielsen (b.1926). Flew is best known for his claim that in the face of counter-evidence, such as disorder in the world, theists regularly qualify their claims to the extent that they no longer have cognitive content. Mackie is noted for arguing that the "logical problem of evil" provides a definitive refutation of monotheistic religions (see Chapter 7 below). That is, he claims that the obvious existence of evil in the world cannot be logically reconciled with the proposition that the world is the work of an omnipotent and all-good God.

Nielsen is significant for arguing that anthropomorphic concepts of God are superstitious and plainly false, while non-anthropomorphic concepts are incoherent—they really amount to a form of atheism. He is particularly important in the current trialogue for coining the term "Wittgensteinian fideism."[2] We consider the appropriateness of this term in section 2.3.

Among evidentialists on the positive side, the most famous in earlier history was William Paley (1743–1805), who wrote a very widely read argument for God's existence based on the apparent design of the natural world, particularly of the fit between organisms and their environments. More recent figures are Basil Mitchell (1917–2011), who claimed that while no single argument for God's existence is sufficient, together they make an adequate "cumulative case" for theism. Using technical probability theory, Richard Swinburne (b.1934) argues that the various individual theistic arguments each make God's existence more probable, but none makes it more probable than not. However, he writes, if we add the evidence of religious experience, this does tip the balance of probability in favor of theism.

2.2 Reformed epistemology

While the school of Reformed epistemology has numerous participants, I shall focus here on the work of Alvin Plantinga (b.1932), not only because he is the most significant of its proponents, but also because his position is too complex to describe briefly, as I have done with several of the evidentialists. Plantinga realizes (correctly, I argue) that "classical foundationalism," if taken as the only account of justification, makes the provision of adequate theistic arguments impossible. Classical foundationalism admits as foundations only premises that are incorrigibly derived from sensations or are self-evidently true; examples are what are now called sense data, such as "I seem to be seeing a tree," and "$2 + 1 = 3$," respectively. If these are the only sorts of "properly basic beliefs," then it is not surprising that no argument for theism can be built upon them, but this stringent requirement also

---

[2] Kai Nielsen, "Wittgensteinian Fideism," *Journal of the Royal Institute of Philosophy*, 42, no. 161 (July 1967): 191–209.

rules out arguments for knowledge of the past, for the existence of other minds, and even, as Hume showed, knowledge that an external world exists at all.

Plantinga first makes a case for the irrationality of classical foundationalism. These foundationalists have no argument or criterion for selection of their categories of basic beliefs, and therefore no proper *foundationalist* justification for their theory. He then goes on to make a positive case for Christian belief. He points out that Christians (other than philosophers) never in fact argue (or even often assert) that God exists. It is not a hypothesis, but a given in the Christian life. So what is there to prevent Christians from counting God's existence as among their properly basic beliefs? His criterion for a justified belief is one that is formed by a person's epistemic faculties when they are functioning properly in the circumstances for which they were divinely designed. If God exists, it is reasonable to assume that God would design people so that they would come to hold the (justified) belief in God's existence. (Note the apparent circularity here: God's existence and likely design explain how we have the capacity to know of God's existence.) This move represents an inheritance from Reformed theology—in particular John Calvin's teaching on the *sensus divinitatis*, an implanted knowledge of God not dependent on human teaching.

However, if God has designed us with the capacity to know him, how is it possible to explain the fact that there are so many unbelievers? Calvin (1509–64) taught that while the human intellect is darkened by sin, the fact that humans are created in God's image implies that the unrepentant still must have some remnant of knowledge of God. Not all recipients cherish this knowledge, but rather cover it over by idolatry or willful self-deception. Here there is a connection with Locke's and Clifford's association of irrationality with moral lapse or sin (an association that goes all the way back to Augustine). Plantinga says that a system of beliefs (a "noetic structure") is rational if it is the product of the individual having done "the right thing with respect to one's believings. It is to violate no epistemic duties."[3] Notice how this account shifts the focus from whether a *belief* is justified to whether *the person who holds it* is justified; that is, within his or her epistemic rights to believe it.

Note also that while Plantinga has given a powerful rebuttal to what he calls classical foundationalism, he still thinks within the general foundationalist model—he argues that belief in God is a "properly basic" belief for Christians, and then uses it as a premise to reach other conclusions. A curious feature of his position, though, is that although belief in God is properly basic, "it is not groundless"[4] because there are circumstances for an individual, such as when one calls on God for help in a time of danger, that presuppose that God can hear and help

---

[3] Alvin Plantinga, "Reason and Belief in God," in Plantinga and Wolterstorff, *Faith and Rationality*, 16–93 (52).
[4] Plantinga, "Reason and Belief," 74.

in such situations, and this presupposition entails that God exists.[5] I believe that a post-foundationalist, "holist" theory of knowledge (see section 4) would better allow Plantinga to make his points while removing what appear to be inconsistencies or circularities in his account of Christian knowledge claims.

2.3 "Wittgensteinian fideism"

I place the heading of this subsection in quotation marks because it is the name given to a position held by some philosophers of religion who base their accounts of faith and reason on Ludwig Wittgenstein's work, but who vehemently deny that they are fideists. Again, I describe here only the most prominent example, D. Z. Phillips (1934–2006).

Phillips is called (pejoratively) a fideist, that is, one who denies that a system of religious beliefs can be tested by any criterion external to itself, including that of rational assessment.[6] There are two aspects of Phillips's work that lead to this charge. The first is that, following Wittgenstein, he has entirely rejected modern foundationalism, particularly the variant that sets philosophy up as a universal arbiter of the rationality of other disciplines. Phillips's rejection of foundationalism in general leads him to deny that religious beliefs should be subject to the same demands for factual support as empirical theories. Thus, a foundationalist such as Nielsen takes Phillips to be saying that there are *no* standards for correct religious statements.

Two further sources of miscommunication between Phillips and his critics come from Wittgenstein's theory of language. I mentioned ever so briefly (Chapter 2, section 5.3) that conservative and liberal Protestants in the USA are divided over the nature of religious language. The conservatives hold to the common modern theory that language gets its meaning from the objects and states of affairs that it describes; the liberals developed a theory whereby religious language is not descriptive of religious objects but rather *expressive* of human religious awareness. One of Wittgenstein's major contributions was to show that neither referentialism nor expressivism (or even the two theories together) could do justice to the complexity of language. To understand language, it is not helpful to attempt to produce *any* theory about it; rather, one has to observe the multifarious ways in which it is bound up with actions in the social world.

Wittgenstein invented the concept of *language games*, with associated *forms of life*—typical patterns of social interactions, such as making purchases in a store, playing guessing games, giving instructions at building sites. In all of these cases, there is the possibility of getting something wrong, but the *game itself* needs no

---

[5] Plantinga, "Reason and Belief," 80.
[6] Anthony C. Thiselton, "Fideism," in *A Concise Encyclopedia of the Philosophy of Religion* (Grand Rapids, MI: Baker Academic, 2002), 102.

justification other than its being something we agree to do. A religion is a large collection of language games and forms of life.

Wittgenstein made a cryptic remark, "Theology as grammar,"[7] which has prompted later writers to compare the teaching of theology to the sorts of corrections we offer beginners—for example: "No, we don't say the Trinity is three Gods in one; we say that there are three persons in one God." So again, criticisms and corrections of various sorts are at home in religious forms of life, but Phillips argues that there is no place to stand outside of religion to call into question an entire religious way of life and thought.

A common mistake in interpreting Wittgenstein's view of religion is to take religion as a whole as an instance of a form of life with its own particular language game. Then it is imagined that religious language is somehow sealed off from all other spheres of life, and so not only immune from the rational assessments appropriate to other spheres, but even *unintelligible* to those who do not participate in it. So, for instance, Edward Wierenga (b.1947) says that Wittgenstein held "that the religious believer's use of language is so different from that of the non-believer that the non-believer is unable to contradict the believer."[8] The brief remark by Wittgenstein that comes closest to supporting Wierenga's claim is the following: "If an atheist says: 'There won't be a Judgment Day, and another says there will,' do they mean the same?—Not clear what criterion of meaning the same is."[9]

Phillips has written much more on this topic; he writes: "In the course of his discussions on the notion of belief as it appears in religious contexts, Wittgenstein . . . wanted to deny that the non-believer contradicted the believer when he said, 'I do not believe in God . . .' One of his reasons for this conclusion was that he did not think that 'There is a God' and 'There is no God' are contradictory statements within the same mode of discourse."[10] Certainly, Phillips says, much meaning is lost when Christian language is torn away from its scriptural contexts. And there are varieties of unbelief ranging from that of a person who knows nothing of the context to one who knows the context quite well, yet refuses to participate in a Scripture-formed life. Wittgenstein's point in the whole of the lecture that gave rise to this discussion[11]

---

[7] Philosophical theologians who have made use of this remark include Paul L. Holmer, *The Grammar of Faith* (San Francisco: Harper & Row, 1978); and Dallas M. High, *Language, Persons, and Belief: Studies in Wittgenstein's Philosophical Investigations and Religious Uses of Language* (New York: Oxford University Press, 1967). See also historical theologian George Lindbeck, *The Nature of Doctrine: Religion and Theology in a Postliberal Age* (Philadelphia: Westminster Press, 1984).

[8] Edward R. Wierenga, "Philosophy of Religion," in John V. Canfield, ed., *Philosophy of Meaning, Knowledge and Value in the Twentieth Century* (London and New York: Routledge, 1997), 429–46 (434).

[9] Ludwig Wittgenstein, *Lectures and Conversations on Aesthetics, Psychology and Religious Belief*, ed. Cyril Barrett (Berkeley: University of California Press, 1967), 58.

[10] D. Z. Phillips, *Religion without Explanation* (Oxford: Basil Blackwell, 1976), 183.

[11] Wittgenstein, *Lectures*, 53–72.

is that belief and action are so closely interwoven that, apart from knowing how the (purported) belief in God or the Last Judgment affects the speaker's life, we cannot judge what, if anything, it could mean to him or her.

I suspect that most readers will find this account of Phillips's work unsatisfying. His ideas cannot be summed up in a neat thesis about faith and reason; in this sense, he is being true to his mentor, Wittgenstein, who believed that the job of philosophy is not to present theories about, say, the essence of language, but rather to attempt patiently to clear up confusions as they arise. Nonetheless, I hope that the Wittgensteinian point of view will become clearer by the end of this chapter. Also, at the end, we should be in a position to explain both the strengths and weaknesses of all the positions surveyed above.

2.4 Excursus: Escaping the Cartesian theater

It is appropriate at this point to note the escape from the modern image of the Cartesian philosopher trapped in his or her own mind, since it was one of the philosophical confusions that Wittgenstein was at pains to cure. As I have noted, in a variety of contexts, Descartes's peculiar image of his true self as being located inside his mind or soul has had disastrous consequences for the whole of modern thought. His inside-out approach led not to the certitude he desired but to even more radical forms of skepticism than had gone before. Hume did the best job of laying out the skeptical consequences of beginning the quest for knowledge with the representations inside one's mind, and at the same time Thomas Reid pointed out that the problems were the result of the misleading way in which philosophers were speaking of perception: interposing a (perceptible) idea between the perceiver and the (now questionable) perceptibility of the object. Arguments over these issues have continued right up to the present.

However, students these days often fail to appreciate the problem. They have to be coached to believe that they are seeing reddish, roundish "sense data" (the twentieth-century version of ideas) rather than a tomato. It has not been long, though, since the inside-out metaphor spontaneously affected (infected?) even children. Philosopher Bryan Magee (b.1930) describes the moment in his youth when this image struck him. He was in chapel when he reflected on the fact that upon closing his eyes all of the other boys disappeared—that is, his visual image of them did. "Up to that moment," he says,

> I had always taken it for granted that I was in immediate contact with the people and things outside of me . . . but now, suddenly, I realized that their existence was one thing and my awareness of it something radically other . . . even now after all these years, what I cannot put into words is how indescribably appalling I found that moment of insight . . . as if I were for ever cut off

from everything that existed—apart from myself—and as if I were trapped for life inside my own head.[12]

In the Introduction to this volume, I contrasted three approaches to philosophy. One takes philosophy to deal with perennial problems. Two more recent approaches to philosophy include the Wittgensteinian and the Popperian. Popper's view (and the one most often illustrated in this text) is that philosophical problems are rooted in urgent questions arising outside of philosophy. We shall see many examples of such problems in following chapters. Wittgenstein took philosophical problems to be largely the result of confusions coming from misuse of language or misleading mental pictures and metaphors. The task of philosophy is to dissolve such problems, not to solve them, by showing how our language has "gone on holiday."

Clearly, the problem recalled in this section is best met with a Wittgensteinian approach, and, in fact, much of Wittgenstein's (later) philosophical work was "therapy" directed at victims like Magee. Wittgenstein and others have been largely successful in dissolving the problem within Anglo-American epistemology. However, philosophical theologians Fergus Kerr (b.1931) and Nicholas Lash (b.1934) find that the inside-out imagery is still quite influential in theology. This may be because of the way liberal theologians developed inside-out theological methodologies. Lash and Kerr help to exorcise the Cartesian self by means of parody. For Lash it is the "anxious little person" trapped in its own head; for Kerr it is "the hermit in the head."[13]

I find that simply making a picture of the mental image helps to free us from its power (Figure 8 overleaf).

A strange fact about recent philosophy is that the "linguistic turn," described at the end of Chapter 2, should have eliminated the skeptical worries arising from the "idea-idea." Recall Gottlob Frege's complaint that the concept of an *idea* had never been clear. If ideas are supposed to represent things or states of affairs, and language represents the ideas, why not eliminate the slippery middle term of the relation? Ideas would become the province of psychology, and philosophy should take the relation between language and world as its central business. This is what has in fact happened in Anglo-American philosophy. What is strange is that worries about a mind- or idea-independent world were transmogrified into worries about a language-independent reality. Richard Rorty (1931–2007) explains as follows: Modern epistemology came into being when Descartes and his followers thought of the mind as a *mirror* of reality. When language replaced ideas as the

---

12 Bryan Magee, *Confessions of a Philosopher: A Personal Journey through Western Philosophy from Plato to Popper* (New York: Random House, 1998), 9–10.

13 Nicholas Lash, *Easter in Ordinary: Reflections on Human Experience and the Knowledge of God* (Charlottesville: University of Virginia Press, 1986); and Fergus Kerr, *Theology after Wittgenstein*, 2nd ed. (London: SPCK, [1976] 1997).

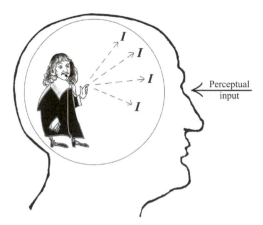

Figure 8 A representation of Descartes's head, the space inside representing his mind. Inside the mind is a miniature figure of (the real) Descartes, examining the ideas he finds there (*I* represents an idea)

main focus of philosophy, the metaphor of a mirror remained, and so the question became one of how language could *mirror* reality.[14]

Kevin Vanhoozer (b.1957) well illustrates veil-of-language skepticism, yet attributes it to Kant, who was writing long before the linguistic turn. Vanhoozer writes:

> The Kantian picture contributes to the epistemological predicament, for he demonstrated that there is a constructive dimension to human knowing. The mind does not simply mirror reality, but rather works reality over . . . Kant could not imagine forms of logic or physics other than those of Aristotle and Newton, yet we now have to contend with alternative forms of logic, geometry, and physics. What Kant took to be universal categories of the understanding have instead turned out to be contingent and historically conditioned. The mind is not a *mirror* but a filter of nature. For post-Kantians, then, the predicament is that we construct the world with historically variable and culturally conditioned conceptual schemes . . .
>
> The Kantian problematic amounts to the fundamental dilemma whether anything . . . is really there . . . or is everything constructed . . .? The difficulty—the Kantian problematic—is that there is no way to get behind or above our language and our conceptual schemes to check whether they fit with reality.[15]

---

[14] Richard Rorty, *Philosophy and the Mirror of Nature* (Princeton, NJ: Princeton University Press, 1979), see in particular p. 211.

[15] "The State of Claims to Truth," in J. Andrew Kirk and Kevin J. Vanhoozer, eds., *To Stake a Claim: Mission and the Western Crisis of Knowledge* (New York: Orbis, 1999), 21.

The problem with this worry is, as Rorty noted, the mirror image and a picture of the knower looking at the world, but now the world is draped or veiled by language. Clearly this is one of the beguiling pictures that Wittgenstein would help us to escape by showing us how language and world are inextricably related. Neither language nor the world is conceivable for humans apart from or prior to the other.

It is true that we cannot know what the world is like apart from our human, linguistically shaped, experience of it, but to want such nonhuman knowledge is to want to be like God and we should lean against this craving. Note that to recognize that human knowledge is not divine knowledge is not to say that it is no knowledge at all.

3 Foundationalism in the twentieth century

Following this excursus, we return to the role of foundationalism in religious knowledge.[16] Plantinga has already made a large part of the argument that I want to make in this section. First, there is his clever use of foundationalism itself to defeat foundationalism: there is no foundationalist argument to support the foundationalist theory of knowledge. As I would put it, the position is self-referentially incoherent. Second, he has noted that classical foundationalism, which recognizes only certain or incorrigible (irrefutable) beliefs as properly foundational (or basic), never enables one to argue to any interesting claims—or even uninteresting ones, for that matter, such as "I ate breakfast yesterday"!

In this section, I recount the history of the rejection of foundationalism, but I shall follow the progression in philosophy of science because it has been clearer and more decisive in this discipline than in others. A parallel story could be presented of the rejection of foundationalism in biblical studies, theology, and other disciplines. Along the way, I shall note some of these parallels.

A second reason for beginning with philosophy of science is that it is very difficult to keep in mind that criticism of a philosophical *theory* of knowledge is not the same as denial of the truth or justification of beliefs that the theory has been used to justify. So, until a newer and better theory of knowledge is brought to bear on Christian belief and theology, the worry easily arises that the beliefs themselves are being called into question. Any such confusion will distract from the philosophical points I wish to make here.

3.1 Logical Positivism

An organized, communal approach to philosophy of science began in the 1920s, largely in Vienna, but also in Berlin and then England. The members of the Vienna

---

[16] These two topics are not unrelated, as Rorty's *Mirror of Nature* amply shows, but the connections need not be pursued here.

and Berlin Circles came from a variety of disciplines, but they shared a common goal of investigating the *foundations* of science. Some members, such as Rudolf Carnap (1891–1970), were what Plantinga calls classical foundationalists. That is, only contemporary reports of simple sensory experiences had the requisite certitude (incorrigibility) to serve as a foundation for empirical knowledge. Carnap's hope was that by means of definitions, statements about ordinary material objects could be constructed from collections of reports of sensual properties at space–time points. However, he soon abandoned this project as hopeless, and accepted the more workable position that sentences describing ordinary, intersubjectively recognizable, states of affairs are sufficiently solid for the foundations of science. So the insistence on absolute certitude for scientific foundations may be one of the shortest-lived philosophical theses in history!

Due to the Nazi takeover of Europe, members of the Logical Positivist school spread widely, to Britain, the USA, and Australia. Along with the allied school of "logical atomism," in England, this was a significant source of what is conventionally called Anglo-American philosophy.

Meanwhile, throughout the modern period there was an attempt to get clear on what it means, in Plantinga's terms, for a statement to be self-evidently true. Plantinga has already noted part of the problem. While "1 + 2 = 3" is self-evidently true for everyone reading this text, for some "21 × 21 = 441" may not be. Thus, while Plantinga speaks in terms of beliefs being properly basic "for me" or for someone else, he is implicitly acknowledging that this sort of individualism is problematic in epistemology—a point to which I shall return (at the end of section 3.3).

To trace the many attempts to pin down self-evidently true propositions would take us too far afield—through the foundations of mathematics, Immanuel Kant's "synthetic *a priori*" knowledge, and finally to a discussion of tautologies and the criteria for synonymy (that is, how to know when two words mean the same). In the end, only tautologies such as "All green things are green" are uncontested as self-evident. But tautologies tell us nothing about the world, since all we know from our example is that *if* there exist any green things then they are green.

So again the quest for foundational statements immune from doubt has led to types of statements that are useless for supporting any interesting conclusions. I have written that the foundationalist faces a corollary of Murphy's Law ("Anything that can go wrong, will"); namely, whenever one finds suitably indubitable beliefs to serve as a foundation, they will always turn out to be useless for justifying any interesting claims; beliefs that are useful for justifying other claims will always turn out *not* to be indubitable, and in fact will be found to be dependent upon the structure they are intended to justify.[17] (We take up this last point in section 4.)

---

[17] See Nancy Murphy, *Beyond Liberalism and Fundamentalism: How Modern and Postmodern Philosophy Set the Theological Agenda* (Valley Forge, PA: Trinity Press International, 1996), 90.

In short, classical, or "radical," or "strong" foundationalism fails entirely as a theory of knowledge.

A parallel with theology is in order here. Strong foundationalism can easily lead Christians to promote an inerrantist doctrine of Scripture. That is, if the possibility of the Bible's containing any error at all is accepted, then a passage that one wants to use to support a theological claim just might happen to be one of the erroneous ones. Doubt creeps in, and for the strong foundationalist, there is no longer any foundation at all.

3.2 Construction problems

In early modern philosophy, two kinds of reasoning were recognized. One is what Descartes called demonstrative reasoning. What he was aiming for was what is now called deductive reasoning, which guarantees that the conclusions that are correctly drawn from true premises will also be true. Again, the history is too complex to follow here. Suffice it to say that since Descartes's day, philosophers and logicians have gotten much more precise about deduction, largely by inventing new forms of symbolic logic. However, as precision has increased, the scope of the applicability of deductive reasoning has shrunk. In particular, it guarantees the transmission of truth only within a formal system, but it loses this character when applied to the real world. A simple example: it is an axiom of Euclidean geometry that parallel lines never meet. But if we take this to mean that two "parallel" phone lines will never meet, we are implicitly adding the (false) assumption that phone lines never sag.

Much of the power of Hume's skeptical arguments came from his recognition that there could never be adequate justification for inductive reasoning—the second mainstay of early modern epistemology. Strictly speaking, induction is drawing universal conclusions from limited sets of instances. The term is also used more broadly to refer to any inferences in which the claim that is made goes beyond what can be deduced from the premises. Examples are arguments on the basis of analogy, predictions of the future, inference to causes, and so forth. Hume's skeptical conclusions exploited the weaknesses of such arguments. For example, to argue from the fact that the sun has always risen in the past to the conclusion that it will rise tomorrow requires the addition of a general premise regarding the uniformity of nature. But what could justify the claim that nature always operates uniformly except an inductive argument from the fact that it has always operated uniformly in the past?

It is common now to dismiss "the problem of induction" as based on a misguided demand that induction provide the same certitude as deduction. Nonetheless, the debates about the legitimacy of induction are important because they alert us to the fact that even indubitable foundations will not ordinarily lead to indubitable conclusions because of the fallibility of the arguments upon which they depend.

At best, in ordinary life, in science, and in theology we have well confirmed conclusions, but never proof.

3.3 The Neopositivist movement

The Logical Positivists had the great intellectual virtues of recognizing their failures and of being willing to move on. Consequently, shortly after the exodus from Germany and Austria, the Logical Positivists evolved into what is now called the Neopositivist movement, which lasted from approximately 1936 through the 1970s. Carl Hempel (1905–97) and Karl Popper were two of the most significant figures.

The standard (foundationalist) model of science for the Neopositivists was called the layer-cake model. The bottom layer was composed of facts, data, observations. This foundation was not thought to be of concrete (to push the metaphor); however, a solid layer of cake is usually sufficient to hold up the rest. The next layer comprised laws or generalizations—the results of induction from collections of particular facts; for example, all gases expand when heated. The top layer comprised the scientific theories that *explained* the regularities described by the laws—for example, the kinetic theory of heat (heat is equivalent to the mean velocity of the movement of gas particles).

Construction from one layer to the next was the main problem for the Neopositivists. I have already mentioned the problem of induction, and much was written about when and why some inductive arguments were legitimate. But no sort of induction could justify the leap from the laws to the explanatory theories. Hempel and Popper both offered important solutions.

Hempel coined the term "hypothetico-deductive reasoning" to name one of the most important forms of reasoning used in science. It is also used (more loosely) in everyday explanations, in biblical interpretation, and theology. In Chapter 4, we see that it is useful for interpreting theistic arguments based on design. Hempel acknowledged that there is no such thing as a logic of discovery; theories in science come from the creative imagination of scientists. What matters is the "logic of confirmation"; that is, the goal is to show that, if the hypothesized theory is true, then we would expect to find the observations and data that we have. For example, if the kinetic theory is true, then increased heat causes faster movements of gas particles, which then collide more often with the walls of the container, and this is measured as increased pressure. Next, further implications are drawn from the hypothesis, ideally by deductive reasoning. If these further consequences are borne out by experience or observation then the theory is confirmed, and if not it is disconfirmed or falsified. Note that the theory is never said to be *proved*, since another, better hypothesis may come along in the future and displace it. So our layer cake now needs to be thought of more as a wedding cake with upper layers supported by dowel rods (Figure 9).

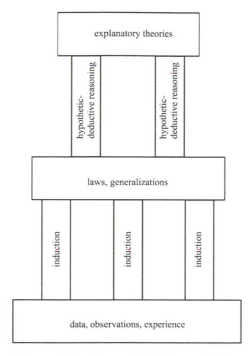

Figure 9 The Neopositivist wedding-cake model of science, with data supporting general laws (by means of induction), and laws supporting theories that explain them (e.g., by hypothetico-deductive reasoning)

Popper is known for his "falsificationism." That is, adding one more confirming instance to a law or theory makes little difference to its justification, but one negative instance can falsify a purportedly universal law or theory. Popper was enormously influential in philosophy of science, and the next generation of philosophers usually took him as their main target. However, for our purposes, he is most interesting because he is clearly hunting for a way beyond foundationalism. Here is a vivid quotation:

> the empirical basis of objective science has thus nothing 'absolute' about it. Science does not rest upon solid bedrock. The bold structure of its theories rises, as it were, above a swamp. It is like a building erected on piles. The piles are driven down from above into the swamp, but not down to any natural or 'given' base; and if we stop driving the piles deeper it is not because we have reached firm ground. We simply stop when we are satisfied that the piles are firm enough to carry the structure, at least for the time being.[18]

---

[18] Karl Raimund Popper, *The Logic of Scientific Discovery* (New York: Basic Books, 1959); quotation from reprint by Harper and Row, 1965, p. 111; tr. Popper from *Logic der Forschung* (Vienna, 1935).

In addition to Popper's obvious discomfort with the foundationalist imagery, note the communal "we" that he employs. By Popper's day, it was widely recognized that science is a communal task—the relevant community of scientists has to judge when the factual support is strong enough. This represents a significant difference in interest from Plantinga's question of when an individual is within her or his epistemic rights to hold a belief. The focus here is on the theories, and whether *they* are well enough justified for the world to accept them. Yet another step away from typical modern accounts of knowledge (and toward the "holism" to come after) was his recognition that a whole system of theories is called into question by a potential falsifier, and the scientific community must judge where a change should be made.

4 The development of post-foundationalist epistemologies

We have seen (in section 2.3 above) that Wittgenstein, already in the 1930s, denied the need for foundations for forms of life, but I date the end of foundationalism to 1951, when W. V. O. Quine (1908–2000) gave his famous lecture, "Two Dogmas of Empiricism." Thus, this section begins with his contributions to "holist" epistemology. Two additional subsections pick out from the works of philosophers of science Thomas Kuhn and Imre Lakatos some important ingredients that will go into the crafting of the theory of knowledge (by Alasdair MacIntyre) that I claim is sophisticated enough to address the question of the rationality of Christian belief.

4.1 W. V. O. Quine's new metaphor

It should be clear from the history I have traced so far that images, models, and metaphors are potent influences in the development of philosophical theories, for example the building metaphor that has shaped modern epistemology. Perhaps, then, Quine's new metaphor for a system of knowledge will turn out to be one of his greatest contributions. Quine rejected Descartes's presumption that a whole system of beliefs could be called into doubt all at once; Quine recognized that doubt is only reasonable when it is based on parts of a system that are not called into question.

Quine's image of knowledge is that of a web or net (Figure 10), with each belief justified if it is tied (by some form of reasoning) to beliefs that we have no reason to question. The net is constrained by (but not tied to) a boundary consisting of the deliverances of the physical senses, thus making Quine a (crude?) empiricist. However, he rejected both of the criteria I listed as identifying foundationalist epistemology. There is no special *class* of beliefs directly tied to experience— beliefs vary continuously in their distance from experience. And even if there were

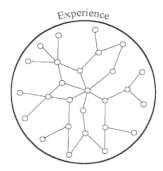

Experience

Figure 10 A Quinean web of beliefs. Note that tiny circles representing beliefs nearest the exterior of the web are not connected to any specific part of the experiential boundary

a set of special experientially certified beliefs, reasoning would not always proceed from that set to the others, because the theoretical knowledge near the interior of the web often determines which putative experiential facts will be taken seriously.

When problems occur within the system, either (1) "recalcitrant experiences"—something like Popper's potential falsifiers—or (2) logical inconsistencies, there will usually be a variety of ways to repair the network, and the choices are usually made on the pragmatic basis of wanting to disturb our shared belief system as little as possible.[19] Quine's new picture of knowledge is salutary for religion scholars. No longer is there a need to find an unquestionable starting point, a theological foundation, before one can begin the task of theology proper. And of course this eliminates the need to choose between scriptural and experiential foundations. So Quine's model removes 300 years' worth of epistemological headaches. However, it still does not provide adequate guidance for theology: what use are theologians to make of Scripture and religious experience? And what of history?

4.2 Thomas Kuhn's revolutions

Quine emphasized the tendency to seek solutions to epistemological problems that disturb our system of belief as little as possible. Thomas Kuhn's interest was in the (relatively rare) cases of radical change. He introduced "paradigm" as a technical term in philosophy of science and recounted the history of science as a series of revolutions in which one paradigm replaces its predecessor. Kuhn was a historian of science, not a philosopher, and his work was intended to counter textbook accounts of science in terms of cumulative growth. In Chapter 2, we have already

---

[19] W. V. O. Quine, "Two Dogmas of Empiricism," *Philosophical Review* 40 (1951): 202–43; and Quine and J. S. Ullian, *The Web of Belief* (New York: Random House, 1970).

seen something of one paradigm change, that from Aristotelian and Ptolemaic science to atomistic and Copernican systems.

Paradigms incorporate the data, laws, and theories recognized by the Neopositivists. But an interesting addition, and one that is crucial for a deeper understanding of the failure of foundationalism, is his (and others') recognition of *theories of instrumentation*. These are part of the *network* of theories (note the holism) that explain why the classes of data used in the paradigm are legitimate. For example, telescopic observations were crucial to the Copernican revolution, but a theory of optics needed to be incorporated into the new paradigm to explain why images seen through these new tubular devices should be taken to be superior to those seen by the naked eye.

In addition, a new paradigm usually involves a shift in metaphysical conceptions of the very nature of reality. Think of the shift from Aristotelian hylomorphic concepts of the material world to modern atomism. It should be of interest to theologians that scientific paradigms have their own authoritative texts, such as Newton's *Principia Mathematica*, and the task for scientific practitioners is to apply the formative text to outstanding problems. Note also the critical role Kuhn gives to the tie between language and practice: paradigmatic experiments (like those done by students in physics labs) tie the theoretical language to ways of interacting with the world and thereby flesh out the meaning of the theories.[20]

Kuhn's *Structure of Scientific Revolutions* is said to be the most widely read text in philosophy of science of the last 30 years of the twentieth century, but he was inundated with criticisms. Many, perhaps most, of these addressed what readers took to be relativistic implications of his work. For one thing, he noted that ideals of good science varied (somewhat) from one paradigm to another—there is no single account of scientific rationality. He likened the scientist's change from one paradigm to another to religious conversion, claiming that the change "transform[s] the scientific imagination in ways that we shall ultimately need to describe as a transformation of the world within which scientific work was done."[21] This sounds reminiscent of Paul's assertion (as translated by John Howard Yoder), that "If one is in Christ, behold a whole new world!" (2 Cor. 5.17).[22]

4.3 Imre Lakatos and scientific rationality

Imre Lakatos (1922–74) was primarily a philosopher of mathematics, but he presented an account of change in science that built on Popper's falsificationism,

---

[20] Thomas S. Kuhn, *The Structure of Scientific Revolutions*, 2nd ed. ([1962] Chicago: University of Chicago Press, 1970).

[21] Kuhn, *Structure*, 6.

[22] John H. Yoder, *The Politics of Jesus* (Grand Rapids, MI: Eerdmans, 1972), 189, n. 43; his justification for this translation is on pp. 226–7.

especially on its holist elements, and provided a counterpoint to what he saw as Kuhn's irrationalism.[23]

In place of Kuhn's successive paradigms, he developed an account of the history of science in terms of competing research programs. His goal was to argue that despite Kuhn's having shown that there are no theory-independent data, and that standards for good scientific research are paradigm-dependent, it was still possible to judge which is the most rational to pursue. His central insight is that research programs can be compared on the basis of *how they change over time* in response to problematic empirical discoveries.

Lakatos described a research program (Figure 11) as follows: There is a network of theoretical assertions supported by a body of data. One theory, the "hard core,"

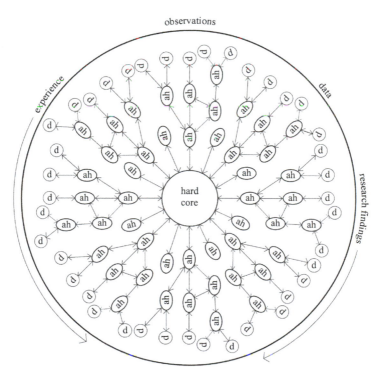

Figure 11 A (simplified) temporal cross-section of a Lakatosian scientific research program showing the hard core, a web of auxiliary hypotheses (*ah*), and data (*d*)

[23] Imre Lakatos, "Falsification and the Methodology of Scientific Research Programmes," in Lakatos and Alan Musgrave, eds., *Criticism and the Growth of Knowledge* (Cambridge: Cambridge University Press, 1970), 91–196; reprinted in Lakatos, *The Methodology of Scientific Research Programmes: Philosophical Papers, Volume 1*, ed. John Worrall and Gregory Currie (Cambridge: University of Cambridge Press, 1978), 8–101.

is central to the research program. Conjoined to the core are a set of "auxiliary hypotheses" that together add enough information to allow the data to be related to the core theory. Examples of types of auxiliary hypotheses are the theories of instrumentation that Kuhn recognized, lower-level theories that apply the core theory in different kinds of cases, and so forth. The auxiliary hypotheses form a "protective belt" around the hard core, since they can be modified when potentially falsifying data are found. A research program, then, is a temporally extended network of theories whose core remains the same while auxiliary hypotheses are successively added, modified, or replaced, in order to account for problematic observations.

The problem in evaluating research programs is that, given enough ingenuity on the part of scientists, any conflicting datum (anomaly) can be made consistent with the program by adding theoretical explanations. To illustrate his point without getting into technicalities from the history of science, Lakatos tells a parable of "planetary misbehavior." A physicist uses Newton's laws to calculate what ought to be the path of a newly discovered planet, but the planet deviates from the predictions. Instead of taking Newton's laws to be refuted, he adds a new auxiliary hypothesis: there is another planet, too small to be observed, whose gravitational pull disturbs our new planet's orbit. So a larger telescope is built, but there is no additional planet found. Maybe a cloud of gas is hiding it . . . And so the story goes on. Lakatos's point is that if one of these new hypotheses is confirmed, then there has been significant progress in astronomy—the research program is "progressive" (Figure 12). But if no such confirmation ever takes place, the program is merely creating face-saving devices—it is degenerating—and ought to be rejected if there is a more progressive one available.

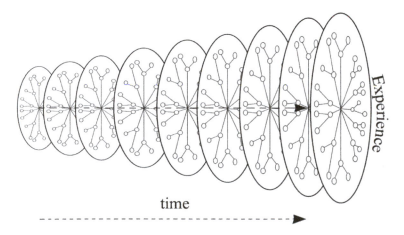

time

Experience

Figure 12 A (simplified) temporally extended Lakatosian scientific research program. The increasing diameter of the circles is intended to represent progress; that is, increasing empirical content

An autobiographical note may be in order here. I studied philosophy of science at the University of California, Berkeley, but then went to the Graduate Theological Union to study theology. I had not been particularly interested in Lakatos's work at Berkeley, but I studied it avidly and wrote a dissertation on it at the Graduate Theological Union because I could see that theologians and biblical scholars are tempted to use the same *ad hoc* or "face-saving" style of reasoning as are scientists in order to defend their positions against potentially falsifying data. Here the theories are Christian doctrines and the data could be from Scripture, history, or religious experience. I argued that theological schools could be described in ways parallel to scientific research programs.[24] The parallels with scientific theories of instrumentation in theology are theories of revelation and interpretation that justify and guide the use of textual data, and a theory of discernment that guides communities in recognizing which putative religious experiences are actually telling us something about God and God's will.

The important point to be gained from Lakatos's account of scientific rationality is that justification of a paradigm, scientific research program (or theological program?) must be narrative in form. It must evaluate how the program has changed over time in the face of intellectual difficulties. However, philosopher of science Paul Feyerabend raised a problem for Lakatos's account. Lakatos claimed to have given us a way to show, sometimes, that one program is rationally superior to its rival, but Feyerabend pointed out that there are examples in the history of science in which one program degenerated for a long period of time, but suddenly a new idea came along and it became strikingly progressive. Unless Lakatos could tell us how much time to give a program before rejecting it, he had not in fact offered the scientist any guidance. Lakatos never provided a satisfactory response.

4.4 Foundationalism's failure

I began section 4 by endorsing Plantinga's critique of classical or strong foundationalism. It has not been possible, over these past 300 years, to find a category of belief that is (1) not in need of justification on the basis of other beliefs, (2) indubitable, and (3) useful for supporting even minimal additional knowledge claims.

"Soft" foundationalists have had to recognize that their foundational beliefs could be called into question, and also that reasoning from the foundation to further knowledge claims never amounts to proof. If these were the only problems with the foundationalist theory, and especially if we had no other available theories of knowledge, it would be reasonable to accept this chastened form of foundationalism. However, as I have illustrated from developments in philosophy of science, there is an insurmountable problem for foundationalists. Science cannot simply

---

[24] See Nancey Murphy, *Theology in the Age of Scientific Reasoning* (Ithaca, NY and London: Cornell University Press, 1990).

begin with facts because recognition of relevant facts depends on prior theoretical knowledge. Theories of instrumentation are needed to tell us what observations are reliable. In fact, extremely complex networks of theory go into the design of scientific instruments and the interpretation of their readings. So it is said that the facts themselves are "theory laden." This means the end of foundationalism in that there is no clear differentiation between two types of knowledge—factual and theoretical—and reasoning in science is a dialectical process back and forth between theory and observation or measurement. If we were forced to maintain the building metaphor, we would have to say that the superstructure holds up the foundation as much as the foundation supports the superstructure (Figure 13). Fortunately, we can simply abandon the foundationalist imagery in favor of holist images.

4.5 Theological uses of holist epistemology

I have already indicated that something like Hempel's hypothetico-deductive reasoning is common in theological disciplines, but the parallels with science are

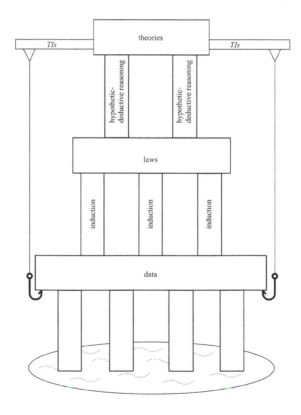

Figure 13 A whimsical representation of scientific "foundations" partially hanging from theoretical "balconies" (i.e. theories of instrumentation, *TIs*)

usually not noted. However, there have been explicit uses of Quine's, Kuhn's, and Lakatos's work in theology.

Ian Barbour (1923–2013) argues that religions can be understood as analogous to Kuhnian paradigms.[25] However, a religion as a whole does not exhibit the logical consistency or agreement among its practitioners that Kuhn took to be hallmarks of scientific paradigms. In addition, the central purpose of science is the pursuit of knowledge, and this is not the case for most religions. A much closer parallel is Hans Küng's (b.1928) comparison of theological schools with paradigms.[26] He suggested that theologians such as Thomas, Calvin, and Luther initiated new paradigms in Christian theology.

Theologians such as Philip Clayton (b.1956), Philip Hefner (b.1932), and Robert John Russell (b.1946) have used Lakatos's concept of a research program to describe theological schools. The limitations here are that Lakatos's requirement for new data to confirm a research program is difficult to meet in theology—the best that can usually be asked for are new insights regarding the applicability of already known information—for example, a new interpretation of a biblical text that suddenly shows its relevance to a theological theory.[27] In addition, Lakatos's work only helps to illuminate (second-order) theology, not first-order belief.

The most insightful use of holist epistemology may be that of Ronald Thiemann (1946–2012) in his book *Revelation and Theology*.[28] His work is useful for understanding both first- and second-order religious claims. Thiemann argues that the concept of revelation has been distorted by the modern attempt to use Scripture as an epistemological foundation; he sets out to explain it instead in the traditional term of God's *prevenience*. He explains prevenience as follows:

> Christian theology has traditionally been guided by the conviction that faith's knowledge of God is a gift bestowed through God's free grace. Our thought and speech about God are not simply the free creations of human imagination but are developed in obedient response to God's prior initiative. Theologians have commonly referred to this prior act of God as revelation.[29]

Thiemann first gives an account of holist justification of a theological claim, then uses that method to show the warranted assertability of the doctrine of God's prevenience. Borrowing from Quine, Thiemann states that holist justification consists in seeking the relation between a disputed belief and the web of

---

25 Ian G. Barbour, *Myths, Models, and Paradigms* (New York: Harper and Row, 1974).
26 Hans Küng, "Paradigm Change in Theology," in Küng and David Tracy, eds., *Moving Toward a New Theology* (Edinburgh: T. & T. Clark, 1988), 3–33.
27 See Murphy, *Theology in the Age of Scientific Reasoning*, 87.
28 Ronald F. Thiemann, *Revelation and Theology: The Gospel as Narrated Promise* (Notre Dame, IN: University of Notre Dame Press, 1985).
29 Thiemann, *Revelation*, 2.

interrelated beliefs within which it rests. Quoting Quine, he says: "We convince someone of something by appealing to beliefs he already holds and by combining these to induce further beliefs in him, step by step, until the belief we wanted finally to inculcate in him is inculcated."[30]

Thiemann notes that belief in God's prevenience is logically tied to both beliefs and practices that are not in dispute among Christians and, further, that these beliefs and practices are so central to Christian identity that to give them up would constitute a drastic change in Christian identity. Praise, supplication, thanksgiving, all become meaningless without the presupposition of God's prior reality and action.

While deeply indebted to Quine, Thiemann's account of theological method is actually more sophisticated in at least four ways than Quine's epistemology. First, he recognizes the intrinsic relations between knowing and doing. It is not merely consistency among beliefs that rationality requires, but also consistency between belief and action (a Wittgensteinian point).

Second, Thiemann recognizes a historical dimension in the justification of beliefs: webs of belief endure and change through time, and part of what consistency requires is congruity with (but not slavish repetition of) past formulations. This is a more sophisticated version of Quine's recognition of the value of conservatism in matters epistemological.

Third, Quine counts the laws of logic as part of the web of belief. This claim needs to be extended to recognize that all sorts of standards of rationality are internal to traditions, as Thiemann recognizes in claiming that part of the theologian's description of the "internal logic of the Christian faith" is recognition and employment of "criteria of judgment internal to the Christian tradition."[31]

Finally, the critical problem with using Quine's model of holist epistemology is that it leaves one open to a radical form of relativism. Since Quine considered knowledge to consist of only logic, science, and everyday beliefs based on experience, it never occurred to him to worry about radically different and competing webs of beliefs. A topic to be covered in this text, though, is the problem of religious pluralism. Christians are well aware of these competitors, and so we need some guidance for adjudicating among them if we are to be able to claim that the Christian web is more rational, and therefore the true one. So while holist epistemology offers valuable resources for the theological task, none of the models we have examined here is entirely adequate.

---

[30] Thiemann, *Revelation*, 75–6; quoting from Quine and Ullian, *The Web of Belief*, 127.
[31] Thiemann, *Revelation*, 74.

5 Retrospect and prospect

The foregoing section may seem puzzling to some students because these problems of modern philosophy are not their own. Also, the extensive use of philosophy of science in a philosophy of religion text may seem odd. However, I believe we need to know these bits of history in order both to appreciate the difficulties Christians have had throughout the modern period in defending their beliefs, and also to appreciate newer and more sophisticated theories of rationality.

We have seen some value in the works of Quine, Kuhn, and Lakatos for understanding theological reasoning, but none of these theories is entirely appropriate for describing theology. For example, Kuhn's emphasis on authoritative texts may be useful for thinking about Scripture, but neither Quine nor Lakatos have guidance here. In addition, none of these theories provides a model to allow theologians to address the relation between first- and second-order religious language.

Fortunately for us, Alasdair MacIntyre has incorporated the best insights from these holist epistemologists, and from Wittgenstein as well, into a new theory that will turn out to fit a religious tradition like a glove.

4

Faith and reason for the twenty-first century

1 Introduction

In this chapter, we come to the high point of this part, which is titled "A brief history of reason." The central focus of the chapter will be a description of Alasdair MacIntyre's account of the role of "large-scale traditions" in human reasoning. From this perspective we shall be able to see some of the developments covered in previous chapters in better light. MacIntyre's work also provides, in large part, the rationale for the choice of topics in the remainder of this text.

I begin here with a very brief reminder of what has come before. We first saw some accounts of reasoning that are far removed from our own. Histories of philosophy usually begin with the thinkers who sought "true knowing" as opposed to the "much knowing" that came from experience, and, in general, they turned away from the senses and sought it within their own minds/souls. While some of our contemporaries in mathematics and physics find this approach congenial, we live in a world in which (once again) knowledge is taken to be largely dependent upon sensory experience. The rise of empiricism in the modern era required a drastic change in methods for justifying religious claims.

The prevalence of atheism and agnosticism in intellectual circles in our day is in large part due to the conclusion that no such justification is possible. My own thesis, however, is that philosophical theories of justification have, until now, been too crude to make them the arbiters of theological rationality. The rejection of foundationalism and the development of holist theories of knowledge, particularly by late-twentieth-century philosophers of science, have been important steps in the right direction. However, Paul Feyerabend may well have been correct in his day in claiming that there still were no adequate criteria "sly and sophisticated enough" for justifying scientific theories (paradigms, research programs). And, I add, if this is true, still less was there a theory of reason sophisticated enough to apply to a system of religious beliefs.

Then MacIntyre comes on the scene. When progress in philosophy of science had ground to a halt he published "Epistemological Crises, Dramatic Narrative, and the Philosophy of Science," in which he explained the failure of this philosophical debate to move forward and provided his own account of how it is possible (sometimes) to show that one paradigm or research program represents a permanent gain in understanding relative to its competitor.[1] In the briefest terms, the theory that can explain its rival's successes and (acknowledged) failures in a way that the rival cannot shows itself to be an intrinsically richer understanding of reality than the rival.

The first task of this chapter, then, will be to explain MacIntyre's theory of tradition-constituted reasoning, including his accounts of justification and truth. Along the way, I shall use examples from Christian thought, not only to illustrate MacIntyre's positions, but also to show how easily his work applies to the central question of this book: how to provide a rational justification of the Christian faith.

Now, here is an interesting question: Can MacIntyre's theory of rational justification be applied to itself? Does it measure up to its own standards? Showing that it does will involve using it to explain both the successes and failures of MacIntyre's predecessors—first, the earlier holist philosophers (Quine, Kuhn, Lakatos). Second, a more interesting question for readers of this book is as follows: There seems to be something right about each of the predominant recent approaches in philosophy of religion (evidentialist, Reformed, Wittgensteinian) described all too briefly in Chapter 3. Yet proponents of each approach have provided devastating critiques of the others, and the discussion may have reached a stalemate. Can we use MacIntyre's theory of rationality to explain what each position gets right, but also why it cannot seem to satisfy its critics?

I end this chapter with an overview of standard types of arguments for the existence of God. However, I give much less space to this topic than do typical texts in philosophy of religion. I provide examples to show, first, that the point of such arguments is different in different intellectual milieus. Second, I believe that in light of MacIntyre's work we can see why these arguments have turned out to be so unconvincing in our own era.

2 Alasdair MacIntyre as philosopher of science

Alasdair MacIntyre was born in Glasgow in 1929. He first studied classics at the University of Manchester and then analytic philosophy at Oxford. He began teaching at Manchester in 1951 and since then he has held numerous academic positions in a surprising variety of disciplines, first in the United Kingdom and then in the United States.

---

[1] Alasdair MacIntyre, "Epistemological Crises, Dramatic Narrative, and the Philosophy of Science," *Monist* 60, no. 4 (October 1977): 453–72. Reprinted in Stanley Hauerwas and L. Gregory Jones, eds., *Why Narrative: Readings in Narrative Theology* (Grand Rapids, MI: Eerdmans, 1989), 138–57; page references are to this reprint. It is also reprinted in Gary Gutting, ed., *Paradigms and Revolutions: Applications and Appraisals of Thomas Kuhn's Philosophy of Science* (Notre Dame, IN: University of Notre Dame Press, 1980), 54–74.

MacIntyre has had a complex relationship to Christianity. He studied for the Presbyterian ministry in his early years and in the process read a great deal of Karl Barth's theology. However, he soon concluded that Christian theology was philosophically indefensible and abandoned it. MacIntyre was also long concerned with Marxism and briefly joined the Communist Party. His rejection of both liberal Protestantism and Marxism was based on a Popperian insistence that no system of beliefs is worth holding that is not open to falsification. Later, in the process of writing *Whose Justice? Which Rationality?*, in which he set forth his own account of rational justification, he became convinced that Thomist Christianity was the most intellectually defensible tradition available and joined the Catholic Church.[2]

MacIntyre attributes what he sees as a "clumsily patched together" set of beliefs in his early career to his immersion as a youngster in "two antagonistic systems of belief and attitude."[3] One was the Gaelic oral culture captured in stories and poetry; the other was the Anglo-Saxon culture expressed in academic English.

MacIntyre is now best known for his work in philosophical ethics. However, a chronological account of his work would provide a skeleton for addressing many of the interesting changes in philosophy of the past 60 years. In this section we pick up the story with his response to the philosophy of science of the 1970s.

During the 1970s, both Feyerabend and Kuhn (independently) developed concepts of *incommensurability*. This concept is based on the recognition that some points of view (scientific paradigms, worldviews) are embodied in such different sets of concepts that there can be no simple rendering of one into the terms of the other. (Feyerabend's contrast between archaic and classical Greek thought is an illustration (see Chapter 1, section 2.1).)

Incommensurability is the problem underlying the debates over the justification of scientific theories described in Chapter 3. The concepts used in different paradigms are so different that they cannot be defined in terms of one another. Consider the shift from medieval hylomorphism to modern atomism. There is nothing in the new worldview that is equivalent to an Aristotelian *Form*. And even though both Aristotle and Copernicus use the (equivalent of the) term "matter," it means something different in each case.

An even deeper problem is that concepts of doing good science change, too. We have already seen that medieval *scientia* means something quite different from modern "science." The very concept of sense perception has changed: In medieval optics, the *Form* of a thing was actually transmitted to the mind via the visual

---

[2] Alasdair MacIntyre, *Whose Justice? Which Rationality?* (Notre Dame, IN: University of Notre Dame Press, 1988).

[3] Alasdair MacIntyre, "Nietzsche or Aristotle," in Giovanna Borradori, *The American Philosopher: Conversations with Quine, Davidson, Putnam, Nozick, Danto, Rorty, Cavell, MacIntyre, and Kuhn* (Chicago: University of Chicago Press, 1994), ch. 8 (142, 139).

system. In early modern science, vision must occur by means of atoms striking the surface of the eye. Having lived in incommensurable cultures in his youth, MacIntyre came to this discussion already understanding this most pressing problem: incommensurable standards of justification, knowledge, truth.

In his essay on epistemological crises and philosophy of science, he begins by invoking incidents that lead an *individual* to fear that he or she has radically misinterpreted (or been deceived in) a social situation, such as someone who has believed that she was a highly valued employee and is suddenly fired. In a shared culture we operate on the basis of shared "schemata" that make our behavior intelligible and relatively predictable to one another. When a schema breaks down, the possibility of rival schemata arises, and this creates an *epistemological* crisis because, without knowing which is the appropriate schema, one does not know what facts are relevant, and without knowing what to treat as evidence one cannot tell which schema to adopt. Mystery novels trade on just this sort of confusion. MacIntyre's point could be put as follows: the end of the novel comes at the point where an expanded narrative establishes which details were and were not clues, and thereby can resolve the problematic relationship between what *seemed* to be and what *is*.

The example MacIntyre uses in order to apply this insight to science is the triumph of Galileo's science over the Aristotelian–Ptolemaic science of the late Middle Ages. The Neopositivist theory of theory choice required that the change come about because of either greater evidence for the Copernican system or more evidence in conflict with the Ptolemaic. However, Kuhn argued that such radical changes can never be made on the basis of the evidence because what counts as evidence differs in the two paradigms. Furthermore, Feyerabend is but one of several historians who have pointed out that it was only much later that empirical results favored the new cosmology; in fact, Feyerabend claimed that no general theory of scientific rationality could be given that would account for the change having occurred *when* it did.

MacIntyre sets out to explain this "premature" acceptance of the Copernican system and uses his explanation to illustrate his general thesis about rational choice between rival systems of thought. He says that when Galileo entered the scene "he was confronted by much more than the conflict between the Ptolemaic and Copernican astronomies."[4] The Ptolemaic system was inconsistent not only with empirical observations, but also with widely accepted Platonic standards for true science, and with some aspects of Aristotle's physics.

MacIntyre points out that Galileo had to do more than appeal to the facts, because he was working at just the time when a modern conception of what it means to appeal to the facts was being established. He was able to win favor for his new conception of science, along with the Copernican cosmology, because

---

4   MacIntyre, "Epistemological Crises," 145.

together they allowed him to make sense of the successes and failures of the older science:

> The criterion of a successful theory is that it enables us to understand its predecessors in a newly intelligible way. It, at one and the same time, enables us to understand precisely why its predecessors have to be rejected or modified and also why, without and before its illumination, past theory could have remained credible. It introduces new standards for evaluating the past. It recasts the narrative which constitutes the continuous reconstruction of the scientific tradition.[5]

For a simpler illustration of MacIntyre's point than the one he presents, consider a classroom with physical models of both the Ptolemaic and Copernican systems. The Platonic element of the former was the assumption that the heavenly bodies, being near the top of the hierarchy of beings, must have perfect, that is, circular motions. The stars do appear to move in circles around the earth, but "planets"—meaning wanderers—exhibit retrograde motion. That is, while they generally travel westward with the stars, they sometimes appear to stop and move east for a time. To explain this, Ptolemy hypothesized that they are carried on a small sphere, an epicycle, whose center moves along another circle around the Earth. This added rotation would involve the planets sometimes moving backwards relative to the fixed stars. However, to attempt to match empirical observations, the system had to be made more and more complicated, with epicycles on epicycles (Figure 14).

Now, once we have the model in which Earth is one planet circling the Sun, the "retrograde motion" is simply an illusion caused by the different speeds of the planets—with the Earth either overtaking or being overtaken by other planets. So from the point of view of the Copernican model, it is easy to see why the Ptolemaic model could have remained credible, but also to see what caused its most striking anomalies and, ultimately, its failure. To be able to give a historical narrative that makes the acceptance of the new astronomy intelligible is exactly to give a rational justification of the new theory.

So MacIntyre has in common with Lakatos the recognition that science does not consist of a collection of static theories but, rather, clusters of theories that change over time. These clusters must be evaluated in terms of *how* they change through time. But he has now been able to answer Feyerabend's challenge. Recall that Lakatos had offered an account of rational choice in science: the research program that needs fewer *ad hoc* adjustments to account for the data is more progressive and therefore the more acceptable one. Feyerabend's challenge was to point out that there is never a guarantee that the less progressive will not suddenly

---

[5] MacIntyre, "Epistemological Crises," 146.

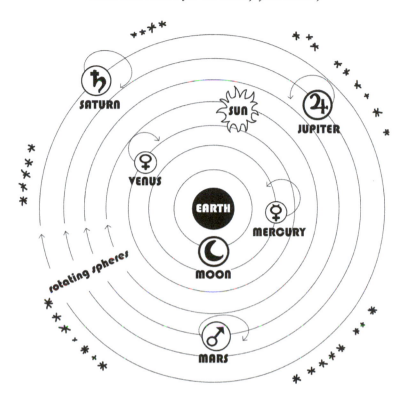

Figure 14 The Earth-centered (Ptolemaic) model of the universe, with epicycles to account for retrograde motion of (other) planets

become more progressive than its rival. MacIntyre's point is that in Galileo's day, the Copernican model had its own problems—in particular, it needed to replace circular with elliptical orbits. However, the Ptolemaists, with their principled commitment to circular motion, could never have *diagnosed* the Copernicans' problem. So there is an asymmetry in the explanatory power of the two theories. Both may explain *the world* equally well, but *one can also explain the other's successes and failures in a way that the other cannot.* This is one of MacIntyre's principal insights, and I believe that the reason for the scant attention paid to his contribution here is because he is usually not read in the context of this epistemological crisis in philosophy of science itself.

3 The nature of large-scale traditions of enquiry

In a *theological* context, the word "tradition" is often used to refer to church teaching, either oral or written, that complements (or competes with) the teachings of Scripture. The *ordinary* English use of the word comes closer to MacIntyre's:

"tradition" is defined as the handing down from one generation to another of beliefs and customs, practices, attitudes, and institutions. He provides, for his philosophical purposes, a more specific account of traditions, which, in the case of Christianity, would have roles for both Scripture and the narrower theological sense of "tradition."

In "Epistemological Crises," as we have seen, MacIntyre shows that a scientific theory needs to be situated in a larger scientific (and philosophical) tradition in order to be evaluated. His next major work led him to describe traditions of *moral* reasoning. In *After Virtue* he identified two moral traditions in the landscape of Western thought: the virtue tradition, going all the way back to Homer, and the moral tradition that developed during the Enlightenment. A central purpose of the book was to claim that the Enlightenment Tradition has failed, in that it has led to inescapable moral relativism. Furthermore, this tradition *had* to fail *by its own standards* because it was unable to understand itself as a tradition, but aimed instead at universal and timeless truth. MacIntyre's solution was to show that the virtue tradition, whose finest exemplar was Aristotle, could be revived to take its place.

MacIntyre was criticized for attempting to avoid relativism with regard to specific moral issues but, in so doing, of creating relativism on a grand scale. If a particular issue can only be resolved by locating it in the context of the moral tradition within which it arose, then the much larger question is raised of whether and how it is possible to choose rationally between rival traditions. To this question MacIntyre turns, first, in a postscript to the second edition of *After Virtue*[6] and then in two successive books: *Whose Justice? Which Rationality?*[7] and *Three Rival Versions of Moral Enquiry*.[8] In the process, he has developed his account of the nature of large-scale traditions of enquiry.

3.1 The origins and development of traditions

Traditions generally originate with an authority of some sort, usually a text or set of texts. In his *God, Philosophy, Universities*, MacIntyre says:

> All human beings, whatever their culture, find themselves confronted by questions about the nature and significance of their lives: What is our place in the order of things? Of what powers in the natural and social world do we need to take account? How should we respond to the facts of suffering and

---

6 Alasdair MacIntyre, *After Virtue: A Study in Moral Theory*, 2nd ed. (Notre Dame, IN: University of Notre Dame Press, [1981] 1984). Note that while we usually cite the first edition in academic references, this is the correct one to cite because of the importance of the postscript in the second edition.

7 Alasdair MacIntyre, *Whose Justice? Which Rationality?* (Notre Dame, IN: University of Notre Dame Press, 1988).

8 Alasdair MacIntyre, *Three Rival Versions of Moral Enquiry: Encyclopaedia, Genealogy, and Tradition* (Notre Dame, IN: University of Notre Dame Press, 1990).

death? What is our relationship to the dead? What is it to live a human life well? What is it to live it badly?

Yet characteristically these existential questions are raised for most human beings in the early history of humankind not as questions to be asked, let alone puzzled over, but as questions that have already received definitive religious answers. Those answers have of course varied from culture to culture. And they are generally presented through rituals, myths, and poetic narratives, which constitute the collective response of a culture to those questions.[9]

Thus, all traditions begin with an authority of some sort, oral or written, that answers life's major questions, and for a time is not called into question. But at some point the authorities will be questioned, and this creates the first epistemological crisis. It is an *epistemological* crisis because it calls into question at the same time what it is to *know* (anything) if not on the basis of these authorities. If it is possible to resolve *this* crisis with augmented intellectual resources, then a mature tradition is born. Traditions develop by means of successive attempts to interpret and apply their authoritative texts in new contexts. Application is essential: traditions are socially embodied in the life stories of the individuals and communities who share them, in institutions, and social practices.

While MacIntyre developed his account of traditions primarily through his study of the Hellenistic sources of Western culture, his account serves well to describe the development of Christianity. The first Christians, of course, were a part of the Jewish tradition, and took over from it its formative text: what we now call the OT. This collection of books provided the basic worldview for Christians: concepts of God, of social powers, of morality, of death. What we see in the NT writings are responses to major intellectual crises occasioned by the teaching, death, and resurrection of Jesus. How could it be that the long-expected Messiah suffered the ignominious death usually reserved for treason? Who is this man who put himself above the law, yet was vindicated by God raising him from death?

Gradually, the Christian Tradition became separate from Judaism both because its authoritative canon shifted to include and prioritize the NT; and because new forms of social practices, such as worship and evangelism, were established. Institutions were formed to carry these practices on from one generation to another. The history of theology and apologetics is the history of successive attempts to interpret and apply the church's formative texts in new contexts (see Figure 15 overleaf). Epistemological crises involved real or apparent inconsistencies within the Christian web of beliefs, encounters with rival traditions, both religious and philosophical, and new historical situations that seemed not

[9]   Alasdair MacIntyre, *God, Philosophy, Universities: A Selective History of the Catholic Philosophical Tradition* (Lanham, MD: Rowman and Littlefield, 2009), 9.

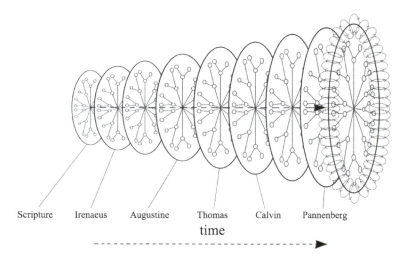

Scripture   Irenaeus   Augustine   Thomas   Calvin   Pannenberg

time

Figure 15 The Christian Tradition. This (simplified) representation of the Christian Tradition shows Scripture as its formative text(s); a series of increasingly comprehensive theological systems, based on interpretation and application of Scripture; and ends with a picture of a contemporary theological web informed by its predecessors, but not bounded by experience. The curling lines around the edge are meant to illustrate the going out into the world in Christian practices and the bringing in of better understanding of Christian teaching

to be explainable in the Christian Tradition's terms. The remainder of this text will focus on addressing crises that arose in the modern period.

A caveat is in order here: While it makes sense in some contexts to speak of *the* Christian Tradition, what we actually have is a tangle of Christian subtraditions (see Figure 2 on p. 11). In addition, traditions admit of containment relations. So, for instance, Lutheranism is a subtradition within Christianity. Liberal Protestantism is another kind of subtradition, and some, but not all, liberal Protestants are Lutherans. Thomas Aquinas's moral theology contributes both to the Christian Tradition and to the tradition of moral philosophy that focuses on the virtues. So the containment relations are not simple ones as with a set of Russian dolls.

3.2 Justification and truth

The mention above of rival traditions, of course, brings us back to the epistemological question: can one large-scale tradition be shown to be rationally superior to others? Apologists through the centuries have taken on this task. What makes the task more challenging today is the recognition, first with regard to science, and now, by MacIntyre (and others) with regard to all knowledge, that standards of rationality and concepts of truth differ (somewhat or to a great extent) from one tradition to another. The historical sketches in Chapter 1 were meant to illustrate this problem. And MacIntyre is featured here because he provides the best answer *so far* to this problem. He claims that despite the lack of a universal account of rational justification it is (sometimes) possible to show that one tradition (tradition A) succeeds on its own terms better than a rival (tradition B) does on its own terms.

The justification of tradition A would involve creating narratives of both A's and B's development, showing the extent to which each has encountered crises and has or has not been able to reformulate itself in order to resolve the crises. If A has a better track record than B, then there is some reason to think that A's account of reality is true, but then we are faced with a Feyerabendian problem: how do we know that B will not overcome its problems in the future? MacIntyre's answer, as in his example of Galileo and Ptolemy, is to ask whether A is able to explain not only B's successes—that is, why things appear as they do from B's point of view— but also B's failures, in a way that B itself cannot do. That is, part of knowing how things *are* is being able to say how, in consequence, they must *appear* from a range of different, limited, local points of view.

It is important to note that MacIntyre requires judgments regarding the limitations or failures of a rival tradition be made from the point of view of the rival itself. This is often difficult, due to the fact that the two traditions offer rival and *incommensurable* conceptual systems. The investigator must have the interest, empathy, and patience to learn the new system as a "second first language." He says that if some tradition

> has successfully transcended the limitations of its predecessors and in so doing provided the best means available for understanding those predecessors to date *and* has then confronted successive challenges from a number of rival points of view, but in each case has been able to modify itself in the ways required to incorporate the strengths of these points of view while avoiding their weaknesses and limitations *and* has provided the best explanation so far of those weaknesses and limitations, then we have the best possible reason to have confidence that future challenges will also be met successfully, that the principles which define the core of a [tradition] are enduring principles.[10]

This is the best criterion we can have for claiming that the tradition's general account of reality is *true*.[11]

---

[10] MacIntyre, *After Virtue*, 270.

[11] See Nancey Murphy, *Anglo-American Postmodernity: Philosophical Perspectives on Science, Religion, and Ethics* (Boulder, CO: Westview Press, 1997), ch. 6 for a more extensive account of the relation between justification and truth.

3.3 Testing the truth of Christianity

If MacIntyre is right, we can see rationales for all of the disciplines in the theological curriculum. They are social practices partially constitutive of the Christian Tradition. A tradition is defined as an ongoing argument about how to interpret its formative texts. Thus, we see the role not only for study of the Bible itself but for involvement in arguments about *how* to study the Bible. But note that there is no need to begin with foundationalist-style prolegomena to argue for the authority of the Bible since every tradition has its own formative texts. To be a member of a tradition just *is* to take its formative texts as authoritative.

A tradition is socially embodied in institutions and practices. Thus, there is the study of church polity and of the various practices that are the life of the tradition: worship, evangelism, discipleship. One aspect of participation in a social practice is ongoing discussion of the goods at which the practice aims. So the curriculum includes discussions of the purposes and best approaches to these practices. A tradition is an argument about how to apply its formative texts. Thus, we have the discipline of Christian ethics—what does participation in this tradition require regarding relations within the church and to action in the world?

A tradition faces new intellectual challenges in new contexts. Therefore, theology is always in need of development and, perhaps, repair. A tradition can be trusted to be true if it has overcome its crises in the past, so knowledge of the history and development of theology and church life is essential, *with particular attention paid to points of crisis.*

In addition, when traditions confront new crises, some of which are due to the pressure of rival traditions, some to internal incoherence, or conflict with new sources of knowledge, some discipline—philosophical theology, philosophy of religion, apologetics—is needed to attempt to resolve crises and challenge rivals.

I believe it is no accident that apologetics has largely disappeared from the theological curriculum. If all of the disciplines listed so far are crucial for the intellectual health and rational justification of the tradition, then no single scholar or small set of specialists can be expected to do the work that a MacIntyrean account of justification and truth requires. Nonetheless, this text is intended as a very modest contribution to the apologetic task. Now that we have seen one part of that task to be the attempted resolution of intellectual crises, the remainder of the book will focus on what may be judged to be the most pressing issues of the present and recent past.

4 MacIntyre as philosopher of religion

In section 1, I raised the question of whether MacIntyre's account of justification could be used reflexively to justify itself. I believe I have shown that his account of justification and truth provides a solution to an impasse in philosophy of science—a point at which the discipline by its own standards had ceased to make progress. The justification of his contribution (as his own theory says should be the case) was his ability to explain *why* the parties in the debate were unable to come to agreement about the nature of scientific rationality. (I have given a shorter and somewhat different account of his contribution at the end of section 2 above.)

If my judgment is correct, the evidentialist versus Reformed versus Wittgensteinian debate has likewise come to a point at which it is questionable whether enquiry into the justification of religious beliefs has a way forward. I want to try to show that a MacIntyrean perspective can incorporate the strengths of each position but also explain why each position is not fully adequate. At the same time, I shall be able to provide an account of the relation between the justification of theological programs (what I have called second-order religious language) and justification of the (first-order) religious beliefs of individuals, in which these philosophers of religion are primarily interested.

I shall begin with the evidentialists' challenge to those whom they designate as fideists. D. Z. Phillips describes their challenges as follows:

> To talk of distinctive language games in relation to religion, it is thought, is to claim that only religious believers understand religious belief, that religious belief or believers cannot be criticized, that anything called religion determines what is meaningful, and that religious belief cannot be overthrown by any personal or cultural event.[12]

Let us take up first the question of whether non-believers can understand religious language. Phillips has written that there are degrees to which a non-believer may fail to understand. If we place this question within a MacIntyrean framework, in which the possibility exists of incommensurable traditions, then in some cases it will be a monumental task to come to understand the language of the rival tradition. MacIntyre believes that people with the empathy and imagination to do this are rare. So there may well be inhabitants of other traditions who, apart from such meticulous work, will fail to grasp the meaning of Christian claims. I have had the experience of speaking with people from remotely related religious traditions and failing to be able to make sense of their claims.

The second charge made against real or imagined fideists is that they claim that their beliefs are not open to rational criticism. A MacIntyrean answer to this charge is also relevant to Alvin Plantinga's claim that for Christians, belief in God is "properly basic," and thus not open to refutation. Without using Plantinga's foundationalist language, I endorse his claim that for adherents of the Christian Tradition, belief in God is so central that to call it into question is to question the tradition as a whole.

---

12 D. Z. Phillips, *Wittgenstein and Religion* (New York: St. Martin's Press, 1993), xii.

The issue of "Wittgensteinian fideism" is one that MacIntyre himself worked through many years ago. MacIntyre says in an interview:

> For a time, I tried to fence off the area of religious belief and practice from the rest of my life, by treating it as a *sui generis* form of life with its own standards internal to it and by blending a particular interpretation of Wittgenstein's notion of "form of life" with Karl Barth's theology . . . When I came to reject this strange philosophical mixture of a misunderstood Wittgenstein and an all-too-well understood Barth, I mistakenly rejected the Christian religion along with it.[13]

It is interesting that Barth has himself been classified as a fideist.[14]

MacIntyre has been highly critical of any system of belief that has managed to make itself immune to criticism. While he believes this to be true of some Christian subtraditions, his response in general to the "fideist" challenge is that (apart from these exceptions) the Christian Tradition has such a good track record of facing and overcoming intellectual challenges, individual adherents are—as the Reformed philosophers would phrase it—"within their epistemic rights" to believe the central teachings of the tradition.

This is not to say that individuals cannot suffer epistemological crises. We have in MacIntyre's work some valuable resources for addressing the relation between individual religious convictions and theological programs. For the individual, the presence of rival traditions (with their interpretive schemata) puts one's own interpretations in question. I suspect that true intellectual crises result not so much from pure rational reflection, but autobiographically: How have I understood my own life as a believer, and can I make of it a coherent narrative? For example, can I continue to see myself as a descendant of Adam and Eve while I devote myself to the study of evolutionary biology?

The theory of evolution has never been a problem for me, but a real crisis arose during my theological studies: Can I continue to participate in the re-enactment of the Last Supper when I identify myself as a feminist and note that there are no women mentioned in this high point of the Jesus story? This latter question created an *epistemological* crisis: There seemed to be four possibilities, none of which justified my continued participation in the church: (1) some feminists claim that the Scriptures are so biased by patriarchal assumptions that they are not trustworthy sources of *knowledge* of Jesus or the early church. But (2) if they *are* trustworthy, then are they not painting a picture of Jesus as excluding women from the high points of the story? And if Jesus was

---

[13] MacIntyre, in Boradori, *American Philosopher*, 142.
[14] Anthony C. Thiselton, *A Concise Encyclopedia of the Philosophy of Religion* (Grand Rapids, MI: Baker Academic, 2002), 102.

a misogynist (which I take to be sinful), then (3) either he is not an adequate source of knowledge of God, or else (4) God, too, is a misogynist. Elizabeth Schüssler Fiorenza's (b.1938) book, *In Memory of Her*, solved this crisis for me by providing a reading strategy for the NT texts that takes the charge of patriarchalism into account, but uses it against itself to justify the claim that Jesus' ministry did include, and even sometimes favor, women. Note the relevance of MacIntyre's claim that traditions often progress by arguing for better ways of *interpreting* their formative texts.[15]

So the question is not: Can I justify the existence of God? but rather, Can I identify myself as a rational person and continue to live out my life using the interpretive resources of the Christian Tradition? But no individual should be expected to answer this question without the resources provided by others, including scholars. This brings our focus back from the level of individual epistemic crises to that of the conflict of large-scale traditions. In light of MacIntyre's account of the process of defending a tradition against rivals, I have noted the relevance of the variety of theological disciplines, understood as practices partially constitutive of the tradition. It is not the job of each individual believer to justify her or his convictions, but it is a task to which the Christian academy is regularly contributing, by showing the justification of theological claims both within, and by the standards of, a particular Christian subtradition.

Less often, theologians and philosophers contribute to the task of justifying Christianity vis-à-vis rival traditions. Assorted modern attempts to show the superiority of Christianity to other religions (largely in the nineteenth century) came to appear invidious in the twentieth century, when greater attention was given both to ecumenism within Christianity and to interreligious dialogue. MacIntyre is sometimes accused of encouraging conflictual relations between rival points of view, but his central point in urging the mutual testing of rival traditions is that its purpose is not so much to show the rivals to be inadequate, but rather to test the strength of one's own tradition. For Christians, this means testing our own tradition by means of facing the challenges that the other traditions raise for us.

A rival tradition that is ripe for criticism is what I shall call the Naturalist Tradition, which has grown up in Europe and the USA beginning in the eighteenth century. This topic will merit a detailed examination of its own in Chapter 10. I claim that if there are to be "arguments for the existence of God" in our day, they need to be reconceived as arguments *against* non-theistic traditions.

---

[15] Elizabeth Schüssler Fiorenza, *In Memory of Her: A Feminist Theological Reconstruction of Christian Origins* (New York: Crossroad Publishers, 1983). I had the opportunity to sit next to her at a conference shortly after reading the book and told her how much it had meant to me. She said that many women had told her that.

In sum, from MacIntyre's perspective, we can say that the evidentialist challenge is warranted and important, but it cannot be taken as a challenge to every individual. As both Phillips and Plantinga maintain, for the adherent of the Christian Tradition, God's existence is not a hypothesis. But for scholars to make truth claims for Christianity's account of reality, the hard work needs to be done of first exploring other traditions, understanding them from the inside, and then assessing how well they stand up to their own standards of rationality.[16] And the language of a rival tradition may indeed be incomprehensible to those who are unable imaginatively to enter into a different worldview. My conclusion, then, is that MacIntyre represents the best response so far to questions relating to the rationality and truth of the Christian belief system.

5 Arguments for the existence of God

Nearly all texts in philosophy of religion include one or more chapters on arguments for God's existence. Typologies are not entirely uniform, but I consider three types: ontological arguments, cosmological arguments, and arguments from design. Two types that I shall not describe are moral arguments and arguments based on religious experience. Much has been written either to defend or to show the arguments to be invalid, and contemporary philosophers seek to reformulate earlier arguments in brilliant ways so as to avoid previous objections. This section, therefore, should be thought of merely as a sampling of this vast literature. I consider Anselm of Canterbury's version of the ontological argument; three of Thomas's "five ways" of proving God's existence under the heading of cosmological arguments. However, I reserve comments on his fifth way for the subsection on design arguments, since the differences between his and modern versions is instructive. I report on objections to the argument that have widely been seen as refutations. However, my real interest in this section is to show how different these arguments look in their own contexts, rather than extracted and compared under the single category of "arguments for the existence of God."

5.1 Anselm's ontological argument

Anselm (1033–1109) was born in what is now Italy; he became a monk and then abbot of a Benedictine monastery in Normandy until he was installed as Archbishop of Canterbury in 1093. He left a number of writings: treatises and dialogues, meditations and prayers. An ontological argument (also called an *a priori* argument because it is not dependent on *prior* experience) is described as one

---

[16] For one contribution to this monumental task, see David J. Brewer, "Mutual Constructive Engagement: A MacIntyrean Approach to Theology of Religions – Christianity and Islam in Conversation," PhD thesis, Fuller Theological Seminary, 2016.

that begins from the very concept of God and then seeks to show that internal consistency requires this being to exist. I quote one contemporary philosopher's version (by Philip Quinn, b.1940) of Anselm's argument (taken from Anselm's *Proslogion*, ch. 2):

> We understand God to be a perfect being, something than which nothing greater can be conceived. Because we have this concept, God at least exists in our minds as an object of the understanding. Either God exists in the mind alone, or God exists both in the mind and as an extramental reality. But if God existed in the mind alone, then we could conceive of a being greater than that than which nothing greater can be conceived, namely, one that also existed in extramental reality. Since the concept of a being greater than that which nothing greater can be conceived is incoherent, God cannot exist in the mind alone. Hence God exists not only in the mind but also in extramental reality.[17]

I have used another scholar's language (an acknowledged expert) to describe the argument because of textual and translation problems. Anselm wrote in terse Latin, and even adding an editorial comma in an English translation can change the appearance of what Anselm was attempting to do.

During the Enlightenment, arguments for God's existence came under attack by a number of philosophers, particularly David Hume and Immanuel Kant. To some extent, theologians' acceptance of these negative conclusions was responsible for the character of nineteenth-century liberal theology. That is, Friedrich Schleiermacher and his followers sought a grounding for theology other than reason. Kant's short response to Anselm was to point out that existence is not a predicate. That is, for example, to say that my desk is heavy, made of oak, *and existent* does not make sense. My own concern with Anselm's position is that it trades on the idea of a hierarchy of beings/reality, such that ideas in the mind and things in the world can be compared as greater or lesser, more or less "real."

However, criticizing Anselm's argument may be beside the point, since Anselm Stolz (1900–42) had already argued in 1933 that this piece is primarily an exercise in mystical theology.[18] The most famous reinterpreter of Anselm's intentions was Barth, and Barth's theology is said to be heavily indebted to his reading of Anselm. Anselm was working within the tradition of the church fathers who wrote to believers to increase their understanding, and this ability to show the reasonableness (*ratio*) of their faith was intended to produce joy. Barth insists that the order of a Christian's development is and must be, first, faith, which is a straining toward

---

[17] Philip Quinn, "Philosophy of Religion," *Camb. Dict.*, 607–11 (608). Here is an example of the way that *degrees* of reality were assigned in ancient and medieval thought.

[18] Jasper Hopkins, "Anselm of Canterbury," *Routledge*, 1:283–97 (288).

God, an act of will. But a rational creature's faith aims at understanding. Both the faith itself and the understanding are gifts of God, so the point of Anselm's "proof" is a prayer of gratitude.

Barth ends his book with the warning to contemporary readers not to read back into Anselm's work the modern notion of an ontological proof of God's existence; it is different altogether from the well-known arguments of René Descartes and G. W. Leibniz (1646–1716). He says that what "Kant put forward against these doctrines—all that is so much nonsense on which no more words ought to be wasted"[19]—as I, of course, have done here.

5.2 Cosmological arguments

Cosmological arguments begin with some observation(s) of the world (the *cosmos*) and conclude God's existence therefrom. At the beginning of his magnificent *Summa Theologiae*, Thomas has five arguments regarding God's existence, commonly referred to as his "five ways." The arguments are not particularly original: for example, similar ones are found in the writings of Aristotle and Ibn Sina. The first three are commonly taken to be cosmological arguments. The first way is from motion to a "first mover moved by no other." The second argues from observed causes to a first cause, and the third from contingent beings (that is, those that are generated but then corrupted) to a necessary being. Here is how philosopher of religion Louis Pojman (1935–2005) reconstructs Thomas's second way:

1. There exist things that are caused.
2. Nothing can be the cause of itself.
3. There cannot be an infinite regress of causes.
4. There exists an uncaused first cause.
5. The word *God* means uncaused first cause.
6. Therefore, God exists.[20]

As with Anselm's argument, there are reasons to think that Thomas had a purpose here different from proving (to anyone who does not already believe it) that God exists. Notice the difference between the ending of Pojman's reconstruction of Thomas's argument and the typical way Thomas ends his own arguments. In all five cases, Thomas ends by saying that what he has proved is "understood by everyone to be God," or is "spoken of" as, or is "called" God.

A rough way of putting the matter is to say that Thomas was not proving God's existence, but rather showing the compatibility of Aristotle's manner of reasoning (and the system of knowledge to which it led) with the Augustinian tradition.

---

[19] Karl Barth, *Anselm: Fides Quaerens Intellectum*, tr. Ian W. Robertson ([1931] Richmond, VA: John Knox Press, 1958), 171.
[20] Louis P. Pojman, *Philosophy of Religion* (Mountainview, CA: Mayfield Publishing Company, 2001), 21.

I ended Chapter 1 with a section (section 7.1) on Thomas's work, emphasizing the intellectual crisis that the recovery of Aristotle's system had created for theology. For Augustine, divine illumination was essential for attaining truth, yet God played no role in Aristotle's account of knowledge. The standards of truth and rationality of the two systems were different and incompatible. The positioning of the five ways near the beginning of Thomas's *Summa Theologiae* is significant. It is a textbook for theology students at the University of Paris, who would have just completed their studies in the Faculty of Arts, dominated by Aristotle's system. Thomas's first question in the *Summa* is on the nature of theology. As a good Augustinian, he says that theology in the mind of God is *scientia*, but notes that in the history of thought, humans begin with only a vague idea of God based on experience. In this context, the five ways set out the best account of God that human reasoning alone can provide (first mover, first cause, not determined by anything else). What comes after this beginning is both an integration of theology with other deliverances of human reasoning (Aristotle's and others') and, much more importantly, an investigation into that which can only be obtained by revelation, by Augustinian divine illumination. Theology thus becomes the highest science in Aristotle's hierarchy and the final end (*telos*) of Aristotelian enquiry.[21]

Paul Seungoh Chung (b.1978) makes the point that Thomas's five ways are strikingly *un*original.[22] Fergus Kerr says, for example, that the fifth way is found wherever religion flourishes.[23] What accounts for the fact that in their day these were so uncontroversial and yet, today, pages and pages have been written to criticize them?

A helpful set of concepts is provided by philosopher Stephan Körner (1913–2000).[24] He was a Kantian scholar but recognized that Kant was wrong in supposing there to be one universal and unchanging set of concepts or categories that account for human capacities for knowledge. In contrast, Körner recognized the possibility, and actuality, of multiple "categorial frameworks." Specifying a categorial framework involves listing all of the maximal categories—the major classifications—that are needed for describing the whole of reality, along with their subordinate genera, and the criteria for membership in those categories. It also involves stating the logical assumptions to be employed in reasoning.

Körner notes that the manner in which communities classify the objects of their experience into higher categories, the standards of intelligibility that they apply, and the metaphysical beliefs that they hold are intimately related. For example, a community that has the category of *causally determined* events will be

[21] Paul Seungoh Chung, *God at the Crossroads of Worldviews: Toward a Different Debate About the Existence of God* (Notre Dame, IN: University of Notre Dame Press, 2016), 148.

[22] Chung, *God at the Crossroads*, 169–70.

[23] Fergus Kerr, *After Aquinas: Versions of Thomism* (Oxford: Blackwell, 2002), 70–1.

[24] Stephan Körner, *Categorial Frameworks* (Oxford: Basil Blackwell, 1970).

committed to the demand that all or some *explanations* be causal, and to the belief that nature is at least partly a *deterministic system*. These metaphysical beliefs so involve each other that they are either all present in a community's thinking or else all absent from it. To possess a category such as *cause* commits a community to certain propositions about reality. This is due simply to the "grammar" (in the special sense used by Ludwig Wittgenstein) governing the relations among the concepts, and to logic. Körner describes such metaphysical claims as "internally incorrigible"; that is, necessarily true so long as the categorial framework is not changed.

My point in including this detour on Körner's thought is that it explains why arguments for God's existence appear to be so compelling to those who share the categorial framework. Both Anselm and Thomas can be seen as spelling out how the concept *God* functions within the Christian categorial framework. "God is the first cause of everything that exists" is internally incorrigible. Only an outsider could intelligibly raise the question of who or what caused God. We can also re-describe Anselm's ontological argument in Körner's terminology: *God* is a maximal category of the Christian framework and the criterion for membership in this category is being "that than which none greater can be conceived." Furthermore, "objects that exist independently of thought are greater than those that are merely objects of thought" is a part of the grammar of words such as "object," "reality," and "existence" in Anselm's day, although they are not a part of ours today. The point to be made here is that claims that are internally incorrigible in one categorical framework (medieval Christianity) may appear unintelligible, questionable, or obviously false from the point of view of a different framework. We could make this same point using MacIntyre's technical account of a tradition.

5.3 Design arguments

I have made a point throughout Part I of illustrating the fact that what counts as rational, logical, justified, true, has varied through history. My discussion of design arguments will provide another illustration of the problem modern Christian scholars had in coming to terms with the new sense of "probable reasoning." To do so, I contrast Thomas's fifth way with modern design arguments. Here is Thomas's fifth way:

> The fifth way is taken from the governance of the world. We see that things which lack knowledge, such as natural bodies, act for an end, and this is evident from their acting always, or nearly always, in the same way, so as to obtain the best results. Hence it is plain that they achieve their end, not fortuitously, but designedly. Now whatever lacks knowledge cannot move toward an end, unless it be directed by some being endowed with knowledge and intelligence; as the arrow is directed by the archer. Therefore some

intelligent being exists by whom all natural things are directed to their end; and this being we call God.[25]

Notice that it is not the (apparent) design of the world that Thomas takes to call for a designer. Rather, it is the fact that there are things in the world that act for a purpose. Due to both Aristotle's influence and his own theology, Thomas would have seen the world as suffused with purpose to a far greater extent than we can today (his was a different categorical framework from ours). For example, according to Aristotle, even the fall of a heavy object exhibits purpose—the earthy substance is *seeking* its natural place at the center of the universe. Two important features shared by all the medieval arguments are that they are intended as strict *proofs* (that is, deductive arguments) and that they trade heavily, as we have seen, on metaphysical principles. Modern design arguments take empirical features of the world as *evidence* for God's existence and are free of such *obvious* metaphysical presuppositions.

The most widely read of modern design arguments was William Paley's in a book the very title of which indicates the empiricist shift in modern thought: *Natural Theology: or Evidences of the Existence and Attributes of the Deity, Collected from the Appearances of Nature* (London, 1802). However, for brevity's sake I shall quote a brief and elegant example from David Hume's *Dialogues Concerning Natural Religion*. Here is Hume's version, put into the mouth of his character Cleanthes:

> Cleanthes: . . . Look round the world: contemplate the whole and every part of it: You will find it to be nothing but one great machine, subdivided into an infinite number of lesser machines, and even their most minute parts, are adjusted to each other with an accuracy, which ravages into admiration all men, who have ever contemplated them. The curious adapting of means to ends, throughout all nature, resembles exactly, though it much exceeds, the production of human contrivance; of human designs, thought, wisdom, and intelligence. Since therefore the effects resemble each other, we are led to infer, by all the rules of analogy, that the causes also resemble each other, and that the Author of Nature is somewhat similar to the mind of man– though possessed of much larger faculties, proportioned to the grandeur of the work, which he has executed. By this argument *a posteriori*, and by this

---

[25] Thomas Aquinas, *Summa Theologiae*, part I, question 2, 3rd article.

argument alone, do we prove at once the existence of a Deity, and his similarity to human mind and intelligence.[26]

Despite the fact that Cleanthes describes his argument as a proof, it is clear from the fact that it is an argument from analogy that it is not meant to be taken as a deductive proof of the existence of God. In fact, in the remainder of Hume's *Dialogues* he pointed out that the hypothesis of an intelligent designer is only one possible explanation of the origin of the world and depends upon our first construing it as a machine or mechanism. If instead we construe it as more analogous to an organism, then it could be produced by propagation. Because the hypothesis of an intelligent and morally good creator is not the only possibility, the final verdict must take into account all of the relevant evidence, and the existence of evil in the world is *prima facie* strong evidence against this traditional conception of the creator. (We consider the problem of evil in Chapter 7.)

Both Hume and Kant have arguments based on the concept of *causation*, which were taken by many of their followers to entirely rule out design arguments. However, we shall see in the following pages (Chapters 7 and 8) that changes in science and in other aspects of scholarship have brought the question of design back to the table again.

By Hume's day, skepticism about theological matters had grown to be significant enough that it is not unreasonable to take him to be considering whether God's existence could be proved or not. However, some interpreters see him as having had more modest goals in mind—namely to show the limits of human reasoning within the areas of religion and politics, and, especially, in metaphysics. However, from Paley's day on, atheism was coming to be a live option, and arguments such as his did have apologetic purposes. We look at the development of secularism and atheism below (Chapter 10).

6 Retrospect and prospect

Given my rather skeptical evaluation of the standard arguments for the existence of God in the previous section—and, in fact, my calling into question whether early arguments even have the same purpose that is usually attributed to them by modern readers—what then could it mean to argue for God's existence?

---

[26] David Hume, *Dialogues Concerning Natural Religion*, probably written in the 1750s and published posthumously in 1779, part ii. Hume has a passage in *Dialogues* meant to be scathing criticism of Christian belief. Philo sets up analogies in nature, such as that between the rotting of a turnip and the structure of human thought, and then asks whether the designer might bear also some equally remote analogy to any of these processes. I think it is a *great* piece of theologizing: God's intelligence is to ours as ours is to the rotting of a turnip? Reprinted in Richard Wollheim, ed., *David Hume: On Religion* (Cleveland and New York: Meridian Books, 1963), 193–4.

The conclusion expressed in this chapter is that nothing short of comparison of large-scale intellectual traditions, in the way MacIntyre has described, could possibly suffice. To "argue for the existence" of the Christian God would be to show that at least one Christian subtradition has in fact demonstrated its possession of sufficient intellectual richness to have overcome its crises in the past. Success of this sort, then, offers hope that it will continue to do so, even and especially, if it is open to dialectical challenges from rival traditions, whether theistic or atheistic.

So the remainder of this book (Part II) will be devoted to recent and contemporary intellectual crises that the Christian Tradition has had to face.

Part II

CRISES IN MODERN CHRISTIANITY

Overview of Part II: Crises in modern Christianity

We have considered throughout Part I issues of "faith and reason." I put this phrase in quotation marks because, as we have seen, both "faith" and "reason" can be used in a variety of ways. Many pages have been devoted to changes in conceptions of the nature of human reasoning—of ways of acquiring knowledge—over the centuries, and to how these changes have affected, in turn, conceptions of Christian knowledge. The influences have gone both ways, however, as in the case of Augustine's revision of the Platonic theory of knowledge.

It is not germane to the purposes of this text to survey the history of changes in the *content* of the faith. That is a topic requiring multiple books by historians and theologians. However, I ended my account of the development of epistemology with MacIntyre's conception of large-scale traditions, which implies that the content of Christian teaching should be expected to change as we struggle to apply our formative texts in new contexts and to new problems. His work also implies that historians should be especially attentive to crisis points in the development of doctrine and to the ways in which Christian scholars have (or have not) been able to respond to these crises. This is because the first step in arguing for the truth of a tradition is exactly to tell the story of the intellectual problems it has faced and the resources it has found to solve them.

Therefore, Part II of this text will be an overview of major crises facing Christians in the modern period. It should be noted that some earlier crises have been alluded to or described in Part I. The earliest was the problem of reconciling the teaching and life story of Jesus with the authoritative texts of the Jews of his day. But as the church expanded into the Gentile world, the outstanding problem became that of relating the Christian faith to an intellectual world deeply formed by Greek philosophy.

Chapter 5 will offer an overview of three major modern intellectual crises: (1) what I call the 300 years of epistemological problems; (2) the crisis created by the application of critical studies to the Scriptures; and (3) the modern challenge of religious pluralism. These will only be discussed briefly; the first is largely a recapitulation of material from Chapters 2 and 3. The two others will be treated all too briefly because doing them justice would each take at least a book in itself.

Chapter 6 describes the problem of special divine action. First, we shall see why God's action in the natural world became an especially challenging problem in the modern era. Second, I argue that limited options for responding to this crisis had significant effects on the development of modern theology, and (I speculate) even contributed to the development of atheism. Finally, I comment on current attempts to reconcile a robust account of God's special divine action with our contemporary worldview, particularly as it has been influenced by science.

Chapter 7 addresses a perennial problem for Christians, that of reconciling evil and suffering with the goodness of God. However, the problem of evil only became an intellectual crisis in the modern period. It has been traditional, at least since Augustine's day, to distinguish between moral evil (sin) and natural evil (suffering from natural causes). Augustine explained the second as a consequence of the first, but his solution is now widely rejected, and a new approach is needed. I argue that considerable resources are now being provided by developments in science. Augustine had a third concept, metaphysical evil (weakness), and contemporary science contributes here, as well.

Chapter 8 describes the conflicts (real or merely perceived) between Christian thought and science. Two basic theses are advanced. One is that most of the real conflicts were minor, and had a great deal to do, in the first instance, with the drastic worldview changes accompanying the scientific revolution—they were not Christianity versus science, but the old science versus the new science. Later (perceived) conflicts had much to do with authority over educational institutions—from clergy to science-minded leaders. Second, there have been exciting positive relations between Christian theology and contemporary scientific developments.

Chapter 9 describes what may be the most likely perception of science–theology conflict, revolving around the Christian concept of body–soul dualism and the increasing evidence from the cognitive neurosciences that the concept of an additional entity, a mind or soul, is not needed to account for human higher capacities.

Chapter 10 describes what may be the most daunting ongoing challenge to the Christian Tradition: the development of a rival Naturalist Tradition. As I claimed in Chapter 4, to "argue for the existence of God" now can be seen as an argument for the rational superiority of a theistic tradition to its most powerful (non-theistic) rivals. And a preliminary step to such an argument is to come to understand the rival. A tiny step in understanding the Naturalist Tradition is all that will be possible in one chapter.

A conclusion to the book will attempt a judicious assessment of the successes (and failures?) of the Christian Tradition to find resources within itself to resolve these crises.

5

Three epistemological crises for Christianity in modernity

1 Introduction

First a brief (and perhaps tedious) reminder of what we have covered so far and the distance we have to go: Recall that Part I was dedicated to arguing that Alasdair MacIntyre's method for testing the rational credentials of rival traditions is the best account of rationality that we have to date. This involves (1) an account of the crises one's own tradition has faced, and the extent to which the tradition has (or has not) had the resources to resolve them; (2) a sympathetic assessment of the most significant rival traditions, the extent to which they suffer crises, and either have or have not demonstrated the resources to overcome them;[1] and, finally, (3) an explanation, on the basis of one's own tradition, of why the rivals failed, and had to fail, just at the point they did. If so, one's tradition is justified in claiming that it is rationally superior—that is, it offers a better account of reality than the partial and perspectival accounts of reality provided by other traditions. In such a case, the scholars of one's own tradition have met the criteria for claiming the truth of the central tenets of that tradition.

So, the first step in the process is to review the intellectual crises one's own tradition has faced and recount the narrative of whether and how it has had the resources to overcome the crises. I hope that this will be one of the major contributions of this text. Note, however, that sympathetic narration of the intellectual histories of all of contemporary Christianity's major rivals is far beyond the scope of this book. Even less will it be possible to explain, in Christian terms, the rivals' failures. With the exception of Chapter 10, which will suggest prospective problems for the contemporary Naturalist Tradition, this comparison will not be definitive.

However, as this text does intend to illustrate, Christians have been very quick to recognize their own intellectual problems. As noted in the Overview to this Part of the text, we can see NT authors already struggling to reconcile the events of Jesus' life with their authoritative Hebrew texts, and Chapter 1 focused specifically on two different versions of the problem of reconciling Christian theology, first, with

---

[1] Denying that one will always see one's own tradition to be entirely in order, while rivals will always appear to be deficient, is one of MacIntyre's claims, and one that is both essential to the defeat of relativism, and one that the material in the remainder of this text is meant to demonstrate.

Platonic thought and then Aristotelian. As the pace of scholarship speeded up in the modern period, so did the pace of scholarly work dedicated to addressing the problems and epistemological crises that modernity produced.

The purpose of this Part of the text, then, is to provide an overview of what I take to be the major crises facing modern and contemporary Christian thinkers.[2] Three problems are addressed briefly in this chapter. The first is the 300-year struggle to reconcile theological reasoning with the forms of reasoning that have developed over the course of the modern period. Much of this will recapitulate material from Chapters 2 through 4. Second, I present an all-too-brief account of the crisis presented by the development of critical biblical studies; an adequate account would require at least an entire book in itself. Third, while Christianity has always been surrounded by competing religious systems, I point out how religious plurality became an epistemological *crisis* in the modern period and recount a bit of the history of how it has been addressed. Again, at least an entire book would be needed to cover this issue adequately.

As described in the Overview of Part II, the remaining chapters will address at greater length the problems of divine action; of evil, particularly natural evil; real and perceived conflicts between science and Christian theology; a potential conflict regarding the nature of human beings; and the development and evaluation of the current Naturalist Tradition.

As I have struggled to think how to organize this Part of the text, I have become fascinated by the ways in which each problem relates to some or all of the others. Thus, the organization is somewhat arbitrary because each problem could be seen as leading to another. However, if I were to try to draw a network representing the interconnections, there would be two important hubs: the modern epistemology already discussed, and the problem of divine action.

2 Three hundred years of epistemological problems

I begin this section of the chapter with a review of issues described in Part I, which I shall together call the epistemological problem. I recounted in Chapter 1 how theological method had been integrated with the ancient and medieval epistemological categories of *scientia* and *opinio*. While theology had the status of *scientia* only in the mind of God, studying and reconciling the authorities allowed nonetheless for human knowledge of Christian doctrine.

I also described (in Chapter 2) the role of the Reformation in dismantling the medieval concept of probable knowledge (*opinio*). In short, the Reformation

---

[2] These issues will be seen to line up rather well with the topics addressed in typical philosophy of religion textbooks, but they are addressed not as individual (and perhaps perennial) problems but as the steps in one continuous argument.

created the problem of conflicting authorities, and there appeared to be no way to answer the question of which authorities to believe. I described the transition from the medieval sense of "probable" as that approved by authority to the modern sense of knowledge based on the weight of evidence.

2.1 The foundationalist challenge

In Chapter 2, I traced some of the consequences of Descartes's foundationalist metaphor for developments in theological method. I claimed that different choices for foundations (Scripture or a peculiar sort of inner experience) created two types of theology, particularly among Protestants in the USA. I made a rather tentative suggestion (in section 5.3) that both foundationalist methodologies have come to dead ends. However, using the critique of foundationalism developed in Chapter 3 (esp. section 4.4), I can now be more specific in explaining why neither scriptural nor experiential-expressivist foundationalism could ever have succeeded.

Scriptural foundationalists expected that the text would provide a factual foundation from which theology could be constructed reliably by means of induction or mere organization. However, current biblical scholars and theologians present us with a much more complicated picture. Recall Karl Popper's comment that the facts supporting a scientific theory are more like pilings driven into a swamp. Recall also that inductive reasoning never provides a certain means of construction, that scientific theories are hypotheses creatively devised by scientists to explain regularities, and, finally, that the choice of what to count as data depends on theories of instrumentation, which in turn are often dependent on the theory being tested.

Theology is even more complicated. From a huge number of copies of ancient scriptural texts, it is necessary first to construct a critical text—the one that is judged to be closest to the original. Doing so relies on a number of assumptions. For example, a copyist might well insert a marginal note into the text, but it is very unlikely that any part of the sacred text would (intentionally) be omitted. Therefore, as between a shorter and longer version of the same text, prefer the shorter.

Next (for most scholars) these texts need to be translated, and again there is sometimes no obviously correct translation; it is a matter of judgment. The texts must then be interpreted, and it is well recognized that there is a hermeneutic circle: the theological presuppositions of the interpreter often shape the interpretation. Finally, parallel to science's theories of instrumentation, a number of theological factors go into selection of texts to use (canon), methods of interpretation, and so forth, so we end up with an unstable-looking monster here, just as we do if we still try to represent science as a building or layer cake (Figure 16 overleaf).

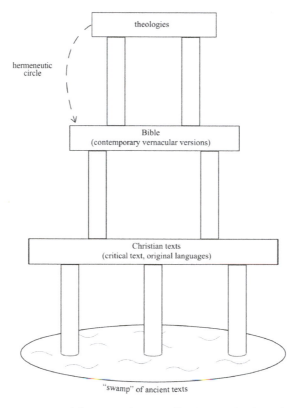

Figure 16 A monstrous model representing complications in theology if pictured using a foundationalist model

A similar sort of circularity is now recognized when one attempts to find an *experiential* foundation for theology. The recognition, description, and even qualitative feel of an experience are now recognized to be dependent, to a greater or lesser extent, on the language and concepts one has available. How could Friedrich Schleiermacher have recognized his feeling of absolute dependence as a *religious* experience without all of the theology he had learned? And there is no way to know (or perhaps even make sense of) the existence of a *universal* experience that is always only experienced as it is transformed by the person's *particular* culture and religion.

2.2 Holism to the rescue

As described in Chapter 3 (section 4.3), I have spilled much ink in arguing that the rational structure of theology ought to be envisioned holistically. In particular, I have argued that theological schools can be seen as analogous to Imre Lakatos's scientific research programs. Furthermore, a theological research program, according to its own standards of reasoning and judgments regarding reliable sources of data, can in fact stand up to current standards of probable reasoning.[3]

Having now read MacIntyre's work, I would say that *doing* systematic theology is one of the *social practices* in which the Christian Tradition is embodied—it is a crucial part of ongoing arguments about how best to interpret and apply Christianity's formative texts. But to show that this one practice has, or could have, standards equivalent to those of scientific practice still leaves open the question: Why bother? That is, if Christianity as a whole has been supplanted (or made merely a matter of private values and meaning) then the whole practice of theology is parochial.[4]

Obviously (at least I hope it is by now) we need a way of showing the Christian worldview to be rationally superior to its major competitors. And if MacIntyre has given us a means to do this, then at last, after 300 years, *we have a theory of rationality sophisticated enough to justify the general truth claims of the Christian worldview.* Insofar as I am successful here, this text is itself a *very* small contribution to the solution of the epistemological crisis created by the development of modern epistemology.

3 Biblical criticism as an epistemological crisis

Recall that when MacIntyre speaks of an *epistemological* crisis he is not referring to a run-of-the-mill intellectual problem, but to one that threatens the very mode or sources of rational justification that, prior to the crisis, one would have used to solve the problem. We have seen that the loss of the epistemological category of authority provided one such crisis for the Christian Tradition, and I have suggested that attempts to find ways out of the crisis by adopting Descartes's foundationalism and inside-out reasoning have run into insuperable obstacles. The development of historical-critical methodology was the source of a subsequent epistemological crisis. For (however one understands the epistemological role of Scripture: as chief authority or as foundation), calling both its truth and its status as revelation into question is devastating, especially for Protestants.

3.1 Crisis created

We have already seen (in Chapter 2, section 4.4) that David Hume was able rather easily to undermine John Locke's apologetic for the revealed status of the Christian Scriptures. And notice that he did so exactly by employing the

---

[3] Nancey Murphy, *Theology in the Age of Scientific Reasoning* (Ithaca, NY and London: Cornell University Press, 1990).

[4] Money was given for Oxford University to endow a chair in religion and science. A well-known (but not to be named here) professor of philosophy was heard to say something like: "A chair in religion and science? As well endow a chair in phrenology and psychology!"

standard of rationality developed in the Port Royal *Logic*. Testimony regarding the existence of a miracle can never serve as a *foundation* for a system of religion. Miracles he took to be, by definition, violations of the laws of nature. The laws of nature are established by uniform experience. If it is uniform experience that warrants belief in the probability of an event's occurrence, then belief in the violation of a law of nature (a miracle) is just what is least likely ever to be supported by good reasons. He reinforced this argument by adding a low assessment of the credibility of the putative witnesses to miracles on the basis of the Port Royal *Logic*'s criteria. Because the alleged witnesses are not known to be numerous, intelligent, well-educated, evidently honest, in the position of having something to lose if the account proves false, and operating publicly in a well-known part of the world, we have especially good reason, Hume concluded, to disbelieve their accounts.[5]

In addition, to argue from the miracle accounts or fulfilled prophecies *in* Scripture for the truth of Scripture is viciously circular.

By the time Hume was writing (late eighteenth century), critical study of the biblical texts themselves was well underway. Techniques for ascertaining the authenticity of, for example, legal documents could just as well be applied to biblical texts. I shall not say much about the *development* of historical criticism since this is not relevant to my point here. My purpose has been in part to tie the issue to the epistemological developments associated with Port Royal.

The essential conclusion to draw is to note how well the modern struggle with the import of critical study of the Bible illustrates MacIntyre's concept of an epistemological crisis. Hans Frei (along with a number of others) points out that before the modern age most Christians read the Bible primarily as a kind of realistic narrative, with an overarching story from creation to last judgment, and often understood their lives by locating themselves in the context of this larger story.[6]

To use MacIntyre's language, the modern scientific worldview (including "scientific" study of the Bible) provided a new schema. To put the alternatives perhaps too starkly, the older schema led scholars to attempt to fit current events (*including the rise of science*; e.g., describing study of the laws of nature as discovering the mind of the creator) into the biblical storyline. The new schema understands the world "scientifically"—in terms of facts, the universal laws of nature, and so forth—and so the Bible becomes an *object* of such study. In an epistemological crisis one does not know what to take as evidence without resolving the question of which schema is correct, and one cannot decide on the proper schema without knowing what to take as evidence. So the dilemma is this: Does the

5   David Hume, "Of Miracles," in *An Enquiry concerning Human Understanding* (1748), section x.
6   Hans W. Frei, *The Eclipse of Biblical Narrative: A Study in Eighteenth and Nineteenth Century Hermeneutics* (New Haven, CT and London: Yale University Press, 1974).

scientific study of biblical texts destroy the Bible's authoritative status for telling us the most important truths about reality? If so, how then do we make sense of reality and of our own lives? An epistemological crisis is a breakdown in what we think we know about *how to know*. (See my own account in Chapter 4, section 4.)

3.2 Crisis resolved?

Developments of methodologies in biblical criticism in more recent years have done much to refocus attention on biblical narrative as opposed to mere historical factuality. More important is the fact that a variety of scholars are calling us back to the attempt to interpret the world in terms of biblical narrative. David Kelsey (b.1932) writes that to take the Christian Scriptures as normative is simply what it *means* to be a Christian.[7] George Lindbeck (b.1923) calls for an "intratextual" approach to Scripture. He compares religions to languages, which provide the concepts for construing the nature of reality and thus provide guidance for the living of life.[8] He concurs with Frei in urging that we once again allow the biblical narrative to absorb the world.[9]

Of course, all of this is consistent with MacIntyre's writings. One of the *virtues* he recommends is being aware of the tradition(s) one inhabits; and to be a participant in a tradition is to participate in the attempt to apply the tradition's formative texts in one's current context. Difficulties remain, of course, and an essential *communal practice* is to attempt to resolve differences. There are striking differences in views on how to practice biblical criticism.

Another difference within the Christian Tradition regards views on the extent to which contemporary science can be incorporated into the Christian worldview. For this reason, I devote the whole of Chapter 8 to issues in science and Christianity. However, differences regarding the compatibility of Christianity with science depend in large measure on views of divine action. Therefore, Chapter 6 will consider this topic.

4 The modern challenge of religious pluralism

The existence of other religions is nothing new for Christians. We saw in Chapter 1 that our current distinction between philosophy and religion was not made in ancient times: Pythagoreanism and Neoplatonism, for instance, were as much religious as philosophical (in our current senses).

---

[7] David H. Kelsey, *The Uses of Scripture in Recent Theology* (Philadelphia: Fortress Press, 1975), 99.

[8] George A. Lindbeck, *The Nature of Doctrine: Religion and Theology in a Postliberal Age* (Philadelphia: Westminster Press, 1984), 64–6.

[9] Lindbeck, "The Church's Mission to a Postmodern Culture," in Frederic B. Burnham, ed., *Postmodern Theology: Christian Faith in a Pluralist World* (San Francisco: HarperCollins, 1989), 37–55.

Christianity related to these other systems in a variety of ways: outright rejection; intentional incorporation of some of their resources; accidental incorporation of their interpretations of reality, often due to an apologist in one generation adopting the opponent's language, and then having it read later as representing authentic Christian concepts. Christian *holy* days were sometimes created intentionally to compete with or replace pagan *holidays* (how did they know Jesus was born almost exactly on the winter solstice?). Pagan practices (worship of trees) were "baptized." And some would say that certain doctrinal formulations were designed to turn political enemies into heretics.

There was, of course, terrible fighting between Christians and Muslims in the Middle Ages, and the Jews were sorely persecuted. But meanwhile, during the high Middle Ages Thomas and Maimonides (1135–1204) were working appreciatively with Islamic commentaries on Aristotle.

4.1 Religious plurality becomes an epistemological crisis

If the plurality of religions was more of an interest or a mixed blessing than an intellectual problem in the high Middle Ages, how did it become an epistemological crisis in early modern thought? I believe that there are at least seven factors, some of which will already be familiar.

The change described above (Chapter 2) from an epistemology based on authority to one based on the preponderance of evidence is certainly central: if there is no clear answer to the question of how to give rational support to the central claims of Christian thought, then all the less could there be a way to show the rational superiority of the Christian faith to any of its religious rivals. But an important factor, even before this change was complete, was sixteenth-century Renaissance apologetics. During the Renaissance, sandwiched between medieval and fully modern thought, the writings of ancient skeptics were discovered and translated. One form, called academic skepticism, insisted that no knowledge was possible. The other and more useful version was called Pyrrhonian skepticism. This is the view that there is no sufficient evidence to support significant judgments such as those regarding the truth or falsity of a religious system. Michel de Montaigne (1533–92) employed this form of skepticism effectively in favor of the Catholic Church. If there was no rational means of choosing between the criteria for truth used by Protestants versus Catholics, then the most reasonable thing to do would be to accept the laws and customs of one's community, which for Montaigne was Catholicism.[10]

Another, closely related contributory factor, as we have already seen, was a deep mistrust of the Christian Scriptures, brought about by the change from the

---

[10] Richard Popkin, *The History of Skepticism from Savonarola to Bayle*, rev. and expanded ed. (Oxford: Oxford University Press, [1979] 2003), 51.

epistemological category of authority (the chief of which had been the Bible) to that of empirical evidence. When the canons of empirical evidence were applied to the Bible itself, first, arguments such as Locke's for its status as divine revelation were easily called into question as by Hume. Then particular claims within the texts became subject to empirical evaluation and, again, Hume stands out (in the English-speaking world) as particularly adept in questioning the scriptural narratives.

A third factor was increased knowledge of the existence of other religions and accounts (real or exaggerated) of how radically they diverged from Christianity. This was to an extent the effect of the great seagoing expeditions already begun in the fifteenth century. And if neither Catholicism nor Protestantism can be shown to be true, perhaps neither are any of the newly recognized religions of other cultures.

A fourth factor was arguments *against* the existence of God. While Hume's and Kant's arguments could have been seen to be equally effective against other con-ceptions of God, given the Christian context, they were taken as arguments spe-cifically against the God Christians worshiped: "creator of heaven and earth." In fact, in Hume's *Dialogues Concerning Natural Religion*, his character Philo points out that a designer is only one possible explanation for the existence of the world, and, furthermore, even if it is designed, the disorder in the world needs to be taken into account as well, and might rather suggest a team of superannuated deities; the suffering might suggest a malevolent deity.[11]

A fifth factor, also found in Hume's work (as well as in other writers) was on the nature of history. He wrote a six-volume work, *The History of England*,[12] with the purpose of demolishing the Christian *providential* view of history, a view firmly established in Hume's time, both in popular consciousness and in the meta-physical framework within which the scientists of the age worked. Joseph Priestley (1733–1804), for example, believed that history promised to provide the most important source of insight into divine activity and plan; as we learn more of history we see more and more clearly the perfections and providence of God.[13] Hume set out to show that history could be understood perfectly well in terms of the regularities of human behavior.[14]

---

[11] David Hume, *Dialogues Concerning Natural Religion*, probably written in the 1750s but published posthumously in 1779.

[12] David Hume, *The History of England, from the Invasion of Julius Caesar to the Abdication of James the Second* (1668).

[13] Joseph Priestley, *Lectures on History and General Policy* (Dublin, 1777).

[14] So another topic that should be given much more attention here is the methodological naturaliza-tion of the discipline of history. While students often object to methodological naturalism in the natural sciences, they might even more strenuously object that the histories of the church and of the development of doctrine never include phrases such as "and then God did . . ." Here is another point at which the problem of special divine action bears strongly on modern and contemporary accounts of Christianity.

Finally, these arguments against the truth of Christianity and particularly against the existence of God raised the question of why religion even exists, if it is not due to God's actions and revelation. Hume published his *Natural History of Religion* in 1757, arguing that religion is a consequence of fear of the unknown. It usually begins with polytheism, and then evolves into monotheism. In France, Paul Henri Thierry, better known as Baron d'Holbach (1723–89), published what is known in translation as *The System of Nature*.[15] The entire second volume comprises his naturalistic account of the origins of religions and criticisms of Christianity.

So the factors I have mentioned here first called into question the possibility of giving rational justification for Christian belief, but by eroding the role of God in revelation and history, and in religion in general, finally promoted the view that all religions are merely human phenomena. This raised the question of whether there was any point in attempting to evaluate or choose among them, and certainly removed religion as an authoritative source of knowledge about the nature of reality (the epistemological crisis).

All of these factors are equally relevant to the rise of a competing Naturalist Tradition, especially d'Holbach's *System*, since it *was* an attempt at a comprehensive explanation of reality without God, souls, or other non-material beings. As will appear in Chapter 10, very often the solutions Christians offered to these problems lent themselves to skepticism with regard to Christian claims, making atheism a live option, and opening the way for a competing Naturalistic Tradition.

4.2 Early theological responses to religious plurality

In response to "the cultured despisers of religion" in his own day, Friedrich Schleiermacher took on the topic of religious plurality in an appreciative way at approximately the same time as Hume's devastating attacks were being appreciated in Britain. In his *Speeches*, he distinguished between formalized religions and the essence of religion itself.[16] In most of the book, he emphasized that no single manifestation, either in an individual or in a social group, could show forth the whole of religion; therefore, the fact of the variety of religions was a good thing: each could add another glimpse of the whole. Nonetheless, in his Fifth Speech he described Christianity as the superior religion because of its recognition of the way everything finite resists the unity of the whole and of how the deity brings about reconciliation. In his mature work, translated as *The Christian Faith*, he

---

[15] Baron d'Holbach, *The System of Nature, or, The Laws of the Moral and Physical Worlds* (London, 1795–6); reprinted as Paul Henri Thierry, Baron d'Holbach, *The System of Nature*, 2 vols. (Sioux Falls, SD: NuVisions Publications, 2007).

[16] Friedrich Schleiermacher, *On Religion: Speeches to its Cultured Despisers*, tr. John Oman ([1799] New York: Harper and Row, 1958). There are more recent editions, but some experts consider this the best translation.

was much more explicit about the superiority of Christianity to other developed religions, due to its being influenced by the God-consciousness of Jesus, who was unique in the fact that his consciousness never waned (as ours does). And Protestantism is a higher form of Christianity than Catholicism because there is no church mediating one's consciousness of God.[17]

There were other fair and sensitive treatments of other religions at the time, but academic study of religions is said to have begun in earnest only around 1870. Claude Welch says that the Romantic movement "freed the European mind to become . . . curious about other people's religions . . . [and] appreciative of their ways of *expressing* the human experience." Earlier intolerance he attributes to the insistence that only one religion could be *true*.[18]

Another factor that led to the development of comparative religion as a recognized discipline was the explosion of information about the religions of the world, through both the acquisition of books and archaeological work. Professorships were established in universities, and there were two principal goals. One was to seek out the roots of religion by the study of "primitive" religions. The other was to compare Christianity to the other developed religions and (whether or not this was admitted) to show, in one way or another, the "absoluteness" of Christianity. This was a term borrowed from G. W. F. Hegel (1770–1831) and was meant as a replacement for apologetics based on any sort of supernatural basis such as miracles. The work of Ernst Troeltsch (1865–1923) is often considered the culmination of the quest for absoluteness.

Later in the twentieth century the study of religion was established in secular universities. For example, Ninian Smart (1927–2001) established the first religious studies department in the UK at the University of Lancaster in 1967. In these departments, there is a firm intention to *avoid* claims for the superiority of any one religion.

4.3 Recent developments in philosophy of the religions

The topic of religious pluralism does not appear in many textbooks on the philosophy of religion,[19] but rather appears more often in entire books devoted to various positions, which might be classified as either philosophical or theological.

---

[17] Friedrich Schleiermacher, *The Christian Faith*, ed. and tr. H. R. Macintosh and J. S. Stewart ([1928] Edinburgh: T. & T. Clark, 1999); translated from *Der christliche Glaube*, first published in 1821.

[18] Claude Welch, *Protestant Thought in the Nineteenth Century*, 2 vols. (New Haven, CT and London: Yale University Press, 1972, 1985), 2:104. My italics in the quotation; this is intended to remind the reader of the distinction, described in Chapter 2 (section 5.3), between the experiential-expressivist (liberal) and cognitive-propositionalist (conservative) types of modern theology.

[19] A notable exception is Michael Peterson, William Hasker, Bruce Reichenbach, and David Bassinger, *Reason & Religious Belief: An Introduction to the Philosophy of Religion*, 4th ed. (New York and Oxford: Oxford University Press, [1991] 2009). Pagination is based on the 4th ed., and I shall refer to the text simply as Peterson's.

It is common to classify positions on religious plurality as one of three types: exclusivism, pluralism, or inclusivism. This simple three-way distinction is complicated, though, by the fact that some scholars are concerned primarily with the question of truth, and others with the question of salvation. However, if part of what a religion teaches concerns the conditions or paths to salvation, or if faith (in the sense of true belief) is taken as a requirement for salvation, then the two topics become entangled.

The simplest position to explain is *exclusivism*: only one religion (and here I shall focus on Christian positions only) can be true, and a significant part of what Christianity (truly) teaches is that only Christians can be saved through the work of Jesus Christ. There are usually provisions made to soften this stance on salvation, such as allowing that faithful Jews before the time of Christ were saved as well, and there is often recognition that other religions contain *some* true teachings.

Pluralism is more complicated to explain because there is a plurality of versions of it. Pluralists tend to begin by affirming that different religions may well offer paths to salvation. Then the question arises of what to say about their different systems of beliefs. The example most often cited is in John Hick's *An Interpretation of Religion*.[20] Hick argues that the infinite Reality is unknowable as it is in itself. We can only speak of it as experienced from within our own cultural ways of knowing and being. Thus, only formal ("empty") concepts such as *the infinite Reality* or *the Transcendent* can be applied literally to God. All of the rest of our religious language is best understood as mythological. He defines mythic truth as follows: "A statement or set of statements about X is mythically true if it is not literally true but nevertheless tends to evoke an appropriate dispositional attitude to X." Since myths do not correspond in any way to the reality to which they refer, the usual rules regarding logical consistency and contradiction do not apply: "Myths, functioning in their separate mythic spaces, do not clash with one another."[21] Thus, there is no need to select one of the many religions as true and reject all others.

In addition, he maintains that all of the major religions are salvific. He understands salvation as transformation of the person from an absorbing self-concern to a new centering in the Real. This transformation is readily observable by its moral fruits—growth toward an ethical ideal common to all of the great traditions. With salvation so understood, it is a simple step to argue from the observed transformation of devotees of the various religions to the conclusion that those religions are all paths to salvation.

So, to sum up, Hick solves the problem of truth by explaining religious knowledge in such a way that apparently contradictory claims can all be true; Christianity

---

[20] John Hick, *An Interpretation of Religion* (New Haven, CT: Yale University Press, 1989).
[21] Hick, *Interpretation*, 348, 15.

is true (in the mythic sense of "true"), but not the only truth. Doctrines regarding the status of Christ (for example, that he is the only incarnation of the second person of the Trinity) can be mythically true if they evoke appropriate religious attitudes toward God and neighbor. However, Hick warns, taking such doctrines to be literally true can lead Christians to feel uniquely privileged and therefore free to patronize and exploit the non-Christian majority of the human race. Michael L. Peterson (b.1950) makes an important point here. He and his co-authors sharply distinguish between the question of how a person of one religion should approach a *person* who advocates a different religion and the question of how to approach the *truth claims* that the other person advocates.[22]

A legitimate criticism of Hick, I believe, is that he fails to do justice to how most religious believers understand themselves—that is, they believe that they are describing divine realities. Also, Hick has been accused of simply inventing a new religion with a very definite view of salvation and a very definite *agnosticism* about nearly everything else.

Inclusivism is a sort of hybrid position. It is (exclusively) through the redemptive work of Jesus Christ that salvation is possible, and Christians, of course, are the only ones who know this truth. But God's graciousness extends salvation to faithful practitioners of other religions, even though they are ignorant of Jesus' role in their salvation. On this view, all religions may lead to salvation. The problem of the truth of the various religious systems need not arise if one is an experiential-expressivist. As Welch said of nineteenth-century interest in religious plurality, following Schleiermacher, there are a number of ways of *expressing* consciousness of the divine. Catholic theologian Karl Rahner (1904–84) was the best-known exponent of this view, calling those in other religions who are saved "anonymous Christians."[23]

Much has been written on this topic, and it is clear that many of the differences are due to the liberal versus conservative leanings of the authors. Has the discussion stalled or is there a way forward?

4.4 The way forward?

The Peterson text ends its chapter on religious pluralism with the conclusion that despite brilliant attempts (some briefly surveyed here, and at greater length in its own chapter) it is simply not possible to evade the truth question. And MacIntyre reminds us that this is not merely a philosophical puzzle. He writes:

All human beings, whatever their culture, find themselves confronted by questions about the nature and significance of their lives: What is our place

---

[22] Peterson, *Reason*, 292.
[23] See, for example, Karl Rahner, "Christianity and the Non-Christian Religions," in *Theological Investigations* 5, tr. Karl-H. Kruger (Baltimore: Helicon Press, 1966), 115–34.

in the order of things? Of what powers in the natural and social world do we need to take account? How should we respond to the facts of suffering and death? What is our relation to the dead? What is it to live a human life well? What is it to live it badly?[24]

Peterson rightly notes that the attempt to evaluate individual religious beliefs outside of their context is impractical because many of them are not even meaningful outside of a particular religious tradition (recall the claims and counterclaims concerning D. Z. Phillips in Chapter 3, section 2.3). Thus, the task is to evaluate the various *traditions*, in the hope of showing that one is as true (or truer than) the others. They endorse criteria for evaluation provided by Keith Yandell (b.1938). His criteria include internal consistency among the major claims of the tradition, as well as failure to contradict well-established data from other fields such as the sciences and psychology. *Ad hoc* reasoning in order to attempt to avoid contradictory evidence counts against a tradition, and the system should be able to account for broad reaches of human experience.[25] Peterson adds another criterion: "It should satisfy some basic moral and aesthetic intuitions and provoke and inspire persons to live more morally responsive and responsible lives."[26]

I have already noted that both philosophers and theologians have written on the problem of religious plurality (and as we shall see in Chapter 10, this is a topic addressed by naturalists). I have speculated that theological differences such as those between experiential-expressivists and cognitive-propositionalists influence scholars' choices among inclusivism, exclusivism, and pluralism. We have also seen the difference between the nineteenth-century attempts to place Christianity at the top of a hierarchy of religions, in contrast to the twentieth-century university departments that strictly avoid such judgments. So religious convictions can be seen to make a difference in dealing with this philosophical issue.

It used to be the case that philosophy of religion and philosophical theology were taken to be different disciplines, even though they often considered the same problems. The assumption was that philosophers of religion studied the issues objectively, while philosophical theologians did so (as suggested above) from a convictional starting point. Now, however, there is a growing recognition that all of us work from within *some* worldview or tradition.[27] The Enlightenment, with its goal of leaving behind all tradition and pursuing objective and universal

---

[24] Alasdair MacIntyre, *God, Philosophy, Universities: A Selective History of the Catholic Philosophical Tradition* (Lanham, MD: Rowman and Littlefield, 2009), 9.

[25] Keith E. Yandell, "Religious Explanation and Rational Appraisal," *Religious Studies* 8 (June 1974): 185–6. On this last criterion, see Chapter 3, section 4.3.

[26] Peterson, *Reason*, 308.

[27] See James Wm. McClendon, Jr. and James M. Smith, *Convictions: Defusing Religious Relativism* (Valley Forge, PA: Trinity Press International, 1994); a revision of *Understanding Religious Convictions* (Notre Dame, IN: University of Notre Dame Press, 1975).

knowledge, can now itself be seen as the Enlightenment *Tradition*! I dedicated Part I of this text, in part, to showing that down-home philosophical concepts such as *truth, justification, knowledge, rationality* in fact have histories. Therefore, to take a stance on the meaning of any of these (e.g., to assume that "truth" simply means, and has always meant, correspondence of a proposition to some fact) is to be standing in convictional territory—modern Enlightenment territory.

This growing recognition of the convictional nature of *all* traditions has led to new developments in the academic world—a much more forthright *theological* approach to the topic of the variety of religions. There seem to be two movements developing: One is to attempt to give a theological explanation for the variety of religions. This has been attempted by means of pneumatological, Christological, and theocentric approaches.

Despite the objections in other religions to Christian Trinitarianism, it may nonetheless turn out that a Trinitarian explanation works best. For example, Mark Heim (b.1950) raises another criticism of Hick's and others' claim that all major religious traditions may be equally salvific in that they lead (in an observable way) to salvation, defined as the transition from self-concern to a new centering in the Real. Heim argues, though, from a Christian Trinitarian perspective, that the highest form of religious fulfillment is eschatological communion with the Trinitarian God, not added extrinsically at the end of this life, but pursued throughout this life by means of appropriate practices. However, he recognizes that there are a variety of other forms of religious fulfillment that are more or less worth pursuing. Christians, he says, can broaden their own understanding of truth and deepen their practice of faith by encountering other paths of faith. He calls his position "orientational pluralism."[28]

Veli-Matti Kärkkäinen (b.1958) also insists on a Trinitarian basis for interfaith dialogue. He points out that "in the triune God there is both unity and plurality, communion and diversity. The Trinity as communion allows room for both genuine diversity . . . and unity."[29] He, too, resists the pluralist tendency to deny genuine differences among religions, but carefully examines each of the major faith traditions not only to note the differences, but also to search for common themes such as the monotheism shared among Christians, Jews, and Muslims. All three share concerns with creation, the nature of the human person, sin, salvation, and eschatology.[30] Dialogue can contribute to the recognition that opposition between religions is sometimes based on heretical interpretations of one's own tradition.[31]

The second movement, again theological rather than philosophical, is the attempt to do Christian theology in light of the teachings of at least one other

---

[28] S. Mark Heim, *Salvations: Truth and Differences in Religion* (Maryknoll, NY: Orbis, 1995), ch. 6.

[29] Veli-Matti Kärkkäinen, *A Constructive Christian Theology for the Pluralistic World*, 5 vols. (Grand Rapids, MI: Eerdmans, 2017), 5:451.

[30] Kärkkäinen, *Christian Theology*, 5:467.

[31] For example, Kärkkäinen, *Christian Theology*, 5:459–60.

major religion. This new movement is called comparative theology. It begins with reading the texts of other religions with the same sophistication that Christian theologians bring to their own. Francis Clooney (b.1950) suggests that a consequence may be that when Christians return to their own texts they may find themselves reading them in new lights.[32]

A more striking change is the attempt to revise one's constructive theology in such a way as to harmonize it as well as possible with the teachings of other traditions. Keith Ward (b.1938) has written a four-volume theology that compares Christian doctrines with teachings from a variety of other religions and then seeks common themes that Christians can endorse.[33]

A problem that Clooney describes is one now familiar to readers of this text. Although he does not use the word "incommensurability," he says that "close attention to another tradition's theology may in fact lead to basic scepticism about the viability of concepts and words across theological boundaries." He fears that this will make it impossible to come to any conclusions about the answers to the great questions. He says: "Perhaps we must simply be patient for a century or two, until the implications of comparison become more familiar and coherent."[34]

The Peterson text ended its discussion of Yandell's suggestions for evaluating religions by saying that further reflection on his criteria is warranted.[35] My proposal (not coming as a surprise at this point, I suspect) is that, of all of the scholars who *have* thought further about Yandell's criteria, MacIntyre's reflections will be the most useful. While he has not participated in the discussion of rival *religious* traditions, he has argued for the rational superiority of the Thomist (Catholic) tradition over its *philosophical* competitors, and I see no reason not to extend his methods for testing traditions to other religious traditions as well.

This is no quick and easy task. In *Whose Justice? Which Rationality?*, MacIntyre spent 400 pages just on the Aristotelian/Thomist and Enlightenment Traditions of ethics.[36] The sort of insiders' appreciation of a rival tradition that is required before one can even begin to criticize it can take years. Learning the history of its crises and successes, and *sometimes* recognizing that one's own tradition can better

---

[32] Francis X. Clooney, sj, "Comparative Theology," in John Webster, Kathryn Tanner, and Iain Torrance, eds., *The Oxford Handbook of Systematic Theology* (Oxford: Oxford University Press, 2007), ch. 36 (659).

[33] Keith Ward, *Religion and Revelation; Religion and Creation; Religion and Human Nature;* and *Religion and Community* (Oxford: Oxford University Press, 1994, 1996, 1998, 2000).

[34] Clooney, "Comparative Theology," 667.

[35] Peterson, *Reason*, 308.

[36] Alasdair MacIntyre, *Whose Justice? Which Rationality?* (Notre Dame, IN: University of Notre Dame Press, 1988). Note that Lesslie Newbigin, in *The Gospel in a Pluralist Society* (Grand Rapids, MI: Eerdmans, 1989), does in fact describe and use MacIntyre's insights in discussing the rationality of religious traditions. He also reinforces Heim's insight that not all religions are pursuing salvation, as Christians understand it, and makes a case for the importance of the topic of the next chapter, that of special divine action.

understand the crises, provides a non-tradition-dependent criterion for claiming that the basic understanding of reality that one's own tradition provides is as close to truth as one can get at this point in history. So if I am correct about "the way ahead," Clooney may be right about the time span required.

5 Retrospect and prospect

I grew up in a Catholic home and attended Catholic schools from kindergarten through university. My family lived on a cattle ranch far out in the country, so I had little time to interact with children outside my school. In those days, the world was divided between Catholics and non-Catholics, and the differences among the non-Catholics did not register.

I went directly from (Jesuit) Creighton University in Omaha to a PhD program in philosophy at Berkeley and found that my professors (and most fellow students) were not religious; the only difference among them was whether they thought that arguing *against* religion was still worth the time. Growing up in my Catholic cocoon, I was unaware of having missed one of the greatest revolutions in Western thought: the 300-year-long dismantling of the Christian worldview.

What I have attempted to do in this chapter is to provide a sketchy overview of some of the intellectual factors that made it harder and harder to justify, or even understand, the various forms of Christianity. I touched briefly (again) on the difficulties Christian thinkers have had in adjusting to the new modern standards of rational argument. (And I have made the bold claim that this text itself provides a blueprint, finally, after 300 years, for how to do this.) I also addressed one of the most critical epistemological challenges of modernity, the development of critical biblical scholarship, but although there are hopeful signs, I do not hazard an opinion on whether this crisis has been solved. Finally, I addressed the problem of religious pluralism, which can be expressed crudely in the question of why believe that Christian teaching is right when there are so many other options. With enough time and work, that question might be answered, again, using the blueprint laid out by MacIntyre.

However, I have not done justice to the two challenges that I believe have done the most to promote the rejection of the Christian worldview: One is the problem of special divine action: is there really a God who interacts personally with me? And this, of course, is a problem closely related to questioning the divine credentialing of the Christian Scriptures. The second challenge is the problem of suffering: "If there is a God he doesn't take as good care of us as I do my cats!" These will be addressed in Chapters 6 and 7, respectively.

A (to me) surprising number of Christians and secular scientists believe that Christianity and science (especially evolutionary biology) are incompatible, so I hope to dispel this impression in Chapter 8. A widely debated topic at present is a variant of the Christianity and science question: do neuroscience and Christian anthropology present incompatible accounts of human nature—neuroscience being based on the assumption that humans are purely physical, in contrast to the long-held Christian view of humans as unities of bodies and souls? This will be the topic of Chapter 9.

Finally, one cannot do without a worldview. As MacIntyre says: "To be outside all tradition is to be a stranger to enquiry; it is to be in a state of intellectual and moral destitution."[37] So the final chapter will be the best account I can provide of the development of a tradition to replace Christianity. In general, I shall call it the Naturalist Tradition, but it has subtraditions, as does Christianity. There are humanist strands, Marxist strands, and, most prominently today, a scientistic strand.[38]

The changes that made a naturalist worldview intellectually acceptable took a considerable amount of time. James Turner (b.1946) argues that it was only during the years from 1865 to 1890 that it became respectable to be an unbeliever (agnostic or atheist) in the USA.[39] Charles Taylor (b.1931), in *A Secular Age*, has written 850 pages to explain why it was *impossible* in 1500 *not* to believe in God, while in 2000, even believers recognize that their system is but one option among others.[40] While the crises I attend to here are certainly significant, one factor stands out in Taylor's account. I quoted MacIntyre as saying that basic human questions involve that of what it is to lead a good (or bad) life. Peterson and co-authors add to Yandell's criteria for a true religion (or, I would say, any kind of tradition), that it should satisfy basic moral intuitions and provoke and inspire persons to live more morally responsible lives. Christianity had offered powerful versions of an answer to the questions of why I am here and how I should live in order to make life worthwhile. Taylor believes we are only now finding replacements for these Christian answers.

Of course, the reason Taylor's book is so long is that this basic set of questions is intimately related to a number of others, which I hope to condense to the space of one chapter. In any case, I hope to provide a sympathetic account of the development and status of our new modern and contemporary Naturalist Tradition—sympathetic enough that we might perceive some budding epistemological crises. However, it does not appear to me that these problems have been given as serious attention as the various crises facing modern Christianity that I shall have described here. So only time will tell.

---

[37] MacIntyre, *Whose Justice*, 367.

[38] Note the difference between "scientific" and "scientistic." The latter makes claims for the importance of science that go well beyond those we usually make for science itself.

[39] James Turner, *Without God, Without Creed: The Origins of Unbelief in America* (Baltimore and London: Johns Hopkins University Press, 1985).

[40] Charles Taylor, *A Secular Age* (Cambridge, MA and London: Harvard University Press, 2007).

6

The problem of special divine action

1 Introduction

I ended Chapter 5 by noting that I had missed out, in my otherwise excellent Catholic education, on accounts of how developments in modern thought could be seen to count *against* belief in the Christian God. So while no overt conflict appeared between theology and modern science, I was unaware of the assumptions lying behind the development of science that created a number of sound reasons for the rejection of Christianity. I mentioned above that the problem of special divine action is one of the pivots around which many of these reasons turned (and still turn).[1] A fine expression of the centrality of this problem is found in the Introduction to Brian Hebblethwaite (b.1939) and Edward Henderson's (b.1939) book, *Divine Action*:

> The topic of divine action in the world has rightly come to occupy centre stage in both doctrinal and philosophical theology. Whatever theological question is raised, some conception of God's action in the world will turn out to be involved in any answer proposed. The issue of objective theism— whether God-talk refers to transcendent reality or is only a symbolic expression of our highest aspirations or basic life attitudes—may seem at first to be an exception to this. It soon becomes apparent, however, that the question of divine action bears critically even on this apparently prior dispute.[2]

The list of consequences of this problem is extensive, but my focus here is on the MacIntyrean question of why it constitutes an *epistemological* crisis. I have already discussed divine action briefly in Chapter 2 (section 5.3). The role of Immanuel Kant was crucial in (apparently) barring the door to special divine action in the world. The problem, as he formulated it, was that the concept of *causality* only applied in the phenomenal (perceptible) world, but not to noumenal realities such as God. So at the end of modernity there appeared to be only three options: to ignore Kant and hold on to both general providence and special divine action

---

[1] Recall that I prefer the term "special divine action" to that of "miracle" because the latter term has been corrupted by early modern thinkers *identifying* miracles with violations of the laws of nature.

[2] Brian Hebblethwaite and Edward Henderson, eds., *Divine Action: Studies Inspired by the Philosophical Theology of Austin Farrer* (Edinburgh: T. & T. Clark, 1990), 1. See my brief remark at the end of Chapter 2, section 5.3, and especially section 6.3 below.

(interventionism); to attribute God's action only to creating and upholding the existence of the world (immanentism); or Deism (God creates the world along with the laws that govern it but has no further role apart from that of final judge). I take this split over divine action to be at the root of the (perhaps more obvious) differences in attitudes toward Scripture and biblical language.

The plan for this chapter will be, first, to explain a bit about the transition from medieval to modern thought that made special divine action into an epistemological crisis, whereas it had not been before. Section 3 will describe an interesting set of intermediate positions (which I shall refer to as physico-theologies) that gradually resulted in development of the concept of the laws of nature. It is ironic that while this concept was initially designed to account for God's constant providence, it eventually came to be one of the most powerful obstacles to any account of special providence or special divine action.

Section 4 provides a brief account of a varied collection of positions called Deism, which was thought by many to be superior to Christianity in that it evaded the problem of divine action and, more importantly, could also be touted as a rational religion.

Section 5 attempts to make clear the radical difference between the positions of the physico-theologians, for which I shall borrow Charles Taylor's term, "providential deism," and the immanentism of the liberal theologians following Kant and Friedrich Schleiermacher. Section 6 describes mid-twentieth-century crises within liberal theology itself involving the coherence of a theological system that omits any sort of special divine action.

I finish (in section 7) with accounts of two current research projects that may have a potential to eliminate, or at least ameliorate, the problem of special divine action created in early modern science by invention of the concept of the laws of nature. One I call the "Order Project," arising from philosophy of science; and the other, the "Divine Action Project," a series of attempts to bring recent scientific advances to bear on the problem.

2 The demise of the Thomist option

I addressed Thomas's appropriation of Aristotle's hylomorphism in Chapter 1 and mentioned that his work provided a systematic organization of all known branches of knowledge, as well as justification for the hierarchical structures of both the church and society. According to the Aristotelian–Thomist system, immanent Forms gave natural entities their characteristics, including whatever causal powers they possessed.

For Thomas, God, as creator, was the ultimate source of the Forms and thus the cause of the regular behaviors of created beings. However, Thomas maintained, God could use created beings for special purposes, in which cases God was called the primary cause and the creature, the secondary cause. This is a position still argued today, especially by some Catholic scholars.[3]

The Copernican revolution in the seventeenth century was the most notable blow to the Medieval Synthesis. Aristotelian physics was based on the concept of the Forms of the elements determining their natural motions (for example, the motion of "earthy" things downward toward the center of the universe); an entirely new approach to physics had to be developed if the Earth was no longer the center. This led to the revival of (ancient) atomism, and, most important for the topic of this chapter, the development of the concept of the *laws of nature*. As noted above, it is ironic that while the concept of laws of nature was developed for specifically Christian reasons to account for God's omnipresent providential role in the created world, it came, in later centuries, to be seen as the primary reason for rejecting special divine action and thus special providence. I take the problem of divine action to be a genuine *epistemological* crisis because failure to solve it calls into question the revealed status of Scripture and raises the question of whether this collection of texts tells us about God's role in history and nature, or only about Hebrews' and early Christians' *beliefs* about God.

Of course, to speak of *the* Medieval Synthesis is a vast oversimplification, and it is equally misleading to speak as though the change in worldview from medieval to modern happened suddenly with the rejection of hylomorphic metaphysics in favor of atomism. Historian of science Stephen Gaukroger (b.1950) states that Aristotelian natural philosophy did displace other philosophies because of its notable systematicity, but the alternatives never disappeared entirely.[4] Although Plato's own works were not commonly known until the fifteenth century, Neoplatonic ideas were transmitted through Augustine and other church fathers. When Neoplatonic thought was combined with ideas from other sources, too many varieties of philosophies and theologies were produced even to list here. I shall only discuss one below (section 3.2.1).

A few of the other complicating factors leading from medieval thought to modern include the following. One has to do with the powerful metaphor of nature as the second book of God's revelation. Gaukroger writes that the "understanding of the physical world fostered in the Church Fathers was one in which an explanation of physical phenomena took the form of an account of what those phenomena signified . . . and what is important is not what causes physical things to behave the way they do . . . Origen [*c.*195–*c.*254] in particular maintained that both the world and Scripture were symbolic through and through."[5]

---

[3] Michael J. Dodds, OP, *Unlocking Divine Action: Contemporary Science and Thomas Aquinas* (Washington, DC: Catholic University of America Press, 2012).

[4] Stephen Gaukroger, *The Emergence of a Scientific Culture: Science and the Shaping of Modernity, 1210–1685* (Oxford: Clarendon Press, 2006), 133.

[5] Gaukroger, *Emergence*, 135.

The second factor is the issue of "realism." The word was used quite differently in the late Middle Ages than it is now. John Duns Scotus (*c*.1266–1308) and other nominalists of the fourteenth century called into question the necessity of postulating the *reality* (thus, "realism") of either Platonic or Aristotelian Forms. God, being omnipotent, could simply create whatever beings he chose, and our language classifies them (names them—thus "nominalism") according to their similarities.[6] Nominalism is closely tied to voluntarism (to be explained further below). This is the emphasis by William of Ockham (*c*.1285–*c*.1349) and others on God's will. Voluntarists argued that God would not be omnipotent if subject to any prior rationality or pre-existing pattern of goodness. If the voluntarists were correct, then everything in the world is contingent, and there could be no *a priori* knowledge. Therefore, nothing but experience could reveal the nature of the world to us.

Nominalism and voluntarism return us to the topic of causation. If there is no Aristotelian immanent Form to account for movement and the causal capacities of different life forms, then what? During the Renaissance, the Stoic idea of *forces* was revived. Historian Amos Funkenstein (b.1937) says: "The war between the Aristotelian adherents of form and the new adherents of force was fought in Italian universities in the generation before Galileo, at times with bare fists."[7]

Another factor was the Reformation emphasis on the literal sense of the texts of Scripture—as opposed to Origen's and others' views of both nature and Scripture as needing to be interpreted symbolically. So, step by step, the understanding of nature as symbolic shifted, with Thomas as an intermediary figure, to an understanding of the world in terms of causal forces.

Much more should be said about developments in the late medieval worldview. However, I move on, now, to modern developments, noting some intermediate movements between medieval thought and the rise of (what we now call) modern science.

3 Physico-theology and providential deism

The earlier thinkers in the modern era whom we now classify as scientists were not at all antagonistic to theology, and, using medieval terminology, called themselves natural philosophers. Their entanglement with natural theology has resulted, more recently, in their being called "physico-theologians."[8] These include Galileo, Boyle, Kepler, Newton, and many others. This entanglement was because, as historian John Hedley Brooke (b.1944) writes, "where natural philosophers referred to *laws*

---

6 Amos Funkenstein, *Theology and the Scientific Imagination from the Middle Ages to the Seventeenth Century* (Princeton, NJ: Princeton University Press, 1986), 57–8.
7 Funkenstein, *Scientific Imagination*, 67.
8 See for example, Gaukroger, *Emergence*, 149–53.

of nature, they were not glibly choosing that metaphor. Laws were the result of legislation by an intelligent deity. Thus . . . Descartes . . . insisted that he was discovering the 'laws that God has put into nature."[9] However, historian James Byrne (b.1956) writes that from the seventeenth to the eighteenth centuries, this concept of reason will undergo "a subtle but decisive shift." Reason will come to be seen not so much as a way of penetrating to the eternal truths of the divine mind, but rather as a way of investigating the here and now of the empirical world.[10] The decisive split between philosophy and theology on the one hand and science on the other—that is, science as we know it—will come later, heavily influenced by Kant and Schleiermacher.

3.1 Varying strategies among physico-theologians

The physico-theologians worked out a variety of ways of understanding the relations between God and the natural world. Historian Michael Buckley (b.1931) describes three strategies. Galileo (1564–1642) emphasized the introduction of mathematics into physics, claiming that math was the language in which the Book of Nature was written. He claimed that natural philosophy says nothing about religion. Theology and each of the sciences have their own special methods. This does not mean that God is absent from Galileo's thought: "the heavens are prized as the creation of the omnipotent craftsman" and the highest object of philosophy is turning to the great Book of Nature—that is, the Bible.[11] Science and theology do not interact, but each contributes to the general advance of knowledge.

Johannes Kepler is Buckley's second example. It seems (to me) that Kepler is given disproportionately little attention in current accounts of the rise of science; I suspect that this is because one cannot explain his reasoning in astronomy without admitting his indebtedness to theology. He reasoned that the most perfect God could only create a most beautiful world. The most beautiful world is manifested through its agreement with geometry, the signature of God. For example, there are five intervals between what were then thought to be six planets, and this is consistent with Euclid's demonstration that there are only five perfect geometric solids. Concerning the role of specifically Christian theology, Kepler wrote that from the doctrine of the Trinity one can show why there are three and only three stationary realities in Galileo's astronomy: the sun, the fixed stars, and the intermediate space between them. One can see why a contemporary secular historian of science would not go into these details.

---

[9] John Hedley Brooke, *Science and Religion: Some Historical Perspectives* (Cambridge: Cambridge University Press, 1991), 19.

[10] James M. Byrne, *Religion and the Enlightenment: From Descartes to Kant* (Louisville, KY: Westminster John Knox Press, 1996), 99.

[11] Michael J. Buckley, sj, *Denying and Disclosing God: The Ambiguous Progress of Modern Atheism* (New Haven, CT: Yale University Press, 2004), 7.

Newton is Buckley's third example. Newton (1642–1727) argued that the universality of the fundamental coordinates of the universe demonstrated the existence of God, but one could also argue from the existence of God for the universality of mechanics. God's role in Newton's system is not only to set the universe in motion, but continuously to keep the universe from collapsing in on itself due to the force of gravity. He repeatedly asserted that the main business of his mechanics was to culminate with the first cause.

I have now illustrated two important characteristics of early natural science: its *slow* development away from medieval natural philosophy and its *lack* of antipathy toward Christianity. A third characteristic was its regular incorporation of elements that most today would reject on both scientific and theological grounds. These included alchemy, magic, astrology, and a surprisingly widespread acceptance of the legendary writings of Hermes Trismegistus, who was thought to have influenced both Plato and Moses. (In fact, there were a variety of authors of the so-called "hermetic texts," which are now taken to have been written during the first few centuries of the Christian era.) More on these issues below.

3.2 Robert Boyle and providential deism

I shall borrow a term from Charles Taylor, "providential deism,"[12] not to be confused with the much more commonly recognized Deism (to be described below in section 4). This term aptly describes the various understandings of the physico-theologians mentioned above. These scholars were often rather traditional in their Christian beliefs, and accommodated Christianity with the new sciences specifically by means of the concept of the laws of nature: the laws are God's *providential* ordering of the cosmos for the good of human beings. Taylor says that these scholars' works are essential for understanding the transition from a concept of God as "an agent interacting with humans and intervening in history" to a God as "architect of a universe operating by unchanging laws."[13] The concept of providential deism became widely accepted in the seventeenth century, and served as a transition to the "legal–mechanical" world-picture represented in later modern science. Robert Boyle (1627–91) is a particularly fine exemplar.

I shall largely follow historian Eugene Klaaren's (b.1937) book, *Religious Origins of Modern Science* in sections 3.2.1 and 3.2.2.[14] Klaaren's central thesis is that the "legal–mechanical" view that prevailed in science as we now know it was the result of rejection not only of the medieval system, but also of a third option, which he calls the Spiritualist Tradition. He argues that what I am calling

---

[12] Charles Taylor, *A Secular Age* (Cambridge, MA and London: Harvard University Press, 2007), see esp. 233.

[13] Taylor, *Secular Age*, 270.

[14] Eugene M. Klaaren, *Religious Origins of Modern Science: Belief in Creation in Seventeenth-Century Thought* (Grand Rapids, MI: Eerdmans, 1977).

providential deism won out over the Spiritualists largely for theological reasons, and I would add that these were specifically Calvinist reasons.

3.2.1 The Neoplatonic–spiritualist option

I shall first present here an account of Spiritualism and then follow with theological objections to it, primarily as seen by Boyle.

Klaaren describes the Spiritualism of the seventeenth century as "a relatively amorphous yet influential cluster of ideas and practices."[15] Its sources included varieties of Neoplatonism; mystical strands in Catholic, Protestant, and Jewish thought; and the supposed writings of the legendary Hermes Trismegistus. The "hermetic texts" incorporated magic, alchemy, and astrology, and enjoyed renewed interest in the seventeenth century.

Klaaren's representative of the Spiritualist Tradition was primarily Johan Baptist von Helmont (1577–1644). Helmont was a Flemish physician and chemist, who is best known for his contributions to medicine.[16] However, in retirement he came under the influences of Paracelsus (1493–1541), a Swiss alchemist and physician, and the hermetic writings. He held that the world was composed of matter (either water or air), and an efficient cause—his own version of a world-soul. He believed that life results from a vegetative soul and that every organ of the body "has its own *archaeus insitus* that determines its special function."[17]

Helmont's writings were translated into English by his son, Franciscus Mercurius (1614–98) and became available in England in 1648. The younger Helmont may be an even better representative of the Spiritualists' theological positions regarding the relations of God and the world that his Calvinist contemporaries found entirely unacceptable: a Neoplatonic–kabbalistic theory of monads that emanate as pure spirits from the divinity—thus making the world itself, in a sense, divine.[18]

For the purposes of my narrative, the Spiritualist view of divine action is most important: According to Klaaren, for the Spiritualists, "all created entities are forms of the divine Spirit." God is in all cases the total cause of everything that happens. He perpetually creates all things *ex nihilo*.[19] All order and motion in nature are attributed directly to God.[20] Thus, knowledge of the world comes as much from inspiration as from empirical observation. Klaaren comments on the lack of references to this particular group:

---

[15] Klaaren, *Religious Origins*, 53.
[16] Gaukroger, *Emergence*, 348–9; Giorgio Tonelli, "Helmont, Jan Baptista van," in Macmillan, 3:471.
[17] Macmillan, 3:471.
[18] "Helmont, Franciscus Mercurius van," Routledge, 4:340–2.
[19] Klaaren, *Religious Origins*, 59.
[20] Klaaren, *Religious Origins*, 62.

Spiritualism in this context raises difficult problems for the historian not simply because of its immense diversity and extent, but also because it did not closely adhere to fairly compact or relatively well-known traditions ... Spiritualist theologies were part of a movement which rose and fell, flamed and dimmed, rather than a tradition characterized by relatively measured growth and decline ... Moreover, the scholarship devoted to the movements of Spiritualism is relatively recent, and has merely begun to map out its cultural significance, especially for the rise of science.[21]

Klaaren published his book in 1977 and so there has been a significant amount of time since then for further research on Spiritualism. However, there are almost no references to it in later histories of the rise of modern science, although there is much mention of Neoplatonism in general, and particularly of the peculiar role that the hermetic tradition, alchemy, and magic had during this period.

3.2.2 Physico-theology and the legal–mechanical option

While the elder Helmont may not have been the best choice as a representative of the Spiritualists, given his near invisibility in the literature, Klaaren's choice of the revolutionary chemist, Robert Boyle, as their opponent is certainly well justified. Boyle was as opposed to this Spiritualist worldview as he was to the Medieval Synthesis. He is now remembered only as a scientist, but this, of course, is anachronistic since in the seventeenth century there was not yet a sharp distinction among theology, philosophy, and science.

Here is how historian of science Ronald Numbers (b.1942) describes Boyle's motivations and accomplishments:

The English chemist Robert Boyle (1627 – 91)—as ardent an advocate of the mechanical philosophy as Descartes yet as pious as Pascal—viewed the discovery of the divinely established laws of nature as a religious act ... He sought to explain natural phenomena in terms of matter in motion as a means of combating pagan notions that granted nature quasi-divine powers, not as a way to eliminate divine purpose from the world ... [V]iewing the cosmos as a "compounded machine" run according to natural laws struck Boyle as being "more consistent with biblical statements of divine sovereignty than older, non-mechanistic views" of an intelligent nature. "By denying 'Nature' any wisdom of its own, the mechanical conception of nature located purpose where Boyle believed it belonged: over and behind nature, in the mind of a personal God, rather than in an impersonal semi-deity immanent within the world."[22]

---

[21] Klaaren, *Religious Origins*, 54.
[22] Ronald L. Numbers, "Science without God: Natural Laws and Christian Beliefs," in B. L. Gordon and W. A. Dembski, eds., *The Nature of Nature: Examining the Role of Naturalism in Science* (Wilmington, DE: ISI Books, 2011), 62–80 (64).

Here is why I find Taylor's term "providential deism" so useful. Boyle (and the contemporaries he represented) were not the Deists who rejected the divinity of Christ, revelation, and thus (nearly) all of the content of Christianity. Boyle was thoroughly Christian in his theology, believing in God's revelation in Christ and even the resurrection. In contrast to the Deists' absentee God, Boyle argued for the continued dependence of creation on God. And it was for theological reasons that Boyle emphasized both the existence and inviolability of the laws of nature. He was opposed to the Spiritualists' "diffusions" of God in the world such as Johan Helmont's world-soul.[23] The concept of the laws of nature served as an intermediary between a thoroughly transcendent God and his creation. The inviolability of the laws was based on God's omniscience; Boyle wrote:

> The omniscient author of things, who, in his vast and boundless understanding, comprehended at once the whole system of his works, and every part of it, *did not mainly intend the welfare of such or such particular creatures*, but subordinated his care of their preservation and welfare to his care of maintaining the universal system and primitive scheme or contrivance of his works . . .[24]

Boyle's physico-theology was typical, in his day, of the legal–mechanical tradition that has come to define science for us today. This concept of nature was seen by some as a threat to religion, particularly in the wake of Newton's successes. However, it was easily turned into an apologetic: Wallace Matson writes that the

> defense dwelt on the sublime conception of God to be derived from the majestic, inexorable, harmonious system of nature—God's creation—revealed by Science . . . In previous ages the occurrence of miracles had provided proof of the existence, power, intelligence, and goodness of God. Now the nonexistence of exceptions to the order of nature proved the existence, power, intelligence, and goodness of God.[25]

4 Deism

The simplest option for "solving" the problem of divine action is simply to do away with it. This was the choice of a movement called Deism.[26] James Byrne writes that the term "Deism" is conventionally used "to describe the views of a

---

[23] Klaaren, *Religious Origins*, 99.

[24] Klaaren, *Religious Origins*, 168, my italics.

[25] Wallace I. Matson, *A New History of Philosophy*, 2 vols. (San Diego: Harcourt Brace Jovanovich, 1987), 2:336–7.

[26] Not all authors capitalize "Deism," but I shall do so to help to keep clear its difference from the providential deism described above.

range of thinkers who loosely subscribed to . . . a rejection of revealed religion yet who consistently held to the existence of a Creator."[27] In the late seventeenth and the eighteenth centuries key doctrines of Christianity such as the Trinity, the divinity of Christ, and original sin were rejected by many in favor of what could be known by reason alone. Reason did seem to certify a supreme being that was necessary to maintain the laws of nature.

Byrne writes that "Deism" is "a notoriously imprecise term which cannot capture the myriad differences between these thinkers themselves, between them and certain forms of Christianity, and them and some barely undisguised forms of atheism."[28] However, a review of a variety of sources provides a somewhat standard account. What is most often immediately associated with the term is the view that God initially created the laws of nature but has no further role in the world's operation. However, this "absentee God" was still needed to mete out reward or punishment in the afterlife. Deism flourished largely in Britain in the eighteenth century, although there are some parallels in France and Germany, and its influence in the USA came after its decline in England.

Most histories present Lord Edward Herbert of Cherbury (1583–1648) as an early influence in promoting Deism. He claimed that there are "common notions" in all religions, which can be demonstrated rationally. There are five central principles: (1) there is a Sovereign Deity; (2) this Deity must be worshiped; (3) piety is closely linked to virtue, to good living; (4) wrongdoing must be expiated by repentance; (5) there is reward or punishment after this life.[29] These rational notions prepare the ground for modern natural theology, specifically without the necessity of special revelation.

Two prominent eighteenth-century Deists were the Englishman Matthew Tindal (1653–1733), and the Irishman John Toland (1670–1722). Toland published an influential book, *Christianity not Mysterious*, in 1696. He claimed that Christianity is a naturalistic religion that requires no mysterious explanations—that is, whatever *is* mysterious or miraculous in Christianity must be discarded. This gave Toland's readers a means of continuing to believe in God while justifying the futility of disputes between the Christian sects. Tindal's book, *Christianity As Old as the Creation* (1730), was known as the Deists' bible.[30] He argued that what is true in Christianity has always been available to rational people, and so religion has no need of revelation at all.

Throughout the eighteenth century there were ongoing arguments between the Deists and their more orthodox counterparts, and beyond disputes about the doctrines that the Deists rejected, there appeared to be a critical problem regarding

---

[27] Byrne, *Religion and the Enlightenment*, 100.
[28] Byrne, *Religion and the Enlightenment*, 100.
[29] Herbert of Cherbury, *De Veritate* (1624)
[30] Byrne, *Religion and the Enlightenment*, 110.

morality. It was assumed by most that bare naturalistic religion could not provide grounding for ethics. This was a topic addressed directly by Anthony Ashley Cooper, Earl of Shaftesbury (1671–1713). He advocated a naturalistic morality that celebrated human nature; the virtue of self-love would naturally give rise to the love of others and would therefore be beneficial to society.

Byrne describes Deism as a halfway house between orthodox Christianity and outright atheism. He concludes that it emerged in the eighteenth century for two reasons:

> The first is that in the dawn of the new science in which the universe was seen to be governed by laws which were rational and consistent, it was inconceivable to most people that an ordered cosmos could have arisen without the help of a Designer; hence the new scientific discoveries of Newton and others enabled freethinkers to reject traditional Christianity, but also impelled them toward deistic forms of belief.
>
> The second reason has to do with morality. As an intimate link between morality and religion was more or less taken for granted by everyone—mainly through the perseverance of the vivid reward and punishment imagery of heaven and hell in Christian piety—few of even the most radical thinkers could envisage a purely secular ethics which would replace the clearly successful role of the Christian churches in this regard . . . Hence the idea of a Deity continued to serve a useful social function, even for those who were in the process of divesting their enlightened minds of what they considered as nonsense.[31]

For more orthodox Christians, "Deism" became a term of abuse, referring to those who believe in an "absentee God." I speculate that it served as a stepping-stone to atheism in large part because a God who is never seen to *do* anything in the world becomes one in whom it is very easy to *disbelieve*. Deism also paved the way for German biblical criticism a century later, with its own detrimental effects on orthodox belief.

5 The revolution: From providential deism to immanentism

The beginning of liberal theology in "the turn to the subject" has been described as the equivalent of a Copernican revolution. I want to make clear how revolutionary this theology was compared to that of the earlier providential deists. For the physico-theologians, right up through Newton, science was a means of doing natural theology. Newton saw his inertial account of matter and motion as the basis of an argument for the existence of God, not only as source of the laws of

---

[31] Byrne, *Religion and the Enlightenment*, 121.

nature and as the first cause of motion, but continually involved in preventing gravitational collapse of the universe.

After the revolution represented in liberal theology, science is entirely irrelevant to theology, and theology's starting point is human religious awareness. I suggested above (Chapter 2, section 5.3) that the most significant difference between conservative and liberal theologies (at least as we find them in the USA) is their different understandings of divine action.

The liberals' immanentist view of divine action was a reaction both against Deism, with its view that God is not active at all within the created world, and against the conservative theologians' view that God performs special, miraculous acts. The liberal view emphasizes the universal presence of God in the world, and God's continual, creative, and purposive activity in and through all the processes of nature and history.[32] This view made it possible to understand progress, both evolutionary progress in the natural world and human progress in society, as manifestations of God's purposes.

A primary motive for emphasizing God's action *within* natural processes was the acceptance of the modern scientific view of the world as a closed system of natural causes, along with the judgment that a view of divine activity as intervention reflected an inferior grasp of God's intelligence and power. That is, it suggested that God was unable to achieve all of the divine purposes through an original ordering, and also that God was inconsistent in willing laws and then also willing their violation. In short, the higher view of divine action was thought to be one in which God did not need to intervene. Thus, the interpretation of divine activity in terms of miracles tended to disappear in the liberal tradition.

We find variations on these themes from Schleiermacher up through the present. Schleiermacher claimed that divine providence and the operation of causal laws entirely coincide; the word "miracle" is just the religious word for "event." Furthermore, he argued that it can never be in the best interests of religion to interpret an event as a special act of God in opposition to its being a part of the system of nature, since to so interpret it works against the sense of the absolute dependence of the *whole* upon God.[33]

The mid-twentieth-century NT scholar Rudolf Bultmann (1884–1976) argued for the "demythologization" of Christianity. Views of divine action as intervention in the chain of finite events are mythological, he claimed, in that they make God a cause among causes. A non-mythological account of divine action requires that we think of God not as acting between events in the chain of natural causes, but as acting within them. Bultmann says:

---

[32] See Owen Thomas, ed., *God's Activity in the World: The Contemporary Problem* (Chico, CA: Scholars Press, 1983), 3.

[33] Friedrich Schleiermacher, *The Christian Faith* (Edinburgh: T. & T. Clark, 1928), secs. 46 and 47.

[F]aith acknowledges that the world-view given by science is a necessary means for doing our work in the world. Indeed, I need to see the worldly events as linked by cause and effect not only as a scientific observer, but also in my daily living. In doing so there remains no room for God's working. This is the paradox of faith, that faith "nevertheless" understands as God's action here and now an event which is completely intelligible in the natural or historical connection of events. This "nevertheless" is inseparable from faith.[34]

Faith, by which he means a person's existential orientation, is the essence of religion. From this it follows that:

First, only such statements about God are legitimate as expressions of the existential relation between God and man. Statements which speak of God's actions as cosmic events are illegitimate. The affirmation that God is creator cannot be a theoretical statement about God as *creator mundi* in a general sense. The affirmation can only be a personal confession that I understand myself to be a creature which owes its existence to God. It cannot be made as a neutral statement, but only as thanksgiving and surrender.[35]

Another recent example is Maurice Wiles's (1923–2005) claims that removal of the need for God's correction of the irregularities in Newton's model of planetary motion has been the removal of a problematic concept of a "God of the gaps." "This process has not meant, however, that it has become impossible to speak in any way at all of God in relation to the natural world. Rather, . . . it has made possible the reaffirmation of a more profound concept of God as the transcendent ground of there being a world at all."[36] Wiles argues that to speak of God acting *in history*, then, is in fact to speak of the varying human response that is elicited by the unvarying divine presence in historical events. Some events more than others elicit the response of faith—especially the events surrounding Jesus Christ. Thus, the distinction between general and special acts of God does not pertain to a difference in God, but to a difference in human perception.

Gordon Kaufman (1925–2011) was one of the most strident in rejecting special divine action. In 1968 he well expressed the seriousness of the problem of divine action, saying that unless it can be resolved "we are condemned either to live in an intolerable tension between our religious language and life and the rest of experience . . . or to give up Christian faith and talk as outmoded and no longer relevant to the actual structures of our lives and the world."[37]

---

[34] Rudolf Bultmann, "The Meaning of God as Acting," in Thomas, *God's Activity*, 61–76 (64).

[35] Bultmann, "God as Acting," 66.

[36] Maurice Wiles, "Religious Authority and Divine Action," in Thomas, *God's Activity*, 181–94 (183).

[37] Gordon D. Kaufman, "On the Meaning of 'Act of God,'" in Thomas, *God's Activity*, 137–61 (153).

Kaufman claims that particular acts of God performed from time to time in history and nature are not just improbable or difficult to believe, but "literally inconceivable."[38] For this reason, if we are to understand the phrase "act of God," we should use it to designate the "master act" in which God is involved, namely, the whole course of history. God's action consists in giving the world its structure and giving history its direction.

This concept of divine action provides a "more austere" account of providence, without [God] "violently ripping into the fabric of history or arbitrarily upsetting the momentum of its powers."[39] Kaufman's language gives evidence of a measure of scorn for Christians with more robust views of divine action and also a sense (somewhat surprising for a pacifist) that God's involvement in particular events could only be violent. It is interesting to note that over the course of his career, Kaufman changed his mind about the subject matter of theology: in his later years it was not God, but merely "the *concept God.*"

I quoted Brian Hebblethwaite and Edward Henderson above in saying that whatever theological question is raised, some conception of God's action in the world will turn out to be involved in any answer proposed. To see how the topic of divine action pervades the entire theological enterprise, consider again Bultmann's claim (above) that statements about God are legitimate only as expressions of the existential relation between God and man. He goes on to say:

> Moreover, statements which describe God's action as cultic action, for example, that He offered His Son as a sacrificial victim, are not legitimate, unless they are understood in a purely symbolic sense. Second, the so-called images which describe God as acting are legitimate only if they mean that God is a personal being acting on persons. Therefore, political and juridical conceptions are not permissible, unless they are understood purely as symbols.[40]

This is a clear example of the way a theory about how God acts influences the very meaning of doctrinal statements: the doctrine of the atonement cannot be an objective statement about a cultic or juridical act of God in the past if it is the case that God acts only upon individual persons in the immediacy of a personal relationship.

It will already be apparent that one's theory of divine action has consequences for how one regards religious language. Bultmann reasons that if the doctrine of atonement could not refer to an objective past act of God, then any language that gives this impression must be purely symbolic. This factor has conspired with another to result in a typical liberal understanding of religious language as

---

[38] Kaufman, "Meaning," 148.
[39] Kaufman, "Meaning," 157.
[40] Bultmann, "God as Acting," 66.

separate from and incommensurable with the language of science. The other factor, of course, is that all events are assumed to be both natural events and divine acts. Thus, any event can be described in scientific terms, which link it to antecedent conditions and natural laws, or it can be described as it fits into God's purposes. But great confusion arises if these two separate linguistic frameworks are mixed. The religious description must be kept in a compartment separate from the scientific description.

So in contrast to the physico-theologians, with their varied entanglements of the new science with theology, their nineteenth- and twentieth-century successors developed a theology that completely eliminated science (or, one might say, a concept of science that completely eliminated theology).

6 Mid-twentieth-century crises for immanentist theologies?

In this section, I shall attend briefly to three problems (or, perhaps, crises) confronting the liberal, immanentist view of divine action. The first is the question of how to account for the traditional authoritative role of Scripture in Christian thought and practice. The second is a question of the coherence of twentieth-century neo-orthodox accounts of "act of God" with the immanentists' concept of the universe as a closed causal order. The third is a question of the very significance of a liberal, immanentist theology.

6.1 Immanentism and the authority of Scripture

I pointed out above that the most obvious *apparent* difference between liberals and conservatives is the role of Scripture. But I hypothesize that the different status each attributes to the Bible is in fact due to the contrasting theories of divine action. For Christians who believe in special divine interventions there are a variety of ways of explaining how one particular set of books can constitute revelation, ranging from divine dictation, to a looser sense of inspiration, to the causation of revelatory events in history.

For liberals, Scripture is important for theology, but not its ultimate source. For Schleiermacher, it was important because it contained expressions of the religious awareness of those who knew Christ directly. Wiles held that God enacts the whole of history but does not perform any special divine acts. However, recognizing the typical connections between doctrines of revelation and interventionist accounts of divine action, he set out to argue that one can nonetheless attribute *some* authority to Scripture even if God only acts uniformly in all events. His strategy was to claim that while God acts uniformly in all events, some people respond more fully to God's presence, and their words provide authoritative guidance for others. The most important of such events, for Christians, of course, is the life of Jesus. Thus, Wiles writes:

If certain events [such as the life of Jesus] can be given such special importance without implying a different kind of activity on God's part in relation
to the worldly occurrences concerned, then clearly the records which partly
record and partly constitute such events can properly be regarded as having religious authority without that fact implying any special interventionist
activity as responsible either for their composition or for their recognition as
authoritative.[41]

So Wiles is confident that an immanentist account of divine action is compati-
ble with granting the Scriptures the status of "a religious authority of the utmost
importance."[42] However, such a view allows one to ascribe some measure of religious authority to the scriptures of other faiths, as well.

Depending on where one stands regarding the role of Scripture as a source for
Christian theology, this may be only a minor problem to address in a few pages of
an essay (as with Wiles) or it may be seen as an epistemological crisis, calling into
question the very possibility of Christian theology, as Claude Welch implies in the
quotation on the first page of Chapter 2.

6.2 The coherence of theology with the modern causal order

Protestant theology in the twentieth century was largely shaped by Karl Barth's
rejection of nineteenth-century liberal theology, his development of the movement of neo-orthodoxy, and its influence on the biblical-theology movement of
the 1940s, which reaffirmed the centrality of biblical testimony to God's action in
history. Barth stressed the sovereignty of God, who is wholly other. However, in a
well-known article written in 1961, Langdon Gilkey (1919–2004) raised the question of whether neo-orthodoxy and biblical theology succeeded in producing a
credible interpretation of an act of God.[43] Gilkey argued forcefully that they did
not. Robert Russell summarizes Gilkey's argument as follows:

According to Gilkey, neo-orthodoxy is an uneven composite of biblical/
orthodox language and liberal/modern cosmology. It attempts to distance
itself from liberal theology by retaining biblical language about God acting
through wondrous events and by viewing revelation as an objective act,
not just a subjective inference. Yet, like liberalism, it accepts the modern
premise that nature is a closed, causal continuum as suggested by classical physics. The result is that, whereas orthodoxy used language uni-
vocally, neo-orthodoxy uses language at best analogically. Worse since its

---

[41] Wiles, "Religious Authority," 191–2.
[42] Wiles, "Religious Authority," 193.
[43] Langdon B. Gilkey, "Cosmology, Ontology, and the Travail of Biblical Language," *The Journal of Religion* 41 (1961): 194–205.

language has been emptied of any concrete content, its analogies devolve into equivocations.[44]

Gilkey says: "Thus the Bible is a book descriptive not of the acts of God but of Hebrew religion . . . [It] is a book of the acts Hebrews believed God might have done and the words that he might have said had he done and said them—but of course we recognize he did not."[45] So, while neo-orthodox theologians distance themselves from the liberal theology of the nineteenth century, neither they nor the liberals, according to Gilkey, have a coherent account of the meaning of "act of God."

The coherence problem is closely connected to the question of the use of Scripture in theology. Russell's last comment, regarding the emptying of biblical language of concrete content, relates directly to the third problem (or crisis) I present here.

6.3 Evacuation of the content of liberal theology

My account of the potential for the liberal, experiential-expressivist approach to theology to lead to unbelief is simplistic, but sometimes a caricature can highlight important features. If theology's subject matter is human religious awareness, it has been all too easy, beginning with Ludwig Feuerbach in Schleiermacher's own day, to say that religion is nothing but a creation of human thought and feeling. So the shift to experiential-expressivism was an immediate stepping-stone to atheism for a few, but I believe there have been more subtle and equally deleterious effects in the twentieth century.

First, the liberals' immanentist account of divine action made God invisible. James Byrne claims that the "pivotal point in the fall from power of the concept of God" was a matter of Newton's concept of divine activity. Newton believed that the "workings of the universe should portray the infinite power and presence of God. But where Newton saw the power of God, others saw natural processes."[46] There can be no difference in the objective appearance of the world for an immanentist, a Deist, or an atheist.

Second, the restriction of religion to individuals' private inner experiences has made it appear to many to be at least uninteresting or, more harshly stated, vacuous. Jeffrey Stout in his book *Flight from Authority* writes of the liberal turn in theology that it "threatened to reduce the content, and therefore the interest, of theism as much as Deism had . . . The price of saving theism was to isolate it

---

[44] Robert J. Russell, Introduction, in R. Russell, Nancey Murphy, and C. J. Isham, eds., *Quantum Cosmology and the Laws of Nature: Scientific Perspectives on Divine Action* (Vatican City: Vatican Observatory Press, 1993), 7.

[45] Gilkey, "Cosmology," 198.

[46] Byrne, *Religion and the Enlightenment*, 178.

from the theoretical life of the culture and to confine its import for the most part to private . . . existence."[47]

Alasdair MacIntyre, speaking of liberal theologians such as Paul Tillich and Rudolph Bultmann, was even harsher: "any presentation of theism which is able to secure a hearing from a secular audience has undergone a transformation that has evacuated it entirely of its theistic content."[48] MacIntyre published this in 1968, before the appearance of the new atheism, and he attributed the lack of arguments against religion in that period to the fact that "theists were giving the atheists less and less in which to disbelieve."[49]

Are these problems true epistemological crises, in MacIntyre's sense, or do the critiques I have made in this section merely represent acceptable shifts in the nature of the Christian Tradition? Obviously, there will be no consensus here.

7 Two recent options for non-interventionist special divine action

Theological literature from the second half of the twentieth century has recognized the critical nature of the problem of divine action, and some valuable clarifications have been provided through theological and philosophical analysis. However, I claim that no true solution will be found without addressing the scientific worldview that largely created the problem in the first place. Thus, I shall attend here to two attempts to address the issue from the point of view of science and philosophy of science. The first, termed the Order Project in the introduction to this chapter, arose largely within philosophy of science; the second, the Divine Action Project, largely from interactions between theologians, philosophers, and scientists.

7.1 The Order Project

Although few have called the 400-year-old concept of the universe as being governed by natural laws into question, there have been significant problems throughout this history. One is the question of the ontological status of the laws; for Boyle, they were summaries of God's regular actions, but for Deists and for both liberal and conservative Christian theologians they are God's creatures with some sort of (unspecified) ontological status. They can be overridden by God or they stand as obstacles to God's special divine action. For atheists, surprisingly few questions seem to have been raised about the origin and status of the laws. In all of these cases (except Boyle), there is the question of *how* the laws prescribe physical events.

---

[47] Jeffrey Stout, *The Flight from Authority: Religion, Morality, and the Quest for Authority* (Notre Dame, IN: University of Notre Dame Press, 1981), 10.

[48] Alasdair MacIntyre, "The Fate of Theism," in MacIntyre and Paul Ricoeur, *The Religious Significance of Atheism* (New York: Columbia University Press, 1969), 25–6.

[49] MacIntyre, "Fate," 24.

Philosophers of science have argued extensively about how to define a law of nature, particularly because it is necessary to distinguish a law-governed regularity from an accidental one.

Finally, there is the fact that almost no laws are perfectly exemplified in natural processes. For example, friction plays a role in movements of objects, so Newton's laws of motion are idealizations. By 1989, philosopher of science Bas van Fraassen (b.1951) had concluded that "no philosophical account of a law of nature does or can succeed."[50]

This brings us to the Order Project, involving meetings of a core group of scholars, along with invited participants with special expertise in the relevant topic, both in Oxford and the University of California at San Diego, over a four-year period (2009–13). Project director Nancy Cartwright (b.1944) summarizes its point by noting that there has been little challenge to the assumption that if God is the source, then nature will be completely ordered, regimented under natural law. In the last decade and a half, however, a quiet revolution in Anglophone philosophic thought about the character of the laws of nature and the order they describe has cast serious doubt on whether the sciences describe a uniformly law-governed world. This questioning of the order of science has not come along any one fissure, nor has it been provoked by any one great discovery in science such as quantum mechanics. It has come rather from highly detailed analyses of successful scientific practice across the disciplines, from fundamental physics through biology to political economy. Cartwright claims that now, in philosophy of science, it is no longer assumed without question that the order of nature is complete and that its laws are universal and exceptionless.

Much of the analysis of scientific practice has been done by Cartwright herself. She claims that typical scientific explanations are based on the natures of things. This involves understanding the capacities of the components of organized systems that behave in regular ways. Much of science involves *creating* "nomological machines," which are fixed arrangements of components or factors with stable (enough) capacities that in the right environment will, with repeated operation, give rise to the kind of regular behavior that we can then represent in our scientific laws.[51]

Another significant contributor is William Bechtel (b.1951), who argues in a somewhat parallel fashion that scientific practice involves discovery of mechanisms, which consist of particular parts that carry out specific operations, organized so as to produce a given phenomenon. These explanations are not dependent on abstracting general principles; rather they are often developed by means of

---

[50] Bas C. van Fraassen, *Laws and Symmetry* (Oxford: Clarendon Press, 1989), vi.

[51] Nancy Cartwright, *The Dappled World: A Study of the Boundaries of Science* (Cambridge: Cambridge University Press, 1999), 50.

visual representations, and a major advance in recent years has been the possibility of animating diagrams to show how operations are orchestrated in time.[52]

So in both cases, the behavior of physical entities is not to be conceived of as somehow being derivable from universal laws; rather, the regularities that humans describe in nature result from the entities and systems themselves when they operate in consistent manners. So is this the beginning of the end of the concept of universal, pre-existent, prescriptive laws? Perhaps.

Note, however, that even without the obstacle of laws of nature in describing possibilities for divine action in the world, there is still the problem of the point of contact between God and world. How is one to describe God's action as anything but meddling, and perhaps reducing divine action to a mere cause among causes?

7.2 The Divine Action Project

The most sustained attempt to give a scientifically coherent account of special divine action was a 25-year research project sponsored by the Vatican Observatory and the Center for Theology and the Natural Sciences in Berkeley, CA. From the beginning, the participants in the Vatican project (theologians, philosophers, and scientists) recognized that the problem itself originated with the law-governed and mechanistic picture of the world developed from Newtonian physics—exactly the worldview that the participants in the Order Project are calling into question. Our approach was to ask whether, given that science itself had progressed so far beyond Newton, there are recent scientific advances that might contribute positively to understanding special divine action. A series of conferences addressed divine action in light of quantum cosmology, cosmological fine-tuning, complex and chaotic systems theory, contemporary biology, neuroscience, and quantum theory. The theologians involved in the project were educated in the liberal tradition, and thus intent on avoiding interventionism, but they were equally dissatisfied with the immanentist approach, wherein there are no "objective" special divine acts, but only something like Wiles's account of events in which some people are more apt to perceive God at work.

Out of this project there emerged three significant approaches to *noninterventionist*, special divine action. One was John Polkinghorne's (b.1930) theory of divine action in chaotic systems; he claimed that in chaotic systems there is genuine indeterminacy, and thus a place for God's action that would not involve violation of any natural laws. A second approach was Arthur Peacocke's (1924–2006) theory that God's action could be understood by analogy to the way complex systems, such as human beings, exercise "top-down" control over their own parts. He argued that while God is immanent in the world, the world is also,

---

[52] William Bechtel, *Mental Mechanisms: Philosophical Perspectives on Cognitive Neuroscience* (New York and London: Routledge, 2008), 4, 13, 20.

in a sense, in God. Therefore, the system of God-and-the-world is the most complex system possible, and there should be top-down effects from God on the world itself. The third approach was to hypothesize that God works at the quantum level of nature, determining otherwise indeterminate processes. By proper orchestration of countless micro-events, God produces special effects in the macro-world.

Many participants judged that both Polkinghorne's and Peacocke's theories ultimately fail in that neither can specify the actual point of causal contact with nature. Both theorists have suggested that God's action in the world might be via an input of information, but *in* the world, information flow is always by means of the transfer of energy or matter, and so the problem simply arises again at another level. The intractability of this problem led a number of us to conclude that any notion of divine causation "from the outside" is problematic.

The thesis that God acts by determining otherwise indeterminate quantum events has been appealing to a number of theorists because quantum events obey only statistical laws, and there is no way to violate a statistical law. However, this approach can appear to be an *ad hoc* solution: the problem of divine action is a result of the world's being governed by natural laws, so the solution is to find some "opening" for God where deterministic laws do not obtain.

To avoid the charge of *ad hoc* reasoning, I set out to devise a theory of quantum divine action based primarily on a theological argument and concluded that what one needs is a much *stronger* version of immanence than that of liberal theologians.[53] In fact, despite their use of the term "immanence," many liberal theologians, when thinking of the universe as a closed causal order, seem, at least subconsciously, to picture God as outside of it. For example, Kaufman described special divine acts as God violently ripping into the fabric of history.

Prior to the development of modern liberal theology, immanence involved much more than keeping things in being and upholding the laws of nature. It has been common at least from Augustine's day (fifth century) through the Reformation to define God's action in all entities in terms of three concepts: sustenance, cooperation, and governance. So God constantly keeps all things in being and cooperates with their natural causal powers. My account is based, first, on the tautological statement that if God is immanent in all creatures, then God is immanent in the most basic entities and structures constituting the physical world. Second, it is based on the fact that God could work at the quantum level to provide a measure of governance without overriding the natural, God-given, *causal powers* of these entities—note the difference from not overriding natural *laws*.

---

[53] Nancey Murphy, "Divine Action in the Natural Order: Buridan's Ass and Schrödinger's Cat," in Robert J. Russell, Nancey Murphy, and Arthur R. Peacocke, eds., *Chaos and Complexity: Scientific Perspectives on Divine Action* (Vatican City: Vatican Observatory Press, 1995), 325–57.

There have been numerous criticisms of quantum divine action theory. One is that if God is working in all quantum processes then God is determining all events, and this would amount to what theologians call occasionalism. This is a position Thomas rejected in the Middle Ages because it clashes with the doctrine of creation according to which creation involved making entities with their own causal powers. I have been criticized, also, because it is claimed that my position would deny human free will. My response is that this causal cooperation and governance is always restricted by respecting the natures of creatures. I said above that this theory provides for "a measure of governance" because I postulate that God works only by determining the what and when of the behavior of quantum-level entities, not interfering with their intrinsic properties. For instance, God does not give electrons positive charges. Further, I argue that while God may affect human thought and imagination, God never acts coercively in human life. By analogy, God never acts coercively in nature.

I believe that the most important criticisms involve interpretations of quantum mechanics itself, in particular settling the question of what counts as a measurement, and the related question of how the quantum world creates the macro-physical world. In both cases, it is difficult to settle the question of whether divine action at the quantum level could have significant enough effects at the macro-level to matter to the theologian. These issues in physics and philosophy go beyond my ability to adjudicate. However, several proponents of quantum divine action who do have the expertise in physics do not see any criticisms so far as fatal. For example, Robert Russell has worked out an account of ways in which quantum-level events could be involved in producing mutations and thus subtly affecting the process of evolution.[54] Some complex dynamical systems are sensitive enough to initial conditions that God could be conceived as working within chaotic systems by determining these conditions.

I noted above that convincing arguments such as those made by participants in the Order Project against the universal-law-governed character of the universe would seem to dissolve the main obstacle to making further progress on the problem. In fact, several participants in the Vatican project had already come to a different understanding of what "natural law" means: we speak of lawlike regularities in nature, but these are seen as products of divine action within the limits imposed by created entities. The laws are not decreed once and for all, governing processes from "outside." Rather the lawlike appearance of the world is a consequence of the cumulative actions of God within creatures. Because of the regularity of these actions, it is possible to describe them using representations

---

[54] Robert J. Russell, "Special Providence and Genetic Mutation: A New Defense of Theistic Evolution," in Russell, *Cosmology from Alpha to Omega: The Creative Mutual Interaction of Theology and Science* (Minneapolis: Fortress Press, 2008), 212–25.

that we call laws. Thus, for theological reasons I had come to a conclusion similar to Cartwright's—that regularities are results of the natures of structures, not the cause of the natures themselves.

So the scientific and philosophical arguments defended in the Order Project are obviously quite relevant to the problem of divine action. However, I claim that the theory of quantum divine action is still necessary to address the question of the locus of divine action. Even without the obstacle of laws of nature in describing possibilities for divine action there is still the problem of the point of contact between God and world. I have approached it by emphasizing a strong doctrine of divine immanence.

Notice, though, that this understanding of the operation of the physical world is contrary to Boyle's and his contemporaries' drive to understand God as entirely transcendent. It puts God back into matter in a way somewhat akin to the rejected Spiritualist Tradition's "diffusions of God in the world." The physico-theologians made a choice about *the very nature of matter*, for theological reasons. They rejected the Spiritualists' quasi-animist account of nature in favor of a theology that sharply distinguished between nature and God as all-powerful creator. This resulted in an understanding of the world that allowed science to proceed as though atheist materialism were true.

The resulting sharp separation of science from religion, along with the widespread rejection of religion in our day, means that there can be no turning back at this point: no theological arguments for a different understanding of matter will ever make a difference to the scientific understanding of matter. However, the quantum divine action project might offer new starting points for theologians finally to put their own house back in order at the end of the Newtonian age.

Notice, also, that quantum divine action theory offers places for both Polkinghorne's and Peacocke's theories. A complex system can serve as a vehicle to amplify to the macro-level an event at the quantum level. Also, if God acts immanently and everywhere in quantum events, is that not an instance of Peacocke's downward causation?

8 Retrospect and prospect

In this chapter, I have argued that different strategies for addressing the problem of special divine action, until recently, have resulted in a serious epistemological crisis for the Christian Tradition. The history of the problem involves the gradual development of a view of the universe as strictly governed by universal laws of nature. It is ironic that while this began as a theological strategy to understand God's pervasive providential action in the modern world, it later became an obstacle to understanding God's ongoing role in earthly affairs, after the universe and its laws had been created.

There were three major responses: Deism was one popular option—God simply has no ongoing role. A second was (and still is) conservative theologians' assertion that if God is the author of the laws, then God can and does contravene them for special purposes. It is seen as necessary to maintain this position, or else the whole concept of salvation history is lost, and so is God's role in revelation.

However, third, authors such as Leibniz argued that the concept of a God who first decrees the laws of nature and then proceeds to violate them by means of miracles represents God as inconsistent and is utterly unacceptable. Kant's sharp distinction between the phenomenal and the noumenal (Chapter 2, section 5.2), and his attributing causation only to phenomena, was seen by his liberal theological followers as ruling out all special divine acts. They therefore stressed God's immanence in the *whole* of the world process. The problem, then, is how to maintain an account of the significance of Scripture. Wiles expressed particular concern about how it could be possible to attribute authority to the Bible without presuming some kind of special divine action. His solution was to claim that, while God acts uniformly in all events, some people respond more fully to God's (immanent) presence, and their words provide authoritative guidance to others. Each of these responses has consequences for the role of God in revelation, and so each is relevant to the epistemological status of the Christian Tradition.

In section 7, I offered a tentative proposal about how God might be understood to act *objectively* in the world without, as Kaufman says, ripping violently into the fabric of history. I call this a tentative proposal because it is not widely accepted. Thus, the jury is still out on whether Christian scholars have resolved this crisis.

The problem of special divine action is correlated with a number of others. One is the problem of natural evil: if God *can* act in special events, why do we see so little response to events that cause human and animal suffering? This will be the topic of Chapter 7. Also, disagreements about divine action have resulted in our day in different understandings of the relation of Christianity to science; this will be the topic of Chapter 8. A special instance of the problem of divine action arises with the increasing acceptance of an account of humans not as dualities of body and soul, but as entirely physical. A dualist can claim that God acts in human life by affecting the person's soul, but for a physicalist, an account of divine action in material substances is essential. This will be the topic of Chapter 9. The final chapter will draw together from all of the previous material an explanation for the development, beginning in modernity, of a competing Naturalist Tradition, and offer a tentative evaluation of the relative merits of Naturalistic and Christian Traditions.

7

Modern problems of evil and suffering

1 Introduction

Whence evil? The problem of reconciling the existence of evil and suffering with belief in the goodness and omnipotence of God has plagued both sufferers themselves and theologians from the beginning. In fact, John Bowker (b.1935) writes that "[t]here are few better ways of coming to understand the religions of the world than by studying what response they make to the common experience of suffering."[1] In accordance with the purpose of this book, I shall pursue the problem largely as it appears in Christianity. And furthermore, the point of this chapter will be to describe how the problem, once the lesser theological question of how to show the coherence of Christian concepts of God and creation with the obvious facts of evil and suffering, became a genuine epistemological crisis (in MacIntyre's terms) in the modern period.

1.1 Varying interpretations of the problem

While "the" problem can be stated simply, there are helpful distinctions among (at least) three interpretations: (1) The *logical* or *deductive* problem is the claim that if there is a God who is omnipotent and omnibenevolent, then God would be able to, and would desire to, eliminate all evil. But clearly evil exists. Therefore, this system of beliefs is inconsistent and must be rejected. (2) The *empirical* or *inductive* problem is based on the claim that if the order and goodness of the world provide evidence for God's existence, then evil and disorder provide significant counter-evidence. (3) There is also the *experiential* or *existential* challenge of maintaining "vibrant faith and trust in God given the evils [people] actually experience."[2]

It has long been common to distinguish among three kinds of evil: the first is moral evil, that is, human sin; the second is natural evil, that is, suffering of humans and animals due to natural causes, such as tsunamis, earthquakes, famine, diseases; and the third is metaphysical evil, that is, the trying sorts of limitations to which humans are subject. Moral evil is relatively easy to reconcile with God's

---

[1]   John Bowker, *Problems of Suffering in Religions of the World* (Cambridge: Cambridge University Press, 1970), 2.

[2]   Thomas P. Flint, "Evil, Problem of," in *Oxford Companion*, 222–4 (222).

goodness on the assumption that humans just *will* misuse their freedom, and freedom is a necessary condition for the kind of loving and reciprocal relation that God offers.

Recently, however, metaphysical evil is often not mentioned, but structural, systematic, societal evil is included. All of these types interact, of course. For example, warfare often leads to famine and disease.

1.2 Responses

The logical problem of evil can be resolved, most simply, by rejecting the premise of the existence of God. Other options are to deny the complete goodness of God. For example, Manichaeism, an important competitor to Christianity in early centuries, postulated that the deity had a dual nature, both good and evil. Process theology today limits the power of God: God provides an array of possibilities for creatures but only acts *persuasively* to bring about good. Finally, in some versions of Eastern religions it is possible to argue that suffering is illusory. This is not possible, straightforwardly, for Christians, for whom human sin and suffering are central, due especially to the suffering of Jesus. However, arguments can be made that sin and suffering bring about greater good, and therefore only appear to be evil if that greater good is not recognized. Thus, the commonest approaches among Christian theologians and philosophers are not to deny any of the premises that go into the logical problem of evil (existence of God, omnipotence, omnibenevolence, reality of evil) but rather to add arguments to the effect that God has sufficient reason to permit sin and suffering.

Christopher Southgate (b.1953) and Andrew Robinson (b.1964) list three types of what they call good–harm analyses (GHAs). "1. Property-consequence GHAs: a consequence of the existence of a good, as a property of a particular being or system, is the possibility that possession of this good leads to it causing harms." The classic instance of this is the free-will defense in respect to moral evil. "2. Developmental GHAs: the good is a goal which can only develop through a process which includes the possibility (or necessity) of harm." The most familiar version of this is John Hick's "Irenaean" theodicy, which regards the world as a "vale of soul-making," in which virtue is learned through a process that involves suffering. "3. Constitutive GHAs: The existence of a good is inherently, constitutively, inseparable from the experience of harm or suffering."[3] The authors' exam-

---

[3] Christopher Southgate and Andrew Robinson, "Varieties of Theodicy: An Exploration of Responses to the Problem of Evil Based on a Typology of Good-Harm Analyses," in Nancey Murphy, Robert John Russell, and William Stoeger, sj, eds., *Physics and Cosmology: Scientific Perspectives on the Problem of Natural Evil* (Vatican City and Berkeley, CA: Vatican Observatory Foundation and Center for Theology and the Natural Sciences, 2007), 67–90 (76).

ple of this type is Simone Weil's experience of the presence of God in and through times of suffering.[4]

Both "the free-will defense" and "soul-making" are familiar and will be discussed below. However, I believe that Southgate and Robinson's concept of a constitutive GHA is a valuable contribution to the literature, so I shall try to spell out more fully an example below.

1.3 Overview of this chapter

Given the structure and audience of this book, the appropriate starting point would seem to be either with the formative texts of the Christian Tradition, or with an account of how the problem of evil became an epistemological crisis in the modern period. Nonetheless, the chapter will begin with the work of Augustine. He not only set the terms of debate for the following centuries, but also hugely influenced the interpretation of Scripture (for many) to this day. It will be important to see ways in which his intellectual context contributed to his approach to the problem.

Only with Augustine's work as background can we see how modern developments in epistemology and the scientific worldview turn the theological problem of evil into an epistemological crisis. I shall briefly survey a few modern responses, noting strengths and weaknesses, including Alvin Plantinga's solution to the logical problem of evil and John Hick's proposal that the world needs to incorporate as much evil and suffering as it does for the purposes of "soul-making"—that is, the production of true virtue (what Southgate and Robinson would call a developmental GHA).[5] Although critical of Hick on several accounts, I shall make use of his description of Augustine's position, given the saying that anyone who claims to have read all of Augustine's writings is a liar. (I have also come to suspect that, given the vast literature on evil in the Christian Tradition, anyone who claims to have read it all must also be a liar!)

The main point of this chapter, however, is to show that in the modern and contemporary worldviews, Augustine's assorted solutions are no longer sufficient. I shall survey some of the scientific and worldview changes that turned the problem of evil into a genuine epistemological crisis. After a brief survey of some of the most noted modern responses, I shall argue that even if these are adequate to account for moral evil, they are anthropocentric and fail severely to account for what Augustine called natural evil, including especially the suffering of sentient animals.

There are two promising contemporary routes to better understandings of natural, metaphysical, and structural evil: One route is scientific and (rather surprisingly)

---

4   Southgate and Robinson, "Varieties," 78.
5   John Hick, *Evil and the God of Love* (London: Macmillan, 1966; rev. ed., New York: Harper and Row, 1977). Quotations will be from the revised edition.

supports the claims of G. W. Leibniz that the more we understand the world, the more clearly we see that physical causes of suffering could not be changed without changing nearly everything else, as well as his much maligned philosophical and theological reasoning that this must be the "best of all possible worlds."

The second promising route is purely biblical and theological: It is the recognition and exploration of the brief mention by Paul that the whole creation "waits with eager longing for the revealing of the sons of God . . . because the creation itself will be set free from its bondage to decay and obtain the glorious liberty of the children of God" (Rom. 8.19, 21 RSV). Thus, many contemporary theologians stress that no true response to evil and suffering can succeed without incorporating it into the theological doctrine of eschatology. In fact, I shall argue that the entire structure of systematic theology can be reorganized to show that the "research program" as a whole is in fact an explication of salvation that responds to all aspects of evil.

2 Augustine: The fountainhead

Augustine "stands at a watershed in the history of Western thought between the classical world of the Roman Empire and the middle ages."[6] His influence has been unsurpassed due to the fact of his ability to systematize so much of the theology and apologetics that went before him, as well as to the fact that he had, and still has, much influence in both Catholicism and mainline Protestantism.[7] There are three worldview issues that are essential for understanding his thinking regarding evil and suffering.

2.1 Augustine's inherited worldview

In my study of ancient and medieval thought I have found that a picture or idea of a "hierarchy of beings" helps to make sense of a variety of philosophical and theological positions. However, as I set out to affirm my judgment of its importance, "hierarchy of beings" is seldom found in reference works, except under the name given it by Arthur Lovejoy (1873–1962) in his book *The Great Chain of Being*.[8] I believe that this fact illustrates a claim that Lovejoy himself makes in his opening chapter: there are endemic assumptions or intellectual habits that are not specifically enunciated and yet shape people's reflections on almost any subject.[9]

---

[6] Carol Harrison, "Augustine," *Oxford Companion*, 52–5 (52).
[7] Not, however, in the Radical Reformation tradition.
[8] Arthur O. Lovejoy, *The Great Chain of Being: A Study of the History of an Idea* ([1936] Cambridge, MA and London: Harvard University Press, 1964). Quotations are from the 1964 edition.
[9] Lovejoy, *Great Chain*, 10.

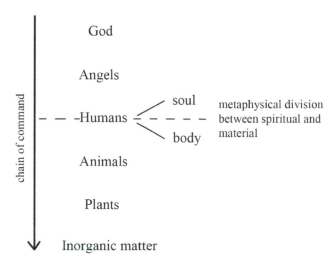

Figure 17 A simple form of the ancient and medieval Christian hierarchy of beings

The simplest form of the hierarchy for Christians places inanimate entities at the bottom, with plants and then animals above. Humans have a special place, in that their bodies fall below the all-important distinction between the material and the spiritual, while their souls are above. Other spiritual beings are fallen angels, obedient angels, and finally God (Figure 17). There were all sorts of elaborations, but this conveys the basic concept. The criteria for height within the hierarchy of goodness were powers; permanence or immutability; and measure, form, and order. Note that these last criteria explain Greek and Roman ideas of beauty—for example, pleasing proportions in architecture rather than, say, colorful painting.

This concept of the hierarchy of beings was related to two others that were essential for Augustine's teaching on evil. One is the idea of the plenum; that is, a world with all "rungs" of the hierarchy filled made for a better world than one without. This explains, for example, why there are flies in addition to butterflies. It also explains why there needed to be humans with *immortal* souls, not just humans who could die like animals. The third related concept was modified from the Neoplatonist idea that as one went down the hierarchy from the spiritual to the material, no goodness remained. Augustine's doctrine regarding the goodness of creation prevented him from accepting the evil of matter itself, but he did accept the view that evil is not a thing, a creature, but merely the lack or *privation of good*.

2.2 The depth of the Fall

Historian Peter Brown (b.1935) writes that the idea that some great sin lay behind the misery of the human condition was widely shared among both pagans and

Christians in late antiquity.[10] While it was common in Hellenistic thought to describe this as the Fall of the soul from the transcendent realm into the material body, Augustine's Christian sources led him to conclude that it was first the Fall of some of God's angels, "a willful misuse of their freedom" in a "revolt from blessed dependence" on God in order to "be lords of their own being."[11] The notion of the Fall of angels appears in the NT only in one verse (Jude v. 6), but has roots in the apocryphal book of 1 Enoch (chs. 6–7). The importance of this for Augustine is that it serves as his explanation of natural evil, in that angels had been put in charge of *the elements of nature* (seen in Revelation). Thus, Augustine could take the defection of (some) angels to be the explanation of the disordering of an originally perfect *natural* world, which now included plagues, droughts, earthquakes, and so forth.[12] These sources of suffering are also explained as suitable punishments for fallen humans.

The hierarchy of being is an important determinant of this collection of ideas. It is a hierarchy of causation and authority from top to bottom. If angels, comparable to military commanders, reject the authority of God, then the chain of command, to that extent, is broken and these angels then cease to control the natural elements according to God's will. The concept of the hierarchy is also important in that only God, at the top, is entirely immutable. The immutability of the angels, which is equivalent to their free will, is what accounts for their turning away from God's authority, and more precisely for their desire to climb to the top of the hierarchy so as to be "the lords of their own being."

This aspect, regarding the angels, is not given much attention in modern thought, but it beautifully illustrates the way in which Augustine could use the philosophical assumptions of his day (hierarchy, mutability, and Fall) to explain how a perfectly created natural world could turn out to produce so much suffering.

It is not surprising, then, that the Genesis account of Adam's sin could be embellished in such a way as to explain moral evil. Adam, as did the angels, sought to "be like God, knowing good and evil" (Gen. 2.5). In other words, he sought a higher place in the hierarchy of being.

I warn the reader that the following is my own speculation. Why is it Adam's sin that condemns all future humans rather than the earlier sin of Eve? In the hierarchy, humans are also ordered, with men above women because, while both are composed of form and matter (recall Aristotle's hylomorphism. (See Chapter 1, section 6) men were thought to be more "form-ish" than women, who were more

---

[10] Peter Brown, *Augustine of Hippo: A Biography* (Berkeley and Los Angeles: University of California Press, 1967), 388.

[11] Hick, *Evil*, 61.

[12] Jean-Louis D'Aragon, sj, "The Apocalypse," in Raymond E. Brown, ss, Joseph A. Fitzmyer, sj, and Roland E. Murphy, o.carm, eds., *Jerome Biblical Commentary*, 2 vols., Englewood Cliffs, NJ: Prentice-Hall, 1968), 2:467–93 (477, 486).

material because of their biological functions. If we tie this to the common understanding that in reproduction the male "seed" provides form while the woman only provides the matter in pregnancy, then it is only Adam's defection from the chain of command that matters. Here ends my speculation.

Compare the following, embellished, description Augustine presents of the state of the first couple in the garden with the much simpler account in Genesis 2.15–25:

> In Paradise, then, man . . . lived in the enjoyment of God, and was good by God's goodness; he lived without any want, and had it in his power so to live eternally. He had food . . . , drink . . . , the tree of life that old age might not waste him. There was in his body no corruption, nor seat of corruption, which could produce in him any unpleasant sensation . . . [I]n Paradise . . . , its inhabitants were exempt from the vicissitudes of fear and desire. No sadness of any kind was there, nor any foolish joy . . . The honest love of husband and wife made a sure harmony between them. Body and spirit worked harmoniously together, and the commandment was kept without labour. No languor made their leisure wearisome; no sleepiness interrupted their desire to labour.[13]

Read now Genesis 3.16–19. Compare this to Augustine's account of the consequence of sin and his reading of Genesis. His emphasis is on the fact that when they had eaten the fruit they knew that they were naked and covered themselves with fig leaves. Hick says that Augustine describes Adam and Eve as having been *ashamed*. The shame that comes from the uncontrollable stirring of the genitals is both clear evidence of, and fitting punishment for, the crime of disobedience.[14]

The lasting effect on the human race also depends on hierarchical ordering. The soul is supposed to be in charge of the body; the soul itself is a hierarchy of will, intellect, and appetites. When the will is no longer subject to God, the intellect is darkened and thus will and intellect together can no longer control either appetites or bodily functions—the relations among will, appetites, and body have been disordered, and this disorder is called concupiscence. Although Augustine ties concupiscence so tightly to disordered sexual desire, theology students may experience it more powerfully in an inability to stay awake when necessary and an inability to fall asleep when appropriate—the body does not obey the will. Note Augustine's embellishment of the pre-fallen couple as suffering no languor or sleepiness. It is this disorder of the hierarchy from will, to appetites, and then body that has been passed on to all future humans.

---

[13] Hick, *Evil*, 65; quoting Augustine's *City of God*.
[14] Hick, *Evil*, 388.

Thus, for Augustine, all subsequent evil is due to sin of both angels and humans. The human Fall had the causal consequence of the deformation of the will, such that only grace can turn it back to God from desire for lesser things. Particular sins cause suffering, and God permits suffering and death as due punishment for sin. The Fall of the angels is the cause of cosmic disorder and the suffering and limitations that follow.

2.3 Criticisms

Terrence Tilley (b.1947) and others criticize Hick's book because he pulls together strands of thought from a variety of Augustine's writings to make it appear that he had an organized and consistent theory to explain why God was not responsible for evil and suffering. Other criticisms are that it is not in fact coherent; that it is not faithful to the NT; and that it has had ill effects on society.[15] Tilley claims that because it is such an amalgamation of writings from various periods and with varying purposes, it is not really Augustine's. Tilley considers what Augustine did say about evil in his most important instruction to Christians, his *Enchiridion*.[16] However, I shall not pursue this here, since it is the amalgam of ideas that has influenced so many later thinkers.

I stated above that moral evil is relatively easy to reconcile with God's goodness by emphasizing free will and its inevitable sinful consequences. However, this aspect of an Augustin*ian* response has been called into question. First, it is not universally agreed that humans have free will. Second, Anthony Thiselton (b.1937) writes that the most fundamental and far-reaching criticism of "the free-will defense" comes from Antony Flew (1923–2010) and J. L. Mackie (1917–81), who write that God "could in principle have created free beings who always do what is right."[17] A counter-response, though, is that if God's primary purpose is to evoke free and uncompelled love and trust, then God's purpose would be frustrated by creating humans so that they can do no other than make this response.[18] I am persuaded by this response and will add to it below (section 4.2) an argument similar to Hick's "Irenaean" or "soul-making" theodicy to the effect that conceptually there can be no such thing as virtue without the genuine possibility of behaving in a non-virtuous manner; and also, as already mentioned, a related and extended example of Southgate and Robinson's constitutive good–harm analysis.

---

[15] Terrence W. Tilley, *The Evils of Theodicy* (Washington, DC: Georgetown University Press, 1991), 114.

[16] Tilley, *Evils*, 125–36.

[17] Antony C. Thiselton, *A Concise Encyclopedia of the Philosophy of Religion* (Grand Rapids, MI: Baker Academic, 2002), 87. See especially Antony Flew, "Divine Omnipotence and Human Freedom," in Flew and Alasdair MacIntyre, eds., *New Essays in Philosophical Theology* (London: SCM Press, 1955), 144–69.

[18] John Hick, "Evil, the Problem of," in Macmillan 3:136–41 (138).

3 From theological puzzle to modern epistemological crisis

I have already noted that (despite having spent so much space on ancient theology) my main purpose in this chapter is to indicate how it came to be that reconciling the amount of evil and suffering in the world with the existence of an already-believed-in benevolent God turned into a fierce set of arguments, in the modern period, regarding the very existence of God.

I see three major factors. The first is the shift described in Chapter 2 from an epistemology understood primarily in terms of rational arguments and *authority* to one understood primarily in *empirical* terms. The churches have lost their authority to stabilize belief, and meanwhile it has become apparent to many that there is insufficient *evidence* for God's existence. Regarding this issue, I shall limit my attention to aspects of the writings of three authors: David Hume, G. W. Leibniz, and Voltaire (1694–1778). Although Hume was born a year after the most relevant of the writings of Leibniz, I shall nonetheless begin with him.

The second factor, not so often noted in discussions of the modern crisis of evil, is the disappearance of the ancient and medieval background assumption of the hierarchy of beings, so crucial to Augustinian accounts, especially of natural evil. I take this up in section 3.3 below. The third, closely related to the second, was the development of biblical criticism, calling into question the historicity of the story of Adam's sin (and Augustine's exaggerated account of its consequences, as well).

3.1 David Hume

Recall the three interpretations of the problem of evil listed in section 1.1 above: logical, empirical, and existential. Given that Hume was writing when knowledge was understood largely in terms of proportioning one's beliefs to the strength of empirical evidence, arguments for God's existence increasingly shifted from the logical type to the empirical type—that is, design arguments. Hume was not the first to note that if the order and goodness of the world were taken as evidence for the existence of the Christian God, then evil and disorder needed to be weighed in as well.

Hume was cautious, as was typical in his day, in making outright statements regarding his belief or non-belief in God. Nonetheless, he was continually at variance with official Christianity and died "condemned by most of the devout."[19] He is considered by many philosophers today to have provided "a definitive refutation"[20] of any argument from "alleged" design in nature to an infinitely wise, powerful, and good God.

---

[19] J. C. A. Gaskin, ed., *Varieties of Unbelief from Epicurus to Sartre* (New York: Macmillan, 1989), 68.
[20] Wallace I. Matson, *A New History of Philosophy,* 2 vols. (San Diego: Harcourt Brace Jovanovich, 1987), 2:366.

The most significant of Hume's writings for present purposes is his *Dialogues Concerning Natural Religion*, published posthumously in 1779. Three characters participate: Demea, who is conservative and orthodox, and argues that the foundation of religion is faith; Cleanthes, who urges some form of design argument; and Philo, who opposes design arguments, arguing, first, that they require that the universe be conceived of on analogy to a mechanism, while this is but one possibility, and, second, noting that, due to its imperfections it might better be hypothesized to have been produced by an infant deity, or a deity in his dotage, or even by chance.

Some commentators conclude that Philo's rebuttal of design arguments represents Hume's own position.[21] If Philo does speak for Hume, note, though, that due to Hume's skepticism, even if we conclude that the universe may have a creator we can know nothing of the creator's nature. Other commentators believe that it is not possible to identify Hume with any of the three characters.[22] This is actually a more interesting conclusion for the purposes of this chapter because in Part X of the *Dialogues* all three characters agree on the prevalence of misery in the world, suggesting that it is as pressing a problem for orthodox Christians as it is for proponents of a bare natural religion.

3.2 Leibniz and Voltaire

Thomas Flint (b.1954), in his essay describing the three forms of the problem of evil, writes that the existential or experiential problem is probably the most grievous form. Even if theologians and philosophers find suitable answers to the logical and empirical problems, these same thinkers can still find themselves "floundering in feelings of estrangement and abandonment in the wake of particularly crushing instances of evil."[23] And the theoretical responses are often counterproductive in pastoral care.

The existential problem's contribution to the epistemological crisis in the Christian Tradition can best be seen in a confluence of factors: the writings of Leibniz, who coined the term "theodicy" and published his *Essays on Theodicy* in 1710; the writings of Voltaire, including his viciously satirical novel *Candide* (1759); and an intervening event, the great Lisbon earthquake in 1755.

Leibniz was born and educated in Germany, and has been so influential that no course on the history of modern philosophy can omit him. As was typical of his day, he wrote on a great variety of subjects. His work resembled the argumentation style that preceded the decisive shift to empiricism as evidenced in

---

[21] E.g., Matson, *New History*, 2:364.

[22] E.g., Richard Wollheim, in his introduction to *Hume on Religion* (Cleveland and New York: The World Publishing Company, 1963), 17.

[23] Flint, "Evil," *Oxford Companion*, 224.

Hume's writings. His argument for God's existence was of an ontological sort and involved one of many uses of "the principle of sufficient reason." That is, for any contingent statement to be true (in this case the existence of the universe itself) there *must* be a sufficient reason. As Wallace Matson summarizes:

> The sufficient reason cannot be found in the universe ... Therefore, the sufficient reason ... must be a non-contingent ... necessary being, that is, God. Now, we find in the world power, knowledge, and will. The Being Who is a sufficient reason for these must also be endowed with these attributes and in the highest degree ...[24]

God's infinite knowledge means that God could imagine all possible worlds, and God's goodness entails that the actual universe is the best of all possible worlds.

I stated in Chapter 1 (note 7) that I would not clutter this text with qualifications and counter-positions unless I judged them to make a substantial difference for the purposes of this book. There is a significant difference between two interpretations of Leibniz's claim that this must be "the best of all possible worlds." For example, Matson's first explication of the phrase is that this must be "the one with the greatest surplus of good over evil."[25] Other interpreters emphasize that this frequently used phrase has only the "rarefied metaphysical sense of greatest variety of phenomena consonant with greatest simplicity of laws."[26] The different explications, however, fail to note that Leibniz has actually made both claims:

> It follows from the supreme perfection of God, that in creating the universe he has chosen the best possible plan, in which there is the greatest variety together with the greatest order; the best arranged ground, place, time; the most results produced in the most simple ways; the most of power, knowledge, happiness and goodness in the creatures that the universe could permit.[27]

We shall see that placing the emphasis on one or the other of these explications makes a great deal of difference in assessing the lasting importance of Leibniz's contributions regarding the problem of evil.

The great Lisbon earthquake of 1755 was one of the deadliest recorded in history. Its magnitude is estimated to have been 8.5–9.0; estimates of the number of people killed vary considerably, but a recent author, Niels Christian Hvidt

---

[24] Matson, *New History*, 2:327.
[25] Matson, *New History*, 2:328. Cf. Michael Peterson, William Hasker, Bruce Reichenbach, and David Basinger, *Reason & Religious Belief: An Introduction to the Philosophy of Religion*, 4th ed. (New York and Oxford: Oxford University Press, [1991] 2009), 157.
[26] Nicholas Rescher, *The Philosophy of Leibniz* (Englewood Cliffs, NJ: Prentice-Hall, 1967), 19.
[27] G. W. Leibniz, in "The Principles of Nature and of Grace, Based on Reason," (1718), reprinted in Philip P. Weiner, ed., *Leibniz: Selections* (New York: Charles Scribner's Sons, 1951), 528.

(b.1969), estimates that a third of Lisbon's 275,000 inhabitants were killed, and others died as far away as Spain and Morocco. He notes that it not only shook the ground for miles around in Europe and North Africa, but also "shook the ground under Leibnizian optimism."[28]

François-Marie Arouet wrote prolifically under the pen name Voltaire. In his early years he was influenced by optimistic philosophers, including Leibniz. Note that if we place emphasis on Leibniz's concern with God's selection of the best possible laws of nature, his work falls well within the category of *providential* deism, and he is even less willing than Robert Boyle and his contemporary physico-theologians to countenance miraculous interventions to remedy the suffering of individuals. By the time Voltaire wrote *Candide*, after the earthquake, all notions of providence had dropped out of his thinking. The main character, Candide, and his tutor Pangloss (a parody of Leibniz) are shipwrecked off the coast of Portugal. Only they and an evil sailor survive, just in time to view the destruction of the earthquake. Yet Pangloss announces that all that is, is for the best. "It is impossible that things should be other than they are; for everything is right" (ch. 5).

Despite Voltaire's pessimism having developed a half-century after Leibniz's *Theodicy*, scholars credit Leibniz with creating the modern crisis in theology. Jeffrey Stout writes that:

> The problem of evil is no longer a problem of figuring out what God is up to, given all the theology we already believe. In a context shaped by the new probability, it is a problem of figuring out what kind of God—*if any*—is plausible as an explanation of the origins of the universe as we find it. Given the existence of earthquakes, plagues, and the suffering of innocent children, the existence of a supremely perfect personal God seems unlikely.[29]

Tilley writes that during the eighteenth century the burden of proof shifted to showing how worldly evil is consistent with "providential theism"—of showing that it is *not* improbable that God exists.[30] So both Tilley and Stout are confirming my claim above (section 3) that the development of empirical or "probable" reasoning was a significant factor in the shift from problem to crisis. Hvidt notes that Leibniz was trained in the discipline of law rather than theology. So whereas earlier thinkers saw God as judge of human sinfulness, now "God is in the seat of the accused, charged for being the cause of evils in the world. The judge is human reason."[31]

---

[28] Niels Christian Hvidt, "Historical Development of the Problem of Evil," in Murphy et al., *Physics and Cosmology*, 1–34 (26).

[29] Jeffrey Stout, *The Flight from Authority: Religion, Morality and the Quest for Autonomy* (Notre Dame, IN: University of Notre Dame Press, 1981), 123.

[30] Tilley, *Evils*, 226.

[31] Hvidt, "Historical Development," 23.

3.3 Worldview changes

Lovejoy writes that the great chain of being was discussed more in the eighteenth century than at any other time in history[32]—it was no longer an "endemic assumption ... which if made explicit would amount to a large and important and perhaps highly debatable proposition in logic or metaphysics."[33] In the eighteenth century, the new empirical-scientific mindset was already clashing with this metaphysical assumption, and it is interesting that the sources he quotes who still held to it were predominantly literary figures. For example, it was a major theme in *Essays on Man* (1733–4) by Alexander Pope (1688–1744), who even repeats Augustine's assumption that a break in the chain of being would create cosmic disorder.[34]

Loss of this concept of a break in the chain of command from God to the natural world, attributed to angelic and human disobedience, and then combined with such a dramatic focal point (Lisbon) for recognition of the "prevalence of misery in the world,"[35] caused the existential problem of evil to bare its teeth in a new way: what can account for a universe designed to produce such massive suffering?[36] Especially important is that it defeated the Augustinian answer to the problem of animal suffering.

4 Recent approaches to the problem of evil

I believe that two of the best-known recent writers on the problem of evil are Alvin Plantinga and John Hick. Plantinga is taken by many to have solved the logical problem. Hick's has been one of the most debated instances of Southgate and Robinson's developmental good–harm analyses. I report on these only briefly because this material is available in so many other resources. What I believe is not prominent in the literature are accounts in terms of constitutive good–harm analyses, so I report on one, by Diogenes Allen, at greater length. I end with a critique of both Hick and Allen, which I believe would apply much more generally to modern responses: they are anthropocentric, only (partially) justifying human suffering, and (almost) entirely failing to address animal suffering.

4.1 Plantinga and the logical problem

Plantinga has written voluminously on the problem of evil, so I hope that this brief summary is accurate even though it does not incorporate all of the nuances of his thought. As described at the beginning of this chapter, the logical problem

---

[32] Lovejoy, *Great Chain*, 59.
[33] Lovejoy, *Great Chain*, 10.
[34] Lovejoy, *Great Chain*, 60.
[35] Hume's *Dialogues*.
[36] Note that Voltaire's Pangloss is as much a parody of Pope as of Leibniz.

is the claim that the statement (1) that there is an omniscient, omnipotent, all-benevolent God is logically inconsistent with the statement (2) that there is evil in the world. Since it is obviously true that there is evil, belief in God must be rejected. Plantinga (and others) point out that the logical inconsistency can be removed by showing that there is a *possibly true* premise (3) that reconciles *1* and *2*. In fact *1* and *3* together imply *2*. Regarding moral evil, Plantinga offers a form of the ancient free-will defense: (3) God has sufficient reason to permit moral evil because a world with free creatures who sometimes do more good than evil is more valuable than one without any free creatures.[37]

As already noted (end of section 2.2), critics claim that God in principle could have created free beings who always do what is right. Plantinga counters that the very meaning of free will involves *not* being determined by God to do only what is moral. I side with Plantinga here, and I will slightly elaborate in my discussion of Hick below. Plantinga's response to natural evil is to postulate as a possible premise that there are free and rebellious spirits who cause natural disasters and suffering.[38]

I mention here only two criticisms of Plantinga's work. First, Thomas Tracy (b.1948) concedes that the logical objection presents the most radical challenge to belief in God; however, it is the easiest to rebut because it only requires the provision of claims that may *possibly* be true, but need not be shown to be true. He turns to the existential problem: what religious believers want is more than a defense of the possibility of belief in God in the face of evil, but "some understanding of the way these beliefs cohere within an explanatory story that is at least a viable candidate, a 'live option' for winning assent. The story will not only need to be internally consistent, but also consistent with the network of beliefs" that are actually held.[39]

Note the congruity between Tracy's recognition of the need for an approach to the problem of evil that coheres with the rest of one's theology and the holist epistemology advocated in this text. Another way to make the point is that solution to the logical problem by importing highly dubious premises is, in Imre Lakatos's terms, *ad hoc.*

Tilley's critique of Plantinga is quite relevant here. Philosophers have a variety of terms for and definitions of free will. The version that Plantinga needs for his free-will defense is most often called libertarian free will and, in short, this means that one acted freely only if one could have in fact acted differently.[40] Tilley argues that liber-

---

[37] Alvin Plantinga, *The Nature of Necessity* (Oxford: Clarendon Press, 1974), 166–7.

[38] Alvin Plantinga, *God, Freedom, and Evil* ([1974] Grand Rapids, MI: Eerdmans, 1977), 55–9.

[39] Thomas F. Tracy, "The Lawfulness of Nature and the Problem of Evil," in Murphy et al., *Physics and Cosmology*, 153–78 (158).

[40] See Nancey Murphy and Warren S. Brown, *Did My Neurons Make Me Do It? Philosophical and Neurobiological Perspectives on the Moral Responsibility and Free Will* (Oxford: Oxford University Press, 2007) for a critique of the common conceptions of free will as either libertarian or "compatibilist": we argue that complex adaptive systems with sophisticated linguistic capacities become agents in their own right, adapting causally determined processes for their own purposes.

tarian free will is incompatible with the mainstream theological accounts of human nature in Plantinga's own tradition, including those of Augustine, Aquinas, Luther, and Calvin.[41] The key theological cost seems to be that *grace* simply drops out of the picture, because of the traditional claim that without grace the effect of sin is bondage of the will such that we find ourselves drawn to what is wrong.[42] And, in fact, if Plantinga did emphasize the traditional concept of grace, would this not itself interfere with the exercise of libertarian freedom?[43]

My judgment is that, given the recent change to holist epistemologies, the logical problem of evil has been reduced simply to a philosophers' puzzle and is not particularly important for defeating or defending a Christian theological tradition.

4.2 Hick and the vale of soul-making

John Hick's and others' arguments known as the soul-making defense are relevant here. The perfection of human creatures does not take place at the species level by a natural and inevitable evolution, "but through a hazardous adventure in individual freedom."[44] Hick rightly regards human goodness, slowly built up through personal histories of moral effort, as more valuable in God's eyes than humans with a nature created good.

I would go much further here and say that human nature created *de novo* with good moral character is an incoherent idea. Certainly, children are born with more or less suitable temperaments for developing moral goodness. But the concepts of character and virtue are "past-entailing predicates"; that is, they cannot apply now if certain things have not been true in the past. Virtues are *acquired* human characteristics; the virtue of courage is to be distinguished from innate fearlessness because to be courageous is to have the capacity to feel fear and yet to have developed the capacity to act in face of that fear as one knows one ought to act. Thus, Hick is correct in saying that dangers, hardships, pain, and other kinds of suffering are necessary conditions for development of the moral character prized by God.

However, there are three major problems to be noted immediately. One is that suffering sometimes does not lead to virtue, but rather to various forms of self-destruction, or to death of children before they reach the age of character development. Second, many have questioned why there seems to be so much more suffering in the world than would be necessary for soul-making, and third, the one with which I am most troubled, is the anthropomorphism of his account. We now know from biology that animal suffering and death preceded the appearance

[41] Terrence W. Tilley, "Towards a Creativity Defense of Belief in God in the Face of Evil," in Murphy et al., *Physics and Cosmology*, 195–215 (200).

[42] Tilley, "Creativity," 200–1, referring to Plantinga's *Warranted Christian Belief* (New York: Oxford University Press, 2000), 206–8.

[43] Tilley, "Creativity," 200, n.15.

[44] Hick, *Evil*, 256.

of humans by billions of years: death by approximately 3.5 billion; because of disagreements about what kinds of life forms are capable of pain and other sorts of suffering, we are unable say when suffering emerged.[45]

4.3 A constitutive good–harm analysis

Recall that Hick's account is an instance of Southgate and Robinson's developmental GHA. They provide brief mention of what might count as a constitutive GHA, one of which is Diogenes Allen's account of Simone Weil's (1909–43) claim to have experienced God in the midst of suffering.[46] I present here in much more detail a striking example found in a tiny (but I believe very important) book, also by Allen, *The Traces of God in a Frequently Hostile World*.[47]

Allen's example comes from the life of Iulia de Beausobre (1893–1977), a rather ordinary Russian woman imprisoned and tortured under Stalin's regime. In two books she writes about that experience and the insights she gained regarding the Christian idea of redemption.[48] The victim must try to respond to the tormenters, she says, in a "redemptive" manner. One does this by making oneself "invulnerable." This does not mean to dull oneself to the pain; rather, it is a refusal to be hurt, to be damaged by it. The effort of keeping a clear awareness of her surroundings, she says, makes her go cold with clammy sweat. The victim must attempt to understand the tormenters without becoming sentimental and concealing their responsibility. All passions such as fear, self-pity, and despair must be controlled. Not everyone can do this. But for those who do, such an effort has two results:

> You realize that you have been privileged to take part in nothing less than an act of redemption. And then you find that, incidentally and inevitably, you have reached a form of serenity which is, if anything, more potent to counteract sadistic lusts than any barren impassivity could be. But to your mind, now, that is a minor matter. The direct and positive work of an effort applied in this way towards redeeming the deed is far too big and too thrilling for anything else to matter to you very much at the moment.[49]

She explains how this is an act of redemption in a passage where she imagines a conversation between herself and her "Leonardo"—the person she aspires to

---

[45] Meric Srokosz and Simon Kolstoe, "Animal Suffering, the Hard Problem of Consciousness and a Reflection on Why We Should Treat Animals Well" *Science & Christian Belief* 28, no. 1 (April 2016): 3–19.

[46] Diogenes Allen, "Natural Evil and the Love of God," in Marilyn McCord Adams and Robert Merrihew Adams, eds., *The Problem of Evil* (Oxford: Oxford University Press, 1990), 189–207.

[47] Diogenes Allen, *The Traces of God in a Frequently Hostile World* (Cambridge, MA: Cowley Publications, 1981), ch. 5.

[48] Iulia de Beausobre, *The Woman Who Could Not Die* (New York: Viking Press, 1938) and *Creative Suffering* (London: Dacre Press, 1940).

[49] Quoted by Allen, *Traces*, 63.

become. A great bond is formed, he says, "between the man who is tortured day in, day out, and the man who day in, day out, tortures him . . . If you ponder on this you may find the justification for your apparently absurd suffering."[50] She responds that surely there is no justification for a crowd of well-fed, strong men bullying a weary, undernourished, half-demented woman. Leonardo replies:

> If you want to understand, to know the truth about this sort of thing, you must rise higher and look deeper. If you do, you can transform the ghastly bond into that magic wand which changes horror into beauty . . . [W]hen you overcome the pain inflicted on you by them, you make *their* criminal record less villainous? Even more, you bring something new into it—a thing of precious beauty. But when, through weakness, cowardice, lack of balance, lack of serenity, you augment your pain, their crime becomes so much the darker, and it is darkened by you. If you could understand this, your making yourself invulnerable would not be *only* an act of self-preservation; it would be a kindness to *Them* . . . Look right down into the depths of your heart and tell me—Is it not right for you to be kind to them? . . . Particularly to them, perhaps? Is it not right that those men who have no kindness within them should get a surplus of it flowing towards them from without?

She recounts that "[t]he whole of me responds with a 'Yes!' like a throb of thundering music. It is so shattering that it makes me stagger . . . Drowsily I think: 'Oh, Leonardo, what if we are both only mad after all, my dear'?"[51] Next she despairs. But then Christ becomes present to her; she finds in him her security, her invulnerability. She feels joy, serenity, and is empowered to love.

In the example cited here, we learn a great deal about God's response to evil, about God's love for both victim and villain, and gain insight into the meaning of Jesus' death on the cross. It is a powerful example of a constitutive GHA: without the torture and other forms of suffering, the change that Iulia recounts never could have happened.

4.4 Social evil: The principalities and powers

I mentioned above that in modern times the Augustinian concept of metaphysical evil has received little attention, and social or structural evil has come to be treated more extensively. One approach has been the "contagion model," according to which individual sin spreads by example from one person to another. Plantinga offers one example:

> We human beings are deeply communal; we learn from parents, teachers, peers, and others, both by imitation and by precept. We acquire beliefs in this

---

[50] Allen, *Traces*, 63.
[51] Allen, *Traces*, 64.

way, but just as important (and perhaps less self-consciously), we acquire attitudes and affections, loves and hates. Because of our social nature, sin and its effects can be like a contagion that spreads from one to another, eventually corrupting an entire society or segment of it.[52]

Tilley, however, responds that contagion models "obscure the huge number of economic, social, religious, industrial, and other structures and practices that combine to make an engine of social evil so powerful."[53]

Long before Plantinga began to write, there had already been a recognition that the contagion model was inadequate to account for social sin. Walter Rauschenbusch (1861–1918) did not hesitate to retain the term "original sin" to describe corporate sinfulness everywhere present and persisting through long ages.[54] James McClendon (1928–2000) describes his position as follows:

> He commended the traditional doctrine for its practical recognition that others' sin can cause our own, not merely by the force of evil example, but by creating depraved social conditions. Under these, cruelty, or misuse of sex, or lynchings or blood feuds, or gluttonous acquisition of wealth, or oppression and economic strangulation fester. Righteousness is discouraged. Often enough such conditions are the consequence of the sin of more recent foreparents than Adam; transmitted from generation to generation, these conditions grow or wither as functions of each new generation.[55]

McClendon makes use here of the biblical concept of the "principalities and powers"; however, I shall present John Howard Yoder's (1927–97) explication.[56] He raises the question: if Jesus' ministry is to be understood in political terms, where in the NT do we find the equivalent of the concepts of *power* or *structures* as these are used by contemporary social scientists? It happens that in the 1950s and 1960s, NT research by G. B. Caird (1917–84), Hendrikus Berkhof (1914–95), and others began to build a body of exegetical literature regarding a set of terms used by Paul and his school: "principalities and powers," "thrones and dominations," "angels and archangels," "elements," "heights and depths", "law" and "knowledge." In the intervening centuries, many of these terms were taken to apply to demons and angelic beings, and thus fit in well with the Augustinian type of theodicy, but came to be ignored in the modern period as mythological.

---

[52] Plantinga, *Warranted Christian Belief*, 207.

[53] Tilley, "Creativity", 213.

[54] Walter Rauschenbusch, *A Theology for the Social Gospel* (New York: Macmillan, 1917).

[55] James Wm. McClendon, Jr., *Doctrine: Systematic Theology, Volume 2* (Nashville, TN: Abingdon Press, 1994), 128–9.

[56] John H. Yoder, *The Politics of Jesus: Vicit Agnus Noster* (Grand Rapids, MI: Eerdmans, 1972; 2nd enlarged ed., 1994), ch. 8.

Apparently, the NT concept of the powers developed from concepts of the alien gods of other nations in OT understanding—hence there is a lingering sense of their being spiritual realities. However, the most significant function of the terms is to apply to what we would now call power structures: human traditions, the state, class, economic structures, and religious institutions, to name a few.

If we can make this connection between Paul's peculiar set of powers and our contemporary concept of power structures, we are in a position to appreciate Paul's sociopolitical theory and to see their relation to structural sin. The powers were created by God for good purposes, since human social life is impossible without them. However, they are "fallen" in the sense that they do not serve the good of humankind for which they were created, but seek instead their own self-aggrandizement. They have become idols in that they require individuals to serve them as though they are of absolute value.

Christ's role in relation to the powers was to destroy their idolatrous claims. In his public ministry, he showed that it was possible to live a genuinely free life in spite of the powers. He conquered the powers through his death, in that the worthiest representatives of Jewish religion and the Roman state conspired to put him to death and thus revealed their true colors. Christ "disarmed the principalities and powers" by stripping them of their ability to create an illusion of absolute legitimacy; he made a public spectacle of them and thereby triumphed over them (cf. Col. 2.15). In the time between Christ's victory on the cross and the eschaton, the powers linger on, but their absolute sway over Christians is broken.

If Yoder and others are right,[57] we have not only an analysis of social structures, but also a powerful insight into the meaning of Jesus' death. Christians' response to the powers must sometimes be to refuse to cooperate with them, even though this may well lead to suffering. The church is meant to be a new social reality in the midst of the world that unmasks the powers by its very existence and provides a laboratory for imagining and practicing new forms of social life.

4.5 Criticisms: Anthropocentrism and the possible evils of theodicy

As I confessed at the beginning of this chapter, I find the amount of literature on the problem of evil to be unmanageably large (and perhaps the very length of this chapter helps to substantiate this claim). Consequently, my criticisms here will not involve critiques of particular authors. Rather, I shall make two general points. The first is the likely inadequacy of all of the good–harm analyses offered: for example, the virtues and other goods enabled by free will and soul-making may

---

[57] See especially the trilogy by Walter Wink, *Naming the Powers: The Language of Power in the New Testament, Unmasking the Powers: The Invisible Forces that Determine Human Existence,* and *Engaging the Powers: Discernment and Resistance in a World of Domination* (Minneapolis, MN: Fortress Press, 1984, 1986, and 1992, respectively).

be hugely outweighed by the evils and destruction of human lives "on the other side of the ledger." So one might be justified in asking whether a good God would indeed instigate these processes at all. Augustine's followers did have an answer: all humans are implicated in sin (original sin) and so whatever befalls them in this life is justified punishment. However, add to this Augustine's estimate that only about 5 percent of Christians (not to mention others outside the church) would be saved—the rest consigned to eternal punishment—and the problem of suffering is unimaginably magnified!

A pertinent point here is the movement to reject the whole project of (modern) theodicy as itself an evil. Tilley summarizes his arguments as follows: the abstract theological and philosophical discourse "misportrays and effaces genuine evils . . . It silences powerful voices of insight and healing." It comes close to denying that there is genuine evil in the world.[58] In addition, the academic *practice* of theodicy tends to displace the various practices to which Christians are called that attempt to *remedy* the evil and suffering in the world.

The second point of this section is to criticize the extreme anthropomorphism of modern theodicies. It is widely recognized that theology in general took an anthropocentric turn in the modern period. In fact, some theologians would say that the subject matter of theology is *human* religious awareness. Thus, it should not come as a surprise that modern theodicies have paid scant attention to animal suffering. Most of the authors I have described here have something to say about animal suffering, but I find it shocking that they say so little. Hick devotes nine pages to animal suffering and suggests that the whole material world (including sentient and suffering animals) might have further meaning for God than simply to provide an environment for us, but if so, we can only glimpse God's purposes as they directly concern us.[59]

The topic of animals appears in only a few indices of books in my (confessedly small) library and only one reference book: *The Oxford Companion to Christian Thought*. Andrew Linzey (b.1952) writes that non-canonical gospels embellished the small amount of material in the NT on Jesus' relating to animals, and there has since then been a tradition of hagiography that emphasized saints' celebration of animals as fellow creatures. However, Scholastic theology emphasized the difference between humans and (other) animals in that they lack a rational soul, and thereby reinforced the hierarchical (and instrumental) reading of creaturely relations.[60]

Linzey's account of the history skips from Scholasticism to late modernity, leaving out the dreadful and widely held Cartesian belief that animals were

---

[58] Tilley, *Evils*, 1.
[59] Hick, *Evil*, 309–17.
[60] Andrew Linzey, "Animals," *Oxford Companion*, 22–3.

incapable of feeling pain. A number of "scientists" performed vivisection on animals. Dogs' front and back paws were nailed to wooden boards in what might be called a cruciform pattern. Charles Darwin (1809–82) stated that "everyone has heard of the dog suffering under vivisection who licked the hand of the operator" until it had been muzzled.[61]

I was surprised to learn that benevolence in general, and revulsion toward animal cruelty, *began* to realign moral principles only in the eighteenth century. James Turner writes that from then on suffering "even of strangers or animals, provoked . . . revulsion; the infliction of it stank of grave sin."[62]

Another, related, point made by Turner is that, in the nineteenth century especially, a combination of emphasis on benevolence, with the quest for a rational religion and a belief in inevitable progress led increasingly to rejection of the "doctrines" of original sin and eternal damnation. He writes that "eternal damnation and original sin in particular jarred humane sensitivities and stumped rational minds."[63]

Knowledge of Darwinian theory and the results of German biblical criticism converged at approximately the same time in the United States. Biblical critics largely rejected the historicity of the first chapters of Genesis, and thus the idea of a historical Fall of the first humans. All the more so did they reject the idea of the Fall of the angels. The fundamentalist movement arose largely in reaction against these developments, but another reaction was to shift the focus of Christian teaching and preaching away from doctrinal orthodoxy in favor of an experiential and moralized interpretation of the Christian message. Again, most of the attention focused on what these changes meant for *humans*. One exception was an increased perplexity regarding belief in the benevolence (or existence) of God in light of an evolutionary theory most often interpreted for the public in Alfred Lord Tennyson's terms of "nature red in tooth and claw."[64]

It is noteworthy that a small stream of books have begun to appear calling into question the images of animals as beastly and of humans as humane. Mary Midgley's *Beast and Man* is a classic.[65] More recently there is Frans de Waal's (b.1948) *Good Natured*, criticizing the tendency in ethology to describe accounts

[61] Charles Darwin, *The Descent of Man and Selection in Relation to Sex*, 2 vols. (London: John Murray, 1871), 1:40.

[62] James Turner, *Without God, Without Creed: The Origins of Unbelief in America* (Baltimore and London: Johns Hopkins University Press, 1985), 70.

[63] Turner, *Without God*, 71.

[64] See my chapter, "Science and Society," in James Wm. McClendon, Jr., *Witness: Systematic Theology, Volume 3* (Nashville, TN: Abingdon Press, 2000), sec. 2.

[65] Mary Midgley, *Beast and Man: The Roots of Human Nature* (Ithaca, NY: Cornell University Press, 1978).

of animals' prosocial and proto-moral behavior as naïve sentimentalism.[66] Elizabeth Johnson's (b.1941) *Ask the Beasts: Darwin and the God of Love* criticizes scholars' nearly complete focus on humans "while the great biblical theme of cosmic redemption flew by in silence."[67] Andrew Linzey's *Why Animal Suffering Matters* does a remarkable job of taking all of the arguments against moral and theological consideration for animals and turning them on their heads to show that animals (like small children) are particularly deserving of human care.[68]

It is worth noting that while Western Christianity, as Linzey claims, beginning with Scholasticism, has denigrated animals, there has been a subtradition, beginning in approximately 1525, that has incorporated an opposing tendency. Already suspicious of the Augustinian notion of original sin, its general tendency has been to focus on individuals' choice to follow or reject the way of Jesus, and the way of Jesus generally led to the cross. A number of these (pejoratively termed) Anabaptists (re-baptizers) or Radical Reformers preached not only the gospel of Christ crucified, but the Gospel of all creatures. Taking into account the suffering of animals and the fact that they were forced into servitude for humans, they claimed that the suffering of animals conforms to the pattern of redemption through suffering and therefore in its own way preaches the gospel of Christ crucified.[69]

Contemporary ecological ethicist Holmes Rolston (b.1932) expresses this theme so beautifully that I have quoted him in a number of my own publications. He emphasizes our continuity with the rest of the biological world and at the same time reconciles evolutionary "morals" with a Christian ethic of self-sacrifice. In both cases, in the life we are called to live as followers of Jesus and in the biological realm, there is an analogy with the self-sacrificing character of God. Rolston teaches us to see the work of God not in the predator, but in the prey.

> The Earth is a divine creation and scene of providence. The whole natural history is somehow contained in God, God's doing, and that includes even suffering, which, if it is difficult to say simply that it is immediately from God, is not ultimately outside of God's plan and redemptive control. God absorbs suffering and transforms it into goodness . . .[70]

---

[66] Frans de Waal, *Good Natured: The Origins of Right and Wrong in Humans and Other Animals* (Cambridge, MA: Harvard University Press, 1996).

[67] Elizabeth A. Johnson, *Ask the Beasts: Darwin and the God of Love* (New York and London: Bloomsbury, 2014), 2.

[68] Andrew Linzey, *Why Animal Suffering Matters: Philosophy, Theology, and Practical Ethics* (Oxford: Oxford University Press, 2009).

[69] See e.g., George Huntston Williams, *The Radical Reformation*, 3rd rev. ed. (Kirksville, MO: Sixteenth Century Journal Publishers, [1962] 1992), esp. 442, 1269.

[70] This is consistent with Yoder's description of nonviolence (in a number of writings) as a call for Christians to "absorb evil" rather than to augment it, as well as with de Beausobre's understanding of "invulnerability."

Rolston describes nature itself as cruciform. The world is not a paradise but a theater where labor and suffering drive us to make sense of things. "Life is advanced not only by thought and action, but by suffering, not only by logic but by pathos."

> This pathetic element in nature is seen in faith to be at the deepest logical level the pathos in God. God is not in a simple way the Benevolent Architect, but is rather the Suffering Redeemer. The whole of the earthen metabolism needs to be understood as having this character. The God met in physics as the divine wellspring from which matter-energy bubbles up . . . is in biology the suffering and resurrecting power that redeems life out of chaos.

Rolston suggests that, in faith, the secret of life is seen to lie not in natural selection and the survival of the fittest; rather "the secret of life is that it is a passion play. Things perish in tragedy.

> [T]hings perish with a passing over in which the sacrificed individual also flows in the river of life. Each of the suffering creatures is delivered over as an innocent sacrificed to preserve a line, a blood sacrifice perishing that others may live. We have a kind of "slaughter of the innocents," a nonmoral, naturalistic harbinger of the slaughter of the innocents at the birth of the Christ, all perhaps vignettes hinting of the innocent lamb slain from the foundation of the world. They share the labor of the divinity. In their lives, beautiful, tragic, and perpetually incomplete, they speak for God; they prophesy as they participate in the divine pathos. All have "borne our griefs and carried our sorrows."

The abundant life that Jesus exemplifies and offers to his disciples is "a sacrificial suffering through to something higher . . . The cruciform creation is, in the end, deiform, godly, just because of this element of struggle, not in spite of it."[71]

This interpretation of suffering is consistent with Anabaptist thought, in which the suffering of Christians is not generally seen as a punishment for sins, but rather as redemptive participation with Christ in the expected consequences of obedience to God in the midst of a sinful world.

The foregoing excursus on Anabaptist thought provides a contrasting interlude in the midst of a chapter in which I claim that most treatments of evil as unduly anthropocentric. It relates animal suffering to that of humans, in a theological context that places great emphasis on what Paul mentions briefly: "I rejoice in my sufferings for your sake, and in my flesh I complete what is lacking in Christ's afflictions" (Col. 1.24 RSV). But still, does this explain animal suffering? It only

---

[71] Holmes Rolston, III, "Does Nature Need to be Redeemed?" *Zygon: Journal of Religion and Science* 29, no. 2 (1994): 205–29 (quotations 218–20 *passim*).

suggests that there may be a meaning to God that, as Hick says, we can "glimpse only" as it directly concerns ourselves.

So I come back to the problem that without the Augustinian concept of the Fall of angels disrupting the natural order, we have seen very little by way of attention to animal suffering, and certainly no robust explanation or justification of it. For this reason, I take up two topics in the next section: a scientific explanation of the suffering of animals (and humans); and a widespread emphasis on the necessity of theological eschatology to provide justification.

5 Contemporary movements

This section focuses on recent scholarship that pertains equally to animals and humans. The first subsection brings up to date and unifies earlier arguments that explain suffering as a necessary consequence of the kind of universe needed for life. For example, pain is required to keep higher forms of life from harming or killing themselves. Science's contribution is to consider the lawlike character of natural processes, recognizing that much suffering is simply the consequence of the regularities of nature. In addition, recent work on the "fine-tuning" of the constants and basic laws of physics suggests that the laws themselves had to be almost exactly as they are in order that life exist in the universe.

Section 5.1 will present my attempt to sum up what we can say at this point about necessary preconditions for the loving communion of creatures (humans, again) with God. Tracy notes, however, that the central concern of the biblical tradition is not to explain evil, but rather to describe what God is doing to address evil. The topic of section 5.2, eschatology, is relevant here. Tracy says that the Bible is concerned with salvation,[72] and I shall argue (with the help of several theologians) that it has been an egregious error to think of salvation primarily or solely in terms of humans getting to heaven in the end. The section focuses on the importance of a broader, richer eschatology in order to address the problem of evil. I conclude that systematic theology can be "arranged" so as to show that nearly all of it is relevant to God's addressing the various forms of evil (see Figures 18–19 pp. 176–7).

5.1 Evil as a necessary by-product of God's benevolent purposes

I happened to be writing a chapter for a book on natural evil when the tsunami of December 26, 2004 hit Southeast Asia.[73] Kenneth Woodward (b.1935) asked scholars how adherents of various faiths in the region would likely respond to the questions: Why us? Why here? Why now? Hindus could resort to concepts of

---

[72] Tracy, "Lawfulness of Nature," 159–60 (155).
[73] Nancey Murphy, "Science and the Problem of Evil: Suffering as a By-product of a Finely Tuned Cosmos," in Murphy et al., *Physics and Cosmology*, 131–51.

destructive deities such as Shiva; Buddhists could resort to the doctrine of karma; Muslims could reply that God was testing survivors' faith.[74]

My immediate response was not to turn directly to a theological consideration, but to recognize that events such as this, as well as others such as famine and disease, are results of the same lawlike regularities that make the goods of this world possible. So this chapter naturally follows Chapter 6, examining the rise of the concept of the laws of nature in the early modern period.[75]

My chapter (among others) offered an alternative account, in which humans still play an essential part, but suffering is seen not so much as *a means to good* for humans but as an unwanted but unavoidable *by-product* of conditions in the natural world that have to obtain in order that there be intelligent life at all. That is, the better we understand the interconnectedness among natural systems in the universe, and especially their bearing on complex life, the clearer it becomes that it would be impossible to have a world that allowed for a free and loving response to God, yet one without natural or any other type of evil.

Note that this pattern of reasoning is consonant with Leibniz's argument for "the best of all possible worlds" (in the sense of recognizing the interconnectedness of events such that removal of an instance of evil would result in a variety of other changes) but enhanced by considering *current* understandings of the interconnectedness of natural systems, especially as seen in arguments for the "fine-tuning" of the laws of physics and the constants of nature.

In an attempt to sum up this argument, I created a diagram that is, first, something of a decision tree expressing, to the best of our current knowledge, a series of options in which only one could be expected to produce creatures capable of a loving response to God. It also shows by-products of these efficacious options that lead to the four types of evil categorized here: moral, natural, metaphysical, and social. However, the diagram (Figure 18 on p.176) is not adequate because it does not incorporate laws of special sciences such as geology or biology.

It is anthropocentric, of course, to present the following as sets of options for God but, being a mere *Anthropos* myself, I have no better way of making the following points. The first choice is to create a cosmos or a chaos—that is, in contemporary terms, a universe that is or is not lawlike in its operations. Although this may seem to be a clear distinction, from the point of view of contemporary science, there are a variety of ways it could have been chaotic, such as having an incoherent jumble of laws or laws that changed from moment to moment. In

---

[74] Kenneth L. Woodward with Sudip Mazumdar, "Countless Souls Cry out to God," *Newsweek*, January 10, 2005, 37.

[75] Note that I say "lawlike regularities" rather than "laws of nature" for assorted reasons spelled out above.

fact, Paul Davies (b.1946) says, ours is highly ordered with well-defined, dependable laws.[76]

Even more interesting is William P. Brown's (b.1958) description of the first creation account in Genesis in terms of God acting to bring increasing order out of "a primordial state of 'void and vacuum' . . . a dark, watery mess . . . a primordial soup."[77] Brown notes further that "the uniform 'chaos' of Genesis 1:2 . . . shares virtual semblance with the uniformity that scientists posit about the primordial 'soupy' state of the universe at its inception."[78]

The reasons why a non-lawlike universe would fail to result in creatures able to relate to God are too many and, I presume, too obvious to spell out.

The second set of options is based on the (apparent) fine-tuning of the laws and cosmological constants. Leibniz's speculations are, again, quite relevant here: an omniscient God would be able to survey all possible worlds and choose the one that best suited divine purposes. There have been a variety of arguments over the years noting ways in which Earth is especially suited for human habitation. For example, the fact that ice is less dense than water prevents bodies of water from freezing all the way to the bottom and then never melting, leaving too little liquid water available for life. The day after the *Newsweek* piece described above, the *New York Times* Science Section ran an article by William Broad (b. 1951) explaining that earthquakes like the one on December 26 are a crucial part of the constant recycling of planetary crust, which has the effect of producing a lush, habitable planet.[79]

However, the most notable contribution to arguments such as this is relatively recent. During the 1980s, astrophysicists Brandon Carter (b.1942), Bernard Carr (b.1947), and Martin Rees (b.1942) compiled impressive lists of calculations showing that life depends very sensitively on the particular form of the laws of physics, and on some "seemingly fortuitous accidents in the actual values that nature has chosen for various particle masses, force strengths, and so forth."[80] In 1986 John Barrow (b.1952) and Frank Tipler (b.1947) published *The Anthropic Cosmological Principle*, with page after page of calculations showing that even *very* slight differences in the laws or constants would produce a universe in which no conceivable kind of life is possible.[81] I believe that the best list of factors that were necessary to produce a habitable universe (and most accessible for non-mathematicians)

---

[76] Paul Davies, *The Mind of God: The Scientific Basis for a Rational World* (New York: Simon and Schuster, 1992), 195.

[77] William P. Brown, *The Seven Pillars of Creation: Bible, Science, and the Ecology of Wonder* (Oxford: Oxford University Press, 2010), 36.

[78] Brown, *Seven Pillars*, 53.

[79] William J. Broad, "Deadly and Yet Necessary, Earthquakes Renew the Planet," *New York Times*, January 11, 2005, Science Section, 1, 4.

[80] Davies, *Mind of God*, 199.

[81] John Barrow and Frank Tipler, *The Anthropic Cosmological Principle* (Oxford: Clarendon Press, 1986).

is John Leslie's (b.1940). One example: after the Big Bang the cosmos could have re-collapsed within a fraction of a second or else expanded so fast that galaxy formation would be impossible. Therefore, the rate of expansion at early instants "needed to be fine tuned to perhaps one part in 10^{55} (which is 10 followed by 54 zeros)."[82]

There are four basic forces in the universe: gravitation, electromagnetism, the nuclear weak force (which controls radioactive decay), and the nuclear strong force (which binds nuclei together). All of these forces needed to be precisely balanced. For example, if the nuclear weak force had been stronger, the Big Bang would have burned all hydrogen to helium, and there could be no long-lived stable stars.[83] Without stars, and the precise value of the nuclear strong force, carbon, so essential to life, could not form. Leslie concludes that very small changes in fundamental constants could have meant "not merely slight changes in the cosmic picture but rather the destruction of its foundations."[84] A complete description of the fine-tuning of the laws of our universe would take the 680 pages devoted to it by Barrow and Tipler.

So the claim of authors writing on fine-tuning is not simply that there could be no humans as we know them, but rather that there could be no life of any conceivable sort. In my chapter, "Suffering as a By-product," I concentrated on answering questions that would undermine the usefulness of the discovery of the fine-tuning for addressing the problem of evil. Returning to Leibniz's claim noted above, we can now see that even the *smallest* change to reduce suffering produced by the regular operation of nature's laws would result in catastrophic disruption of the entire universe.

My diagram (Figure 18) shows the second law of thermodynamics as an intermediate step between fine-tuning and life. This is the law that results (in all but exceptional cases) in systems changing irreversibly from order to greater disorder unless there is an injection of energy. Robert Russell has pointed out that it is more appropriate to include the laws of thermodynamics as an aspect of fine-tuning and has detailed a number of reasons why the second law is essential for the existence of life. For example, our sun radiates energy at a great cost in entropy, but it is this energy that fuels biological organisms.[85]

Nonetheless, I have set the second law of thermodynamics apart from the other elements of fine-tuning for visual reasons. It is valuable to be able to show its particular relevance to the issues of both metaphysical evil and suffering. The effects

---

[82] John Leslie, *Universes* (London and New York: Routledge, 1989), 3.

[83] Leslie, *Universes*, 4.

[84] Leslie, *Universes*, 52.

[85] Robert John Russell, "Entropy and Evil: The Role of Thermodynamics in the Ambiguity of Good and Evil in Nature," in Russell, *Cosmology from Alpha to Omega* (Minneapolis, MN: Fortress Press, 2008), 226–48 (235).

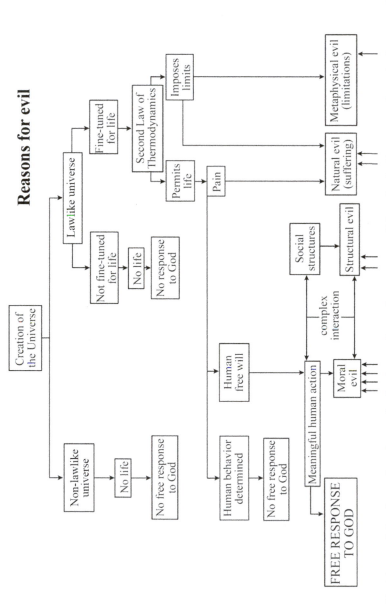

Figure 18 A "decision tree" showing various forms of evil as by-products of necessary conditions for God's purpose of creating humans who could freely respond to his love

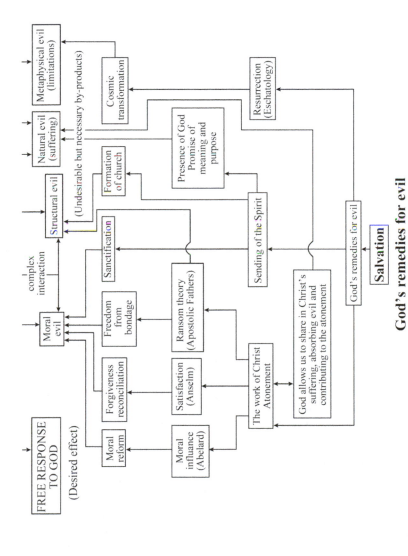

God's remedies for evil

Figure 19 A representation of the organizing of theology to show salvation as a response to all types of evil. Rather than a decision tree, however, the options here are all additive. Note that the remedies line up precisely with the evils in Figure 18

of entropy, limiting human (and animal) life, are everywhere: the need for food and consequent suffering from hunger pangs; certain forms of disease; predation; the need for clothing and shelter to conserve energy; fatigue; aging; and ultimately death. These limitations in human life are not moral evils but certainly provide much of the motive for sin, from instances simply of being too tired to do a good deed (what Augustinians would call metaphysical evil), to robbery, murder, and many wars.

The next set of options is a universe with only simple organisms versus one in which higher forms develop as well. I have represented the capacity to feel pain both as a consequence of complex neural systems and also as a necessary condition for the existence of complex organisms. Very simple organisms can be hardwired to withdraw from harmful stimuli, but this only allows for a simple repertoire of responses that are adequate in a narrow range of environments. For great flexibility in behavior we need *motivation* to avoid self-destructive situations. Pain (or something equally noxious, such as fear) is necessary for higher organisms' survival. And of course, it is just these capacities that allow for suffering.

The animal capacity for flexible action, in turn, is one of the building blocks for human free will. "Free will" is inserted in the diagram in deference to the important place the free-will defense has traditionally played in Christian discussions of the problem of evil.

Another factor that is both a consequence of and a precondition for complex life, and especially for human free will, is the existence of social structures. Warren S. Brown (b.1944) and I have argued that complex language is a prerequisite for free will, and language can only develop within a community. Sophisticated language allows for the creation of abstract concepts such as morality, evil, and sin.[86] Free will, along with social structures, allows for meaningful human action, which allows in turn for a free and loving response to God. However, a by-product of social structures, as we have seen, is structural evil. A major by-product of free will is sin.

So metaphysical evil (limitation) is built into the universe by the law of entropy, and various limitations contribute to suffering for sentient creatures. Social structures contribute to structural evil. Free will allows for sin. Especially now, when humans have such an impact on one another and on nature, all forms of evil interact in various ways, often producing horrendous evil.

Again, I warn that the following is speculative on my part: The story of Adam and Eve depicts pain in childbirth, harsh conditions of labor, and death as consequences of the first sin (Gen. 3.16–19). While pain, toil, and death are not caused by sin, they are not causally unrelated. Toil and death are the consequences of the finely tuned laws of physics that allow us to be here. The pain of childbirth is due

---

[86] Murphy and Brown, *Did My Neurons Make Me Do It?*, ch. 7.

to the large heads of human infants, which are necessary to house brains large enough to learn language, and ultimately to pray, and write theology—but also, tragically, to sin.

5.2 Theological responses and eschatological hope

Both the problems of religious plurality and of evil have been treated, since the beginning of the modern period, by both philosophers and philosophical theologians, and both have also shaped recent doctrinal theology. This subsection can be briefer than the preceding, because comparable treatments can be found in a number of recent theologies.

I suggested above that Christian theology could be organized in such a way as to show that it provides an account of what God has done, is doing, and will do in the future to address all forms of evil and suffering. A number of current theologians point out that older responses to evil have been backward-looking and anthropocentric. The topic of evil has been treated under the heading of creation (and subsequent Fall), and within the doctrine of theological anthropology, thus focusing on human sin. There appears now to be a growing consensus that the first direction to look is, instead, to the future—to recognize that the problem of evil can only be fully addressed by means of an adequate doctrine of *eschatology*. This includes the recognition, as N. T. Wright (b.1948) says, that salvation needs to be understood more broadly than as an expression of humans' hope of "going to heaven when they die."[87] James McClendon structured his volume, *Doctrine*, by beginning with eschatology, and nesting the doctrines of salvation and creation within the framework that eschatology provides.[88] Wolfhart Pannenberg (1928–2014) states that "it is only the union of creation and redemption against the background of eschatology that makes possible a tenable answer to the question of theodicy."[89] Wright, McClendon, and Pannenberg all object to the anthropocentricity of earlier treatments of evil and promote the expectation of a transformation of the entire cosmos: as Russell writes, a "vision of the mercy of God the Creator and of Christ's suffering on the cross as extended to all of life through the power of the Holy Spirit, bringing all living creatures, all of the 'sparrows who fall' (Matt. 10:31) immediately into the endless joy of the eschatological New Creation."[90]

Veli-Matti Kärkkäinen so objects to the anthropocentrism of discussions of evil that in his treatment his *main* focus is on nonhuman creatures, but with attention

---

[87] N. T. Wright, *New Heavens, New Earth: The Biblical Picture of Christian Hope* (Cambridge: Grove Books, 1999), 5.

[88] McClendon, *Doctrine*.

[89] Wolfhart Pannenberg, *Systematic Theology*, tr. Geoffrey W. Bromiley, 3 vols. (Grand Rapids, MI: Eerdmans, 1991), 2:164.

[90] Robert John Russell, *Time in Eternity: Pannenberg, Physics, and Eschatology in Creative Mutual Interaction* (Notre Dame, IN: University of Notre Dame Press, 2012), 193.

to human-caused damage to them. Finite creatures "praise God in their perishing, because this is part of their finitude."[91] In elaborating on Paul's cryptic statement in Romans that "the creation waits with eager longing for the revealing of the sons of God; . . . because all the creation itself will be set free from its bondage to decay and obtain the glorious liberty of the children of God" (Rom. 8.19, 21), and congruently with my emphasis on the law of entropy in the preceding subsection, Kärkkäinen, Russell, and a number of others associate the final overcoming of evil and suffering with the overcoming of entropy.

My brief notes here are not intended to suggest that previous attempts to address the problem of evil are ignored or rejected. Rather, it is claimed that they simply do not go far enough to address the suffering of creatures who are innocent and have no capacity for benefiting from suffering.

I have attempted to indicate, again in a simplistic diagram, the organizing of doctrinal theology so as to show some of the multiple ways in which God has been and will in the future provide remedies for evil. In contrast to Figure 18, it is not a decision tree: all of its branches are additive, and most of the four forms of evil are addressed by multiple routes.

"Salvation" is taken to refer to the past, present, and future remedies God provides. The work of Christ is often addressed under the heading of atonement. It has become common since the publication of Gustaf Aulén's (1879–1978) *Christus Victor* to speak of three types of atonement theories: the Anselmian or substitutionary theories; the Abelardian or moral influence theories; and the "classical" ransom or conflict theories, according to which the work of Christ is interpreted in terms of conflict with and triumph over cosmic evil powers.[92] A variety of versions of the latter were developed during the early centuries of the church: Christ as a ransom paid to the devil; a transaction wherein God used Christ as "bait" to deceive the devil; and a political form in which the devil lost his rightful dominion over sinful humankind by abusing the sinless Christ.

While the classical theory clearly has NT support, it has been seen as objectionable because it involves the concept of the devil, which many now take to require "demythologization." Aulén had argued that the mythological language of the conflict theory could simply be dropped, leaving the theory intact. But then it is no longer clear what is meant by "cosmic evil powers."

I followed Yoder, above, in giving an account of recent exegesis of the Pauline language of the powers, so I follow him again here in his updating of the classical motif. Yoder's central understanding of atonement fills the gap left by the excision of a mythical devil by means of the interpretation of the principalities and powers

---

[91] Veli-Matti Kärkkäinen, *Creation and Humanity: A Constructive Christian Theology for the Pluralistic World*, 5 vols. (Grand Rapids, MI: Eerdmans, 2015), 3:206–7.

[92] Gustaf Aulén, *Christus Victor*, tr. A. G. Herbert (New York: Macmillan, 1931).

described above. These superhuman power structures are the forces with which Jesus came into conflict, and from which he has freed humankind, both by his example (and here the moral influence theory gets its due) and by stripping them of the illusion of absolute legitimacy, precisely because their most worthy representatives (the Roman state and the Jewish religion) abused him in his innocence. The cross has as much significance in this theory as it does in the substitutionary theory, but for different reasons.

Yoder does not ignore personal sinfulness, but he gives it neither the significance nor the inevitability that it has in Augustinian Christianity. His focus instead is on institutionalized sin; the remedy for it is found in freedom from bondage to the principalities and powers, and especially in the creation of a new social order, the church. So the moral influence motif predicts (a degree of) moral reform, and thus a (partial) remedy for sin. The substitutionary motif emphasizes forgiveness for sin and thereby reconciliation (at-one-ment) with God. The conquest motif frees us from bondage to the powers.

The sending of the Spirit provides individuals with power to overcome sin, but also creates the church as a new social reality, providing an alternative social order to compete with corrupted social structures. The church, in addition, supports its members in living lives of discipleship, and discipleship is largely focused on the relief of suffering. As exemplified in de Beausobre's encounter with the Spirit of Christ, the Spirit's presence also relieves suffering directly.

The resurrection of Christ is interpreted by Pannenberg and others as the entry into the middle of world history of a foretaste of the world's eschatological fulfillment—its transformation into a cosmos with no sin, no suffering, no decay or death, and with the final transformation of the powers, and thus the overcoming of moral, social, natural, and metaphysical evil. God's final word: hope!

6 Retrospect and prospect

So the problem of evil is not to be dissolved, nor solved in a merely abstract theological or philosophical manner, but tackled by Christians following the costly way of discipleship, empowered by Jesus' spirit, and anticipating the end of the journey, as Wright proclaims, in God's bringing about "a new, or renewed, heaven and a new, or renewed earth, with these two integrated together."[93]

In the next chapter we turn to the relations between theology and some of the natural sciences. Chapter 9, on human nature, incorporates one particular relation, that between Christian anthropology and recent developments in the cognitive neurosciences.

---

[93] Wright, *New Heavens*, 5.

8

Science and Christianity

1 Introduction

As I have written (*ad nauseam*), beginning in Chapter 4, one of the criteria for judging the rationality of a large-scale tradition is to recount a historical narrative of the epistemological crises it has faced, and of the extent to which it has (or has not) overcome them, but without losing its identity. And, as it happens, the usual topics covered in individual chapters in a typical philosophy of religion text line up rather nicely with the topics described in Chapters 5–10 of this text, which many would count as prominent crises Christianity has faced (or is still facing) beginning in the modern period. One exception, of course, is a text whose major focus is specifically on the rationality of religion. So in a sense, the whole of this text is an attempt to provide the best account that can be offered (at this point in history) of the rationality of the Western Christian Tradition.

For a number of years I thought of studying the relations between theology and science as a mere hobby for a philosopher. However, at this point in my career, I am convinced that none of what we now distinguish as philosophy, science, or theology can be understood adequately apart from knowledge of the other two. So, as indicated by the title of this chapter, I shall here address the relations between Christian theology and modern and contemporary natural sciences.

It is widely believed (especially in the USA and in other countries where conservative American Christians have had a strong influence), by both Christians and some scientists, that Christian theology and modern science are incompatible; that the church regularly opposes scientific advances; and that, in case after case, the church has (usually belatedly) backed down. So, in a text largely devoted to epistemological crises in the modern and contemporary periods, it is very much to the point to put this view to rest. However, I shall argue below that it is not so much the science itself, but rather the *perception* of incompatibilities that creates an intellectual challenge to the Christian Tradition.

These *perceived* conflicts between science and Christian belief, particularly evolutionary biology, are having a devastating effect in many churches. Biology professors report that college freshmen often begin with the conflict view and assume that they have to choose whether to believe in Christianity or "believe in" evolution. And at the end of a good science education they abandon Christianity in large numbers.

Section 2, "Christianity and the warfare myth," then, will address the question of whether the rise of modern science has, in fact, amounted to an epistemological crisis for Christianity, or whether the conflict narrative regarding relations between the two has turned out to be, as the title of the section indicates, myth. When taken as a grand narrative regarding the *necessary* conflict of science with religion (each usually treated as monolithic in nature), I take this conflict thesis indeed to be mythological, both in the sense of just plain false and in the anthropological sense as a story that provides meaning to people's lives.

As will be shown in sections 3–5 (as well as in Chapter 9 below), scientific developments (or interpretations) and particular interpretations of Christian doctrine often result, usually temporarily, in mere accommodations, but also in *positive* reinterpretations of Christian thought. However, section 2 will also point out that (largely philosophical) assumptions or entailments of modern science have produced tremendous crises for Christianity. Prominent among these was the epistemological shift (described above in Chapter 2) from ancient and medieval concepts of knowledge, based on demonstrative reasoning and authority, to the modern concept of probable knowledge based (largely) on the weight of empirical evidence. This crisis, I have been arguing, can now be brought to an end. Equally difficult has been, and continues to be, the problem of special divine action, created by the development of a worldview based on laws of nature, determinism, and reductionism (as reported in Chapter 6).

Section 3 will address the Galileo "affair." The most obvious issue was a conflict between Galileo and church authorities on how to interpret Scripture and on who had the authority to do so. If this were all it involved, though, it might now be a forgotten (or even amusing) episode in history. What really mattered was that acceptance of the new astronomical theory resulted in a revolution throughout the entirety of Western culture.

Section 4 will address the Darwinian revolution in the biological sciences. Here I shall provide reminders regarding the providential-deist phase of the gradual separation between what we now conceive of as science and as theology, in which it was argued that the grander idea of God was of one who could establish universal laws at the beginning of creation that would serve to fulfill all of the divine purposes—in contrast to a God who needed to tinker with the system along the way. I suggest that controversies from Darwin's day to our own essentially reflect, on the one hand, the admiration for a majestic God as designer of the laws of evolution, and on the other, rejection of the apparent moral implications of a God who would initiate, and not intervene in, a wasteful and miserable biological history.

Section 5 will turn from considerations of the negative to the positive and focus specifically on a number of ways in which recent scientific cosmology has (or should have) provoked deeper insights into the doctrine of creation. Whereas many modern theologians have made the doctrine of creation to be all about us, reflective interpreters of contemporary science, especially cosmology, are attempting to bring out the religious meanings of (1) debates regarding the temporality of the universe; (2) various concepts of the finitude of the universe and of the possible emergence of the universe out of "nothing"; (3) the possible role of cosmological fine-tuning with regard to the goodness of creation (as already described in Chapter 7); (4) the status of the laws of nature if they are not in fact divine creations; and (5) the place of humankind in God's plans if it becomes evident that there is intelligent life elsewhere in the universe.

2 Christianity and the warfare myth

The title of this section is, I confess, misleading in two ways: "the" suggests, first, that there is a single conflict thesis, and, second, that this thesis is now generally taken as false by the increasing number of historians of the relations between Western Christianity and science.

Geoffrey Cantor (b.1943) writes that there is no consensus over the precise nature of what the conflict actually amounts to. He distinguishes between a strong thesis to the effect that science, in general, and religion in general, are *necessarily* in conflict because of some essential difference between the two. This he contrasts with lists of contingent conflicts, choosing Colin Russell's (1928–2013) four areas of possible disputes as his example. These include: (1) instances of conflict between the worldviews of science and (some) religion; (2) the uses of different methodologies; (3) being backed by or supporting different sets of values; and (4) social conflicts between different groups. Examples of each of these (along with counter-examples) are all easy to find.

1 *Worldviews*: We have already seen an instance of this in Chapter 6. A Christian worldview prior to the development of modern sciences based on inviolable natural laws had incorporated both natural regularities (willed by God, especially due to creatures being created with their own causal powers) as well as miracles, or what I prefer to call special divine actions. The physico-theologians in various ways tried to hold these together, but their positions turned out to be unstable, and I argued that the split (in the USA at least) between modern liberal and conservative Protestants is most basically between those who accepted the scientific worldview incorporating a closed causal order versus those who continue to hold to what are now called "divine interventions."

2 *Different methodologies*: There has been, beginning in the modern period, a developing account of what counts as scientific methodology, from Francis Bacon's

inductivism—that is, to collect the instances of a phenomenon, such as heat, and make generalizations about what they have in common—to Imre Lakatos's account of confirming scientific research programs. It is quite interesting to note that there are instances, throughout this history of developments in theories of scientific methodologies, of theologians arguing that their methods are parallel to science's, from some late-nineteenth-century Princeton theologians' claims that doctrines are produced by induction from the facts to be found in the Bible, to, for example, my call for a closer approximation of theological method to Lakatos's methodology.[1]

3 *Different values*: It is often said that science fosters values of the search for truth, but also of control of nature and practical applications in technology, while religion fosters love of God and neighbor, and an ethical lifestyle. It seems undeniable that the general aims of science and of *religion* are different, while the question of whether they are in conflict is a matter of dispute. However, it is more apt to compare the theoretical aspect of science to the discipline of theology. Here, both value truth and understanding, both have a common ethic of openness and honesty, and both aim to have practical import for human lives.

4 *Social conflicts*: Cantor provides the example of one such conflict in Victorian Britain, when "a group of scientific naturalists sought to wrest power from the Established Church."[2] We shall see below that the strong conflict thesis in the USA largely began as a result of two late-nineteenth-century books, whose authors were particularly concerned with wresting control of colleges from clergymen, in favor of presidents who preferred promotion of science over theology and Christian formation.

   The strong form of the conflict thesis provides a master narrative that does count (for many) as a myth in the anthropological sense. "Myth," here, refers to a story that conveys commonly shared convictions on the purpose and meaning of life. For example, although few outside of biblical studies actually know the Babylonian creation myth (to which OT creation stories are widely believed to be opposed), Walter Wink (1935–2012) cites it as the source of the myth of redemptive violence, which "undergirds American popular culture, civil religion, nationalism, and foreign-policy." All that is needed to see its continuing hold on popular

---

[1]   See Nancey Murphy, *Theology in the Age of Scientific Reasoning* (Ithaca, NY: Cornell University Press, 1990), ch. 3, sec. 4 for an overview.

[2]   Geoffrey Cantor, "What Shall We Do With the 'Conflict Thesis,'" in Thomas Dixon, Geoffrey Cantor, and Stephen Pumphrey, eds., *Science and Religion: New Historical Perspectives* (Cambridge: Cambridge University Press, 2000), 284–5; referring to Colin A. Russell, "The Conflict of Science and Religion," in Gary B. Ferngren et al., eds., *The History of Science and Religion in the Western Tradition: An Encyclopedia* (New York and London: Garland, 2000), 12–16.

culture is to watch cartoons on television, in which "the good guy" overcomes evil by killing "the bad guy."[3]

The strong conflict thesis is a subplot of this storyline. From the science side, it is the story of virtuous seekers of truth defeating the dark powers of superstition and obeisance to inept authorities. Brad Kallenberg (b.1958) has pointed out that depictions on the backs of cars, showing a larger Jesus-fish devouring a smaller Darwin-fish, are a pictorial representation of the conflict myth seen from the Christian side.[4] Thomas Dixon (b.1973) writes that the image of conflict has "been attractive to some religious believers, who use it to portray themselves as members of an embattled but righteous minority struggling heroically to protect their faith against the oppressive and intolerant forces of science and materialism."[5]

I and many others believe that the strong conflict thesis is (and I would go further and say *has to be*) a myth in the sense of "myths" as simply false.

2.1 History of the myth

One important reason for many historians' rejection of the strong conflict thesis is that its influence can be rather precisely dated. David Lindberg (b.1935) and Ronald Numbers write that sustained debate began slightly over a century ago, beginning especially with the two books I mentioned above, published in 1874 and 1896, and to which I return below.

This is not to say that conflicts did not exist regarding Galileo's work, coming to a head with his condemnation in 1633; and after the publication of Darwin's two most influential books, *On the Origin of Species* in 1859, and especially after publication in 1871 of *The Descent of Man*.

So now, back to Lindberg and Numbers: They trace the sustained arguments over the conflict thesis to books by John Draper (1811–82) and Andrew Dixon White (1832–1911). Draper first taught chemistry and physics at New York University but turned to writing history after 1850. By that time, he had abandoned his original Methodist faith in favor of rational theism. He was invited to write his *History of the Conflict between Religion and Science*, in which he especially excoriated the Catholic Church, in part as a reaction to a recent papal decree that elevated revealed doctrine above the *human* (note: not *natural*) sciences.[6]

---

[3] Walter Wink, *Engaging the Powers: Discernment and Resistance in a World of Domination* (Minneapolis, MN: Augsburg Fortress, 1992), ch. 1.

[4] Brad J. Kallenberg, *Live to Tell: Evangelism for a Postmodern Age* (Grand Rapids, MI: Brazos Press, 2002), 48.

[5] Thomas Dixon, *Science and Religion: A Very Short Introduction* (Oxford: Oxford University Press, 2008), 2.

[6] John William Draper, *History of the Conflict between Religion and Science* (New York: D. Appleton & Co., 1874); Andrew Dickson White, *A History of the Warfare of Science with Theology in Christendom*, 2 vols. (New York: D. Appleton & Co., 1986)

The book was quickly and widely criticized because clearly he had illegitimately projected bitter animosity by the Catholic Church toward science all the way back to the fourth century, saying that the hands of the church were "steeped in blood." Nonetheless, he offered praise of other religious bodies, from Islam to Protestantism. Yet the book was widely read—it went through 50 printings and was translated into ten languages.

White's *A History of the Warfare of Science with Theology in Christendom*, however, turned out to be more influential. White was the first president of Cornell University. Lindberg and Numbers say that

> [h]e began writing on science and religion as part of an effort to discredit religious critics envious of the funds given to his new university . . . and distressed by its thoroughgoing secularism, typified by White's stated desire to create "an asylum for *science*—where truth shall be taught for truth's sake, not stretched or cut exactly to fit Revealed Religion".[7]

White's book was initially accepted by many because it appeared to have been well researched; however, throughout the twentieth century, increasingly sophisticated histories were written, such as Robert Merton's (1910–2003) "Science, Technology and Society in Seventeenth Century England,"[8] and followed by an ever-larger body of historical writings by many others. So a second factor in the rejection of the strong conflict thesis was simply the increasing amount and sophistication of historical studies. Nonetheless, the warfare myth still continues on the part of some scientists and in some quarters of Christianity, especially in the USA. This continuation can be partly attributed to the media's tendency to report on conflicts while ignoring positive developments in dialogues between theology and the sciences.

Lindberg and Numbers write that the continued acceptance of White's work, in light of these later histories, "overlooked mounting evidence that White read the past through battle-scarred glasses."[9] What is it that left White "battle-scarred"? In great measure it was the fourth type of (real) controversy described by Russell between conflicting social groups. Frank Turner (1944–2010) points to a shift in prestige and power in colleges and universities from the long-held authority of religious bodies to practitioners of science.[10] Most colleges were founded

---

[7] David C. Lindberg and Ronald L. Numbers, eds., *God & Nature: Historical Essays on the Encounter between Christianity and Science* (Berkeley: University of California Press, 1986), 13; quotation of White by Bruce Mazlish in his Preface to the 1965 ed. of *History of the Warfare*, 13.

[8] Robert K. Merton, "Science, Technology and Society in Seventeenth Century England," *Osiris* 4 (1938): 432–4.

[9] Lindberg and Numbers, *God & Nature*, 3.

[10] Frank M. Turner, "The Victorian Conflict between Science and Religion: A Professional Dimension," *Isis* 69 (1978): 356–76.

by Christian denominations, and their presidents were usually clergymen, who often taught "capstone" courses at the end of the curriculum to put the whole of it into proper denominational context.

There were political overtones to the debate, as well. Upper-class views easily accommodated themselves to a perfectly ordered cosmos. Stephen Toulmin uses the term "Cosmopolis" to refer to a worldview that gives an account of the order of the cosmos and, at the same time, provides rational justification for the order of society. The modern Galilean–Newtonian picture of the cosmos as stable and organized around the sun served as justification for new political arrangements, whose center was the monarch: "the planetary model of society was explicitly *cosmopolitical.* Without such a justification, the imposition of a hierarchy on 'the lower orders' by 'the better sort' of people would be arbitrary and self-serving."[11]

In light of Toulmin's thesis, it should not be surprising that strongest reactions against science in the USA—especially against Darwinian science and "scientific" criticism of the Bible—would come (and continues to come) from among social groups that were already feeling culturally marginalized. Fundamentalism was organized and inspired in large part by a series of pamphlets titled *The Fundamentals,* published by The World's Christian Fundamentalist Association, founded in 1909. The prominence of Fundamentalism has waxed and waned since then, but still provides the most organized opposition to science. Also, not surprisingly, the opposition is most often focused on control of education.

Meanwhile, "liberal" or "modernist" Protestantism adapted both to new societal and cultural transformations and to the new biblical criticism and developments in science. More on this in section 4 regarding the mixed reactions to evolutionary biology.

2.2 This text: Lessons from philosophy

There are two types of lessons regarding theology and science to be drawn from what has been written in this text so far. One is the point, already mentioned above in section 1, that Christian theology and science cannot be conceived as having a conflictual relationship from the beginning because what we refer to as "science" today did not exist before the modern period. The second lesson is that even *if* there have been no real or significant conflicts between the contents of Christian theology and the contents of modern science, the developments in modern *philosophy* occasioned by the scientific revolution have been major sources of crises for the Christian Tradition.

---

[11] Stephen Toulmin, *Cosmopolis: The Hidden Agenda of Modernity* (New York: Macmillan, 1990), ch. 3 (quotation p. 135).

2.2.1 Anachronistic projections

This subsection can be relatively brief, because it amounts to drawing together points already made and simply relating them to the strong conflict thesis regarding science and religion. The Introduction to this volume stressed the fact that terms used in philosophical discussions often have sharply different meanings in different centuries. I quoted with approval MacIntyre's claim that one of the last disciplines to recognize its historicity has been philosophy. He writes: "Philosophers have often been prepared to acknowledge this historical character in respect of scientific theories; but they have usually wanted to exempt their own thinking from this same historicity."[12] MacIntyre published this essay in 1977, and I would quibble with his claim that philosophers had, *at that time*, often been willing to accept the historical character of science. Thomas Kuhn, Paul Feyerabend, and Imre Lakatos have been credited with introducing historicism into philosophy of science, and all were still highly controversial throughout the 1970s. However, there were no debates at Berkeley, of which I was aware, of historicism in philosophy; the only professor who acknowledged it was Paul Feyerabend (see Chapter 1, section 2.1).

For this reason, Jeffrey Stout's argument that the predominant method in Anglo-American philosophy—conceptual analysis—had been completely delegitimized by W. V. O. Quine's "Two Dogmas of Empiricism" in 1951 was a welcome development. He argued that the definition of Anglo-American philosophy as conceptual *analysis* needs to be replaced by the understanding of philosophy as conceptual *archaeology*. One has to enquire, regarding significant philosophical concepts, when and by whom (which culture) the concept was so defined.[13]

Chapters 1 and 2 drew out contrasts between ancient Greek *episteme* and Latin *scientia* versus the concept of science developed in the modern period. So late modern writers such as Draper simply had to be wrong to claim that the Catholic Church opposed (what we now think of as) science since the fourth century. In the next subsection I shall provide brief reminders of what was said in Chapter 6 regarding the slowly emerging distinction between modern science and theology.

Two further points are worth noting here. Historian of science Michael Shank (b.1949) has written that the history of the Galileo affair has been condensed into a (wholly simplistic) narrative: Galileo proved the Copernican theory; the

---

[12] Alasdair MacIntyre, "Epistemological Crises, Dramatic Narrative, and the Philosophy of Science," *Monist* 60, no. 4 (October 1977): 453–72. Reprinted in Gary Gutting, ed., *Paradigms and Revolutions: Applications and Appraisals of Thomas Kuhn's Philosophy of Science* (Notre Dame, IN: University of Notre Dame Press, 1980), 54–74; and also in Stanley Hauerwas and L. Gregory Jones, eds., *Why Narrative: Readings in Narrative Theology* (Grand Rapids, MI: Eerdmans, 1989), 138–57 (page references are to this reprint, 141).

[13] Jeffrey Stout, *The Flight from Authority: Religion, Morality, and the Quest for Autonomy* (Notre Dame, IN: University of Notre Dame Press, 1981), esp. 2.

Catholic Church condemned him for doing so; and thereby astronomy/science was set back. Then this narrative has been used as *the* paradigm to interpret relations between science and Christianity both before and after Galileo's time. One example is the claim that Hypatia, one of the first female mathematicians and philosophers, was killed by Christians in Alexandria in AD 415 because of her *scientific* views. A much better historical hypothesis is that she was caught between two conflicting parties within Christianity.[14] Historian John Heilbron (b.1934) provides a contemporary example. Some creationists have blamed Galileo for his part in "creating the myth" that the Bible is inimical to science.[15]

As will be detailed below (section 3), Galileo's major impact did not so much involve a conflict between science and theology as a clash of worldviews, one based largely on Aristotelian philosophy and a new one based on an equally ancient account of matter (atomism), provided by Democritus and Epicurus (391–270 BC).

The second point worth noting is that while eighteenth-century Deists were often called atheists, genuine atheism only became a live intellectual option in the English-speaking world near the middle of the nineteenth century. A major reason was the belief that, without religion of some kind, morality could not be justified (or enforced by fear of punishment).[16] So the strong conflict thesis, pitting militant *atheistic* scientists against Christian believers, or vice versa, could not be conceivable before that point.

2.2.2 Science and genuine crises

This subsection will also consist largely of reminders of material already presented, but focusing on genuine crises faced by the Christian Tradition beginning in the modern period, and with slightly more attention to the role of science in contributing to (largely) philosophical changes that created the crises.

The two most significant crises stemmed from the shift in epistemology from the ancient and medieval categories of *scientia* and *opinio* to the modern emphasis on empirical knowledge. It is somewhat ironic that some attempts to adapt theology to the new epistemology contributed to the second, equally severe, crisis regarding special divine action. Other, more circumscribed, crises are related to these two: (1) the challenge to biblical authority coming largely from modern historical-critical methods; (2) the critical nature of the plurality of religions; and (3) the powerful skepticism stemming from lack of an answer

---

[14] Michael Shank, "The Long Reach of the Galileo Affair: From Hypatia to Recent Times," unpublished paper presented at The University of Notre Dame, April 3, 2017, typescript pp. 5–7. Published with permission.

[15] John Heilbron, "Galileo: The Man and the Emblem," unpublished paper presented at The University of Notre Dame, April 3, 2017, typescript p. 9. Published with permission.

[16] James Turner, *Without God, Without Creed: The Origins of Unbelief in America* (Baltimore and London: Johns Hopkins University Press, 1985); Charles Taylor, *A Secular Age* (Cambridge, MA: Harvard University Press, 2007). More on these sources in Chapter 10.

to the problem of natural evil. And, of course, we might say that the stark differentiation between science and theology has become a crisis in itself (to be further explored in Chapter 10).

Epistemology. Recall that René Descartes was working before the decisive modern epistemological shift. Seeing no hope for restoring *opinio* due to the conflicting religious authorities of his day, he set out to uphold both theology and science by means of demonstrative reasoning (*scientia* as understood in his day). In the process, he developed his foundationalist metaphor and proposed the clear and distinct ideas in his mind as a source of the new foundation. Both his foundationalism and his inside-out epistemology have been decisively rejected in science. However, they deterred attempts to find acceptable modern justifications for theological knowledge. Descartes's participation in the development of a new (non-Aristotelian) physics encouraged him to believe that universal knowledge, based on human reason alone, was possible.

Between Descartes and David Hume there was the immense influence of *Logic, or the Art of Thinking* (1662) written by authors associated with an abbey at Port Royal in France. Beginning with the metaphor of God's two books, nature and the Bible, it had come to be the case by Hume's day that the "witness" of nature (weight of empirical evidence) had displaced, for many, the witnesses recorded in the Bible. So the shift to modern empiricism came to predominate. The question persists to this day as to whether theology can meet this new standard for justification. Among many philosophers, at least, Hume's multifaceted negative judgment (approximately 100 years after *Logic*) has been taken to be definitive.

I mentioned above that, as theories of scientific justification have developed, there have been corresponding attempts to show that theological reasoning is at least parallel to that of science. More interesting, I believe, were the varying strategies of the physico-theologians to attach theology, one might say, to science's coattails. I believe that my brief account of Robert Boyle's work (in Chapter 6) is sufficient to show the instability of this variegated movement: divine providence (only?) via the laws of nature, but combined with special divine action described in Scripture. Unfortunately, providential deism was an unstable position. How can one hold on to God as a source of revelation, and even as the cause of Jesus' resurrection, as Boyle did, while also ruling out all *special providence* in favor of *general* providence seen in the consequences of the laws of nature? Boyle resolved this problem by conceiving of the laws simply as the regularities in God's usual way of acting, but maintained that God could "intermeddle" in the world in special cases, such as the scriptural miracles.[17]

---

[17] John Hedley Brooke, *Science and Religion: Some Historical Perspectives* (Cambridge: Cambridge University Press, 1991), 134.

Historians such as James Turner, however, write that soon special providence came to be seen as awkward and archaic.[18] At this point, providential deism, leaving no intelligible place for divine effects such as miracles and revelation, was in many cases replaced in the eighteenth century by Deism as usually understood. From the absentee God of Deism, it was a short step to atheism. The shift from providential deism to Deism itself was thus a consequence of the new account of divine action. From the Reformers' view that the age of miracles had passed, the providential deists moved on to question the historicity of the founding miracles of the faith and thus of the whole concept of incarnation.[19] The historicity of all of the Abrahamic religions was marginalized. Also, we still hear the phrase "God of the gaps" to describe Isaac Newton's use of God as needed in his physics.

Immanuel Kant's attempt to rescue religion and morality from Hume's skeptical arguments is taken by many to have definitively distinguished science from religion by placing science in the sphere of knowledge (empirical knowledge of the phenomenal world) and religion within the sphere of doing (ethics based on moral intuitions).[20] The connection to science here is that Kant also intended to save Newtonian physics from Hume's skepticism.

I mentioned early on that I would only describe conflicts among historians and interpreters when they matter for purposes at hand. One that does indeed matter is whether Kant argued that God exists, or only that we need to *presuppose* "the ideas of reason" to make sense of our moral intuitions: these are free will, the immortality of the soul, and the existence of God. I can speak only anecdotally here, but in the very secular philosophy department at University of California, Berkeley, the emphasis was on the necessity only of the *supposition*, along with acceptance of Kant's claim to have rebutted the three major arguments for God's existence: the cosmological, the ontological, and the design arguments. At the Graduate Theological Union the emphasis was on Kant's claim in the preface of his *Critique of Pure Reason* (1781), that he had "found it necessary to deny knowledge, in order to make room for faith."[21] Kant's later work, *Religion within the Limits of Reason Alone* (1793), is notoriously difficult to interpret. So it would take years of study to confirm the suspicion that Christians see Kant as having argued for God's existence, while secular philosophers see him as only pointing out an intellectual condition for understanding morality.

If Kant's rebuttals of arguments for God's existence are taken to be definitive by theologians; if, as Hume and others have done, the criteria proposed in the

---

[18] Turner, *Without God, Without Creed*, 38.
[19] Charles Taylor, *Sources of the Self: The Making of Modern Identity* (Cambridge, MA: Harvard University Press, 1989), 272.
[20] Kant's brief and more accessible account is in his *Prolegomena to any Future Metaphysics* (1783).
[21] Quoted in Wallace I. Matson, *A New History of Philosophy*, 2 vols. (San Diego: Harcourt Brace Jovanovich, 1987), 2:398.

Port Royal *Logic* are applied to Scripture with often drastically skeptical conclusions; and if the existence of a plurality of religions also reduces confidence in the revealed status of the Bible, then we can see why Claude Welch would state that at the beginning of the nineteenth century the question was how (if at all) theology was possible.

Again: what has science to do with all of this? The design argument had become a staple for those seeking a rational religion consistent with science. Hume had called it into question by insisting that when the order or goodness of the world was taken as *empirical evidence* for God's existence, then so too must be the disorder and evil. In addition, Kant's restriction of the concept of *cause* to the phenomenal world entailed that a noumenal God could not be the cause of the world. Finally, the regularities in nature discovered by science called into question anything smacking of the miraculous in the Bible.

Friedrich Schleiermacher followed Kant in taking religion out of the category of knowledge, but instead placing it in the category of judgment or feeling. In so doing he founded Protestant liberal theology, according to which religion is a matter of *human* religious awareness. There is then no possible way for theology to conflict with (or be confirmed by) science. In a sense, then, liberal theology has been much more influenced by science than conservative theology, because the move to evade conflict with science, as well as to solve the epistemological problem of finding a way for theology to stand up to the rational criteria of (scientific) empiricism, led to a complete redefinition of the very subject matter of the discipline.

Divine action: I suggested above that one strategy for meeting the demands placed on theology by the new epistemology was the physico-theologians' various strategies to tie at least some elements of theology to the successful new science. Newton's is the most obvious case, in his asserting that the main business of his mechanics was to culminate with the first cause (Chapter 6, section 3.1 and 5).

In Chapter 6 I gave more attention to Robert Boyle's contribution to what I have termed, borrowing from Charles Taylor, "providential deism." For Calvinist motives, namely to extract as much causal efficacy from creation as possible so as to attribute it to God, he placed more emphasis than many of his predecessors on God's providential ordering of the cosmos by means of the laws of nature. These laws, in accordance with God's omniscience and omnipotence, were taken to be universal and inviolable.

As already noted, providential deism turned out to be an unstable position. Nonetheless, the concept of universal and inviolable natural laws has come to be a staple of natural science. The negative consequences for theology have already been detailed in Chapter 6. I argued that the difference between immanentist and interventionist accounts of divine action is the basis for the split in modern Protestant theology (at least in the USA) between liberals and conservatives. While liberal immanentism has the advantage over conservative interventionism in ruling out science–theology conflicts, it detaches Christian doctrine from traditional accounts of salvation history and makes explanation of the concept of revelation difficult (to say the least). Also, in my view (but supported by MacIntyre, Stout, and others), a theology that pertains only to believers' *interpretation* of their experience and of reality in general is of little interest to those in the secular academy. Meanwhile, skirmishes between theology and science perceived by conservatives continue, usually to be lost, and therefore are also of little interest to most of the secular academy. But now: back to two genuine and persistent (perceptions of) conflict(s)—Galileo and Darwin.

3 The Galileo affair

In the sixteenth century, as most readers probably know, Christians were killing other Christians in great numbers. Copernicus invented his theory of the organization of the universe during that time, but it was not even discussed at the momentous Catholic Council of Trent, which lasted from 1545 to 1563. Yet the Council's emphasis on moral reform and clearly defined doctrines meant that Galileo was born into a much more rigid church a century later. In light of Protestant emphases on the ability of individuals themselves to interpret the Bible, Catholic controversies continued to focus sharply on who *did* have the authority to determine biblical teaching. Animosities toward Galileo came to a head in 1633 on just this matter. This resulted from a spat between him and his old friend, Maffeo Barberini, who later became Pope Urban VIII (1568–1644). Barberini enjoyed scientific arguments and was generally pleased with Galileo's work, so long as he stayed away from pronouncements on how to interpret Scripture. The problem arose when, as Pope, he requested Galileo to add to his *Dialogue Concerning the Two Chief World Systems* (1632) the Pope's own argument that definitive conclusions could not be reached in the natural sciences. Galileo did include the argument, but he put it in the mouth of Simplicio, often cast as the dullard character in the *Dialogue*.[22] The Pope was not amused. If this were all that was involved, it would appear to have been a tempest in a teapot.

However, it is important to keep in mind that acceptance of the Copernican system would, in fact, tear down the entire Medieval Synthesis, which intrinsically ties theology to the sciences, ethics, and political and religious orders. The first problem was to completely revise Aristotelian physics, with its significant ties to the rest of the system. According to Aristotle and the most effective synthesizer of his writings with theology, Thomas Aquinas, all things were composed of the

---

[22] John Brooke and Geoffrey Cantor, *Reconstructing Nature: The Engagement of Science and Religion* (New York and Oxford: Oxford University Press, 1998), 110.

four elements: earth, air, fire, and water. The elements had natural motions: earth downward toward the surface of the Earth, fire upwards toward the heavens, and so forth. But this does not make sense if the Earth is not in the center of the universe. Seventeenth-century scientists had already begun the wholesale rejection of the Aristotelian system, replacing his physics with another ancient philosophy— atomism. But note that this was not in itself a clash of science with theology; it was rather between the *old* science and the *new* science. In Cantor's and Russell's terms, it was a clash of worldviews.

Thomas Kuhn writes that his book, *The Copernican Revolution*, displays the oddity of repeatedly violating "the institutionalized boundaries which separate the audience for 'science' from the audience for 'history' or 'philosophy.'"[23] Despite what I have just written above about Galileo's astronomy and Urban's concerns about biblical interpretation not being a theology versus science issue, the oddity of what Kuhn wrote about his book is that he should have mentioned the violation of boundaries separating science from theology, and also ethics. Max Wildiers (1904–96) writes that the (scholarly) opponents of Galileo acknowledged that his observations were correct, but that they "would not concede that these contained confirmation of the Copernican system. They were simply not prepared to forsake Aristotle, whose philosophy was so closely related to the theology of the time..."[24] In addition, he writes:

> the consequences of the Copernican revolution were also felt in the moral sphere. For centuries morality had been closely allied to a concept of order largely subject to the prevailing cosmology. Thus in his conduct man had to respect the same perfect, hierarchical order that the Creator had established in the world. However, it was just this perfect and hierarchical order that had now become problematic. Was the old idea of order still an acceptable criterion to distinguish good and evil? And if not, on what basis was morality to be founded?[25]

Recall the description of the great chain of being in Chapter 7 (sections 2.1 and 3.3) and its final demise in the eighteenth century. Recall also Stephen Toulmin's description of a Cosmopolis (above, section 2.1), a picture of the cosmos that justifies the political order. Wildiers writes that the new astronomy posed a threat to the very structure of society in that it was thought that society had to observe

---

[23] Thomas S. Kuhn, *The Copernican Revolution: Planetary Astronomy in the Development of Western Thought* (Cambridge, MA: Harvard University Press, 1957), viii.

[24] N. Max Wildiers, *The Theologian and his Universe: Theology and Cosmology from the Middle Ages to the Present* (New York: Seabury Press, 1982), 97.

[25] Wildiers, *Theologian and his Universe*, 106.

the same hierarchical order as exemplified in the cosmos. "A revolution in astronomy thus resulted in a revolution throughout the entire culture."[26]

The atomism that led to such success in physics was therefore extrapolated to all sorts of other areas, in each case replacing the earlier medieval views. For example, philosopher Thomas Hobbes (1588–1644), in his *Leviathan* (1651), described the commonwealth as a collection of atomic individuals, governed by attractive and repulsive forces. Emotions were attributed to particles in motion around the heart; thinking was particles in motion in the brain.

So while it is the Copernican revolution that receives most attention, the revolution from Aristotelian physics and metaphysics to atomism, I believe, has not been adequately appreciated.

4 Darwin's ambiguous contribution to providential deism

The strategy of using the order of creation to reconcile natural science with Christian theology was taken over into the human sciences. Amos Funkenstein writes that a "respectable family of explanations in social and economic thought since the seventeenth century is sometimes known by the name 'invisible hand' explanations, a term borrowed from Adam Smith."[27]

Thomas Malthus (1766–1834), an Anglican clergyman working in the tradition of Smith's laissez-faire economics, published his *Essay on the Principle of Population* in 1798, in which he argued that population, if unchecked, would increase geometrically and food supply, at best, could only increase arithmetically. Here human commerce was understood specifically in terms of providential deism. Malthus's work was a pessimistic statement on the place of humankind in nature, but also a statement on the *divinely appointed* role of struggle, strife, and inequality. It was a theodicy of sorts, justifying suffering and death as the *natural* outcome of the tendency toward overpopulation, but also as the result of divine providence, in that evil produces exertion, exertion produces mind, and mind produces progress. He argued that humans were by nature sinful, sluggish, and averse to work; if population and food supply could increase at the same rate, it is probable that man might never have emerged from the savage state.

Malthus and other theologians of his day later became Charles Darwin's inspiration in discovering the mechanism of evolutionary change in natural selection. Darwin had set out on the *Beagle* expecting to find Paleyan-style evidence of the adaptation of organisms to their environments, and he was not disappointed. But divine design was not needed to account for this adaptation. Only two principles

---

[26] Wildiers, *Theologian and his Universe*, 106.

[27] Amos Funkenstein, *Theology and the Scientific Imagination from the Middle Ages to the Seventeenth Century* (Princeton, NJ: Princeton University Press, 1986), 202.

were needed: variation and natural selection. Selection would be the natural outcome of Malthusian population pressure.

Darwin's two major books, *Origin of Species* and *Descent of Man*, were published in 1859 and 1871, respectively. Why was Darwin's achievement, his new-found ability to account for biological facts in terms of laws of nature, not universally welcomed as a magnificent contribution to providential deism? Surely part of the answer is that Darwin had drawn the language of his theory from his cultural context. Darwin's readers were primed to find in his writings a one-sided picture—to read his often-ambiguous language in a particular manner, drawn from the background of Malthusian negative images of humankind.

Darwin's popularizer, Thomas Huxley (1825–95), wrote that from the moral point of view "the animal world is on about the same level as a gladiator's show." He condemned Christians for worshiping what was plainly unworthy—a God who had created a process in which evil humankind came into existence by virtue of its success over the other animals by cunning, ruthlessness, and ferocity. I believe that in contrast to those who deny the *evidence* for evolutionary theory,[28] the main motives behind attacks today still have more to do with the fear that evolutionary theory, associating us with the "beasts," is destroying the moral fiber of society.[29] What this worry fails to take into account is the extent to which evolution of humans now is to a great extent cultural evolution rather than biological.

From the beginning, however, there have also been enthusiastic and often brilliant moves to reconcile the new biology with Christian doctrine. David Livingstone (b.1953) wrote in his 1987 book that a new wave of evolution phobia was sweeping through Britain and America, and the purpose of his book was to counter the presumption that anti-evolutionists were "guardians of Christian orthodoxy," whereas in fact a "substantial number of the most distinguished representatives of evangelical orthodoxy found the theological resources to absorb the latest scientific findings."[30]

Livingstone's book is a welcome antidote to the assumption that conservative Christians can almost be defined by their objections to evolutionary biology, while liberal Protestants easily accommodated to it. However, another historical

---

[28] E.g., Phillip E. Johnson, *Darwin on Trial* (Downers Grove, IL: InterVarsity Press, 1991).

[29] Phillip Johnson's second book, *Reason in the Balance: The Case Against Naturalism in Science, Law and Education* (Downers Grove, IL: InterVarsity Press, 1995), has in the first chapter approximately 20 references to male and female sex roles, family, monogamy, and sexual behavior. I believe that this illustrates a major motivation for the campaign against evolutionary biology—the belief that it undermines "traditional family values."

[30] David N. Livingstone, *Darwin's Forgotten Defenders: The Encounter between Evangelical Theology and Evolutionary Thought* (Grand Rapids, MI and Edinburgh: Eerdmans and Scottish Academic Press, 1987), ix, xii.

thesis, equally disturbing to the liberal versus conservative assumption, is found in James Moore's (b.1947) evaluation of post-Darwinian controversies. He claims that it was only the more "orthodox" theologies that could accommodate evolutionary theory and that "liberal Christian Darwinism" in the late nineteenth century was actually the imposition on biology of the Romantic worldview of the time, with its emphasis on inevitable progress. He calls the latter "Darwinisticism" to highlight its deep ties to Romanticism. He writes that "those whose theology possessed the resources by which dissonance [between Darwinism and theology] could be reduced . . . would not have needed to . . . reduce their dissonance at the expense of Darwinism; whereas those whose theology lacked these resources would have had to reduce their dissonance by modifying Darwinism to one degree or another."[31]

Moore argues that one of the reasons Darwin's thought was consistent with orthodoxy was that it postulated a universe in which there are meaningful historical processes (in contrast to some Platonic alternatives), and in which humankind was the latest and noblest species, but this was not (as Romanticists would say) the result of necessary progression. Also, Darwin's thoroughly empirical account of biological change eschewed the sorts of occult qualities or vital forces to which the physico-theologians were opposed. And, again, Malthus's principle of population "gave the lie to notions of limitless and automatic progress," and stressed the need for virtue if the evils of overpopulation were to be avoided.[32]

I hope, then, that my brief narratives about Galileo's and Darwin's contexts have done a bit to lessen the image of science–religion warfare. I turn now to but a few of the positive relations between science and Christianity.

5 Positive relations between science and Christian theology

The whole of the next chapter will be devoted to the question of how science, particularly the cognitive neurosciences, can be seen to be consonant with Christian anthropology. I argue for a positive relation, but this is still seen to be controversial in many theological quarters.

It is also possible to use evolutionary theory as an aid to theology in replacing (to some degree) the Augustinian explanation of human sinfulness. For at least 1,000 years the Augustinian understanding of human sinfulness was based on an exegesis of the second creation story in Genesis, attributing the perversion of human nature to Adam's sin. This account has been rejected by countless scholars on the basis of textual exegesis.

---

[31] James R. Moore, *The Post-Darwinian Controversies: A Study of the Protestant Struggle to Come to Terms with Darwin in Great Britain and America, 1870–1900* (Cambridge: Cambridge University Press, 1979), 302.

[32] Moore, *Post-Darwinian Controversies*, 308–12, *passim*.

So if Adam's seed did not sow evil into the hearts of humans, why do we have such remarkable tendencies to go against the teachings of the Bible? Evolutionary theory provides a significant amount of help here. For *Homo sapiens* to have evolved, our ancestors had to have tendencies to retaliate against aggressors, to fight off threats to their children, to hoard food, to defend territory, and so forth. We are still predisposed to these tendencies by our genetic heritage. Recognizing this, we can see why Jesus taught us not to return evil for evil, to share with the needy, to invite strangers into our homes, and so forth. As I said above, our evolution is now largely cultural, and the church is God's gift to culture to recondition us in these ways.

My main focus in this section, however, is the doctrine of creation. In the Middle Ages there was a consensus among theologians that the doctrine of God's creation of the universe was relevant to all sorts of cosmological issues, such as the nature of time and the question of whether the universe had a beginning. However, due to factors in the modern period, described above, many theologians concluded that theology in general and the doctrine of creation in particular are *irrelevant* to the big cosmological questions; theology is basically about *humankind's* relation to God. The ironic development in our own day is that science is now putting all of those big cosmological questions back on the table. And it is an important challenge to current theologians to deal with them.

The following are points upon which theologians largely agreed, from the early centuries of the Christian era through the Protestant Reformation, relating to Christian teaching about creation. First, the universe was created by God out of nothing—the common terminology is the Latin: creation *ex nihilo*. Second, is the conviction that God alone can create. Third, God created freely for the sake of love. Fourth, creation involves temporal origin; and fifth, the universe is essentially good. This very brief summary covers over tensions among these convictions, as well as differences in details of interpretation from one theologian to another. Nonetheless, this consensus provided foundational components of the dominant worldview in Western culture until the Enlightenment.

However, modern developments, both philosophical and scientific, have not only led to the rejection of these assumptions in secular culture, but have so eroded the doctrine's place in theology that, as American theologian Julian Hartt (1911–2010) says, it does not now have a vivid and compelling life in the churches.[33]

The historical factors leading to the loss of consensus on the meaning of creation are many. Jesuit theologian and historian Michael Buckley (b.1931) has argued persuasively that the way was prepared for this breakdown by pre-Enlightenment theologies in which attempts were made to support Christian faith by means of

---

[33] Julian Hartt, "Creation and Providence," in Peter C. Hodgson and Robert H. King, eds., *Christian Theology: An Introduction to Its Traditions and Tasks* (Philadelphia: Fortress Press, 1982), 15–140 (115).

philosophy alone, apart from any theological reasoning. Such arguments could support at best *thin* doctrines of God and creation.[34]

Other factors in the demise of the traditional consensus related in one way or another to the rise of modern science and, in particular, to scientific accounts of the origins of life and of the universe as a whole. And, as already stressed, the response to science that has had the most pervasive effect on mainline theology as a whole, and the doctrine of creation in particular, was the attempt by nineteenth-century liberal theologians to *immunize* theology from science. These strategies, inspired by Kant and following Schleiermacher, led to the so-called Copernican revolution in theology, the "turn to the subject." So the doctrine of creation is an expression of the Christian's *felt awareness* of the absolute dependence of all things on God, and has nothing to do with questions of origins.

In a rich variety of ways, mainline theologies up to the present have followed Schleiermacher in this anthropocentrizing tendency. For example, there is the contemporary American theologian Langdon Gilkey's concentration on the "religious meaning" of doctrines, which he defines as the attitude toward reality, life, and its meaning that the symbol (i.e., doctrine) expresses.[35]

While this turn to the subject began in Protestant theology, it has thoroughly affected (or, as I would prefer to say, *infected*) Catholic theology as well. For instance, in Karl Rahner's *Foundations of Christian Faith* the word "creation" does not occur in the table of contents; instead there is an entry on "Man's Relation to his Transcendent Ground: Creatureliness." Here the focus has shifted from *God's* act as creator to *human* experience of relationship to God.[36]

Much popular writing by scientists and philosophers today might be described, borrowing Gilkey's term, as reflections on the "religious meaning" of current debates in scientific cosmology. In light of the importance of these discussions in contemporary culture, theologians can no longer reduce the doctrine of creation to a reflection on humankind's relation to God, but must return to a consideration of the questions of origins, temporality, finitude, and others that were once thought of as central to the meaning of the doctrine. While science does not always support traditional Christian convictions, it certainly shows that most of the issues comprising the earlier theological consensus are back on the table.

In the remainder of this section, I shall address briefly some of the issues pertinent to the older theological consensus on creation and show how contemporary developments in cosmology have led to the revival of those discussions.

---

[34] Michael J. Buckley, SJ, *At the Origins of Modern Atheism* (New Haven, CT: Yale University Press, 1987).

[35] Langdon Gilkey, "Creation," in Donald W. Musser and Joseph L. Price, eds., *A New Handbook of Christian Theology* (Nashville: Abingdon Press, 1992), 107–13 (108).

[36] Karl Rahner, *Foundations of Christian Faith: An Introduction to the Idea of Christianity* (New York: Seabury Press, 1978).

5.1 Creation in time

The most obvious of the theological issues that has been reopened by developments in cosmology is the question of whether God created the universe in time or
from eternity. That is, did the universe have a temporal beginning, or has it always
existed, with its existence dependent upon God? Recall from what I wrote earlier,
that by the time Schleiermacher published his systematic theology (this was in
the 1830s), it was being argued that whether or not the universe had a beginning
in time was irrelevant to the doctrine of creation. It had been quite otherwise in
earlier Christian thought. For example, in confronting Aristotle's argument for the
eternity of the universe, Thomas Aquinas claimed that Scripture teaches that
the universe was in fact created in time, but he argued that the notion of an eternal
universe is *not* incompatible with the doctrine of creation. This is because the doctrine is essentially about the contingency of the universe, that is, its dependence for
its existence on the will of God. Thus, God could have created from all eternity.[37]
In contrast, Thomas's contemporary, Bonaventure (1221–74), argued that the eternity of the universe was *inconceivable* in that it is impossible to add to an infinite
number or to pass through an infinite series. Thus, if time were eternal the world
would never have arrived at the present day; yet, it is clear that it has.[38]

Copernicus overturned the Ptolemaic conceptions of the organization and
of the motion of the universe but not the conception of the universe as eternal
and static. However, the development of the science of thermodynamics in the
mid nineteenth century presented problems for the assumption of an *eternal*
universe—problems that Bonaventure would have appreciated. If physical systems
can undergo irreversible change at a finite rate, then they will have completed
those changes an infinite time ago and we could not be observing any such changes
today.[39]

In the 1920s astronomers had to give up the idea that the universe is *static*. Its
observable expansion forms the basis for the Big Bang theory of the origin of the
universe. This sudden origin was immediately interpreted by some—believers and
atheists alike—as confirmation of the traditional account of creation as temporal
origination. Cooler heads refused the temptation to claim that science had shown
the truth of the doctrine; Ernan McMullin's (1924–2001) account of the science
and theology as "consonant" has been judged by many to be the most reasonable.
He says that "if the universe began in time through the act of a Creator, from our

---

[37] Thomas Aquinas, *Summa contra gentiles*, 2, 38; *S.T.* Ia, 46, 2. Cf. Frederick Copleston, sj, *A History of
Philosophy*, vol. 2. (New York: Doubleday, 1962), ch. 36.

[38] Bonaventure, *Commentary on Book 2 of the Sentences*, I, I, I, 2, 3; cf. Copleston, *History*, ch. 28.

[39] Paul Davies, *The Mind of God: The Scientific Basis for a Rational World* (New York: Simon & Schuster,
1992), 46.

vantage point it would look something like the Big Bang that cosmologists are now talking about."[40]

More recent (and highly speculative) developments in theories of origins threaten this tidy consonance. A variety of cosmologists have attempted to go beyond what was once thought to be the absolute explanatory limit of science and explain the origin of the Big Bang itself. One of these is Andrei Linde (b.1948), who speculates that our universe started out as a very small bubble in space–time; the bubble's swift inflation produced the Big Bang.[41] While the notion that the universe must have expanded at a "fantastic" rate at the beginning is widely accepted, Linde's assumption that our universe is but one small bubble in an infinite assemblage of universes I take to be highly controversial. For our purposes, though, it is interesting to see how the very possibility raises again the centuries-old questions of whether the universe is eternal and whether an infinite universe is even conceivable—in this case, whether an infinite series of universes is conceivable.

So it is clear that if Linde's cosmology were to become widely accepted it would occasion major rethinking of Christian assumptions. One value I see in his account is as follows: the monotheistic faiths are contrasted with Eastern religions in that the latter assume cyclical recreations of the universe. It has long been argued that the linear view of history associated with the monotheistic religions is required to ensure the meaningfulness of history and of human endeavor. Yet it seems plausible to ask why an eternal God would create only one comparatively short-lived universe. The so-called "principle of plenitude," used by Augustine and others to account for the variety of forms of being *in* the universe, could easily be extended, it seems to me, to allow for the expectation that a God who creates as many forms of being as possible would also create as many universes as possible. Yet, such a plenitude of universes would not count against the meaningfulness of history since each universe would be self-contained and unique.

5.2 Creation out of nothing, contingency, and finitude

In this subsection, I first turn to another development in scientific cosmology: the "quantum cosmology" developed primarily by Stephen Hawking (1942–2018). This theory, whether or not it is ever confirmed scientifically, reopens several of the traditional theological debates.

---

[40] Ernan McMullin, "How Should Cosmology Relate to Theology?" in A. R. Peacocke, ed., *The Sciences and Theology in the Twentieth Century* (Notre Dame, IN: University of Notre Dame Press, 1981), 17–57 (39). However, I would not rule out use of Big Bang cosmology as support for a theological research program that takes its *primary* support from its own proper theological data. See my *Theology in the Age of Scientific Reasoning* (Ithaca, NY and London: Cornell University Press, 1990) for an account of empirical support for theological research programs.

[41] See Robert J. Russell, "Cosmology from Alpha to Omega," *Zygon* 29, no. 4 (1994): 557–77.

Hawking's work (as I understand it) depends on recognition that very early in the history of the universe there was a time when the universe would have been compressed enough in size for quantum effects to be significant. Because quantum events occur without causes in the classical sense, this raises the question whether the origin of the universe can be explained without cause, that is, as the result of quantum fluctuations.

In addition, at this scale, the fluctuations would affect space–time itself. Hawking argues that before 10^{-47} (i.e. 10 divided by 1 followed by 47 zeros) seconds into the universe's existence, space and time would not have been distinguishable as they are now.[42] Paul Davies says: "one might say that time emerges gradually from space," so there is "no actual 'first moment' of time, no absolute beginning at a singular origin."[43] Nevertheless, this does not mean that the universe is infinitely old; time is limited in the past but has no boundary.

A number of authors have commented on possible theological implications of Hawking's work, including Hawking himself. "So long as the universe had a beginning," he says, "we could suppose it had a creator. But if the universe is completely self-contained, having no boundary or edge, it would have neither beginning nor end: it would simply be."[44] Hawking is clearly mistaken in believing that the absence of a temporal starting point eliminates any necessity for a creator since, as we have just seen, traditional accounts such as Thomas's focus on the contingency of the universe: the doctrine of creation is *essentially* an answer to the question of why there is a universe at all, and only *accidentally* about its temporal origin.

However, Hawking's cosmology does legitimately raise a set of related theological issues. The first of these is the traditional emphasis that God's creation is *ex nihilo,* out of nothing. This notion was developed in the second century as the Christian response to a variety of Greek cosmologies. It is based on OT texts that are now seen to reflect explicit rejection of Babylonian creation myths, according to which the world is made of the severed body of a slain goddess. The doctrine of creation *ex nihilo* serves a variety of purposes in Christian theology: It maintains God's transcendence, over against views that the universe is somehow a part of or an emanation from God. It maintains God's sovereignty, over against the view that God's creative activity was constrained by the limitations of pre-existing matter, and thus provides grounds for the goodness of the created world, over against views based on the essential evil of matter itself. Finally, it emphasizes the

---

[42] See C. J. Isham, "Quantum Theories of the Creation of the Universe," in Robert J. Russell, Nancey Murphy, and C. J. Isham, eds., *Quantum Cosmology and the Laws of Nature: Scientific Perspectives on Divine Action* (Vatican City State and Berkeley: Vatican Observatory and Center for Theology and the Natural Sciences, 1983), 49–89.

[43] Davies, *Mind of God,* 67.

[44] Stephen W. Hawking, *A Brief History of Time* (London: Bantam Books, 1988), 141.

contingency of the universe: it could have been the case that there was nothing besides God.

Hawking's proposal does not provide a genuine analogy to the universe's origination out of nothing, since the coming into being of the universe, on his theory, presupposes the existence of a quantum vacuum, as well as the laws of quantum physics.[45] It does provoke some thought about what the word "nothing" really means, and more importantly it provokes thought about the nature and status of the laws of nature themselves, a topic to be addressed shortly. Hawking's work (along with that of many others) does confirm Augustine's insight that space and time must themselves be a part of the created order.

Wim Drees (b.1954) has argued that Hawking's elimination of an initial event with a special status recalls Christians to a traditional emphasis on God's creative activity understood as sustaining the universe in existence. All moments in Hawking's theory have a similar relation to the creator. "It is a nice feature of this quantum cosmology," says Drees, "that that part of the content of creation *ex nihilo* which was supposed to be the most decoupled from science, namely the 'sustaining,' can be seen as the most natural part in the context of the theory."[46]

The most subtle and comprehensive response to quantum cosmology, I believe, is that of Robert Russell. He points out that Hawking's theory requires theologians to make conceptual distinctions that have been passed over in earlier discussions. First, the concept of a temporally finite creation is distinguishable from the claim that there was a first event, designated as occurring at time zero $(t = 0)$. Second, it forces theologians to grapple with the very concept(s) of time that they presuppose.[47] A further conceptual distinction is that between finitude and boundedness, since Hawking's universe is finite but temporally unbounded.[48] Thus, theologians can no longer make a simple distinction, as Thomas and Bonaventure were able to do, between a finite universe created "in time" and an infinite universe created "from eternity."

5.3 The goodness of creation and the problem of evil

Two related aspects of the traditional understanding of God's creative activity support the conviction that the created world is essentially good. As already mentioned, part of the reason for saying that the universe is created out of nothing is to deny the possibility of intrinsic evil in the universe due to the evil or limitation

---

[45] Russell, "Cosmology from Alpha to Omega," 321.

[46] Wim Drees, "Beyond the Limitations of Big Bang Theory: Cosmology and Theological Reflection," *CTNS Bulletin* 8, no. 1 (1988): 1–15 (6).

[47] Robert J. Russell, "Finite Creation without a Beginning: The Doctrine of Creation in Relation to Big Bang and Quantum Cosmologies," in Russell et al., eds., *Quantum Cosmology and the Laws of Nature*, 293–329.

[48] Russell, "Finite Creation," 325.

of any pre-existing materials from which God was constrained to create. Second, God's creation was not *necessitated* by anything within or outside of God. Rather, creation was *motivated* by God's goodness, by love. Thus, Thomas argued that God created in order to diffuse his goodness.[49]

As emphasized in Chapter 7, it is against this theological background that the problem of evil appears. So when theologians address the problem of evil they have traditionally done so in connection with the doctrine of creation. Moral evil—that is, human sin—has always been the easiest to account for. A pressing current problem, though, is to reconcile the supposed free will of human sinners with deterministic natural laws, and this issue will be addressed in Chapter 9.

A brief reminder: Chapter 7 made use of the cosmological concept of the fine-tuning of the laws of nature to suggest that weakness and suffering are necessary, although presumably unwanted, by-products of conditions necessary for the existence of life.

5.4 Continuing creation and the laws of nature

The emphasis in the Christian Tradition on creation out of nothing has tended to obscure the fact that while the Bible does describe God as calling some things into being by his word, it also depicts God as crafting new beings out of pre-existing materials—humans from earth, for instance. Thus, *creatio ex nihilo* needs to be complemented by a doctrine of God's continuing creation. As already noted (Chapter 6), this doctrine, as well as traditional accounts of special providence and miracles, has been difficult to sustain since the rise of modern science due to the concept of the laws of nature.

Here is another area where developments in cosmology have put onto the table for discussion a concept with which theologians must reckon. I have already discussed possible implications of quantum theory. In addition, Davies has devoted an entire chapter in his book, *The Mind of God*, to questions about the status of the laws. He first surveys the history of the idea and points out that the view of laws as imposed upon matter, rather than inherent in it, was originally a medieval theological innovation meant to defend God's sovereignty over creatures. Early modern scientists believed that by discovering these laws they were uncovering God's rational design for the universe. As long as the laws were thought to be rooted in God, their existence was no more remarkable than that of matter. But with the divine underpinning removed, says Davies, "their existence becomes a profound mystery. Where do they come from? . . . Are the laws simply *there*—free-floating, so to speak—or should we abandon the very notion of laws of nature as an unnecessary hangover from a religious past?"[50]

---

[49] Thomas Aquinas, *S.T.* Ia 44, 4.
[50] Davies, *Mind of God*, 81.

Davies's own conclusion is that the laws must be real in somewhat the same way as Plato's Ideas. In fact, he attributes strangely God-like features to them: they are universal, absolute, eternal, omnipotent. However, I believe that there is an insuperable problem for this Platonic account of the laws of nature; it is analogous to the problem of explaining how Plato's transcendent Ideas actually form material beings. Here the problem is *how* such laws "govern" matter. The analogy with laws governing human behavior, upon which the concept was originally based, breaks down when we have inert matter in place of conscious and cooperative agents.

The issues regarding the laws of nature become more complex in discussions of fine-tuning and multiple universes. Some theorists speculate that there is only one logically consistent set of laws. Note that if this is the case, it raises the question of God's freedom in creating. God would still be free to create or not, but not free to choose among possible worlds. Others assume that there are vastly many possible sets of physical laws, as in Linde's multiple-universe theory. If so, are all of those sets of laws "there" from eternity? What causes one or more sets to become instantiated? Or do the laws only come into existence with the world they govern? If so, what *then* determines the character of that world?[51]

I am suspicious that, outside of the theistic worldview in which it was born, the very idea of the laws of nature is incoherent. My own speculations in this area have led me to a position closer to Aristotle's and Thomas's than to Newton's: entities in the world behave the way they do because of innate powers and tendencies. The regularities that we observe are a result of these intrinsic tendencies, not of transcendent laws. And here I am also in agreement with contemporary philosopher of science Nancy Cartwright as well. I have argued that just such a radical reconception of the nature of matter and of causation is needed in order to solve the problem of divine action.[52] This is clearly a topic that needs much further consideration, and, as I mentioned above, may be the most important issue to explore in order to understand God's relation to nature.

5.5 Hierarchy, teleology, and the place of humankind in creation

In Chapter 1, section 4.5, I mentioned the place that the creation of humankind has had in the traditional account of creation. This emphasis clearly derives from the creation stories in the first book of the Bible, but it also follows from teachings about God's motive in creating—namely, love. God loves all creatures, but aims particularly to create beings who can consciously receive and freely return that love.

---

[51] See William R. Stoeger, "Contemporary Physics and the Ontological Status of the Laws of Nature," in Russell et al., *Quantum Cosmology and the Laws of Nature*, 209–34.

[52] Nancey Murphy, "Divine Action in the Natural Order: Buridan's Ass and Schrödinger's Cat," in Robert John Russell, Nancey Murphy, and Arthur R. Peacocke, eds., *Chaos and Complexity: Scientific Perspectives on Divine Action* (Vatican City State and Berkeley: Vatican Observatory and Center for Theology and the Natural Sciences, 1995), 325–58.

The traditional account of creation has also maintained that the wisdom and power of God are manifested in the perfect organization of the whole of the created order. Ancient and medieval theologians accepted the widely held notion of the hierarchy of being, ranging from inanimate material objects through the various levels of living beings to the spiritual. Every kind of being was seen to contribute to the harmony of the whole. Combining this notion with the thesis of the centrality of humankind in God's ordering of creation, it was all too easy to draw the conclusion that the lower orders of being exist primarily for the good of humans.

A number of scientific developments have raised the question of intelligent life elsewhere in the universe. First, our increasing awareness of the size of the universe and of the number of stars leads many to think that there must be other inhabitable planets, and observations are increasingly showing this to be quite likely. Second, if the universe is indeed "anthropic," that is, finely tuned for the production of life, then we should not consider our existence to be a mere accident, an exception, in an otherwise lifeless universe. Finally, if Linde's or any other theory that predicates either vastly many universes or an infinite number of universes is true, then despite the extremely small likelihood of anthropic sets of laws, there are likely to be (or would have to be in an infinite and varied ensemble of universes) others suited to the production of life.

These speculations, I believe, can have a healthy effect on Christian theology. In particular, they force us to "de-anthropocentrize" our theology; that is, they force us to recognize that it may not be *Homo sapiens per se* that represents the goal of God's creation, but rather it is creatures of any sort who have the sensitivity and intelligence to become aware of God's love and the freedom and moral sensibility to respond appropriately.

While the ancient Greek concept of a hierarchy of beings is no longer tenable, current understandings of the relations among the sciences have provided a new conceptual structure—the hierarchy of complex systems. This hierarchy, too, runs from the inorganic to the organic, to the sentient, and finally to the conscious and intelligent. Humans here, too, occupy the highest level among earthly creatures. In light of evolutionary biology and ecology, our dependence on the lower levels is clear, and so one can still say that in some sense the lower levels serve the purposes of the higher. However, there is no justification here for human exploitation of nature.

The topic of God's purpose or goal in creating is the point at which the doctrine of creation is tied to eschatology—that is, Christian teachings about the end of the world. The attempt to reconcile scientific pictures of the end of the universe with hope for human survival has led to the development of what Freeman Dyson (b.1923) calls "physical eschatology." Dyson's theory postulates an open universe that continues to expand and cool forever. It also depends on accepting the premise that a living creature is a type of organization that is capable of information processing. Given this definition of life, he argues that life can continue, throughout the universe, without the conditions needed for terrestrial biochemistry.[53]

Robert Russell notes that there is a dissonance between theories such as Dyson's and Frank Tipler's[54] on the one hand and traditional Christian eschatology on the other. Christian hope for the future is not reducible to unending life, but has to do rather with eternal life, "the full reality of divine time without separations and divisions, weeping and death."[55] In addition, Dyson's theory sees intelligence—in fact, mere information processing—as what makes humans valuable. However, traditional Christian teaching emphasizes love, not intelligence, as that which is central to God's creative purposes.

Russell points out, though, that theories such as Dyson's can remind theologians that eschatology pertains to the whole of the cosmos, not just humans. These theories should prompt us in the church, he says, "to rethink the cosmological implications of just what is at stake if we claim . . . that the groaning of *all* nature will be taken up in and healed by the transfiguration of the universe which has already begun with the Resurrection of Christ."[56]

5.6 Overview

The point of section 5 is to suggest that if you pick up any reference work on the doctrine of creation and read the list of topics discussed in traditional accounts, you will find that each of these issues is being raised afresh by contemporary science. Did the universe have a beginning in time? If so, what occurred before the beginning of the universe? Does it even make sense to speak of its beginning "in time" or is time itself an aspect of the universe? What, really, is "nothing"? Is it true that something can come out of nothing? Does the universe have a purpose and do humans have a special place in it? Is suffering necessary? Could the universe have been better than it is? What is the source of order in the universe? What is to be the fate of the universe and of the human race?

Notice that my interest in this section has not been to engage in what is called natural theology. That is, it has not been my purpose in this section to argue that theological positions can be grounded in scientific results.[57] Rather, I hope to

---

[53] Freeman J. Dyson, *Infinite in All Directions* (New York: Harper and Row, 1988), ch. 6.

[54] Frank J. Tipler, *The Physics of Immortality: Modern Cosmology, God, and the Resurrection of the Dead* (New York: Doubleday, 1997).

[55] Russell, "Cosmology from Alpha to Omega," 571.

[56] Russell, "Cosmology from Alpha to Omega," 572.

[57] However, I have argued elsewhere that such results can be used as supporting data for theological research programs whose primary data come from Scripture, history, and religious experience. See Murphy, "Evidence of Design in the Fine-Tuning of the Universe," in Russell et al., *Quantum Cosmology*, 407–48.

have made three points: First, theologians cannot ignore traditional cosmological questions in treating the doctrine of creation. Second, current debates about the significance of recent scientific theories provide new conceptual resources for theological debate. Third, our contemporary scientific culture is hungry for answers to the big questions—questions bearing on the meaning of life. The door is open to argue for the relevance of traditional Christian teaching in an age when the relevance of religion is as much in question as its truth.

6 Retrospect and prospect

This chapter has had two major goals. The first was to show the historically short-mindedness of theses regarding inevitable or interminable conflicts between science and Christian theology. These have largely been promoted, from the late nineteenth century until today, by people whose concerns are largely related to education: is it more important to promote scientific education (and now STEM education—science, technology, engineering, and mathematics), or humanistic education (largely Christian historical knowledge and discipleship)? Which of these clusters of disciplines leads to a better society and to a better conception of the meaning of life?

The second major goal was to provide a small taste of the fascinating ways in which science and theology can be brought into dialogue, so as to displace the conviction that it is necessary to choose between science and the humanities, science and religion.

Two more chapters will complete this text. Chapter 9 will be addressed to the pressing question today of the implications of the explosion of new knowledge in neuroscience for traditional Christian conceptions of human nature. Chapter 10 will, in its own way, return to "the conflict myth" by arguing that, among competing, rival traditions, the one that is most important to understand in our day is a modern naturalist (as opposed to theistic) tradition that claims to be based on science. We need to answer the question proposed by Yale theologians Hans Frei and George Lindbeck: does the biblical worldview (tradition) have the resources to "absorb the world," including the world as increasingly well discovered and described by science?

9

Christian anthropology, philosophy, and science

1 Introduction

There is a list of topics regarding human nature that have been debated by apologists, theologians, philosophers, and others since the beginning of the development of the Christian Tradition; for example, the meaning of our having been created in the image of God, the sources and consequences of sin, the means by which Jesus has redeemed us, our fate after death. This chapter will concentrate on only two questions: the metaphysical composition of humans (stated most briefly, dualism versus monism) and the closely related question of what happens after death.

In line with the general focus of this text, the *potential* conflict between traditional Christian views of dualism and current neurobiological research suggesting a physicalist view of humans will play a large part, in that *if* this turns out to be an *unavoidable* conflict it has implications that would constitute a significant crisis for the Christian Tradition. It is for this reason that I shall give much more attention to physicalism than dualism in this chapter.

This chapter will begin (in section 2) with the task of sorting through the history of Christian views of human nature. Section 3 presents a small sampling of results from neuroscience that strongly suggest a physicalist view, in that human capacities previously attributed to the soul (or mind)[1] can be shown to depend on quite specific locations or systems in the brain.

While Christian acceptance of a physicalist account of human nature raises, or brings to the fore, a number of philosophical issues, I shall concentrate, in section 4, on the problem of reductionism: that is, how can it *fail to be the case* that all beliefs and actions are simply determined by the operation of our brains. I claim that the answer involves a striking worldview change that is part of the separation of modernity from whatever comes next in Western intellectual history.

2 A patchy history of Christian views of human nature

A number of years ago my colleague in neuropsychology, Warren Brown, warned that a new conflict between Christianity and science, comparable to that between

---

[1] Recall that during part of Christian history these terms could be used interchangeably.

210

creationism and evolutionism, was on the horizon. Most Christians, he said, were substance dualists, while developments in the cognitive neurosciences were strongly suggesting that humans are all of a piece and that our immensely complex brains, conditioned by our immensely complex cultures, were the source of higher human capacities. Some philosophers and scientists were already claiming that neuroscience falsified the beliefs of countless religious people. Brown suggested that we produce a book showing that there is an acceptable Christian account of human nature that is consonant with neuroscience. Recall my mention (in Chapter 8) of Ernan McMullin's concept of *consonance* as the ideal relation between theology and science.

We published chapters by scientists from a variety of relevant disciplines, as well as a theologian, a biblical scholar, and a Christian ethicist, all supporting the position best known in philosophy as "nonreductive physicalism."[2] I had two jobs: One was to write a chapter providing a philosophical argument *against* the reduction of all human capacities and behavior to mere brain processes. I do not judge that chapter to have been successful.[3]

My second job was to write an Introduction to the book incorporating a historical account of Christian views on this particular aspect of Christian anthropology. I found it surprisingly difficult. It made sense to begin with the Bible. Not being a biblical scholar, I resorted to reference works, but concluded that the views *attributed* to biblical authors turned out to be strangely correlated with predominant views of human nature held at the time the reference works were written.

I next attempted to piece together the transition from what appeared to be a monistic Hebraic account in the Bible (to be explained below) to a Platonic-inspired body–soul dualism espoused by Augustine. This, too, proved confusing, as I shall explain below (section 2.2). Much has already been written here (Chapter 1) on the medieval period, in which Aristotelian influences competed with the predominantly Platonic–Augustinian tradition. Section 2.3 will review and amplify contributions from modern philosophy to Christian anthropology and attempt to do justice to contemporary developments.[4]

---

[2] Warren S. Brown, Nancey Murphy, and H. Newton Malony, eds., *Whatever Happened to the Soul? Scientific and Theological Portraits of Human Nature* (Minneapolis: Fortress Press, 1978).

[3] So please do not rely on it in any of your own work. See instead Nancey Murphy and Warren S. Brown, *Did My Neurons Make Me Do It? Neurobiological and Philosophical Perspectives on Moral Responsibility and Free Will* (Oxford: Oxford University Press, 2007).

[4] Since my early attempts to find authoritative and comprehensive accounts of Christian developments in doctrines of human nature, I have discovered Raymond Martin and John Barresi, *The Rise and Fall of Self and Soul: An Intellectual History of Personal Identity* (New York: Columbia University Press, 2006), which covers biblical sources, philosophical sources, and developments up to the present, including those suggested by scientific advances.

2.1 The intriguing tale of human nature in the Bible

While Brown was correct regarding the prevalence of dualism among Christians today, there is another position, nearly as popular, called "trichotomism." This is said to be based on Paul's blessing in 1 Thessalonians 5.23: "May the God of peace himself sanctify you entirely; and may your spirit and soul and body be kept sound and blameless at the coming of our Lord Jesus Christ" (NRSV). However, a more proximate source seems to be the writings of Chinese evangelist Watchman Nee. So there are three major positions among contemporary Christians on the biblical view of human nature. However, a book review claims that 130 different views of the human person have been documented.[5]

An important question for contemporary Christians, then, is whether it is possible to settle differences among monists, dualists, and trichotomists, and if so, how? According to Brown, it is necessary to seek consonance among five sources: Scripture, tradition, science, reason, and human experience. I interpret "reason" to stand largely for philosophy. The structure of this section (as well as of the rest of the chapter) will be heavily indebted to Brown's proposal.

2.1.1 The Bible on monism, dualism, or . . .?

For over 16 centuries the predominant Western Christian view has been that the Bible, both OT and NT, taught some form of substance dualism. This consensus began to be called into question very early in the twentieth century. I have found it important to point out the long history of this shift in Christian thinking in order to try to head off objections that my anti-dualism (and that of other Christians) fits the old canard of theology challenged by science, and theologians then backing down.

I believe that, a century later, there is coming to be a consensus that the Bible does not teach (or even presuppose) any sort of substance dualism. Systematic theologian Veli-Matti Kärkkäinen writes that "a number of more recent, extensive studies have led to verdicts . . . supportive of Paul's essential wholism" and "emphasis on embodied life in this world and the next, while combating body-soul dualism."[6] Nevertheless, Kärkkäinen believes that the term "soul" can and should continue to be used in theology because of its prevalence in the tradition and because it is the theologian's job to help the faithful grasp its redefinition.[7]

---

[5] Review by Graham McFarlane of N. H. Gregersen et al., eds., *The Human Person in Science and Theology* (Edinburgh: T. & T. Clark, 2000), in *Science and Christian Belief* 14, no. 1 (April 2002): 94–5.

[6] Veli-Matti Kärkkäinen, *Creation and Humanity: A Constructive Christian Theology for the Pluralistic World*, vol. 3 (Grand Rapids, MI: Eerdmans, 2015), 333–4; quoting Joel B. Green, *Body, Soul, and Human Life: The Nature of Humanity in the Bible* (Grand Rapids, MI: Baker Academic Press, 2008), 7–8.

[7] Kärkkäinen, *Creation and Humanity*, 345. However, my advice is that it would be better simply to "put the word to bed" for about 30 years, based on my experience that some terms carry so much unhelpful baggage that it is difficult for people even to notice that a familiar term has been redefined.

Joel Green (b.1956) points out that modern thinkers need to recognize that many of the questions we pose were of no interest to biblical authors.[8] Thus, in some cases the questions may turn out to be impossible to answer. The pertinent example is that our contemporary conceptions of human nature are strikingly different from those of the Hebraic tradition.

I describe modern people in the West as thinking of themselves as self-contained in two senses: First, modern individualism, taken over from early modern atomism in physics, assumes that the individual has ontological priority over social groups—that is, I could be the person I am regardless of my social interactions. Second, we have the metaphor of the true self being contained inside the body—a metaphor universalized by René Descartes, but a likely import from the Catholic spiritual tradition, going back to Augustine (see Chapter 2, section 4.1). Philosophical theologians Fergus Kerr and Nicholas Lash describe this as the little person in the head. Phillip Cary emphasizes the modern belief that the little person can never get out.

This is in contrast to interpretations of OT anthropology, such as that of Aubrey Johnson (1901–95): the Hebraic personality was thought to be extended in subtle ways among the community by means of speech and other communication. "Accordingly, in Israelite thought the individual, as a . . . centre of power capable of indefinite extension, is never a mere isolated unit."[9]

One of the questions that has, until recently, seemed impossible to answer has been the long-standing debate regarding Paul: did he hold to the monism of his Hebrew tradition or accept the dualism of Hellenistic philosophers, already prevalent in his context for several centuries?

James Dunn (b.1939) proposes that, while Paul was clearly familiar with both, he found it necessary to craft an account of human nature that was adequate to his theology regarding the impact of divine revelation and grace on the human being.[10] He needed a conception of human life *now* that could support the promise of resurrection. How can we understand ourselves in a way that we can speak of our embodied selfhood in this life, while imagining a new kind of embodiment raised to incorruptibility, glory, and power, patterned on the model of Christ's resurrected body?[11]

For two reasons I have found a distinction of terms used by Dunn particularly useful for understanding biblical anthropology, and also for explaining how

---

[8] Joel B. Green, *Body, Soul and Human Life: The Nature of Humanity in the Bible* (Grand Rapids, MI: Baker Academic, 2008), 12–13; following Klaus Berger, *Identity and Experience in the New Testament* (Minneapolis: Fortress, 2003), 6.

[9] Aubrey R. Johnson, *The One and the Many in the Israelite Conception of God*, 2nd ed. ([1942] Cardiff: University of Wales Press, 1961), 4. See also Robert A. Di Vito, "Old Testament Anthropology and the Construction of Personal Identity," *Catholic Biblical Quarterly* 61, no. 1 (1999): 217–38.

[10] James D. G. Dunn, *The Theology of Paul the Apostle* (Grand Rapids, MI: Eerdmans, 1998), 51.

[11] Dunn, *Paul*, 60.

it could have been possible for Christians, for so many centuries, to believe that the Bible required substance dualism. Dunn distinguishes between what he calls "aspective" and "partitive" accounts of human nature. He writes:

> in simplified terms, while Greek thought tended to regard the human being as made up of distinct parts, Hebraic thought saw the human being more as a whole person existing on different dimensions. As we might say, it was more characteristically Greek to conceive of the human person "partitively," whereas it was more characteristically Hebrew to conceive of the human person "aspectively." That is to say, we speak of a school *having* a gym (the gym is part of the school); but we say I *am* a Scot (my Scottishness is an aspect of my whole being).[12]

Thus, many ancient Greek philosophers were interested in the question: what are the essential parts of a human being? In contrast, for the biblical authors each "part" ("part" in scare quotes) stands for the whole person thought of from a certain angle. For example, Paul's distinction between spirit and flesh is not our later distinction between soul and body; "spirit" stands for the whole person in relation to God. What the NT authors are concerned with, then, is human beings in relationship to the natural world, to the community, and to God. Paul is concerned with two ways of living: one in conformity with the Spirit of God, and the other in conformity to the old eon before Christ.

A second factor in confusions regarding human nature, and perhaps contributing to partitive readings of biblical texts, is the fact that the Scriptures used by early Christian thinkers were those that Christians call the OT. What early Christian apologists had available to them, especially apologists to the world outside of traditional Hebraic Judaism, was the *Septuagint*, a translation of the Hebrew texts into Greek, said to have been done by 70 scholars (thus the name), and completed around 250 BC. Given the vastly different worldviews from which these two languages derived (I might even say, incommensurable worldviews), it was sure to be the case that Greek thought would have entered the texts because of lack of available terminology in Greek to capture the meaning of a Hebrew concept in a single word. For example, one of the words used frequently in the OT, *nephesh*, derived originally from its designation of the throat, was extended to the breath that flowed through the throat, and extended even further to the life force, since the dead no longer breathe. This term was translated into Greek as *psyche*. Thus, early English versions used "soul" almost exclusively to translate it. Newer translations substitute a variety of terms, such as "living being." Even translations made by scholars with a more conservative point of view show a shift toward replacements of "soul" with other, more appropriate, terms.

---

[12] Dunn, *Paul*, 54.

2.1.2 Biblical views of the afterlife

In Jesus' day there were three accounts of what happens at death. One was the predominant view of earlier Hebrew texts: death is simply death, and hope for the future was hope for the future of Israel. Joel Green, following a number of noted OT scholars, notes that there is no well-defined account of what happens after death.[13] However, Jewish scholar Jon Levenson (b.1949) writes that the concept of the dead residing in Sheol reflects an impressively long-standing and broad consensus. The dead do not cease to exist altogether nor are they entirely oblivious, but it is a negative experience.[14] It is the destination of all, both good and bad.

If Levenson is correct here, there are resemblances to numerous other accounts of the netherworld, and the doctrine of Sheol may have been influenced by other ancient cultures in the region. Levenson, in fact, mentions Homer. Recall (from Chapter 1, section 2.1) Paul Feyerabend's account of the incommensurability between Homeric and classical Greek thought. Homeric humans were simple additions of parts: body parts and mental parts; the latter not coming from a unified, invisible, interior entity. Levenson notes one translator of the *Odyssey* who describes the netherworld as "this gloom at world's end."[15]

The second account of the afterlife in Jesus' (and Paul's) day was resurrection. Acts 23.8 makes clear that there was a major controversy between the Sadducees (who rejected it) and the Pharisees (who accepted it). While resurrection only became widely accepted during Second Temple Judaism (515 BC – AD 70), Levenson writes that there are hints of it in the Torah, such as in Psalm 40.2: "He drew me up from the desolate pit, out of the miry bog, and set my feet upon a rock, making my steps secure" (RSV). However, it was thought of only as an unlikely gift from God.[16] The concept of resurrection is usually taken to be clearly endorsed much later in Daniel. Both Levenson and another contemporary Jewish scholar, Neil Gillman (1933–2017), argue that resurrection represents the only authentic Jewish eschatology.[17] Of course, for Christians, the resurrection of Jesus played a great role. The peculiarity for Jewish Christians was that it was expected only at the end of history.

The third option during Jesus' lifetime, for those who had adopted body–soul dualism, was that the soul would continue to exist after the death of the body. For many, the escape of the soul from the body was highly desirable. Perhaps one reason for difficulties in interpreting Paul's second letter to the Corinthians is that

---

[13] Green, *Human Life*, 152–7.

[14] Jon D. Levenson, *Resurrection and the Restoration of Israel: The Ultimate Victory of the God of Life* (New Haven, CT: Yale University Press, 2006), 35.

[15] Levenson, *Resurrection*, 37; citing Robert Fitzgerald.

[16] Levenson, *Resurrection*, 37.

[17] Neil Gillman, *The Death of Death: Resurrection and Immortality in Jewish Thought* (Woodstock, VT: Jewish Lights Publishing, 2000).

he was attempting to write to three audiences at once: those who had no expectation of life after death, those who believed in bodily resurrection but did not have a clear understanding of Jesus' resurrection, and Hellenized Christians who did not understand why returning to bodily existence would constitute good news. Later Christians created a composite account of life after death: the body dies, the soul lives on, and is later reclothed in a resurrection body.

2.1.3 So that what is mortal may be swallowed up in hope[18]

Notice that when Christians focus on resurrection as the hope of what is to come, the old storyline from perfect creation, to fall, to restoration must yield to a storyline from creation, through slow and painful development, from the simple and chaotic to the complex and orderly. But then what? Christian hope for the future is based not on freeing the immortal soul, but rather on resurrection. And the only vision of the end of the world that is fully consistent with the hope of resurrection is a transformation of the whole cosmos, a transformation of which Jesus' resurrection is first fruits. We can say nothing of what this transformation will be like in scientific terms because science is based on the way things are in this eon. But we can say much about the new world in moral terms. It will be a world whose character Isaiah evoked in his prophecy:

> For I am about to create new heavens and a new earth . . . I am about to create Jerusalem as a joy, and its people as a delight . . . No more shall the sound of weeping be heard . . . or the cry of distress. They shall build houses and inhabit them; they shall plant vineyards and eat their fruit . . . Before they call I will answer, while they are yet speaking I will hear. The wolf and the lamb shall feed together, the lion shall eat straw like the ox. They shall not hurt or destroy on all my holy mountain, says the Lord. (Isa. 65.17–25 NRSV *passim*)

If we reject the Neoplatonic vision of the "flight of the alone to the Alone," and return to the biblical view of the rule of God "on earth as it is in heaven," we find a vision of the end time that shows the ultimate value of sociality; that shows that history is meaningful, because past achievements are not left behind but transformed, past sorrows add poignancy to present joy. Finally, it is a vision that shows there to be ultimate value in our care for and harmony with the whole of nature.

2.2 Human nature in the tradition

In this subsection, I try to do justice to ancient and medieval anthropology, to Reformation developments, and to modern and contemporary thought. The last brings us, in a sense, full circle in that contemporary theology and biblical studies

---

[18] 2 Cor. 5.14.

are powerfully shaped by the recovery of a monist anthropology and the centrality of the resurrection.

2.2.1 Ancient and medieval positions

It has been common to describe the demise of dualism and accompanying immortality of the soul as occurring during the first half of the twentieth century: it was seen as Greek corruption of original Hebraic Christianity, with its emphasis on resurrection of the body. However, Green regularly points out that the sharp distinction between Greek dualism and Hebraic monism is an oversimplification. I now know this all too well. In an attempt to give an account of the development from post-NT monism to the Platonic-inspired dualism of Augustine, I discovered that there are a vast number of positions, and that they do not fit into any detectable chronological order, except to say that there was a *general* progression from monism to dualism and toward the addition of a concept of immortality.[19]

I should have expected this, given my emphasis on the need to interpret essential terms in the context of the various authors' overall positions. These positions were developed in response both to a variety of philosophical systems (Platonism and Neoplatonism, but also Stoicism and atomism), and to a variety of religious competitors such as Gnosticism and Manichaeism.

One difficulty for contemporary interpreters lies in the fact that ancient philosophy was still in the process of defining materiality, and it was difficult, then, to imagine the non-material, except in Platonic Forms. Thus, we too easily read into early accounts the radical dualism of material versus non-material. (We should be struggling, ourselves, to redefine the material in light of quantum physics.)

Here are a few examples of uses of words in ancient documents that are at variance with current expectations. (1) Resurrection: In contrast to delicate attempts to read NT accounts of resurrection in terms of a physical *and transformed* body, it could later be understood in a purely spiritualist manner, or, more often, as a mere reconstruction of the physical body. For dualists it can mean resurrection of both body and soul. (2) Dualism: It can be understood entirely in materialist terms; that is, both body and soul are composed of matter. However, there were also instances of a more Platonic account of material body and non-material soul. (3) Immortality: It can be used interchangeably with "resurrection." It can be seen either as a gift of God or as a natural endowment of the soul. (4) The fate of the damned: It can be simply death. Hell can be understood as a quick means of destruction, or as a means of eternal punishment.

---

[19] See Caroline Walker Bynum, *The Resurrection of the Body in Western Christianity, 200 – 1336* (New York: Columbia University Press, 1995) for a detailed account of varying concepts of resurrection and associated anthropologies. Another valuable resource is Raymond Martin and John Barresi, *The Rise and Fall of Soul and Self: An Intellectual History of Personal Identity* (New York: Columbia University Press, 2006).

By Augustine's day, these issues were resolved, and his position continued to influence Christian thinking throughout the Middle Ages. Chapter 1 gave a great deal of attention to the influences of ancient philosophy on major theologians: Augustine and Thomas. However, the emphasis there was on the effects of Greek philosophy on the concepts of reason that they brought to their theologies. I shall mention here a bit more about philosophical influences on their accounts of human nature. Pythagoras is thought to have originated the doctrines of the tripartite soul and of reincarnation, which surfaced again in Plato's thought.

Augustine retained the Platonic notion of the tripartite, immaterial soul, but rejected Plato's view of the soul as eternal, replacing it with mere immortality. He also altered Plato's account of the parts themselves. For Plato, the intellect was the highest level. The intermediate level, *thumos*, is often translated as "spirit" but it is not spirit in the Christian sense, but something closer to what we mean in speaking of a "spirited" horse; and the lowest was appetite. It is said that Augustine invented our Western concept of the will, and for him it was the highest level, followed by intellect and appetite. The Neoplatonism of the early Christian era (Chapter 1, section 4) also contributed to Augustine's understanding of human nature.

Thomas adopted Aristotle's concept of the soul as the immanent, substantial Form of the body, giving the body all of its characteristic capacities. He agreed with Aristotle in attributing souls to all living things: the vegetative soul to plants, the sensitive soul to animals, and the rational soul to humans. These are in a sense cumulative: we share with plants and animals the levels of soul that mirror theirs. However, Thomas had the difficult task of arguing, against Aristotle, that the rational soul could survive death of the body. He did not see this an ideal state, since embodiment, along with all of the other faculties of the soul, are needed in order to function as a complete human being. Thus, resurrection of the body was essential.

As noted (in Chapter 1), Thomas received Aristotelian thought through Islamic intermediaries. I believe that, with their amplifications, Thomas's account of the soul is the most elaborate and interesting to be found in Christian history. I shall not describe it further here, since I use his list of its capacities in section 3 below.

At first, some of the ideas found in Thomas's works were censured by the church, but he was canonized in 1323, and his teachings have been regarded as a touchstone of Catholic thought, especially recognized at the Council of Trent (1545–63). Nonetheless, there were a variety of contrasting conceptions of human nature throughout the medieval period (see Chapter 6, section 3.2.1 on the Spiritualist Tradition to get some idea of the variety).

2.2.2 Reformation reconfigurations

Here I shall distinguish between the well-known Magisterial Reformation, and the lesser-known Radical Reformation. As throughout this chapter, I shall restrict my account to the metaphysical make-up of humans and their fate after death. I shall further restrict my treatment of the Magisterial Reformers to the two most influential: Martin Luther (1484–1546) and John Calvin.

A striking feature, in my view, is that so little can be found in the secondary literature on theories of human nature during this period. Perhaps this should not come as a surprise because the pressing issues had to do, in the case of humans, with sin and salvation. The broader issue, of course, was the question of the authority of the church. However, the principle of *sola Scriptura* meant that any doctrines regarding human nature and the afterlife were supposed to be based on Scripture alone. This certainly required rejecting Thomas's Aristotelian account. However, I believe that by the time of the Reformation it had come to be nearly impossible to read Scripture except in partitive terms, and both Luther and Calvin believed that Augustine had already formulated the biblical view of human nature.

Given so much agreement regarding Augustine's grasp of biblical teaching, there remained few issues separating Luther and Calvin. One was the question of whether the soul was a special creation of God, endowed at conception or, whether it, like the body, is produced by propagation (traducianism). Although Augustine "was inconclusive" on this issue, Luther believed that he leaned toward traducianism, and therefore he accepted it.[20] Calvin was a creationist.

The two Reformers also disagreed on what happens at death. They both believed in resurrection and the existence of the soul. But what happens to the soul between the death of the earthly body and the general resurrection? This is the question of the intermediate state. Are the souls of the just enjoying conscious awareness of God (Calvin's position) or are they "sleeping"? However, because "sleep" is sometimes used as a euphemism for death in the Bible, there were actually two possibilities, either that the soul dies with the body or that it (more literally) sleeps. Luther compares soul-sleep to normal sleep: just as one falls asleep and unexpectedly awakes, the dead, when they rise, will not know how they have come into and through death.

It is clear that interest in this question grew out of Luther's and his followers' objections to the Catholic Church's doctrine of purgatory, for neither position allows that those destined to be saved could suffer through an intermediate period of purifying suffering.

The Radical Reformation, being a highly variegated and decentralized movement, is difficult to date, but perhaps its clearest representative was the Swiss Brethren, who separated from Huldrych Zwingli (1484–1531) and his reformation in Zürich in 1525. Their objection was Zwingli's delaying of reforms to suit

---

[20] George Huntston Williams, *The Radical Reformation*, 3rd rev. and expanded ed. ([1962] Kirksville, MO: Sixteenth Century Journal Publishers, 1992), 793.

the judgment of the city council. After the Swiss Brethren went their own way, they strove to complete a return to NT Christianity, and in the process rejected infant baptism, not only because they believed it was not a biblical practice, but also because it had become the essential marker for citizenship. Thus, they began to baptize themselves as believers, and thereafter were horribly persecuted (as Anabaptists—re-baptizers) both for heresy and for civil disobedience.

I first became interested in Radical Reformation anthropology due to reading about the intermediate state; it was reported that in addition to Luther, many Anabaptists believed in soul-sleep.[21] I assumed then, as many do, that there must *be* a soul that sleeps, and therefore that Anabaptists, too, were (partitive) body–soul dualists. However, this was before learning that "soul-sleep" could also refer to death of the soul along with the body, and also, especially, before I encountered Dunn's partitive/aspective distinction. I have now found evidence that many Radical Reformers were aspective monists.

My first clues came from an issue of a journal, *Direction: A Mennonite Brethren Forum*, which had devoted a number of articles to the physicalism/dualism debate.[22] I found the article by Terry Hiebert suggestive. He states that his general purpose in his review article is to try to answer the question (exacerbated by my book, *Bodies and Souls*) of whether the soul actually exists. More particularly, he says, "it is time to reconsider the admitted paradoxes surrounding Anabaptist views of the soul and death."[23]

Hiebert displays a remarkable breadth of knowledge regarding the Anabaptist tradition. He sketches the positions on the soul and afterlife of three of the most important founders: Michael Sattler (*c.*1490–1527), Balthasar Hubmaier (*c.*1480–1528), and Menno Simons (*c.*1496–1561), stating that they represent a spectrum of views on the nature of the soul and its implications for the afterlife.

> Sattler and Menno refused to speculate on the nature of the soul, but referred to the soul as a believer's openness to God. Flesh and spirit were terms more suitable for describing the Christian life of separation and holiness . . . Sattler expected to die and wait for the resurrection. Hubmaier expected his [immortal] soul to meet God at death and Menno expected to rest in Paradise until the seed of the new body was born at the resurrection.[24]

---

[21] As have other Christian bodies, such as the Quakers, recent descendants of the Radicals have adopted the intentionally pejorative name originally given to them.

[22] Terry G. Hiebert, "Is the Search for the Anabaptist Soul a Dead End? Historic Anabaptism Meets Nancey Murphy's Nonreductive Physicalism," *Direction: A Mennonite Brethren Forum* 47, no. 2 (Fall 2008): 185–200. Here he focuses almost entirely on my *Bodies and Souls or Spirited Bodies?* (Cambridge: Cambridge University Press, 2006).

[23] Hiebert, "Anabaptist Soul," 187.

[24] Hiebert, "Anabaptist Soul," 189.

Later in the article he expresses what I take to represent the "paradoxes" surrounding Anabaptist views of the soul:

> First, historic Anabaptist writers and church confessions were remarkably unified in using the biblical language of the soul. While more research is needed, apparently most Anabaptists, reflecting biblical diversity, were either implicit or explicit dualists. However, their concerns for holiness and discipleship inclined them to talk about the soul in non-speculative and pastoral terms. Anabaptists practiced a restrained use of this interior language of the soul in worship and ministry. They believed in the soul's engagement with God and people through baptism, the Lord's Supper, footwashing, marriage, and pastoral care. *This rich metaphor evokes the moral, emotional, relational, volitional, rational, and spiritual dimensions of human experience.* With the exception of the most explicit dualists, Anabaptists could have affirmed that we *are* souls rather than *have* them.[25]

These long quotations illustrate the value of the aspective/partitive distinction. Apart from Hubmaier, who was an explicit dualist (in fact, a trichotomist), it seems that there is no paradox regarding the (early) Anabaptist concept of the soul so long as it is read aspectively rather than partitively.

A final note on the Reformation: at the Council of Trent, instrumental in the Catholic "counter-reformation," the wakeful sleep of the dead during the intermediate state was affirmed as doctrine.

2.2.3 Modern and contemporary developments

It would take an entire chapter to do justice to theological developments after the Reformation. What can be said, briefly, is that most theologians continued to assume the dualistic anthropology of Catholicism and the Magisterial Reformers into the twentieth century. It also influenced some later Anabaptist theologians. The eschatology that combined an immortal soul with bodily resurrection also continued.

In the seventeenth century, science and philosophy had an impact. The new atomism in physics marked an important turning point for theories of human nature. That is, if the hylomorphic worldview was rejected, then so too must be the Scholastic doctrine that the soul is the Form of the body.[26] There were two major options, which have survived in various forms until today.

As already noted, the Magisterial Reformers had rejected Aristotelian thought in the sixteenth century and returned to the more Platonic dualism of Augustine. Descartes, although a Catholic, chose this route, but created a dualism more radical

---

[25] Hiebert, "Anabaptist Soul," 197; first italics mine.
[26] Nonetheless, many Catholic thinkers still hold this view.

than Plato's.[27] Descartes distinguished between material (extended) substance and thinking substance; the body was the former, the mind the latter. Much of what we now call the philosophy of mind involved an attempt throughout the modern period to explain how these two could interact. Another now familiar influence of Descartes's writings was his importation of Augustine's peculiar form of inwardness from the Catholic spiritual tradition into modern philosophy (see Chapter 2, section 4.1). Fergus Kerr claims that even contemporary theologians who criticize Descartes's philosophy still exhibit the effects of his "inside-out" philosophy in their theological methods.[28]

The second obvious option was to postulate that humans are purely physical. Even though Thomas Hobbes used the word "mind," he believed that thinking was a matter of constructing useful strings of words, and that words represented physical things. Particles striking the senses could have further effects in the heart, and these are called passions. Human bodies, like all bodies, are entirely pushed by forces such as attraction, repulsion, and fear. He believed in souls, angels, and God, but believed that they too were entirely material. Although early church fathers such as Irenaeus[29] and Tertullian (c.150–225) had been materialists, dualism had taken such a strong hold on Christianity in later years that it was Cartesian dualism rather than Hobbes's materialism that influenced most Christian thought.

Historical criticism of the Bible has had a major impact on modern conceptions of human nature, but there have been contradictory tendencies. In the eighteenth and especially nineteenth centuries, many NT scholars cast doubt on the historicity of miracles in general and especially the great miracle of Jesus' resurrection. Skepticism about Jesus' resurrection led to increased emphasis among theologians on immortality of the soul as the only basis for Christian hope in the afterlife. Consider Adolf von Harnack's (1851–1930) neat summary of the kernel of Christian doctrine: The fatherhood of God, the brotherhood of man, and the infinite value of the human *soul*.[30]

Meanwhile—and here is the contradictory tendency—biblical scholars had begun to question whether body–soul dualism was in fact the position to be found in Scripture. One important contribution here was the work of H. Wheeler

---

[27] Green has mentioned on a number of occasions that contemporary readers often read Plato's writings through Cartesian eyes. I add that what it even means to be material was one of the central issues of ancient philosophy.

[28] Fergus Kerr, *Theology after Wittgenstein*, 2nd ed. ([1986] London: SPCK, 1997).

[29] Irenaeus' dates are surprisingly uncertain; his birth is thought to be either between 115 and 125 or between 130 and 142. His death is c.200–3.

[30] Adolf von Harnack, *Das Wesen des Christentums* (1900); translated as *What is Christianity?* (1901); my italics.

Robinson (1872–1945), an OT scholar, who argued that the Hebrew idea of personality is that of an animated body, not (like the Greek) that of an incarnated soul. However, Robinson held to an Idealist philosophy (all of reality is, in some sense, mental), so this was the beginning of a monist, but not physicalist, interpretation of the OT. He also believed that the NT had made a great advance in the belief that the essential personality (soul or spirit) survived death.

A decisive contribution was Rudolf Bultmann's claim in his *Theology of the New Testament* that Paul uses *soma* ("body") to characterize the human person as a whole.[31] In 1955 Oscar Cullmann (1902–99) gave the lectures that were published as *Immortality of the Soul or Resurrection of the Dead: The Witness of the New Testament*. Cullmann effectively contrasted biblical attitudes toward death, along with expectation of bodily resurrection, with Socrates' attitude, given his expectation that his soul would survive the death of his body.[32]

So here we have, in a sense, come full circle to the account of biblical anthropology above (section 2.1), with the mid-twentieth-century emphasis on a holist account of human nature and an emphasis on bodily resurrection. And although we have also seen that the accepted distinction between the Hebraic and Greek accounts of human nature was too sharply drawn, contemporary theology tends toward a more nuanced monism.

I had the opportunity to teach a doctoral seminar on contemporary theological anthropology with my theology colleague at Fuller Seminary, Veli-Matti Kärkkäinen. He rejects dualism and says that the best current theologians do so also. But nonetheless he disliked the term "nonreductive physicalism" because it seemed to emphasize the physical at the expense of all our other characteristics. Another term sometimes used for a non-dualist position is called "dual-aspect monism," meaning that we are unified beings, but we have both physical and spiritual aspects. But this distinction of physical versus spiritual still seems too simplistic. Based on the complex account Scripture gives of the various aspects of human life, we decided that the best term for Christian theology would be "multi-aspect monism." To illustrate, and for a fitting conclusion to this section, I quote Dunn's summary of Paul's conception of human nature:

> Paul's conception of the human person is of a being who functions within several dimensions. As embodied beings we are social, defined in part by our need for and ability to enter into relationships, not as an optional extra, but as a dimension of our very existence. Our fleshness attests our frailty and weakness as mere humans, the inescapableness of our death,

---

[31] Rudolf Bultmann, *Theology of the New Testament*, vol. 1 (New York: Scribner, 1951).
[32] Oscar Cullmann, *Immortality of the Soul or Resurrection of the Dead?* (New York: Macmillan, 1958).

our dependence on satisfaction of appetite and desire, our vulnerability to manipulation of these appetites and desires. At the same time, as rational beings we are capable of soaring to the highest heights of reflective thought. And as experiencing beings we are capable of the deepest emotions and the most sustained motivation. We are living beings, animated by the mystery of life as a gift, and there is a dimension of our being at which we are directly touched by the profoundest reality within and behind the universe. Paul would no doubt say in thankful acknowledgement with the psalmist: "I praise you, for I am fearfully and wonderfully made" (Ps. 139.14).[33]

3 Neuroscience and human nature

This section's purpose is to convey some of the striking correlations between human capacities that have been attributed to the soul (or mind) and highly specific regions or systems in the brain. It is tempting to say that these brain processes are in fact responsible for our "soulish" capacities. However, Warren Brown is correct in saying that a mental process is a *contextualized* brain event—contextualized in the body, with its history of interactions with the world, and especially, for higher human capabilities, contextualized in the social world with its sometimes centuries-old cultural history.

Although I do not have any concept of the soul, and, as you have read above, there is a vast number of such concepts, the one I find most interesting is Thomas's. This is not because of his metaphysical views on what the soul is,[34] but because he and his predecessors, both Aristotle and Muslim commentators on Aristotle's position, were such excellent observers of humans and other organisms. So I shall use Thomas's list of *capacities* to structure my exposition of neuroscientific findings.

3.1 Varied human capacities attributed to Thomas's soul

We have already seen that both Aristotle and Thomas attributed souls to plants and animals as well as humans. The human soul is tripartite, incorporating all the capacities of both plant and animal souls, as well as our own particular rational soul. Here I provide a simple diagram of the levels and capacities of the soul; however, the capacities are not in hierarchical order (Figure 20).

---

[33] Dunn, *Paul*, 78.
[34] There may still be scholarly disagreements here, and the literature is difficult to follow. See, e.g., Anthony Kenny, *Aquinas on Mind* (London and New York: Routledge, 1993).

Rational: will

active intellect

passive intellect

— — — — — — — — — — — — — — — — — — — —

Animal: emotions

four internal senses:

sensus communis (common or unifying sense)

vis memorativa (sense memory)

vis aestimativa (instinctive judgment, estimative power)

phantasia (imagination)

five external senses:

sight, hearing, taste, touch, smell

appetites

locomotion

— — — — — — — — — — — — — — — — — — — —

Vegetable: reproduction

growth

nutrition

Figure 20 Thomas Aquinas's list of the capacities of humans' tripartite soul

3.1.1 The vegetative soul and biology's verdict

The vegetative or plant soul, in the first instance, is simply the life principle. Our word "animate" comes from the Latin for soul, *anima*. However, the question of what makes something alive is now handled by biology. Biologists ask what the minimum requirements are for life. The basics are self-maintenance, growth, and reproduction. Thus, a sphere of proteins and other large molecules is living if, first, it has a membrane separating it from its environment; second, the membrane is permeable enough to allow for intake of nutrients; third, it has the ability to repair itself if damaged; and fourth, the ability to reproduce, even if only by splitting into two spheres, each of which grows large enough to split again.[35] The three functions

---

[35] The quest to discover how RNA-based reproduction could have first begun has been going on for decades. Nicholas Wade, "A Leading Mystery of Life's Origins is Seemingly Solved," *New York Times*, 14 May 2009: A15.

Thomas attributed to the vegetative soul were growth, nutrition, and reproduction. The one feature he failed to note was self-repair.

The physicalist thesis is that as we go up the hierarchy of increasingly complex organisms, all other capacities once attributed to the soul will turn out to be products of complex organization, rather than properties of a non-material entity.

3.1.2 The sensitive soul and subservient neural processes

The faculties Thomas attributed to the animal or sensitive soul were locomotion, appetite, sensation, and emotion. Let us consider some of these. Thomas's distinction between plant and animal on the basis of the ability to move from one place to another is still accepted.[36] The earliest and simplest form of locomotion is found in single-celled organisms equipped with flagella, whip-like structures on the surface of the cells that rotate and drive the cell forward. In humans and other higher animals, locomotion is controlled by a strip of cortex across the top of the brain, appropriately labeled the motor cortex.

Thomas distinguished two sorts of appetite. The sort we share with animals is that which is directed toward sensible objects such as food or mates. Sense-appetite includes a pleasure-seeking drive that inclines animals (and humans) to pursue what pleases their senses and avoid what hurts them, as well as for 11 kinds of emotion, such as love, hate, aversion, fear, despair, and anger.

In higher animals, appetite is mediated by the pleasure centers of the brain. Neuroscience shows these to be dependent on a balance of neurotransmitters—the chemicals that facilitate transmission of impulses from one nerve to another. Sexual desire is highly dependent on hormones. The hormone oxytocin is secreted by the posterior pituitary gland in mammals during sexual intercourse and breast feeding. It has been found to be a significant factor in pair bonding in animals and facilitates mother–infant bonding in humans.

A great deal of research has been done on the role of the brain and extended nervous system in sense perception. For example, visual perception in higher animals has developed from single, light-sensitive cells in primitive organisms. In humans and higher animals, signals are transmitted from light-sensitive cells in the retina via the optic nerve, through a series of processors, to the visual cortex, where additional circuits process it further, ultimately creating visual perceptions.

---

[36] Although Thomas's distinctions among plant, animal, and human capacities is still accepted, there are a few creatures that do not fit easily into one or another category. A lecturer once described a marine organism on the borderline between plant and animal. It spends most of its time attached to rocks, but in one phase of its life it develops a very simple brain, detaches from the rock, and moves to an area with more nutrients. Then it reattaches and consumes its own brain. The lecturer likened it to a professor who had gotten tenure.

The striking difference between lower and higher animals is that while the lower ones can respond to "visual" stimuli in their environments, such as light, they do so without knowing what they are doing—they lack consciousness. There is a phenomenon called blind-sight that helps clarify the difference between conscious and non-conscious perception. Certain victims of damage to the visual cortex are either completely blind or have blind spots in their visual fields. Nonetheless, they are receiving information about their environments. If asked to say where an object is they reply that they do not know, but if told to reach for it they do much better than would be expected by chance. So the value of consciousness is that we not only know things about our environment, but we also know *that* we know.

How consciousness arises from brain function is, as neuroscientists say, the hard problem. Since experts still do not agree on a theory of how this happens, I shall feel free to omit discussion of the current theories. However, it is interesting to note that scientists do not even agree on how far down the phylogenetic tree (of life) consciousness extends. Descartes is infamous for claiming that no subhuman animals had any sort of consciousness, but I do not think that anyone who has had a pet could agree. I have usually assumed that earthworms cannot feel pain, since they have no brain, but there seems to be no agreement as to whether the fish they are used to catch feel pain in their mouths.

Scientists would add at least one other sense: proprioception. This is the ability to detect one's orientation in space. Some religious experiences are thought to result from damping out the brain regions responsible for it.

In addition to the five "exterior" senses, Thomas postulated four "interior senses." These are particularly interesting in that they show Thomas's skill as a cognitive scientist, and also link up with quite detailed work in neuroscience. These are attributes shared with higher animals. Here is Timothy McDermott's (1926–2014) contemporary translation of Thomas's account:

> Higher animals must be aware of something not only when it is present to their senses but also in its absence, so that they can be prompted to seek it. So they not only need to receive, but also to retain, impressions of sense objects presently affecting them.

This ability to retain sense impressions in the absence of the stimulus is the interior sense called *phantasia* in Latin, and often translated as "imagination."

> In addition, animals need to be attracted and repelled not only by what pleases or displeases their senses but by what is useful or harmful in other ways: the straws birds collect must look good for nest-building. So animals must be able to perceive a significance in things that is not merely an externally perceptible quality. In addition to their particular senses . . . for receiving sense

impressions and their imagination for storing them, animals must therefore have an instinctive judgment [the *vis aestimativa*; also translated as "estimative power"] . . . and a memory [*vis memorativa*, or "sense memory"] for storing those . . . Particular senses discern the particular sense-stimuli proper to them, but to distinguish white from sweet we need some common root sensitivity in which all sense-perceptions meet [the *sensus communis*—the "common" or "unifying sense"] . . .[37]

In this last sentence, Thomas is raising the issue that neuroscientists call the binding problem: how is it that we can put together the sound of a bark, the sight of brown hair, the sensation of soft fur, and the smell to recognize that we have before us a dog? This is one of the hardest problems in neuroscience next to consciousness itself.

An important question in neuroscience has been how the brain comes to recognize patterns. It is now believed that recognition tasks ordinarily depend on activation of large nets of neurons rather than on the firing of individual neurons. A "cell-assembly" is described as follows: "Any frequently repeated, particular stimulation will lead to the slow development of a 'cell-assembly,' a diffuse structure comprising cells . . . capable of acting briefly as a closed system."[38] This issue is clearly relevant to understanding Thomas's *phantasia* in that it is the reactivation of such an assembly that accounts for memory of the original set of stimuli.

Thomas's *vis aestimativa* is a particularly interesting faculty from the point of view of neuroscience. Joseph LeDoux (b.1949) is well known for investigating emotion. What he writes about "emotional appraisal" is relevant to distinguishing this estimative power from the *sensus communis*:

When a certain region of the brain is damaged [namely, the temporal lobe], animals or humans lose the capacity to appraise the emotional significance of certain stimuli [but] without any loss in the capacity to perceive the stimuli as objects. The perceptual representation of an object and the evaluation of the significance of an object are separately processed in the brain. [In fact] the emotional meaning of a stimulus can begin to be appraised before the perceptual systems have fully processed the stimulus. It is, indeed, possible for your brain to know that something is good or bad before it knows exactly what it is.[39]

---

[37] St Thomas Aquinas, *Summa Theologiae: A Concise Translation*, ed. Timothy McDermott (Westminster, MD: Christian Classics, 1989), 121. Note that the interior senses must be involved in emotion, since judging and remembering what causes pleasure and pain are essential for the emotions involved in attraction and avoidance.

[38] Alwyn Scott, *The Controversial New Science of Consciousness* (New York: Springer-Verlag, 1995), 81.

[39] Joseph LeDoux, *The Emotional Brain: The Mysterious Underpinnings of Emotional Life* (New York: Simon & Schuster, 1996), 69.

So, using Thomas's terms, the *vis aestimativa* is a separate faculty from the *sensus communis*, and science shows that it works faster.

Thomas emphasized that the *vis aestimativa* is also capable of recognizing intentions. Neuroscientist Leslie Brothers (b.1953) describes the neural basis for such recognition in humans and animals. Social animals come equipped with neural systems that predispose them to pick out faces. The amygdala is necessary for interpreting facial expressions, direction of gaze, and tone of voice. Neurons in the same region respond to the sight of hands, and to leg motions typical of walking. Thus, there are particular neurons whose function is response to visual stimuli indicating intentions of other agents.[40]

LeDoux's research is also relevant to Thomas's *vis memorativa*, the ability to remember the emotional significance of a stimulus. A patient of Swiss physician Édouard Claparède had lost her abilities to create new memories as a result of brain damage. Each time Claparède (1873–1940) walked into the room, he had to reintroduce himself to her. He regularly held out his hand to greet her, but one day, when their hands met, she quickly pulled hers back; Claparède had concealed a tack in his palm and pricked her with it. The next time he returned she still had no recognition of him, but she refused to shake his hand, without being able to tell him why. He had come to signify danger; he had become a stimulus with a specific emotional meaning. She learned that Claparède's hand could cause her harm, and her brain used this stored information to prevent the unpleasantness from occurring again.[41] By investigating fear conditioning in rats, LeDoux has confirmed the crucial role of the amygdala, a distinctive cluster of neurons found in the anterior temporal lobe of each hemisphere, in developing this sort of memory.

3.1.3 The rational soul, still mysterious

For Thomas, the rational soul is what makes us distinctively human. He attributed to it two sorts of intellect, passive and active, and will. Passive intellect is a kind of memory—a memory of facts and ideas. It furnishes the mind with things about which to think. Neuroscientists now distinguish something like a dozen different memory systems. The two sorts of memory that Thomas distinguished are both classified as types of declarative memory and involve the medial temporal lobe of the brain. The *formation* of long-term memory requires the functioning of the hippocampus.

The active intellect is a power humans have, but not animals, of acquiring abstract information from sense experience and forming judgments. Not much is known about actual thought processes, because no brain is "wired" the same as

---

40 Leslie Brothers, *Friday's Footprint: How Society Shapes the Human Mind* (New York: Oxford University Press, 1997), ch. 3.
41 LeDoux, *Emotional Brain*, 180–1.

another. However, Anthony Kenny (b.1931) says that the intellect "is the capacity for acquiring linguistic and symbolic abilities."[42] While very little is understood about the complications of thinking, a great deal is known about the neural bases of language. Peter Hagoort (b.1954) describes the systems that are needed simply to recall and speak one word:

> All core steps in the speaking process are subserved by areas in the left hemisphere, which is the language dominant hemisphere in the large majority of people. Selecting the appropriate concept for speaking . . . seems to involve the left medial temporal gyrus. From there the activation spreads to Wernicke's area, which is pivotal in retrieving the phonological code of a word stored in memory. Wernicke's area plays a crucial role in the whole network of language processing by linking the lexical aspects of a word form to the widely distributed associations that define its meaning. This role is played by Wernicke's area in both language production and language comprehension. The lexical word form information is relayed to Broca's area in the left frontal cortex and/or the middle part of the superior temporal lobe in the left hemisphere. These areas play a role in the conversion of the phonological codes in memory into phonological words from which the abstract articulatory program is derived. In the final phase of preparing for articulation and execution of articulation sensorimotor areas become activated, with the possible additional contribution of the supplementary motor area and the cerebellum.[43]

So we can see the beginning of an understanding of the very complex brain processes that enable us to engage in language-based reasoning.

The third of Thomas's rational faculties was the will. This is the capacity to be attracted to goods of a non-sensory sort. As Kenny says, the will is "a power to have wants that only the intellect can frame . . . We can say roughly that the human will is the power to have those wants which only a language-user can have."[44] Along with intellect, this is the seat of moral capacities. Furthermore, since God is the ultimate good, the will also accounts for the capacity to be attracted to God.

Neuroscience now contributes to our understanding of both morality and religious experience. Antonio Damasio (b.1944) has studied the neural processes that

---

[42] Kenny, *Aquinas on Mind*, 18.
[43] Peter Hagoort, "The Uniquely Human Capacity for Language Communication: From *POPE* to [po:p] in Half a Second," in Robert J. Russell et al., eds., *Neuroscience and the Person: Scientific Perspectives on Divine Action* (Vatican City State and Berkeley, CA: Vatican Observatory and Center for Theology and the Natural Sciences, 1999), 45–56 (53, 55). His choice of the word "pope" was in honor of John Paul II, who had asked the Vatican Observatory to sponsor the series of conferences for which this paper was prepared.
[44] Kenny, *Aquinas on Mind*, 59.

go into practical reasoning, that is, the ability to make both moral and prudential judgments. In his book, *Descartes' Error*, he reports on cases in which brain damage has left cognitive functions, such as attention, perception, memory, reasoning, and language intact. Yet the subjects concerned suffered dramatic character changes afterwards. Hanna Damasio (b.1942) was able to determine from the damage to one such person's skull and from brain scans of others exactly which parts of the brain were destroyed—selected areas of the prefrontal cortices. The Damasios conclude that this area is "concerned specifically with unique human properties, among them the ability to anticipate the future and plan accordingly within a complex social environment; the sense of responsibility toward the self and others; and the ability to orchestrate one's survival deliberately, at the command of one's free will."[45] In short, what Thomas described as the "appetite for the good" appears to depend on localizable brain functions.

Brown and I published *Did My Neurons Make Me Do It?*,[46] in which we relied on the work of philosophical ethicist Alasdair MacIntyre, in his *Dependent Rational Animals*, for a *philosophical* definition of morally responsible action.[47] Our motto, summarizing MacIntyre's definition of the capacity for moral responsibility, is that it is *the ability to evaluate that which moves one to act in light of a concept of the good*. Note that his concern here is to ask the *philosophical* question of the essential requirements for attaining the capacity to act in a fully mature, rational, responsible, and moral manner. Here is how MacIntyre ties together the capacities that comprise moral reasoning:

> as a practical reasoner I have to be able to imagine different possible futures *for me*, to imagine myself moving forward from the starting point of the present in different directions. For different or alternative futures present me with different and alternative sets of goods to be achieved, with different possible modes of flourishing. And it is important that I should be able to envisage both nearer and more distant futures and to attach probabilities, even if only in a rough and ready way, to the future results of acting in one way rather than another. For this both knowledge and imagination are necessary.[48]

---

[45] Antonio Damasio, *Descartes' Error: Emotion, Reason, and the Human Brain* (New York: G. P. Putnam's Sons, 1994), 10.

[46] Nancey Murphy and Warren S. Brown, *Did My Neurons Make Me Do It? Philosophical and Neurobiological Perspectives on Moral Responsibility and Free Will* (Oxford: Oxford University Press, 2006).

[47] Alasdair MacIntyre, *Dependent Rational Animals: Why Human Beings Need the Virtues* (Chicago: Open Court, 1999).

[48] MacIntyre, *Dependent Rational Animals*, 74–5.

Brown and I determined from this overview what *cognitive capacities* are prerequisites for these abilities. We listed six general capacities:

1 A symbolic sense of self.
2 A sense of the narrative unity of life.
3 The ability to run behavioral scenarios and predict the outcome of various actions.
4 The ability to evaluate predicted outcomes in light of one's goals.
5 The ability to evaluate the goals themselves in light of abstract concepts of the good.
6 The ability to act in light of *1* through *5*.

I present only a sample of the neural prerequisites for some of these cognitive abilities. First, a symbolic sense (or concept) of self: This concept arises early in life, simply as the ability to distinguish one's body from the environment, but becomes more complex through maturation. LeDoux stresses the role of memory,[49] and it is also closely linked to a theory of mind; that is, the ability to attribute thoughts and feelings to other people. Shared neural circuits between actors and observers allow us to understand the actions and feelings of others as if they were our own, they prime us to act in similar ways and allow us to anticipate the same sorts of responses to our actions as we have seen in response to others' actions. We *share* their experiences rather than merely understanding them. The brain regions involved are the temporal lobe (more specifically, the middle temporal gyrus), the rostral inferior parietal lobule, and the ventral motor cortex.[50]

Another prerequisite for practical reasoning and moral responsibility is a narrative understanding of the history of one's life and recognition that the narrative will continue into the future, with alternative possibilities for the nature of that continuance. Understanding the narrative unity of our lives depends on the existence of a long-term memory for events from our pasts. This sort of memory is called episodic memory, which appears to develop early in childhood.

Symbolic language enhances mature humans' episodic memory, and also creates the capacity to anticipate stretches of time beyond the present and imaginatively to place ourselves in that future. It allows us to consider the distant consequences of our current actions. Thus, the third cognitive component needed for moral responsibility is the capacity to imagine different possible courses of

---

[49] Joseph LeDoux, *Synaptic Self: How our Brains Become Who We Are* (New York: Penguin, 2002), 9.
[50] Christian Keyser and Valeria Gassola, "Towards a Unifying Neural Theory of Social Cognition," in S. Anders et al., eds., *Understanding Emotions*, Progress in Brain Research vol. 156 (Amsterdam: Elsevier, 2006), 379–401, esp. 379.

action and predict their likely outcomes. Brown and I argue that mental capacities in general are best understood in terms of their role in guiding action. Thus, perceptions and beliefs are cognitive associative networks involving scenarios for potential actions.

Symbolic language is one of the most important sorts of external scaffolding for mental operations; that is, devices we can manipulate in order to increase our capacity to predict consequences of action. The limitless possibilities for combining linguistic elements in new ways enhances humans' abilities to construct an immense number of scenarios for possible future actions.

Sophisticated language allows not only for understanding a variety of abstract possibilities, but also for second-order evaluations of one's own evaluative processes. Brown and I call this the ability for self-transcendence. Humans, like all other organisms, are intrinsically active, and their actions are directed by biological drives and emotions, by immediate desires and longer-term goals, and by social expectations. The forms their action takes are shaped by learning, by imagination, by judgments about what will be effective. *Responsible* action is that which is consequent upon the ability to represent to oneself what one is doing and *why* one is doing it.

Recall that (following MacIntyre) I defined morally responsible action as action undertaken on the basis of evaluation of one's goals in light of *a concept of the good*. *Moral* responsibility, then, depends on the capacity to use moral *concepts* to describe (and *in so doing* to evaluate) one's own actions, character traits, dispositions, and so on. Consider the long history of culture required to possess abstract concepts such as these.

Finally, there is the question of what is required to take one's moral evaluations from the level of thought and put them into action. A long-standing interest in the philosophical literature is the problem of *akrasia*, that is, weakness of will. Why do we so often choose to do things that we know we will regret later?

Mark Hallett (b.1947) has developed a credible model to represent the normal relations among volition, action, and perception of agency, along with suggested neural correlates. Movement begins with motivation, and this leads to planning of a movement. He points out that it may be misleading to look for *an* initial event of willing since the brain is always working and producing actions; thus the relevant question is why the particular action that occurred was selected. When selected, the action can be executed. The perceptual component is alerted to upcoming movement from both planning and execution modules by feedforward signals.

Motivation is associated with limbic and prefrontal regions of the brain. Studies show that selection of the action to perform depends on different regions, depending on whether the choice is *which* action to choose (supplementary motor area, SMA) or *when* to move (dorsolateral prefrontal cortex, DLFPC). It is likely that movement is initiated in mesial motor areas and premotor cortex.

The movement command then goes to primary motor cortex. Corollary discharges appear to come from the SMA and dorsal premotor cortex to parietal areas, and these may be responsible for the sense of volition. Parietal and frontal areas maintain a relatively constant bidirectional communication. It is likely that this network of structures includes the insula. The sense of agency comes from the appropriate match of volition and movement feedback, likely also centered in the parietal area.[51]

This is but one account of brain regions involved in the initiation and completion of an action that one had judged to be moral. Section 3.2 will present a few instances of what is known about how brain functions interfere with proper human functioning, and this will add to an understanding of what needs to go right in order for us to act on our better intentions.

Readers may be thinking at this point that all of this discussion of the brain's relation to the capacities attributed to the soul has missed the most important issue: the soul is our capacity to interact with God. (Note that the issue of the soul's being the part of us that survives death has already been discussed under the heading of controversies regarding the intermediate state.)[52] A number of neuroscientists, however, have begun to study the role of the brain in religious experience. For example, Andrew Newberg (b.1966) has used brain scans to study Buddhist monks during meditation and Franciscan nuns during prayer. These scans show particular regions of the brain to be typically activated.

However, I omit detailed accounts of this research, first, because it takes account of too narrow a spectrum of religious experiences, namely, what spiritual directors call meditation or contemplation. Yet we could provide a long list of much more common activities and experiences that many would count as religious: petitionary prayer, communal worship, singing hymns, Scripture-reading, even pleasure felt while serving meals in a church's pantry. Second if one is a physicalist, then some region(s) or system(s) of the brain would need to be involved in any experience. And would brain involvement in, say, singing a hymn versus a folk song be different? Another field of study, the cognitive science of religion (CSR) is new. I shall report on it and offer a critique below (Chapter 10, sections 2.2 and 6).

---

[51] Mark Hallett, "Physiology of Volition," in Nancey Murphy, George F. R. Ellis, and Timothy O'Connor, eds., *Downward Causation and the Neurobiology of Free Will* (Berlin and Heidelberg: Springer-Verlag, 2009), ch. 7.

[52] There have been many claims that out-of-body experiences and near-death experiences provide empirical evidence for the survival of the soul into the next life. For the most inclusive and convincing argument against these arguments, I recommend Michael N. Marsh, *Out-of-Body and Near-Death Experiences: Brain-State Phenomena or Glimpses of Immortality?* (Oxford: Oxford University Press, 2010).

A final note: I have suggested in a number of my writings that adopting a physicalist rather than dualist anthropology could have important effects on church life. In some cases, it could counteract a tendency to focus on saving souls for the afterlife instead of a focus on discipleship in our own day. However, dualism has been combined with a strong emphasis on reforming the church in this world, as in the career of Teresa of Avila, who provided some of our most beautiful imagery of the soul, and at the same time reformed numerous Carmelite convents in Spain in the sixteenth century. For an excellent account of the consequences of physicalism for the church today, see Brown and Brad Strawn, *The Physical Nature of Christian Life.*[53]

3.2 Brain failure and human impairment

In this section, I shall present some neural causes of impairment, including criminality. These range from some of the most obvious to the more speculative.

We have already considered the work of the Damasios on the effects of damage to the orbital frontal area of the brain. Such cases involve personality or character change. Research suggests that damage to this same brain area also disrupts the ability to experience regret over past decisions and behavior.

A second case of gross brain damage that had clear effects on moral and criminal behavior is that of a 40-year-old man who inexplicably became a sexual impulsive with pedophilia. He had no prior history of sexual misconduct but began to frequent prostitutes and attempted to molest his stepdaughter. He was found guilty of child molestation and sentenced to prison. However, it was soon discovered that he had a large tumor pressing on his right orbital frontal cortex. When the tumor was removed, the patient's sexual impulsiveness diminished. But the impulsiveness later reappeared, and a brain scan revealed that the tumor had grown back. A second surgery again diminished the patient's sexual impulsiveness.[54]

The *New York Times* ran a report on neuroscientists who have found that food and recreational drugs have a common target in the "reward circuit of the brain," and that stress can cause biological changes, making humans and animals more susceptible to addiction. The author, Richard Friedman (b.1956), wrote that "this newspaper estimated that more than 59,000 Americans had died of drug overdoses in 2016."[55]

Stress and lower perceived social support correlate with fewer dopamine receptors, called D2s, in the brain's reward circuit. All rewards—sex, food, money,

---

[53] Warren S. Brown and Brad D. Strawn, *The Physical Nature of Christian Life: Neuroscience, Psychology, and the Church* (Cambridge: Cambridge University Press, 2012).

[54] Dean Mobbs et al., "Law, Responsibility, and the Brain," in Murphy et al., eds., *Neurobiology of Free Will*, ch. 15, p. 250.

[55] Richard A. Friedmann, "What Cookies and Meth Have in Common," *New York Times, Sunday Review*, 2 July 2017: 1, 4 (1).

drugs—cause release of dopamine, which conveys a sense of pleasure and helps to cement memory of the connection between the stimulus and the felt reward. The more D2s that people have, the higher their natural level of stimulation and pleasure. However, there is a vicious cycle: a low level of D2s is associated with lower activity in prefrontal cortex, which would impair judgment and the exercise of restraint. If this leads to use of drugs or overeating, these behaviors further lower the level of D2s.

Dean Mobbs (b.1975) and colleagues report that noninvasive structural brain imaging shows an 11 percent reduction in the amount of gray matter in the prefrontal cortex in patients with antisocial personality disorder. They report, further, that using brain imaging to look at function rather than mere structure reveals stronger relationships between brain and behavior. Using positron emission tomography, neuroscientists have found attenuated blood flow in the frontal lobes of violent individuals. In general, studies suggest that impulsive violent acts stem from diminished recruitment of the prefrontal cortex's *inhibition systems.*[56] Brown has suggested accordingly that studies of neuroscience and behavior should focus on what he calls "free won't" as much as on the traditional problem of free will.

Another area where damage may increase the propensity toward behaviors deemed to be criminal or antisocial is the amygdala. Imaging studies suggest a role of the amygdala in theory of mind, aggression, and the ability to recognize fear and sadness in faces. It has been theorized that perceived fear and sadness ordinarily inhibit aggressive behavior. The amygdala has been a major focus of attempts to understand the poor empathy and fear responses observed in psychopathic criminals. Mobbs hypothesizes that in psychopathic criminals the prefrontal–amygdala connections are disrupted, leading to deficits in contextual fear conditioning, regret, guilt, and affect regulation.

Mobbs also reports that Adrian Raine (b.1954) has used positron emission tomography to tease apart functional differences between premeditated psychopaths and impulsive affective murderers. Compared to controls, the impulsive murderers had reduced activation in the bilateral prefrontal cortex, while activity in the limbic structures was enhanced. Conversely, the predatory psychopaths had relatively normal prefrontal functioning, but increased right subcortical activity, which included the amygdala and hippocampus. These results suggest that predatory psychopaths are able to regulate their impulses, in contrast to impulsive murderers, who lack the prefrontal inhibitory machinery that stops them from committing violent transgressions.[57]

---

[56] Mobbs, "Law," 245.
[57] Mobbs, "Law," 247.

Just a few suggestive statistics: Studies show that 25 percent of defendants are medically and legally incompetent to stand trial. Antisocial disorder is ten times more common in prison populations than in the general population. Childhood trauma and mistreatment can actually stunt the development of the size of children's brains, and this in turn could be the cause of a large number of cases of antisocial personality disorder.

Mobbs concludes two things: First, these studies strongly suggest that some kinds of criminal behavior are associated with dysfunction of different regions of the brain. Second, though, given the role of environmental conditions, it would be inappropriate to expect full neurological localization of criminality.[58] I would add that finding the sorts of brain deficits described earlier does not provide much help in predicting or correcting antisocial behavior.

Again, I have only reported on a few cases of connections between neurobiological deficits or damage that seem to result in ineffective, or even evil behavior, but I hope to have provided enough examples to be convincing.

4 Philosophical issues

We saw (in section 2.2) that philosophical theories of human nature have had very significant influences on Christian anthropology. So I here return to the philosophical aspects of debates on human nature. Section 4.1 provides an overview of historical developments and, again, it is not intended to be a thorough history, but only to provide context for examining contemporary Christian physicalism. Much of this account will consist merely of reminders of relevant material presented previously.

Note that although I have continued to use the most common philosophical term for contemporary non-dualism, "nonreductive physicalism," there are other variants. I mentioned John Polkinghorne's "dual-aspect monism" and Kärkkäinen's proposal, with which I agree, that in Christian theology a more appropriate term would be "multi-aspect monism." Others are theologian Philip Clayton's "emergent monism" (not to be confused with William Hasker's (b.1935) "emergent dualism"); Christian philosophers Kevin Corcoran's (b.1964) and Lynne Rudder Baker's (1944–2017) "constitution view" according to which I am constituted by my physical body but am not identical with it; philosopher John Searle's (b.1932) "biological naturalism"; philosopher Donald Davidson's (1917–2003) "anomalous monism"; and there may be others. Note that "materialism" can be used as a term referring merely to human nature or to an entire worldview. Thus, "nonreductive materialism" is another possibility. "Monism" is another, and although I have used

---

[58] Mobbs, "Law," 252–3.

it to refer to biblical positions, it is ambiguous as to whether it is physicalist or Idealist monism (as H. Wheeler Robinson attributed to the OT).

In section 4.2, I focus on three significant philosophical problems that face the Christian physicalist. I do not pursue the opposite tack of exploring philosophical problems for dualists. These are well represented in modern philosophical literature. And, in fact, it might be said that the inability of some of the best minds, over a period of four centuries, to solve philosophical problems with dualism has been a major motivation for its rejection.

4.1 A sketch of modern and contemporary philosophy of mind

Since the mid twentieth century we have had a discipline called philosophy of mind; before that, pertinent issues regarding human nature were included in the philosophical discipline of epistemology.

We have already seen that atomism in early modern science forced a rethinking (for many) of the nature of the person. Descartes produced a radical substance dualism; the mind/soul is a substance whose essential nature is thinking, and thought comes in various modes: particular ideas, volitions, and passions. In his *Passions of the Soul* (1649), he grouped the passions with sensations, imagination, and perceptions that come from the external world. Now the mind is solely a function of consciousness, and many of its capacities in medieval thought were transferred to the body. And there are no longer animal or plant souls.

We have also seen that Hobbes took another obvious route: to count the whole of the human being as composed of particles. It would not be until later that theories such as his had important proponents and influences.

David Hume proposed that persons or selves *are* their minds, and that minds are merely bundles of perceptions. Minds are bound together only by the relations among the experiences, not by any existent entity that contains or unifies them.

Kant's sharp distinction between the phenomenal (that which was perceivable) and the noumenal (which included the self) provided a reconception of dualism that was as problematic as Descartes's when it came to explaining how the body or external world could causally affect the mind/self.

Even though Idealism could be called the most influential metaphysical stance of the nineteenth century, it is difficult to give a brief overview. T. L. S. Sprigge (1932–2007) writes: "Idealism is now usually understood in philosophy as the view that mind is the most basic reality and that the physical world exists only as an appearance to or expression of mind, or as somehow mental in its inner essence."[59] I shall make no attempt here to give an account of the various Idealists' theories of mind.

---

[59] T. L. S. Sprigge, "Idealism," in *Routledge*, 4:662–9 (662).

The Logical Positivist movement arose as a reaction against Idealism, especially that inspired by G. W. F. Hegel (1770–1831). It would be tempting to say simply that, if the goal is to eliminate the dualism of mind and matter, this was a return to materialism. However, due to the Cartesian notion that perception of the "external" world must be mediated by non-material ideas (or in positivist language, "sense data") in the mind, it did not (in most cases) represent as sharp a break with Idealism as was intended.

Neopositivist Ernest Nagel (1901–85) was a materialist, rejecting the existence of any non-material entities such as minds. However, we see here an early form of nonreductive materialism, in that he takes aesthetic qualities, ideals, suffering, and pleasure to be genuine aspects of experience, yet these are dependent on the temporal and spatial organization of bodies. It is here, I believe, that we begin to find true successors to Hobbes.

Behaviorism is a collection of twentieth-century positions, also aiming to escape from dualism, and perhaps best characterized as denying that mentalist sorts of words should be taken at face value as nouns with referents. Allow me to illustrate using an animal analogy. We would not ordinarily raise the question of whether a horse has a mind. We would certainly describe some horses as intelligent, but that does not imply that they have *something*, an intelligence. Gilbert Ryle (1900–76) and Ludwig Wittgenstein (1889–1951), I believe, have contributed the most in this regard.

In the 1960s and 1970s, the dualism–physicalism issue was expressed in terms of debates between mind–body dualists and mind–brain identity theorists. Arguments for and against dualism, for and against the identity thesis, appeared to be interminable. I believe the reason for this is that Anglo-American philosophical method was understood to be conceptual analysis. That is, in any statement (except tautologies) there were empirical elements (now ceded to science), but also conceptual elements. For example, the empirical question of how we acquire knowledge is empirical, but analysis of the *concept* knowledge was the philosophers' job. A correct analysis was thought to provide universal knowledge immune to scientific refutation. Thus, arguments for dualism were variations on arguments that the concepts *mind* or *mental*, and *brain* were not the same. This could be shown by giving examples of the nonsense that resulted from substituting the word "brain" in sentences where the word "mind" was at home. For example, if a person is seeing an orange-colored after-image it is "in the mind," but there is certainly nothing orange in the brain. So the mind cannot be identified with the brain.

J. J. C. Smart (1920–2012) considered eight arguments of this sort and provided rebuttals to each, thereby supporting the identity thesis. Regarding the example above, he would not say that the after-image is a brain process, but that the experience of having it is a brain process, and the *experience* is not orange.[60]

However, W. V. O. Quine's demolition of the analytic–synthetic distinction made empirical knowledge once again relevant to philosophical arguments. In Jeffrey Stout's terms, conceptual *archaeology* needs to replace conceptual analysis. We need to know what a concept means in a particular era, and for a particular community of scholars (see Introduction and Chapter 2, section 6).

This view of philosophy entails that philosophical arguments based on current linguistic practices are suspect. Paul Feyerabend pointed out that common idioms are adapted to *beliefs*, not facts, and the acquisition of new knowledge (such as neuroscience) ought to be allowed to call such beliefs into question. Feyerabend says:

> It would seem to me that the task of philosophy, or of any enterprise interested in the advance rather than the embalming of knowledge, is to encourage the development of such new modes of approach, to participate in their improvement rather than to waste time in showing, what is obvious anyway, that they are different from the status quo.[61]

So the gradual displacement of conceptual analysis had already influenced a number of arguments for physicalism around 1970 on the basis of brain science. This by no means, however, indicates that there are no significant philosophical problems still to be solved for the physicalist.

4.2 Contemporary problems with Christian physicalism

Yet again, my coverage needs to be selective. What I shall focus on are philosophical problems that arise particularly for Christian physicalists. I shall ask, first, why physicalism should be thought to be true, or at least much more highly confirmed than dualism. Here I employ resources from philosophy of science. Second, there is the question of how to account for personal identity before and after the resurrection, even without a soul upon which to "hang one's identity." The third issue, which I am calling "the deal breaker," is that of reductionism. If there is no credible way to show it is *not* the case that higher human capacities are nothing but brain functions, then Christian faith is untenable.

There are other questions that could be addressed: What does it mean to be created in the image of God? For long periods in Christian history, this image was associated with the soul. Since Descartes's denying of souls to animals, the soul

---

[60] J. J. C. Smart, "Sensations and Brain Processes," *Philosophical Review* 68, no. 2 (April 1959): 141–56 (150–1).

[61] Paul K. Feyerabend, "Materialism and the Mind-Body Problem," in *Realism, Rationalism, and Scientific Method: Philosophical Papers, Volume 1* (Cambridge: Cambridge University Press, 1981), 161–75 (175).

was often counted as the main answer to what makes humans distinctive. If we have no souls, then in what does our distinctiveness lie? However, this chapter has already grown to an unwieldy length, and the three questions I do not cover are being addressed quite well by current theologians.

4.2.1 Epistemological evaluation

I have already discussed a version of Brown's criteria for judging the epistemological merits of physicalism: its consonance (or as Brown himself says, *resonance*) with Scripture, tradition, experience, science, and reason. I noted that this chapter is largely structured accordingly. I proposed that we might interpret "consonance with reason" here as absence of conflict with philosophy. So, in a sense, section 4.2 is my attempt (partially) to meet this criterion.[62]

I wrote above (Chapter 3, section 4.3) that, according to Imre Lakatos, the hard cores (central, unifying theories) of scientific research programs are often philosophical; for example, the atomism that served to structure and guide the development of early modern physics. In Lakatosian terms, it is certainly physicalism that serves as the hard core of the clusters of research programs that make up the cognitive neurosciences. (One exception here was the effort of Sir John Eccles (1903–97) to develop neuroscience on the basis of dualism, but nothing came of it.) So the positive heuristic (plan for continuing development of the program) is the ongoing attempt to explain additional instances of "mental" phenomena physicalistically.[63] Insofar as the physicalist program has been growing phenomenally over the past generation, and does not even have any competitors on the horizon, it is clearly the most highly confirmed, and thus the most rationally credible. I take this as the strongest possible scientific evidence for its truth.

However, my reason for reporting above on Lakatos's philosophy of science was not only to provide the backdrop to MacIntyre's understanding of tradition-constituted reasoning, but because I had found it valuable for understanding other systems of knowledge and therefore applicable to theological schools—theological research programs. So a project for the future might be to attempt to work out a "subprogram" in systematic theology centered on a physicalist anthropology.

4.2.2 Pre- and post-resurrection identity

Another problem for the physicalist is that of personal identity. In philosophical literature, the term "identity" is used in two ways. Numerical identity is distinguished from qualitative identity, and the former is at issue here: what are the

---

[62] Note that there are no sections corresponding to common human experience. This is because, just as language and concepts reflect the beliefs of the communities of which we are a part, so does our experience to some extent, and this is particularly true with something as subtle as our self-perceptions.
[63] I made this proposal in Brown et al., *Whatever Happened to the Soul?*, ch. 6.

criteria by which I am the same person now as I was 40 years ago, even though qualitatively I am quite different?

It is tempting to say simply that philosophers have not been able to solve the problem even for different stages in this life, so the inability of a Christian to account for pre- and post-resurrection identity cannot count as an obstacle to acceptance of a view that is so well supported otherwise. This is especially tempting given the fact that theological language presents more difficulties than does ordinary language, and our language especially breaks down when we come to matters of eschatology, such as the resurrection.

Nonetheless, I shall attempt to sketch a nonreductive physicalist account that is suitable for Christians. I shall conclude that it is not the body *qua* material object that constitutes our identities, but rather the higher capacities that it enables: consciousness and memory, moral character, interpersonal relations, and, especially, relationship with God.

David Wiggins (b.1933) has shown that to say "x is identical to y" requires the specification of a *covering concept*; one needs to be able to answer the question, "the same *what* as y?" Criteria of identity need to be tailored to fit the relevant covering concept. Consequently, it is necessary to ask what are the identity criteria for the covering concept *person* and to expect that these be different from identity criteria for a material object or even for a human body.[64]

There is a rich philosophical literature on personal identity. One long-standing argument is between those who stake personal identity on spatiotemporal continuity of the body and those who tie it to continuity of memories. It is a fact about us *in this life* that continuity of memory depends on temporal continuity of our brains and thus of the rest of our bodies. So these two criteria are essentially related. However, there is more to continuity of consciousness than a bundle of memories. This is the ability to recognize my conscious self over time, which is so unproblematic most of the time (e.g., when we wake up in the morning) that it may go unnoticed.

Recognition of oneself as oneself over time and after interruptions of conscious experience may have been presumed to be part of what philosophers have been referring to all along as the memory criterion, but I want to highlight it; I shall call this additional criterion the continuity-of-consciousness criterion.

I now want to argue that the combined memory–consciousness criterion is still too narrow, in that memory and continuity of consciousness together do not capture all of what we need in order to secure personal identity. Given the moral and social character of the kingdom of God, we need to add "same moral character" to our criterion. I propose that identity of persons depends as much on *character* identity as it does on memory/consciousness and bodily continuity.

---

[64] David Wiggins, *Identity and Spatio-Temporal Continuity* (Oxford: Clarendon Press, 1967), 1, 35–6, 50.

That is, a replica or transformed version of my body with all my memories intact would not be I unless she possessed my virtues (or vices), affections, and moral perceptions.

Another factor that needs to be taken into account in understanding personal identity is relationships. It is clear that a great deal of what makes us to be the persons that we are is our relations with other people, and I especially want to emphasize continuity of one's relations to others in the body of Christ and to Christ himself. Thus, I concur with those who emphasize that God's remembering, recognizing, and relating to me are essential to my post-resurrection identity.

What about bodily continuity? The nonreductive physicalist (or multi-aspect monist) assumption is that on this side of resurrection all of these other criteria are tied to the same body in the sense of same material object. But what if, given our faith in the resurrection, we revise our concept of personal identity accordingly, and define "my body" as that which provides the substrate for all of these personal characteristics? It is that which allows me to be recognized by others; that which bears my memories; and whose capacities, emotional reactions, and perceptions have been shaped by my moral actions and experience. It is these characteristics that make me who I am. So any body that manifests all of these is in fact Nancey Murphy.

This recognition allows us to avoid tortuous attempts, as in the early church, to reconcile resurrection with material continuity. Early theologians raised gruesome questions such as the problem of chain consumption: what if you die and a fish eats your body, then someone else eats the fish. Who gets the matter in the end? These attempts are based on failure to distinguish the covering concepts of *same person* and *same collection of particles*.

In some of my earlier writings, I have used the now popular concepts of *supervenience* and *realization*. "Supervenience" was first used as a technical term to describe the relation between moral properties and non-moral characteristics. The property of being a good person supervenes on properties such as being generous, truthful, etc. I argue (contrary to the most common usage) that the lower-level ("subvenient") properties *constitute* the higher-level properties, *only* given certain suitable conditions. For example, giving all one's money to the poor may *or may not* constitute goodness depending on whether one has a family to support. Supervenient properties are "multiply realizable." That is, there are a variety of different life patterns that constitute goodness.

So what if we say that this physical body *constitutes* me now,[65] but in the next life my personhood will be *realized* by a very different *kind* of body, yet one that still

---

[65] Recall that I mentioned the constitution theory of human nature as comparable to that of nonreductive physicalism (section 4 above).

embodies all of the characteristics I have mentioned above as necessary for personal identity? I am experimenting with language here, but I have already noted that the specification of identity criteria is difficult and controversial in all sorts of cases, and that eschatological language regularly falls short. Our language of bodies is all based on the physical features of this world, but we know that in the next world not just our bodies but all of creation will be as different as the resurrected Christ was from the bruised body laid in the tomb.

My earlier use of the concept of supervenience was in an attempt to evade reductionism with regard to humans, which is the problem to be addressed next.

4.2.3 Reductionism: The deal breaker

Throughout Christian history there have been both monist and dualist positions. For theological reasons, what we might call radical dualism such as Descartes's has been rejected in favor of "wholistic dualism": humans are essentially body and soul.

There is currently a monist position that Christians need to reject on theological grounds: reductive materialism. Otherwise, we lose all of the higher human capacities important to a theological vision of humankind. Recall that according to Dunn, Paul's anthropology emphasized our essential sociality, reflective thought, deep emotions and sustained motivations, and the ability to be touched by the Holy Spirit.

There are a number of reductive materialists in both philosophy and science. However, I report on just one, philosopher Daniel Dennett (b.1942) in his book, *Freedom Evolves*.[66] My account of Dennett's simulacra of human capacities does not line up in direct opposition to Paul's, but I believe it indicates well enough what the reductionist is willing to give up.

Many reviewers of Dennett's book accuse him of "bait and switch" arguments. Human sociality requires "intentionality," in the philosophical sense, including beliefs, desires, and intentions. Dennett claims we do *not* possess these characteristics. However, because attributing them to others allows us to predict behavior so well, this justifies us in taking "the intentional stance" toward others. Also, Dennett substitutes for altruism a concept of "benselfishness." Because of the social pay-off of being perceived as a good person, and the fact that the easiest way to maintain this perception is to actually be a good person, we behave so as to appear to be altruistic, but it is for selfish motives. This has been described as pseudo-altruism. Likewise, he has been accused of providing only for pseudo-responsibility and pseudo-freedom. His account of human thought is based on a view of language as nothing more than computer-like manipulation of strings of symbols. And Dennett, being a strident atheist, does not even think to provide an account of

---

[66] Daniel C. Dennett, *Freedom Evolves* (New York: Viking Press, 2003).

pseudo-spirituality. So the question for this subsection is how to account for the fact that we are not, as Dennett says, at the mercy of an organization of a trillion mindless robots.

My proposal is that the intellectual world is in the process of a rapid change in worldview or, in other words, a Kuhnian paradigm change across all of the sciences. This is the development of "complex (dynamical, self-organizing) systems theory." I shall begin with an account of why reductionism had such a hold on modern thought; however, my central purpose is an attempt to convey the sense in which complex systems theory contributes to a new postmodern worldview.

As already noted, in the mid seventeenth century, Hobbes developed a theory of human nature and society on analogy with atomism in physics. He was also the first to propose the concept of a hierarchy of sciences, reflecting a hierarchy of *complexity*. This is in sharp contrast to the ancient and medieval hierarchy of *beings*, and its significance here is that in the earlier hierarchy, all causation was from the top downward.

In the early days of modern physics, causal reductionism was inevitable. Following Epicurus, the essential assumption was that everything that happens is a consequence of the motions and combinations of atoms, whose behavior was deterministic. The atoms were not thought to be affected by the wholes they composed. Thus, the behavior of the wholes, from the levels of physics, to chemistry, to biology, psychology, and finally to social organizations, was ultimately the product of causation from the bottom up, and complex entities were *not* causes in their own right. So the defeat of causal reductionism in the human case needs to be the defeat of bottom-up causation; or as some would say, of part-to-whole determination.

The most significant criticisms of causal reductionism began with an emergentist movement in the 1920s. It was replaced by the reductionist ambitions of the positivists in philosophy of science. Exploration of a concept of *downward causation* began in the 1970s; and, currently, there are new and impressive attempts to define and defend both emergence and downward causation.[67]

Do these accounts of emergence and downward causation together solve the problems of the reduction of human capacities to biology? At first it may seem so, but then the question arises: How is it *not* the case that humans are, in a sense,

---

[67] In my judgment, the best account of downward causation is by Robert Van Gulick, "Reduction, Emergence, and Other Recent Options on the Mind/Body Problem: A Philosophic Overview," *Journal of Consciousness Studies* 8, nos. 9–10 (September/October, 2001): 1–34; and "Who's In Charge Here? and Who's Doing All the Work?" in John Heil and Alfred Mele, eds., *Mental Causation* (Oxford: Clarendon Press, 1995), 233–58. Both are condensed and reprinted in Nancey Murphy and William R. Stoeger, SJ, eds., *Evolution and Emergence: Systems, Organisms, Persons* (Oxford: Oxford University Press, 2007). On Emergence, see Terrence W. Deacon, "Three Levels of Emergent Phenomena," also in Murphy and Stoeger, *Evolution*, 88–110.

trapped by a combination of downward causation from our environments and the biological factors that do (still) contribute to our behavior? Where is there room for human agency? This is the point at which the resources of complex systems theory are required.

"Systems" thinking has been developing over the past half-century, although it has only recently begun to have a significant impact. Systems theory draws from a number of sources. There are roots in general systems theory, developed from the 1928 through the 1970s by thinkers such as Ludwig von Bertalanffy (1901–72). The idea was that the structure of complex entities, regardless of the academic field they fell into, could be modeled mathematically. Another early source was the study of cybernetics, the study of automated control systems, whether mechanical or biological. Current contributions come from information theory, nonlinear mathematics, the study of chaotic and self-organizing systems, and non-equilibrium thermodynamics.

Examples of the systems of interest range from autocatalytic chemical processes at the most basic, to weather patterns, insect colonies, social organizations, and, of course, human brains. Alwyn Scott (1931–2006), a specialist in nonlinear mathematics and neuroscience, describes nonlinear science as a meta-science, based on recognition of patterns in kinds of phenomena in diverse fields. This paradigm shift amounts to a new conception of the very nature of causality,[68] and he says that it in a way returns us to Aristotelian concepts of causation. Francis Heylighen (b.1960), professor at the Free University of Brussels, has made a bolder claim: systems theory provides the resources for an entirely new worldview, including ontology, epistemology, and ethics.[69] I attempt to set out here some of the essential concepts involved in this change.

Several authors call for a shift in "ontological emphases." Alicia Juarrero (b.1947) says that one has to give up the traditional Western philosophical bias in favor of *things*, with their intrinsic properties, for an appreciation of processes and relations.[70]

Systems have permeable boundaries, allowing for the transport of materials, energy, and information. The boundary is a matter of the tighter coupling of its components with one another relative to their coupling with entities outside of the system. The crucial components of complex systems are not things but *processes*. So, for example, from a systems perspective a mammal is composed of a circulatory system, a reproductive system, and so forth, *not* of carbon, hydrogen,

---

[68] Alwyn Scott, "The Development of Nonlinear Science," *Revista del Nuovo Cimento* 27, nos. 10–11 (2004): 1–115 (2).

[69] Francis Heylighen, unpublished paper written for a "Symposium on Research Across Boundaries," Luxembourg, June 16–19, 2010.

[70] Alicia Juarrero, *Dynamics in Action: Intentional Behavior as a Complex System* (Cambridge, MA: MIT Press, 1999), 124.

calcium. The organismic level of description is largely *decoupled* from the atomic level—that is, if the functional system works, it does not matter what its components are made of.

Systems are different from both mechanisms and aggregates in that the properties of the components themselves are dependent on their being parts of the system in question (e.g., a circulatory system can only *be* what it is within the context of an organism). Philosophers distinguish between internal and external relations. External relations do not affect the nature of the *relata*, but internal relations are partially constitutive of the characteristics of *relata*. An essential assumption of the predominant modern worldview was that the world is composed of *things* related to one another *externally*. Systems theory takes the relations among the constituent *processes* of a system to be *internal*.

Systems range from those exhibiting great stability to those that fluctuate wildly. This is because complex systems are nonlinear, that is, the current state affects the development of each future state. The difference in stability is due to the extent to which the system is sensitive to slight variations in initial conditions, and also to the extent to which there are feedback processes that either do or do not dampen out fluctuations. Systems at the extremes of this spectrum of stability are not of great interest to systems theoreticians. For example, a thermostatically controlled heating system is very stable but produces no novelty because it involves a negative feedback system that keeps the temperature within a set range. Imagine a "reverse" thermostat that provides positive feedback such that the hotter the building becomes, the more it increases the heating. This system is unpredictable, but not likely to last long.

Thus, the systems of interest are those in the middle of the spectrum. Chaotic systems are now familiar to many. They result from having a sensitivity to initial conditions that falls into a narrow range, resulting in their behavior falling into a predictable *range* of states.

More interesting are those at the edge of chaos. Here the system has the freedom to explore new possibilities and may "jump" to a new and higher form of organization. An understanding of how this can happen in terms of physics comes from the study of far-from-equilibrium thermodynamics.[71] Such systems are called complex *adaptive* systems. They are characterized by goal-directedness, at least insofar as they operate in order to maintain homeostasis. In the process of self-maintenance, they may create their own components. For example, in an autocatalytic reaction, molecule A catalyzes molecule B, which catalyzes more of A. The process will stabilize at some point unless additional materials are introduced into the system. In order for the system to maintain itself, the

---

[71] Ilya Prigogine and Isabelle Stengers, *The End of Certainty: Time, Chaos, and the New Laws of Nature* (New York: The Free Press, 1997).

internal dynamics must determine which molecules are fit to be imported into the system and survive.[72]

Complex adaptive systems theory has dramatic consequences for understanding causation. While ordinary efficient causation is presupposed, systems theory developed specifically because such causation is inadequate to describe complex systems. This inadequacy is in part because complex systems operate on information as much as on energy and matter. More important is the fact that the relations among the components of a system need to be thought of in terms of *constraints*. An efficient cause makes something happen. A constraint *reduces* the number of things that can happen, due to the fact that the components are internally related to one another such that a change in one automatically changes the other. Juarrero says that the concept of a constraint in science suggests "not an external force that pushes, but a thing's connections to something else . . . as well as to the setting in which the object is situated."[73] More generally, then, constraints pertain to an object's connection with the environment or its embeddedness in that environment. They are relational properties rather than primary qualities in the object itself.

From information theory, Juarrero employs a distinction between context-free and context-sensitive constraints. For example, in successive throws of dice, the numbers that have come up previously do not constrain the probabilities for the current throw; the constraints on the dice's behavior are context-free. In contrast, in a card game the constraints are context-sensitive: the chances of, say, drawing an ace at any point in the game are sensitive to history because the rules of the game, the number of cards in the deck, and so forth create relations among the possible outcomes such that the probability of one occurrence is related to all of the others. This account suggests that a better term in place of "downward causation" is "whole–part constraint." The "higher-level" system, the whole, does not exert efficient, forceful causation on its components. Rather, global features of the system are such that a change in one component changes the probabilities of the occurrence of other lower-level events.

Due to the role of probability in complex systems, it is necessary to do away with the sharp distinction between determinism and indeterminism, either quantum indeterminacy or complete randomness. The appropriate middle term is "propensity," coined by Karl Popper to mean "an irregular or non-necessitating causal disposition of an object or system to produce some result or effect."[74]

An understanding of the concept of a propensity has been aided by the study of nonlinear mathematics and especially chaotic systems. It begins with a visual

---

[72] Juarrero, *Dynamics*, 126.
[73] Juarrero, *Dynamics*, 132.
[74] See David Sapire, "Propensity," in *Camb. Dict.*, 657.

or imaginary "state space" or "phase space," which is an imaginary "space" with some number of dimensions, in which a trajectory represents possible transitions from one state of the system to another. Chaotic systems theory introduced the concept of a "strange attractor" to describe the development of chaotic systems over time. This is a "shape" in phase space that depicts the boundaries within which the system can be found during its evolution.

From the concept of a strange attractor, the idea of an "ontogenic landscape" has been developed. This is a "topographical map" in which valleys represent areas in phase space in which the system is likely to stay. Peaks represent states in which the system will only be found as a result of a major perturbation, such as the injection of a great deal of energy. So the system has a propensity to remain within the valleys. The topography represents a summation of the general effects of a vast number of contextually constrained interactions among the system's component processes.

Those who are not already familiar with material of this sort may be finding it difficult to follow. My mentor at Berkeley, Paul Feyerabend, once said that significant conceptual changes begin with a group of people speaking nonsense to one another, but it eventually makes sense, and a new paradigm or conceptual scheme is created. I myself believe that I am only now becoming fluent after a number of years.

Now, as noted above, a number of us claim that systems thinking represents a change in worldview. My late husband, James McClendon, and I developed criteria to distinguish modern from postmodern theologies. Modern thought was constrained by a foundationalist epistemology, a general theory of meaning as reference, and an individualist understanding of human nature.[75] We claimed that anyone who simply left all of the arguments relating to these issues behind had escaped from the intellectual "space" of modernity. Epistemological holism left foundationalist arguments behind, the philosophical understanding of language in terms of "meaning as use" left the modern dichotomy of referentialism versus expressivism behind.

While he correctly recognized the important role of individualism in modernity, he claimed that arguments for and against it represented a "metaphysical" axis, but I never knew why he called it that. It has only been in these past 20 years that I came to see individualism as but one manifestation of the metaphysics of atomism and reductionism. And it is only now that I know the escape route from this modern set of arguments, namely complex systems theory.

Brown and I have argued that this set of new concepts, particularly those of complexity theory, gives us the conceptual tools to explain how downward "causes"

---

[75] Nancey Murphy and James Wm. McClendon, Jr., "Distinguishing Modern and Postmodern Theologies," *Modern Theology* 5, no. 3 (April 1989): 191–214.

cause without violating the causal closure of the physical and without postulating causal overdetermination. Humans, who are complex, self-organizing, dynamical, adaptive systems, are partially decoupled from their biology, attend selectively to environmental constraints, and thus are able to become agents in their own right.[76]

However, higher animals possess these features as well. So a remaining question is what distinguishes adult humans' morally responsible actions from those of animals and even small children. See an overview of Brown's and my use of MacIntyre's account of moral agency in section 3.1.3 above. In short, morally responsible action depends on the ability to evaluate one's reasons for acting in light of a concept of the good.

So with this addition to the argument that organisms are (often) the causes of their own behavior—the argument I have made briefly in this subsection—I believe it is possible to make the claim to have eliminated many of the reductionist worries that seem to threaten our traditional theologically informed conception of ourselves.

5 Retrospect and prospect

This chapter has considered four sources that have contributed to Christian conceptions of the constitution and destiny of humans. Scripture is clearly, for many, the first source, but we have seen that later developments have often been read back into the texts. Thus, it is a fair question to ask whether current interests in monist accounts are having such an effect, or is it rather that, as with the cleaning of an old painting, the situation is more like the removal of varnish and smoke that long obscured it?

The theological tradition serves as another source of guidance, and here we find mixed messages. In the ancient period, contrasting philosophies contributed to contrasting theories of human nature. The Reformation provided powerful doctrinal pressures on Reformed and Catholic Christians to argue for substance dualism, while Anabaptists and Lutherans appear to have more options.

What we now call science has had a say in these matters. This is clearest in, first, the adoption of Aristotle's worldview, and then its replacement by atomism in modern science. Evolutionary biology, which is not covered here, drove Christians in two directions. One possibility was to say that if humans are so closely related to animals, and animals have no souls, maybe we do not have them either. The opposite direction has been the claim that it is all the more necessary to postulate the creation of a soul for each individual, in order to account for human distinctiveness among the animals. The question then arises, that given the long,

---

[76] Murphy and Brown, *Did My Neurons Make Me Do It?*.

continuous development of *Homo sapiens*, when should we postulate that God would have begun soul creation?

The science that most affects views of human nature at present is neuroscience. Its striking effectiveness in tracing processes and regions involved in all the capacities that Thomas attributed to the soul leads many to say that "it is the brain alone that does the work." But why should we believe that? Did not the speaker's brain simply cause him to make these noises?

It is essential, then, that one of the philosophical contributions is an argument (or explanation) to show that humans are not merely brain-driven organisms. I repeat here that it has taken a genuine worldview change, beyond the atomist–determinist–reductionist modern worldview; this change is rapidly appearing across all contemporary disciplines.

An explanation of post-resurrection identity that does not rely on a continually existing soul is another important issue. In section 4.2.1, I made the (currently) unusual move of relying on philosophy of science and neuroscience itself to address the question of physicalism, whose philosophical home now is the philosophy of mind.

The following (and last) chapter in a sense ties this text together. The question posed in Part I was whether there is an account of human reason sophisticated enough to evaluate the rationality of Christian thought. MacIntyre's account, I have argued, is the first so far. It involves showing that one's own tradition has had sufficient resources to solve its epistemological crises, and so Part II has examined some of the most significant crises presented by the modern worldview. MacIntyre also insists that self-justification does not end here. It requires opening one's enquiries to rival traditions and judging whether the most relevant rival(s) bring to it additional challenges that one's own tradition is unable to meet. Finally, can one show that one's own tradition has resources to offer the rival in order to solve the rival's own recognized crises, based on inconsistencies, features of the world it cannot explain, or simply its inability to progress further in its enquiries?

So Chapter 10 presents an account, as sympathetic an account as I am able, of the development and flourishing of a rival Naturalist Tradition, while noting the crises it has already faced or may recognize itself to face in the future.

10

Naturalism and Christianity as competing large-scale traditions

1 Introduction

There are three reasons for ending this text with a chapter on naturalism. First, the point of Part II of the book is to examine epistemological crises challenging the Christian Tradition in the modern and contemporary intellectual worlds. One important type of crisis is that which comes from encountering an incompatible rival, so the rise of naturalism (materialism, atheism) in modernity is arguably the most significant crisis to consider. Other challengers, of course, are other religious traditions. However, it is an interesting question as to whether *all* (so-called) religions are rivals.

Second, taking up this topic in the last chapter offers a chance to take stock of the responses Christians have provided to their own *internal* crises, since a part of what is needed to vindicate one tradition over against an *external* competitor is, in fact, to provide a narrative of the crises it itself has encountered and a judgment regarding its success in overcoming them. Further steps in the justificatory process are, first, to provide a *sympathetic* account of the rival's crises and an estimation of its successes *or failures* to overcome them. Finally, the best defense of one's own tradition would be to show that it has resources, as the rival does not, to explain why the rival should be expected to fail, and to fail specifically at the point(s) it does.

A third goal of this chapter is to test my thesis that MacIntyre's concept of tradition-constituted reasoning is indeed applicable to naturalism, as its title suggests. If so, this will have two results: First, it will confirm the claim (Chapter 4) for the value of MacIntyre's work itself, since it will show it to be applicable outside of his own specialization in traditions of moral enquiry—not only to religious traditions (here, Christianity) but to other types as well. Second, it has so far proved difficult to define what naturalism itself is; thus, to use the characterization of a tradition as a sort of template to explicate naturalism may be a contribution in and of itself.

1.1 Complications in defining naturalism

A very brief account of naturalism is that it is one or both of the following: (1) an ontological thesis—the natural world is all that is; (2) a methodological thesis—scientific methods are the only means of gaining knowledge. Here is how John Post (b.1936) elaborates—naturalism is the:

> twofold view that (1) everything is composed of natural entities—those studied in the sciences (on some versions, the natural sciences)—whose properties determine all the properties of things, persons included . . . ; and (2) acceptable methods of justification and explanation are commensurable, in some sense, with those in science.[1]

So far it seems simple enough to define naturalism as either an ontological or a methodological thesis. Yet the ontological and methodological emphases are entangled. Unless one wants merely to define ontological naturalism negatively (e.g., in terms of the *non-existence* of God and all other "supernatural" beings), then claims about what exists are to be adjudicated by science, as can already be seen in the excerpt from Post's article.

However, there is no "science" in general; a reductionistic criterion recognizes the objects and forces as described by physics—but is this the best physics we have now or an *ideal* physics?[2] The reduction of reality to that known only by physics has been called "greedy reductionism," so others would like to recognize the objects picked out by other sciences as well, such as chemistry, biology, and perhaps psychology and sociology (so long as the latter two are versions that do not recognize causation by non-material minds).

Thus, a philosophical account of scientific *methodology* is required; in other words, what Karl Popper and his followers called a "criterion of demarcation," distinguishing genuine sciences from other intellectual enterprises. Two problems arise: first, how is one to determine the criteria for genuine scientific methodology and, second, can those criteria themselves be supported by scientific reasoning? (Here there arises a threat of internal incoherence.) In part for this reason, W. V. O. Quine argued for the *naturalizing* of philosophy. The web of beliefs contains both the sciences and philosophy, two branches of which are ontology and the philosophy of science, and their claims are justified by being connected to beliefs we have no reason to call into question.[3] However, Quine's work is hotly debated.[4]

Notice, though, that scientific naturalists often do not say that their theses must be justified directly by science itself, but (as Post wrote) by methods "commensurable, in some sense, with those in science." Thomas Clark (b.1947) says that

---

[1] John F. Post, "Naturalism," *Camb. Dict.*, 517–18 (517).

[2] Would one not like to define "ideal physics" as that in the mind of God—if only there were a God?

[3] This position is basic to all of Quine's philosophy, but for a short and readable account, see W. V. Q. Quine and J. S. Ullian, "Two Dogmas of Empiricism," sec. 6, in Quine, *From a Logical Point of View* (Cambridge, MA: Harvard University Press, 1953).

[4] See esp. P. M. S. Hacker, "Passing by the Naturalistic Turn: On Quine's Cul-De-Sac," in Georg Gasser, ed., *How Successful Is Naturalism?* (Frankfurt: Ontos Verlag, 2007), 143–81.

naturalism depends on taking rational, evidence-based empiricism, epitomized by science, as our way of knowing.[5] David Papineau (b.1947), in speaking of a Quinean sort of naturalized philosophy, says that philosophy and science are essentially the same enterprise, pursuing similar ends and using similar methods. However, they focus on different questions, and the greater generality of philosophical questions means that philosophers will not ordinarily be engaged in experimental research.[6] We shall have to consider below whether qualifications such as Clark's and Post's can be made clear, and if so, whether they succeed in saving Scientific Naturalism from self-referential incoherence.

A few descriptions in the literature refer to naturalism as a specific movement of self-identified philosophers in the USA in the first half of the twentieth century; however, it is now more common to attempt to explicate it as a set of background assumptions of most current (secular) philosophers and many scientists.[7]

Up to this point, the naturalism described here is scientific (and to a lesser extent, philosophical). Consider, though, that Post's article is followed in the dictionary by a list of five other topics to pursue: The first is: "Naturalism, ethical. See ETHICS, MORAL REALISM." The other four entries are metaphysical, methodological, reductive, and theological naturalisms. The second, third, and fourth are simply synonymous with terms Post has used in his essay. This suggests that additional ground to be covered includes ethical and theological naturalisms. Moral or ethical naturalism is given serious consideration below (section 3.3) so I do not address it here.

It is important to recognize theological naturalism because this makes it clear that naturalism may be an important project in its own right and is not simply a (perhaps) less offensive term for atheism. Willem Drees recognizes a cluster of positions that might be called religious naturalism, but concentrates on the difference between two science-inspired positions: one emphasizes the *integrity* of nature (especially ruling out divine intervention; see Chapter 6); the second asserts the self-sufficiency of nature. Naturalists of the first type can still conceive of a creator, but preferably in the non-temporal sense of asserting the world's constant dependence on a divine being.[8]

---

[5] Thomas W. Clark, *Encountering Naturalism: A Worldview and Its Uses* (Somerville, MA: Center for Naturalism, 2007), 6.

[6] David Papineau, "Naturalism," in Edward N. Zalta, ed., *Stanford Encyclopedia of Philosophy*, first published February 22, 2007; substantive revision September 15, 2015; accessed July 27, 2017, https://plato.stanford.edu/entries/naturalism/.

[7] See, esp. Arthur C. Danto, "Naturalism," in *Macmillan*, 5:448–50; but also Papineau, "Naturalism."

[8] Willem B. Drees, "Naturalism," in J. Wentzel Vrede van Huyssteen, ed., *Encyclopedia of Science and Religion*, 2 vols., 2nd ed. (New York: Macmillan, [2003] 2007), 2:593–7.

Given that the complexities I have mentioned here are but a small sampling, and that entire books and conferences struggle to explain and justify naturalism, I offer the proposal that Naturalism can be *displayed* in an organized manner by interpreting it as a Tradition,[9] and I hope that this provides some clarification regarding the *status* of naturalism. If so, I shall be in position to make a very small contribution to assessing its rational challenge as a rival to the Christian Tradition.

1.2 The roots and branches of the Naturalist Tradition

Just as with Christianity, Naturalism and its history can be represented as comprising several subtraditions, and as drawing from a number of roots. The literature suggests four *current* subtraditions: Scientific Naturalism (the best known outside of academia; consider the "new atheists"), Moral Naturalism, philosophical naturalism (influenced especially by Quine), and theological naturalism. The methodological and ontological emphases interact in various ways in each.

Of these four, I am paying significant attention only to two: scientific and moral naturalism. First, these two are the most influential in contemporary culture. Second, neither philosophical nor theological naturalism provides significant challenges to Christianity. Philosophical naturalism (as shown in Chapter 4) can be incorporated helpfully into the historical development of holist epistemology, culminating in MacIntyre's tradition-constituted rationality; in addition, it involves technical arguments that go beyond the scope of this text. Some of the religious naturalists whom Drees mentions may be rejected by more traditional strands of Christian theology (e.g., process theology), but others (e.g., Arthur Peacocke) have done much to reconcile an unobjectionable theology with contemporary science. Finally, it is difficult to imagine either philosophical or theological naturalism being socially embodied in ways distinguishable from the practices of philosophies or theologies of other types.

The roots of naturalism include modern science, but, given the period of overlap between natural philosophy and natural theology (the physico-theologians, Chapter 6, section 3), there has to be another root, the rise of atheism, in order for science to make its contribution to the most common versions of Naturalism.[10] A third root was Renaissance Humanism, beginning in Italy in the fourteenth century. Because this movement involved a return to classical Greek and Roman writers, we might call this the "tap root." There were both

---

[9] I am attempting to follow a convention here of using "naturalism" when referring to the general subject and "Naturalism" to refer to the Naturalist Tradition.

[10] I do continue to use the term "atheism" because so many proponents of the Scientific Naturalist Tradition profess it, and because, as explained below, a major crisis for Moral Naturalism can be traced to rejection of God as the Ultimate Reality.

Christian and non-theistic versions of Humanism, so this root also needed to become entwined with atheism in order to contribute to Naturalism. Humanism helped to pave the way for modern science, and as we shall see (in sections 2.3 and 3.2), it also contributed to the development of unbelief. So the entwining of (at least) these three roots was necessary to produce Naturalism.

Of these three roots, the one most important for Christian readers is the development of modern atheism. Philosopher Merold Westphal (b.1940) helpfully distinguishes two sorts of atheism. One he calls evidential atheism, which he says is well represented by Bertrand Russell's (1872–1970) account of what he would say if he were to meet God and God asked why he had not been a believer: Not enough evidence God! Not enough evidence![11]

But if religious claims are false, then one needs an *explanation* of why they are so widely believed; just as, if there are no witches, we want to know what caused people to believe there were. David Hume in Britain and Paul Henri Thierry, Baron d'Holbach in France in the eighteenth century began the attempt to explain the origin of religion naturalistically. They argued that religion is a response to fear of the unknown, coupled with superstitious attempts to control or propitiate unseen powers. Such attempts continue today, as I note below (section 5.3.3).

But why does religion persist in the modern world, now that we understand natural causes? The explanations here come from Westphal's second variety of atheists, the "masters of suspicion," Karl Marx (1818–83), Friedrich William Nietzsche (1844–1900), and Sigmund Freud (1856–1939), who practice the hermeneutics of suspicion, the "attempt to expose the self-deceptions involved in hiding our actual operative motives from ourselves, individually or collectively, in order not to notice . . . how much our beliefs are shaped by values we profess to disown."[12] These three develop their suspicion with primary emphasis, respectively, on political economics, bourgeois morality, and psychosexual development, but each also subjects the religion of Christendom to devastating critique.

For this reason, I include each as originators of early Naturalist subtraditions: (1) Marxism, beginning after Marx's death in 1883; (2) a subtradition traced to Nietzsche, but incorporating some current Continental philosophers, so there is a current non-Quinean version of Philosophical Naturalism; and (3) Freudianism, begun during Freud's lifetime.

---

[11] Merold Westphal, *Suspicion and Faith: The Religious Uses of Atheism* (Grand Rapids, MI: Eerdmans, 1993), 13.

[12] Westphal, *Suspicion*, 13.

I would add another earlier subtradition: Positivism. This was largely the work of Auguste Comte (1798–1853), who explained the persistence of religion by postulating that humans, both as societies and individuals, go through three stages: the religious, the philosophical, and the scientific. Believers are those who have failed to make the transition.

It would take another book to explain each of these, and *especially* to chart their multiple interactions, positive and negative. However, a brief presentation may be in order.

Marx's early writings, mostly appreciated only after his death, focused largely on social ethics and ontology (he called himself both a humanist and a naturalist). His main intellectual contribution was his recognition of labor as a *commodity* in systems of exchange. In the *Communist Manifesto* (1848; with Friedrich Engels [1820–95]) he made enthusiastic predictions of worldwide revolution against the concentration of power in the hands of the few who controlled productivity. His famous *Capital* (1868) was moralistic and social scientific.

Marxism is said only to have begun after Marx's death (1883). His writings were appropriated by Vladimir Lenin (1870–1924) for his communist revolution in Russia. He and others created a doctrinaire "orthodox Marxism," of which Josef Stalin (1879–1953) became chief interpreter. Thus, Marxism became associated with totalitarianism. Meanwhile, "Western Marxists" have continued to find philosophical fruit, especially in his early writings. So Marx, *qua* scientific economist, failed to reach the "top of the tree" of Scientific Naturalism; however, he has contributed to both Anglo-American and Continental Naturalist philosophies.

Freud also set out to pursue (Naturalistic) science, first as a neurologist and psychologist, but soon took up (and gradually invented) the practice of psychoanalysis. His theoretical bases shifted over the years, from psychosexual development, to buried memories of trauma, to conflict between instincts and repressive cultural norms. He has had a number of followers up to the present. He made lasting contributions, especially in his recognition of unconscious motives. The very idea of mental *un*consciousness was a direct repudiation of Descartes's definition of the mental in terms of the totality of conscious states.

Freud used his psychological theories to speculate on both morality and religion, which he tended to attribute to early stages of development. While he hoped that his therapeutic practice would lead to liberation of repressed energies, he was ultimately pessimistic about the future of society.

The social embodiment of Freudianism is not as obvious as that of Marxism, but it still exists in ongoing practices, which have involved heated debates concerning their internal goods. It is debated whether the efficacy (and, thus, putative

257

truth) of psychoanalysis could be empirically tested. Nonetheless, in a review of a book of 700 pages recounting Freud's errors, "shafting of loved ones, friends, teachers . . ." the reviewer paraphrases the author, Frederick Crews, as saying that "he is destined to remain among us as the most influential of 20th-century sages" with attention bestowed on him by contemporary scholars and commentators that ranks with that accorded Shakespeare and Jesus.[13]

Positivism, used in Comte's sense, essentially died with him. As did Hume before him, he set out to naturalize the causes of human social behavior. As with Marx, he sought to promote a new social order; in his case, motivated by the disorder following the French Revolution. His six-volume *Course in Positive Philosophy* (1830–42) was to provide a blueprint. This text also included his law of three stages of development, from the theological, to the philosophical, and finally to the scientific. He explained the perseverance of religion by claiming that these are not only three stages of civilization, but three stages in individual development.

For the sake of creating a new political order, he saw the development of altruism as essential and believed that it could be stimulated only by something analogous to the Christianity rejected by the Revolution. Hence, he proposed as a substitute the Religion of Humanity, orienting the will toward the only supreme being, Humanity itself. Note the contrast between his optimism and Freud's pessimism.

His lasting accomplishments were his invention of the term "sociology" and his influence on John Stuart Mill (1806–73), whose own influence on contemporary culture has been immense.

Nietzsche first appeared in this chapter because Westphal included him among the "masters of suspicion" of religion—his answer to the question of why religion continues to exist now that we understand the natural causes of frightening phenomena and have naturalist theories to explain its origin.

I have included his work as the origination of one of the most important earlier Naturalist subtraditions because his books "have left a deep imprint on most areas of Western intellectual and cultural life . . . [making him] one of its most important, if controversial philosophers."[14]

While Nietzsche is difficult to interpret, due to his varied writing styles and the fact that his ideas changed considerably over the (brief) course of his academic career, it is safe to say that he supported a naturalistic methodology and a rejection of God. I must rely on MacIntyre's characterization of his influence as a rival tradition, the "Genealogical Tradition."

---

[13] George Prochnik, "Our Freudian Complex," review of Frederick Crews, *Freud: The Making of an Illusion* (Henry Holt and Co., 2017) in *New York Times Book Review* (August 20, 2017): 1, 20.

[14] Maude Marie Clark, "Nietzsche, Friedrich," *Routledge*, 6:844–61 (844).

In *Rival Versions*, MacIntyre chooses a single formative text for each of the three current rival moral traditions he evaluates (see section 3.5). His choice for the Genealogical Tradition is Nietzsche's *Zur Genealogy der Moral* (1887; translated as *On the Genealogy of Morals*, or *of Morality*), an appropriate choice in that Nietzsche himself considered it his best treatment of morality. It incorporates his sophisticated naturalist epistemology; his perspectivalism (we can only perceive truth from a human perspective, conditioned by our place in history, phrased in terminology provided by our culture, and influenced by our affects); and his rejection of God ("the death of God" reflected his recognition that God no longer made a difference in his nineteenth-century culture).

The book has an intriguing plot. The ancient Greeks discriminated between *good* and *bad*. "Good" referred to the virtues of the nobility, and its contrast was with the poor qualities of the lower classes.[15] Christians being of the lower classes (as Nietzsche believed) resented being thought of as bad. But Christian morality forbade their taking physical revenge, of asserting their will to power. In addition, the priests infected Christian morality with their ascetic values, such that pursuit of natural instincts was sinful; all source of value lay outside of nature. Verbal revenge could then be taken against the nobles by proclaiming them to be *evil*.

However, central to the ascetic ideal was the pursuit of truth. The will to truth eventually led, after Descartes and throughout the Enlightenment, to recognition that rational support for God's existence failed. Thus, there was nothing left but nature. Without God, modern morality fell into a state of crisis, of an ineliminable moral relativism.

1.3 Overview of the chapter

In this Introduction, I have provided a brief descriptive account of the history and diversity of the Naturalist Tradition (Figure 21 overleaf). Of the three roots, I have claimed that atheism is the most important for our purposes, and this is the topic of section 2. In section 3, I first provide a reminder of aspects of a tradition as described by MacIntyre (see Chapter 4, section 1 above) and then discuss the extent to which contemporary Naturalism corresponds to this description. In section 4, I begin the evaluative process by listing the crises faced by, first, Christianity (and thus provide an overview of Part II of this text). I follow this with three crises recognized by naturalists. Section 5 discusses two philosophical moves that offer means of putting Naturalism and Christianity into (perhaps positive) dialogue with one another. It also considers two major questions or conflicts: Does Naturalism or Christianity have closer ties to the sciences? And how do we understand Christianity's (supposed) production of evil in the world?

---

15 Note the Humanist roots in his reference to Greek texts.

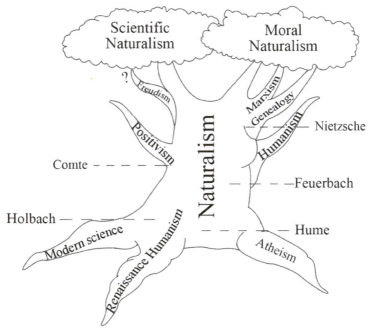

Figure 21 A tree representing the Naturalist Tradition and its roots, with both earlier and contemporary subtraditions

2 The rise of atheism in the modern West

James Turner makes a startling claim in his highly regarded book, *Without God, Without Creed: The Origins of Unbelief in America*. He argues that disbelief was *not* a live option in the USA until roughly between 1865 and 1890.[16] So the task of this section is to trace, first, the "roots" of unbelief in the Reformation and in the apologetics of the Renaissance.

I provide brief reminders along the way of the unintended consequences of René Descartes's efforts to provide a bulwark against Renaissance skepticism. I also briefly review the role of the Port Royal *Logic* in creating the new category of

---

[16] James Turner, *Without God, Without Creed: The History of Unbelief in America* (Baltimore and London: Johns Hopkins University Press, 1985). See also David Berman, *A History of Atheism in Britain: From Hobbes to Russell* (London and New York: Routledge, [1988] 2013). Berman notes that the first atheistic belief system was Baron d'Holbach's *A System of Nature*, published in France in 1770. He sees the transition to avowed atheism in Britain to have begun with Percy Shelley's *The Necessity of Atheism*, for which Shelley was expelled from Oxford in 1811.

"probable knowledge" and the resulting need thoroughly to rethink the nature of theological method.

In section 2.2, I turn to David Hume. I believe that his works are among the best candidates for the formative texts of the Naturalist Tradition. However, if we take the publication in 1779 of Hume's *Dialogues Concerning Natural Religion* to mark the completion of his anti-theistic writings, then what were the obstacles preventing disbelief from becoming a live option until approximately a century later? A number of historians provide accounts of why the transition came about so slowly. We consider Turner himself in section 2.3. Charles Taylor provides a much more extended account, but I reserve his work for section 3.[17]

2.1 Reformation and Renaissance roots

There are (at least) two ways in which the rise of unbelief can be seen as a consequence of the Reformation. One early source was Catholic apologetic strategies during the Renaissance. If one thinks of the agnostic not as one who simply has not formed a judgment on the existence of God, but rather as one who has concluded (positively) that human reason is incapable of making such a judgment, the story traces back to Catholic apologists in the Renaissance such as Michel de Montaigne. These apologists revived ancient skeptical methods to show that there is no rational way to decide between Protestant and Catholic claims. Therefore, the only sensible course of action is to stay within the established (that is, Catholic) faith. The availability of these skeptical arguments helped pave the way for atheism, of course: if one cannot tell whether the Protestant or Catholic version is correct, then maybe none is. But a variety of other factors were needed to justify a positive rejection of religious belief.

I have already described the difficulties created for theologians by the rejection of authority as a proper epistemological category. The irony is that the change can be traced back to Christians themselves for not being able to settle their differences after the Reformation. Recall that it was the problem of *too many* authorities, along with the entanglement of religion with political ambitions, that resulted in the Thirty Years' War and the English Civil War. Both the skeptical climate of the day and the hope of finding a religiously neutral method in the search for truth led Descartes to develop his peculiar modern metaphors regarding knowledge, referred to here as inside-out epistemology and foundationalism. Theologians have struggled to work within the categories inspired by these metaphors throughout the modern period.

Too late to influence Descartes was the Port Royal logicians' development of an entirely new category of knowledge—belief proportioned to the weight

---

[17] Charles Taylor, *A Secular Age* (Harvard, MA: Harvard University Press, 2007).

of *empirical* evidence—and we have seen that modern theologians have also struggled mightily to come to terms with it.

John Locke's apologetic strategy (represented in Figure 5, Chapter 2, section 4.4) nicely shows his dependence on Descartes's foundationalism, as well as his dedication to demonstrative reasoning. The foundation for his argument for God's existence is our *intuitive* knowledge of our own powers, perceptions, and knowledge (ideas he finds *in* his mind?).[18] Port Royal is represented in his turn to sensations (also representations *in his mind*) as the foundation for knowledge of other things. However, humans are not able to reason to a complete moral system, and so revelation, a third type of foundation, is needed. But the Port Royals' caution regarding witnesses requires outward signs to convince us of the "credit of the proposer." Jesus' teaching is accredited by the fact that he fulfills the prophecies about the Messiah, and that his ministry was accompanied by the most wondrous of miracles.

David Hume's various essays successfully undermine (note the metaphor) Locke's apologetic strategy. His further contributions to a secular understanding of reality lead me to propose him as the most significant source (in English) for the Naturalist Tradition.

2.2 Hume and the atheism that dare not speak its name

There is continuing debate on whether Hume was an atheist; anyone in his day would be reluctant to say so.[19] However, many secular philosophers see him as having definitively closed off all avenues to rational support of (Christian) theism. In Chapter 2 (section 4.5), there is a brief account of Hume's attack on Lockean-style apologetics.[20] In his *Dialogues Concerning Natural Religion*, his character Cleanthes (quoted above, Chapter 4, section 5.3) argues that "the Author of Nature is somewhat similar to the mind of man; though possessed of much larger faculties, proportioned to the grandeur of the work . . ." I also mentioned there that design arguments depend on construing the universe as a machine or mechanism, and that alternative construals could point to alternative theories of the universe's origin. It was Hume's (and others') insistence on taking account of all the evidence, including evil and disorder, that turned the problem of evil into an epistemological crisis (Chapter 7, section 3.1).

Notice, though, that Locke did not base his argument for God's existence and much greater faculties on the natural world, but on the specific powers of the human mind. But Philo, in Hume's *Dialogues*, notes the imprecision of making

---

[18] The question mark reflects the difficulty of knowing what anyone means by "intuitive knowledge."

[19] The peculiar title I gave this subsection reflects the difficulty scholars have had in determining whether he was in fact an atheist. (But see the remarks on turnips below.)

[20] Be sure to review this chapter for much more of Hume's thought.

comparisons of degrees of quality, noting that there are certain degrees of analogy among all the operations of nature, "whether the rotting of a turnip, the generation of an animal, and the structure of human thought."[21] So Hume *may* be allowing for a deity that is as much like human intelligence as human intelligence is like the rotting of a turnip.

In addition (in Chapter 5, section 3.1), we have already seen that Hume was arguing, using the new probable reasoning, that in considering the balance of evidence for a law of nature against that of someone claiming to have witnessed a miracle, we could never be justified in using miracle accounts (and likewise prophecies) as a *foundation* for religion.

Also noted above (Chapter 5, section 4.1) was Hume's alteration of the concept of history, showing in his writing of *The History of England* that human history could be understood perfectly well from a secular point of view, in contrast to it being placed in a narrative based on biblical notions of divine plan and providence. Thus, even church history is written today in secular style. Add to this secular approach to historical documents a suspicion of the miraculous, and we have an, at times, radical naturalistic methodology to apply to the Bible.

Three further steps were needed to make atheism a truly viable position. It would be possible to say that religion is an illusion, but a harmless or even beneficial illusion in that it shores up morality. So three sorts of arguments were needed. One was to show that religion did not serve to reveal anything about the moral order that we could not get just as well by the use of human reason. (Most of the work in philosophical ethics during the modern period had this as its aim. The question of whether Hume's or any other philosopher's naturalistic account of morality is adequate will be an important factor in evaluating the Naturalist Tradition.)

Hume's account is as follows: The purpose of Books II and III of his first book, *A Treatise of Human Nature* (1739) and of *An Enquiry Concerning the Principles of Morals* (1751) was to show that philosophical reasoning concerning human conduct has its sole origin in common experience. The moral world is a set of conventions that have developed over time. The sole task of philosophy is to bring to explicit awareness and improve the precision of the standards already implicit in these conventions.

The second step was to argue that a religious system offering divine reward or punishment is not necessary to uphold the moral–political order. In "Of a Particular Providence and a Future State" (1748), Hume claimed that we can see

---

[21] Hume, *Dialogues*, Part XII (only found appended to Hume's 1776 revision, but inserted where planned into the text by editors such as J. C. A. Gaskin, ed., *David Hume: Principal Writings on Religion* including *Dialogues Concerning Natural Religion* and *The Natural History of Religion* (Oxford: Oxford University Press, 1993), 120).

in this life that virtue is attended with its own rewards, namely more peace of mind and a more favorable reception from the world, and that vice leads to misery. Furthermore, any argument to the effect that these earthly rewards and punishments provide evidence for a supreme governor of the world and hence for greater (heavenly) rewards is invalid (as a form of the argument from effects to greater-than-necessary cause) and, in addition, it is unnecessary since the experience of earthly reward upon which it is based is already a sufficient guide to conduct.

A third argument against religion as necessary for morality is to show that religion actually does more harm than good. His milder criticism (in *An Enquiry concerning Human Understanding*) was that religion harms humans by devaluing the goods of this present life in favor of a much more valuable reality in the future. In his *History of England*, he described the positive evils (evident in the previous century): "religions" (Protestant and Catholic political parties) created bigotry and resulted in cruel persecutions.

This last set of arguments, regarding the divine versus human sources of morality, leads directly to the subject of the next subsection: historical accounts of the delay between the articulation of arguments such as Hume's and the cultural acceptability of unbelief in the modern West.

2.3 From atheistic arguments to a full-blown Naturalist Tradition

I considered titling this subsection "How the bishops could still sleep for a century after Hume." Charles Taylor writes that:

> Hume's *Dialogues* . . . may seem to us today a crucial blow in the battle for unbelief. But my hypothesis is, that without the new moral understandings I have been describing, it would have had little impact. Bishops could have slept peacefully in their beds.[22]

Taylor's account goes all the way from 1500, when God's presence was undeniable, to the modern minority elite, such as Hume and d'Holbach, who could deny the existence of God. But to become a way of thinking, feeling, and living acceptable in a culture it was not enough simply to eliminate belief in God. A number of historians provide similar or overlapping accounts of this change from belief to unbelief. Both Turner and Taylor emphasize that the change required not merely the *subtraction* of God from the world, but more importantly, the presence of an alternative.

For brevity's sake, I present only Turner's account of the rise of unbelief in the USA. He focuses on a small sample: the shift from (largely) liberal and Calvinist Protestantism in the New England, New York, and Pennsylvania areas. He claims that the churches themselves laid most of the groundwork for rejection of belief. By

---

22 Taylor, *Secular Age*, 268.

the 1860s, church leaders had responded to the pressures of modernity by increasingly making religion conform to the demands of the modern world "rather than to try to understand that world in relation to a God outside history and beyond human wishes."[23] Turner's own summary of the consequences provides an adequate overview. He writes that a pattern took shape over the space of at least three centuries.

> This configuration makes most sense if cast in terms of the intellectual and emotional functions that belief fulfilled. Roughly speaking, one aspect of God—the Ruler of Nature Who satisfied the desire to understand our surroundings and ourselves—was abstracted into naturalistic scientific explanations.[24] The study of nature yielded no longer evidence of God but simply knowledge of nature. *Another side of God—the Moral Governor Who satisfied the need for good order and the longing for a better—was identified with purely human activities and aspirations. Humanitarianism, science, progress could operate without divine sanction.* A third dimension of God—the mysterious Lord of Heaven Who struck human beings with awe and humility—was much diminished, as believers shifted the main focus of their concern from God's transcendence of earthly things to His compatibility with humanity, its wants, its aspirations, its ways of understanding. What remained of awe before divine mystery was transformed into reverence for such surrogates as nature, art, and humanity itself. In dialectical interplay, each of these "humanizing" trends fostered the others, and thus naturalistic explanations and ideals slowly came to satisfy cultural and personal needs once met by belief in God.[25]

I believe that this is enough said on the atheist "root" of the Naturalist Tradition, so I move on in an attempt to characterize the tradition itself.

3 Naturalism *qua* tradition

It is worth reviewing the features of a large-scale tradition, as this term is being used here (see also Chapter 4, section 3.1). This account has been developed over time in what has been called MacIntyre's trilogy: *After Virtue*, *Whose Justice*, and *Rival Versions*. He began *After Virtue* with the claim that modern moral discourse is in a grave state of disorder. He made a pointed analogy: contemporary moral discourse is comparable to a simulacrum of science after a know-nothing regime

---

[23] Turner, *Without God*, 222.

[24] This is a critique made by Michael Buckley and a number of others. See Michael J. Buckley, SJ, *Denying and Disclosing God: The Ambiguous Progress of Modern Atheism* (New Haven, CT: Yale University Press, 2004).

[25] Turner, *Without God*, 264–5; my italics.

has killed the scientists, burned the books, and trashed the laboratories. Later, fragments of scientific texts are read and memorized, but there is no longer any recognition of the *point* of science.

Similarly, MacIntyre says, our moral language is a holdover from the past, but we have forgotten the original point of morality. In particular, we have forgotten the context that once gave it its meaning. What modern ethics lost is any notion of the ultimate purpose or *telos* of human life. Such accounts of the human *telos* are based on an account of Ultimate Reality, usually provided by religious traditions, but sometimes, as in Aristotle's case, by a metaphysical tradition. MacIntyre argues that the correct form of ethical claims is something like the following conditional statement: "If you are to achieve your *telos*, then you ought to do x."

Traditions are something like worldviews extended over time; they become mature when the original authority upon which they are based is called into question and a methodology for going forward is developed. They are embodied in social practices and institutions. In his historical accounts he shows that variations develop over time, and thus the tradition comes to be made up of subtraditions. Can Naturalism be shown to instantiate all of the elements of this description?

3.1 Ultimate Realities

A proposal for Ultimate Reality as conceived within the Scientific Naturalist Tradition comes rather naturally: it is nature itself, or the cosmos. However, this is not simply to identify it with the totality of entities and forces discovered by science. Ultimate Reality is also that which inspires awe and wonder. Consider the tone of Carl Sagan's (1934–96) PBS series *Cosmos*, aired in 13 parts beginning in 1980. In his article titled "Why Carl Sagan Is Truly Irreplaceable," journalist Joel Achenbach (b.1960) wrote: "We live in Carl Sagan's universe—awesomely vast, deeply humbling."[26]

Mary Midgley (b.1919) has titled a book *Science as Salvation*,[27] and Sagan indeed gives his presentations salvific trappings. His account of salvation is gnostic in character—it assumes that salvation comes from knowledge, in this case scientific knowledge, perhaps advanced by contact with extraterrestrial life forms. He offers a peculiar mix of science itself and concepts drawn from science to fill religious categories that fall into a pattern surprisingly isomorphic with the Christian conceptual scheme. For example, his account of ultimate origins is Evolution with a capital "E." The source of sin is the primitive reptilian structure in the brain.[28]

---

[26] Joel Achenbach, "Why Carl Sagan Is Truly Irreplaceable," *Smithsonian Magazine* (March, 2014).

[27] Mary Midgley, *Science as Salvation: A Modern Myth and its Meaning* (London and New York: Routledge, 1992).

[28] Thomas Ross, "The Implicit Theology of Carl Sagan," *Pacific Theological Review* 18, no. 2 (1985): 24–32.

Midgley writes that Scientific Naturalism supplies two additional psychological necessities—a sense of order[29] (from the laws of nature) and teleology, the belief that there is a final end to life.[30] That such an end, a *telos*, follows from an account of Ultimate Reality will bring us to the next section.

It is much more difficult to determine a concept of Ultimate Reality for Moral Naturalism, and one persuasive explanation for this difficulty will become central in section 4. In fact, nearly everything about Moral Naturalism is difficult to describe because there are so many conflicting positions on nearly every topic. Perhaps this indeed reflects MacIntyre's claim that modern moral discourse is in a grave state of disorder. However, if there is any shared sense of the *point* of moral codes, it is that they are made for humans, by humans, and for the sake of guiding human practice. Thus, I tentatively suggest that if Moral Naturalism has a concept of Ultimate Reality it is humankind itself.

There is a growing sense, however, that drawing the circle of moral concern around humans alone is too narrow. It should include at least sentient animals. Some would say that it should include the whole of our ecology, not merely for the utilitarian purpose of protecting our species' future survival, but for the value of the natural world in its own right. At this point, Moral and Scientific Naturalism would overlap.

3.2 Naturalisms' *teloi*

Both Midgley and MacIntyre have argued that a notion of the ultimate purpose of human life is a necessity. Midgley's argument is more psychological; MacIntyre argues that it is necessary for distinguishing among competing moral theories.

I earlier raised the question of why it took so long for unbelief to become, first, culturally acceptable and, later, widespread in North Atlantic culture (section 1.3). I use Taylor's work in *A Secular Age* in this subsection because I believe the answer he gives for the delay could be described as the long quest for an acceptable *telos* for humankind if God were to be replaced by a different vision of Ultimate Reality.

I have always shied away from speaking about "the meaning of life" because it seems so vague an idea. However, when Taylor claims that it took at least a century to replace Christian *moral* sources, he is not saying that it took that long to replace God as an enforcer of moral norms (as Hume supposed). I believe that he is groping for language to explain what it took to transform North Atlantic conceptions of the meaning of life, that is, a quest for a "fullness, a richness"—a sense that life is fuller, richer, deeper or higher, more worthwhile, more admirable, more what it

---

[29] Midgley, *Salvation*, 127.
[30] Midgley, *Salvation*, 26.

should be.[31] He is attempting to articulate a replacement for the original *telos* of the Christian Tradition. The Christian Tradition had defined a direction of life in terms of loving and worshiping God (17). In Christianity, this did not exclude the willing of human flourishing, but this was because God wills it. Taylor suggests three versions of post-Christian *teloi:* The first of these, and the one that best fits the current Scientific Naturalist Tradition, is the rationalist version. This involves

> an admiration for the power of cool, disengaged reason, capable of contemplating the world and human life without illusion, and of acting lucidly for the best in the interest of human flourishing . . . Indeed, this sense of ourselves as beings both frail and courageous, capable of facing a meaningless, hostile universe without faintness of heart, and of rising to the challenge of devising our own rules of life, can be an inspiring one . . . Rising fully to this challenge, empowered by our sense of our own greatness in doing so, this condition we aspire to but only rarely, if ever, achieve, can function as its own place of fullness, in the sense of my discussion here. (9)

> The great invention of the West was that of an immanent order in Nature, whose working could be systematically understood and explained on its own terms. (15)

Taylor's second version of fullness or *telos* involves needing to receive power from elsewhere than autonomous reason. Sources of this power are found in nature or our own inner depths. It is a development from the Romantic critique of the disengaged reason of the Enlightenment. What he means here is better expressed in his earlier volume, *Sources of the Self.* To find power in nature requires the ability to perceive in ourselves an inner élan, a heightened vibrancy in our lives. But this inner impulse can only be known to us by articulating it. Sometimes the expression itself is a creative process of giving shape to that power.[32] This version is the more appropriate one for Moral Naturalism.

The third possibility, represented in certain forms of postmodernism, involves attempts to undermine the ends of seeking fullness in both reason and nature. This is what MacIntyre calls the Genealogical Tradition: Friedrich Nietzsche and his followers.[33]

The bridge that needed to be constructed from the Christian *telos* to either the scientific or the Romantic substitute was humanism. I have already used Taylor's concept of providential deism in my account of the transition from a concept

---

[31] Taylor, *Secular Age,* 5; further citations to this book will be in parentheses.

[32] Charles Taylor, *Sources of the Self: The Making of the Modern Identity* (Cambridge, MA: Harvard University Press, 1989), 370, 372, 374. Here he also identifies three options, but the third is an identity formed by retaining Christian moral sources.

[33] Alasdair MacIntyre, *Three Rival Versions of Moral Enquiry: Encyclopaedia, Genealogy, and Tradition* (Notre Dame, IN: University of Notre Dame Press, 1990).

of God as actively engaged in humans' daily lives to that of a God whose providence is only expressed in the working of natural laws (Chapter 6, section 3.2). My emphasis in Chapter 6 was on the development of the picture of a law-governed universe; Taylor's emphasis is on the *humanism* that could be developed from the divine *providence* expressed therein. He writes that this issue can be expressed by asking whether the highest and best of life must involve seeking or serving a good that is beyond human flourishing, or can it be found in the pursuit of human flourishing itself.

So, in describing the history of Naturalism, I identified Renaissance Humanism as one of its three roots. While one version of this earlier movement was Christian Humanism, Taylor says, in short, that the transition to a purely secular version of Naturalism was by means of a humanism "accepting no final goals beyond human flourishing."[34] I believe that this work provides an attractive account of the *telos* of Moral Naturalism.

3.3 Modern Naturalist morality and methods

Taylor ends *Sources* with the claim that both Scientific and Moral Naturalists agree on the importance of a morality of universal justice, beneficence, and self-determination. However, he expresses two worries. The first is that both *teloi* have degenerated during the twentieth century, as Western culture has moved further from its earlier basis in Judaism and Christianity. Scientific Naturalism has come to join a lively sense of our powers of disengaged reason to an *instrumental* reading of nature; the study of nature is increasingly used to expand one's own happiness. Moral Naturalism has individualized the pursuit of human flourishing; it has come to be seen more in terms of *subjective fulfillment.*

Taylor's second worry grows out of both of these narrowings of vision. Just as the highest moral aspirations "imposed" by religion in the past were seen in the Enlightenment to result in a renunciation of natural desire, so too in our time the moral demands of justice and benevolence can be seen to stand in opposition to one's happiness and fulfillment.

One of my favorite Naturalist ethicists, Owen Flanagan (b.1949), aptly illustrates Taylor's worry regarding conflicts. Flanagan writes that his rejection of the idea of an immaterial soul raised the question of what makes life worth living: why does anything matter? He concludes that life's meaning comes through being in charge of yourself, and from having chances to express and carry through on projects that have value and worth. However: "Living meaningfully and living morally, as the latter is conventionally understood, can and do conflict."[35]

---

[34] Taylor, *Secular Age*, 18.
[35] Owen Flanagan, *Self Expressions: Mind, Morals, and the Meaning of Life* (New York and Oxford: Oxford University Press, 1996), vii–viii.

Flanagan has written two additional books exploring these and related issues.[36] I have studied his ethics carefully because (in contrast to many Naturalists) his work does not aim at reducing ethics to something else, such as biology. Also, he and I have much in common—both former Catholics, both influenced by MacIntyre. He is particularly relevant here in claiming that we can determine empirically what constitutes human flourishing. His purpose in these two recent books is to show that the pursuit of the good life in *this* life is enough to make it meaningful, without any concept of life after death. The good life essentially involves moral development, and even spiritual practices, but without any form of deity. His empirical studies are supplemented with a review of the great moral philosophies of the West, but also of the literature of some of the great religious systems such as Buddhism and what he calls Jesusism (as opposed to Christianity).

The moral code that Flanagan endorses is not at all out of the ordinary. He argues for the values of friendship, love, kindness, and compassion; for culti-vating the virtues of courage, fidelity, honesty. Flanagan argues that we could develop a science that might be called "eudaimonics," taken from Aristotle's term *eudaimonia*, which means something like flourishing while enjoying one's own flourishing. This would be the science akin to ecology that employs empirical evidence to describe the environments and patterns of behavior that are most conducive to human flourishing. He emphasizes the fact that humans come into the world with some basic moral equipment in the form of emotions and desires that predispose them to social behavior. He does not limit his concerns merely to humans but extends them to other sentient animals, and to nature itself, not for self-interested purposes but because nature itself has value.

The difficulty Flanagan sees is that two quests are often in tension: the quest to be moral and the quest for a meaningful life. His example of such tension is that between, on the one hand, doing philosophy and spending one's salary on living well (which he calls "meaning"), and on the other hand, taking a second job or turning over half of one's salary to help others in need (which he calls morals).

His analysis of what is necessary for a meaningful life begins with morality itself: "across cultures one finds that being moral, that is, being a good per-son, is considered a necessary condition of living a meaningful life. As far as I can tell, it is the only absolutely necessary condition."[37] Good candidates for further conditions are true friendship and what John Rawls (1921–2002) calls the Aristotelian Principle: "Other things being equal, human beings enjoy the

---

[36] Owen Flanagan, *The Problem of the Soul: Two Visions of Mind and How to Reconcile Them* (New York: Basic Books, 2002); and *The Really Hard Problem: Meaning in a Material World* (Cambridge, MA: MIT Press, 2007).

[37] Flanagan, *Problem of the Soul*, 281–2.

exercise of their realized capacities (their innate and trained abilities), and this enjoyment increases the more the capacity is realized, or the greater its complexity."[38] The fact, then, that humans have natural dispositions toward morality means that the quest for higher forms of morality is essential to our human flourishing.

> We are conscious beings on a quest, a quest that achieves its aims when we use our minds to flourish and to be good. These are our most noble aims. They involve striving to become better, individually and collectively, than we are. Insofar as we aim to realize ideals that are possible but not yet real, the quest can be legitimately described as spiritual.[39]

This is by no means an adequate account of Flanagan's work, but he comes surprisingly close to having created an ethical vision that meets the ideals of both the Scientific and Moral *teloi*. He proposes a scientific approach to ethics—using our best rational abilities to come to agreement on what it takes for humans to flourish (without the illusions of God, souls, or immortality).

The account I have given of Taylor's Scientific *telos* is somewhat ambiguous in emphasizing both human frailty and courage. Flanagan uses Taylor's concept of "strong evaluation"; that is, discriminations of right or wrong, higher or lower, that are not rendered valid by our own desires, inclinations, but rather stand independent of these and offer standards by which our choices can be judged.[40] He calls us to apply, to the best of our abilities, judgments of the strong type to our character, our projects, our life decisions. But we do not always possess clear and unequivocal standards, so we do the best we can. We need to live with *unconfident confidence*.[41] He is certainly writing with the intent to *inspire* his readers to invest in the task of formulating increasingly apt rules for life.

Flanagan flatly denies scientism, understood as the doctrine that everything worth saying can be expressed scientifically.[42] What about great art, music, even spiritual experience? What is needed is a "thick description," in anthropologist Clifford Geertz's (1926–2006) terms, of human flourishing. "Meaning is multifarious . . . [it involves] having opportunities to express our talents, to find meaningful work, to create and live among beautiful things," and to live cooperatively in social environments.[43] The very writing of Flanagan's chapter has been an act of *articulating* the inner impulses that give life meaning.[44]

---

[38] Flanagan, *Problem of the Soul*, 284.
[39] Flanagan, *Problem of the Soul*, 319.
[40] Taylor, *Sources*, 4.
[41] Flanagan, *Self Expressions*, 213.
[42] Flanagan, *Problem of the Soul*, 268.
[43] Flanagan, *Problem of the Soul*, 281, 285.
[44] Flanagan, *Problem of the Soul*, ch. 7.

I had intended to include a separate subsection here on Naturalist methods or epistemology, but I believe my account of Flanagan's work has turned out to illustrate at least one fine version. I say more on scientism in section 4.

3.4 Social embodiment

MacIntyre notes that a living tradition is socially embodied in the lives of its adherents, in social practices, and institutions. I shall skip over individual biographies, although many fine examples could be found. It is almost a tautology to say that the most important practices and institutions embodying the Scientific Naturalist Tradition are found in science—but with the caveat that practicing science or supporting it institutionally are not *equivalent* to embodying the Tradition.

Historians may not think of themselves as engaging in a naturalist practice, but, as noted above, one of Hume's chief philosophical goals was to supplant the traditional Christian storyline of creation, Fall, and redemption by a new unity of action based along secular and humanistic lines. Now even Christian historians practice their craft on the basis of naturalist assumptions, and the "methodological atheism" of both historians and biblical critics may have had a much more significant impact on Christian self-understanding than that of the natural sciences.

The above are practices with parallels to those of Christian *scholars*. In addition, of course, there are also now secular versions of practices that used to belong solely to the *church*, such as marriage by a justice of the peace. Psychotherapy competes with spiritual direction. A legal system (institution) has been developed that is independent of canon law. These are forms of secularization, as the term is most often used.

3.5 Authorities?

In presenting Christianity as a MacIntyrean tradition, the easiest question to answer was that of its formative text(s). It is clear that Scripture plays that role, either considered as a canonical whole or as a series of texts, already building a tradition of interpretations of earlier texts. In recognizing the extent to which Christianity has branched out into a number of major subtraditions, it would have been appropriate to consider later authoritative texts through which the Scriptures have been interpreted: the Augustinian corpus, Thomas's two *Summas*, Calvin's *Institutes*, and so forth.

This question should be much more difficult in the case of Naturalism, given that modernity has been cast in terms of the flight from authority. And one surprise, given that "authority" as used by Jeffrey Stout meant religious authority, is that one answer might in fact be Scripture, in that modern Naturalism in the West is, intentionally or not, a substitute for the Christian worldview. This has often been said of Marxism; Turner's account of unbelief is based on his argument that it arose as a result of finding better ways to attain the same goods as those that Christianity (of the time and place he studied) aimed for.

Only Thomas Kuhn noticed that science itself progresses by accepting the worldview enshrined in a formative text, such as Newton's *Principia*. So we should not be surprised that professing Naturalists profess allegiance to no special text.

Let us put these two considerations together and add the fact that in MacIntyre's own *Rival Versions* he selects as formative of three modern and contemporary rival texts that adherents of those traditions may never have heard of. For those continuing to pursue the goods of the Enlightenment, his choice is the ninth edition— specifically the ninth—of the *Encyclopedia Britannica*. For the aforementioned Genealogical Tradition, I have already given a clue: It is Nietzsche's *Zur Genealogy der Moral*. An indication of its continuing relevance is found in Allan Bloom's (loved or hated) book, *The Closing of the American Mind*. Bloom (1930–92) writes that, almost unnoticed,

> there is now an entirely new language of good and evil, originating in an attempt to get "beyond good and evil" and preventing us from talking with any conviction about good and evil anymore . . . The new language is that of *value* relativism and it constitutes a change in our view of things moral and political as great as the one that took place when Christianity replaced Greek and Roman paganism.[45]

And for MacIntyre's argument for the need to recognize that one's conception of the nature of rationality is dependent on the tradition to which one belongs, he chose the late-nineteenth-century encyclical by Pope Leo XIII (1810–1903), *Aeterni Patris*.

All of this leads me to choose as one formative text for the Moral Naturalist Tradition Ludwig Feuerbach's *The Essence of Christianity*.[46] Friedrich Schleiermacher had published his *Christian Faith* in 1834, intending to show that doctrines could be evaluated on the basis of their agreement with (Protestant) Christian feeling or awareness. Karl Barth recommended that all theology students read Feuerbach's *Wesen des Christentums* in order to show, better than anyone else had done, that any theology beginning with human subjective states will necessarily constitute a treatise on anthropology. The essence of Feuerbach's message is humanism: all of the perfections we attribute to God are actually the epitome of the qualities

---

[45] Allan Bloom, *The Closing of the American Mind: How Higher Education Has Failed Democracy and Impoverished the Souls of Today's Students* (New York: Simon and Schuster, 1987), 141. Note that *Beyond Good and Evil* is the English title of Nietzsche's 1886 book, published one year prior to *Genealogy*.

[46] Ludwig Feuerbach, *Das Wesen des Christentums* (1841), tr. George Eliot (i.e., Marian Evans) as *The Essence of Christianity* ([1854] Amherst, NY: Prometheus Books, 1989).

distributed among the human species. Feuerbach's primary concern, then, is ontology; however, he credits his account to an application of empirical analysis of religion, and so we find here too a naturalist methodology.

My attention was drawn to Feuerbach by theologian Owen Thomas (1922–2015) in a comment regarding a paper on naturalism that I composed earlier. He wrote that I should incorporate Feuerbach between my attention to Hume and d'Holbach as earlier contributors, and to Marx and Freud later, because Feuerbach "was the inspiration of the latter two and also the main source of American naturalism."[47]

So I have mentioned the writings of Hume, d'Holbach, Feuerbach, Comte, Freud, and Marx—seven dead white European males.

3.6 A brief postscript

Have I succeeded in this very brief account in showing Naturalism to be a MacIntyrean tradition? One thing missing is a description of anything resembling churches in Christianity. I was surprised to read that Freemasonry, a fraternal order, might be one of the best candidates. Its history has been difficult to trace, but the first grand lodge was established in London in 1717. From the little I know of it, it appears to be an attempt to provide a non-theistic replacement for the pomp and rituals that developed in a number of churches.

I am confident that Midgley would agree with my general claim, even if disputing details. A very fine historian of science and religion, Thomas Dixon, wrote an essay review of a book by John Avise (b.1948) titled "Scientific Atheism as a Faith Tradition."[48] In the end, it is the reader's responsibility to evaluate my arguments here. Mikael Stenmark (b.1962) has provided another rich resource for this view.[49]

4 Traditions and their crises

It will be helpful to review here the complex process of comparing the rational superiority of one tradition to its rival. The first step is to provide a narrative of the crises one's own tradition has encountered and of the extent to which it has (or has not) been able to overcome them.

Second, one needs to consider the rival's crises (from an insider's sympathetic perspective) and judge the extent to which each has been met.

---

[47] Personal communication, June 27, 2008, commenting on my paper now published as "Naturalism and Theism as Competing Traditions," in Gasser, *How Successful is Naturalism?*, 49–75.

[48] Thomas Dixon, "Scientific Atheism as a Faith Tradition," *Studies in History and Philosophy of Biological and Biomedical* Sciences 33 (2002): 337–59: a review of John C. Avise, *The Genetic Gods: Evolution and Belief in Human Affairs* (Cambridge, MA: Harvard University Press, 1998).

[49] Mikael Stenmark, *Scientism: Science, Ethics, and Religion* (Aldershot, UK: Ashgate, 2001).

Third, one ought to be able to show why the rival's crises had not been met, and why the rival should have been expected to fail at just the point it did.

Finally, and ideally, one ought to be able to provide resources from one's own tradition that in fact meet the rival's crises. In this case, one has shown that one's own point of view is superior, not only because it has been successful on its own terms, but also because it can explain why the rival's point of view was lacking, in a way that the rival itself was not able to do.

4.1 Christianity's crises

I considered, up to this point, seven crises Christianity has faced in the modern West, and review here my own judgments of the extent to which each has been met.

1 *The modern epistemological crisis*: Christianity has nearly always sought to justify its claims in terms of the best account of reason available in its culture. The rather sudden rejection of authority as a legitimate epistemological category and its replacement with empirical methods created what some have judged to be an insurmountable epistemological crisis. I argued, however, that while this was true in earlier days, with less sophisticated accounts of reason, it is only now, with the development of MacIntyre's account of tradition-constituted rationality, that we have an understanding of reason capable of doing justice to a tradition such as Christianity, and I offer this book itself as a small step in this justification process.

2 *Biblical criticism*: I presented the development of higher criticism of the Bible as an epistemological crisis, and again one with an emphasis on the qualifier "epistemological" because the texts are our primary public access to the teachings of Jesus and others. I see the radical and quite destructive critiques (prevalent during earlier centuries, but still available today[50]) to be another result of a too-primitive epistemology in the eighteenth and nineteenth centuries, and to an expectation that the texts meet modern standards of historiography. Following Hans Frei and others, I see the resolution to come from a change of perspectives: no longer treating the texts as *objects* of scientific study, but as something like *lenses through which to interpret the world*. I claim below that the biblical worldview is indeed roomy enough, as George Lindbeck says, to absorb the world, and I add, especially the world as science presents it.

---

[50] Consider, for example, John Dominic Crossan's thesis that Jesus' tomb was empty because packs of wild dogs had eaten his body; see, among other works, *Who Killed Jesus? Exposing the Roots of Anti-Semitism in the Gospel Story of the Death of Jesus* (San Francisco: HarperSanFrancisco, 1994), ch. 6.

3 *The problem of religious pluralism*: If my claims in *1* and *2* above are correct, and if those who say that it is an insult to people of other faiths to deny significant differences among religious traditions, then we have a way ahead (a *long* way) to compare and evaluate other traditions, both in terms of their rationality and in terms of the kinds of social embodiment they encourage.

4 *The problem of special divine action*: This is the topic that worries me the most. First, critics of quantum divine action (QDA) are many, and supporters are few. In addition, the de-divinization of nature by the physico-theologians has become scientific orthodoxy, so a proposal such as mine, calling for a new account of the very nature of matter, emphasizing its insufficiency apart from a much stronger doctrine of divine immanence than that of modern liberal theology, has come to be unimaginable outside of a small group of the shrinking population of Christians. And, again, if we cannot make sense of special divine action, I see no way to defend revelation and its reliability as an epistemological resource.

I believe that the most we can say at this point is that the theory of QDA finally allows a new starting point for theologians finally to put their own house back in order at the end of the Newtonian age. I quote a late colleague of mine at Fuller. Theological ethicist Glen Stassen (1936–2014) read my account of QDA and wrote rather lyrically about it. He had started his career in physics and was involved in research using a Van de Graff accelerator (please do not ask me what that is) to probe nuclear isotopes with protons. His theological interpretation of the research is consistent with my theory of QDA:

> The nuclei were telling us specific messages about their binding forces and spins and they were doing this as if alive, as if they were deciding when to split . . . They were . . . speaking our mathematical language, completely understandable, telling us the nature of their binding forces! . . .
>
> For me, it was an experience of God's presence—or openness to God's presence—in the very foundations of physical reality . . .
>
> For a person of faith, this means God is doing new things every moment. Our universe is not a stationary machine; it is dynamic . . . at its very base . . . The nuclei of the atoms, the very building blocks of all nature, are each "deciding" every moment whether to stay the same or whether to split up and go different ways. They are alive and responding to God's will! [51]

So I suppose that work of the sort we have been doing can only be understood as an apologetic strategy within the Christian community; but this is not entirely insignificant.

---

[51] Glen Harold Stassen, *A Thicker Jesus: Incarnational Discipleship in a Secular Age* (Louisville, KY: Westminster John Knox Press, 2012), 85–6.

5 *The problem of evil*: I stated in Chapter 7 that the free-will defense in the case of human evil seems entirely reasonable; I and Warren Brown have done our best to defend free will and moral responsibility against neurobiological determinism.[52] Pure natural evil and human limitation seem indeed to be by-products of necessary conditions for us and for other sentient creatures to be here.

6 *Science versus Christianity*: Insofar as the content of the natural sciences is concerned, conflicts with Christianity—and remember, all Christian theology involves interpretation—have been few and short-lived. Insofar as the success of science has contributed to empiricist epistemology and the desacralizing of nature, it has indeed been indirectly inimical to Christianity.

7 *Neuroscientific monism versus Christian dualism*: Recall that the point of Chapter 9 was not to refute (any of the many versions of) Christian dualism, but only to show that there is an alternative to dualism. This, however, depends on the relative weight one's subtradition places on Scripture and tradition (in the non-MacIntyrean sense).

4.2 A Naturalist reading of Christian crises

There are parts of this subsection that are easy to write. If there is no God, then lack of a suitable epistemology to confirm God's existence or any of the other teachings of the Tradition is to be expected. Biblical texts from thousands of years ago need not be any more flawless then other ancient texts.

No God, then no problem in accounting for divine action. However, some sort of explanation does need to be provided for the countless accounts of humans claiming to experience God at work in their lives and in the world.[53] Readers who have reached this chapter of the book are not likely to accept a simple dismissal of their perceptions as being naïve or deluded.

If the problem of evil is taken as the same as the problem of theodicy: how to reconcile evil and suffering with the (supposed) existence of an all-good, omnipotent God, then it dissolves. However, the suffering is still there; there is still the problem of how to combat it, of why it is so unevenly distributed. And there is no doctrine of sin to explain even a part of it.

There remain serious questions regarding the sufficiency of a purely physicalist account of human nature, but these are raised by some scientists as well as by other Christians.

---

[52] Nancey Murphy and Warren S. Brown, *Did My Neurons Make Me Do It? Philosophical and Neurobiological Perspectives on Moral Responsibility and Free Will* (Oxford: Oxford University Press, 2007).

[53] Review Chapter 7, section 4.3.

If historians are correct in attributing the science–religion controversies largely to power struggles, then Scientific Naturalists are likely to have suffered from these, and, without having read the historians who make this point, will likely see the conflicts in terms of irreconcilable worldviews.

The plurality of religions is an absolute bonus for most Naturalists: if there were a God, could there not be even a bit of consensus? John Hick, premier Christian philosopher of religion, wrote that there is no sufficient reason even to conclude whether God is personal or an impersonal force. However, it will turn out that a new contribution to Scientific Naturalism, the cognitive science of religion (CSR), will provide Christians assistance in defending their Tradition in this regard.

An additional crisis that needs to be addressed is a criticism that Hume did not delve deeply enough into the question of whether Christianity has caused more harm than good. There was a spate of publications between 2000 and 2010, whose authors were called, collectively, the new atheists. Three of the best-selling books are Richard Dawkins, *The God Delusion*;[54] Christopher Hitchens, *god is not Great: How Religion Poisons Everything*;[55] and Daniel Dennett, *Breaking the Spell: Religion as a Natural Phenomenon*.[56] Dawkins (b.1941) is an ethologist by training; Hitchens (1949–2011) was a journalist; and Dennett is a professor of philosophy at Tufts University. The books share many themes: explanations of the origins of religion (none as sophisticated as Westphal's great masters of suspicion); amusing examples of some of the most ridiculous religious movements in history; but also grave criticism: All of the authors attack the idea that good morals depend on religion, and then set out to show that, in fact, most of the evil in the world comes from religion. Hitchens and Dawkins argue that religion can be found lurking behind nearly all of the evils of the world. Where many of us would argue that causes of conflict are economic, political, or ethnic, and that religious differences become tools of one or both sides, Dawkins says that this is "pusillanimous reluctance to use religious names for warring factions. In Northern Ireland, Catholics and Protestants are euphemized to 'Nationalists' and 'Loyalists' respectively." The so-called ethnic cleansing in the former Yugoslavia was really, he says, religious "cleansing"—Catholics, Muslims, and Orthodox.[57] He even has an extended argument that Hitler was a Christian, and that this served as his *main* motivation.

This portrayal of religion, particularly Christianity, as the source of the world's greatest evils is a point of view that all of us need to be aware of and take seriously—even though the atheists' scholarship may be bad. It should not be the

---

[54] Richard Dawkins, *The God Delusion* (Boston and New York: Houghton Mifflin, 2006).

[55] Christopher Hitchens, *god is not Great: How Religion Poisons Everything* (New York: Hachette Book Group, 2007).

[56] Daniel C. Dennett, *Breaking the Spell: Religion as a Natural Phenomenon* (New York: Viking, 2006).

[57] Dawkins, *Delusion*, 21.

case that Christians need to defend themselves by saying that we are not really *as bad as* our detractors say we are, and that atheists such as Stalin are even worse. Here is a call to repentance if ever there was one! An irony here is that Christians *do* have explanations for the real and apparent evils committed in the world; but to dismiss Christian doctrine is to dismiss the explanations as well.

I have spoken with a few scholars about the sudden rush to publication of anti-religious books. Keith Ward, recently retired Regius Professor of Divinity at Oxford University, has made a careful study of the phenomenon. I recommend his book, *The Case for Religion*. In place of the snarling dispositions of the atheistic books considered here, there is Ward's sparkling sense of humor. For example, after pointing out that most universities teach courses in "religion" and that the usual first lecture (or in this case, the Introduction) explains how impossible it is to define "religion," Ward says that: "The courses continue to be called courses on religion, however, because that sounds better than having a course entitled, 'I do not know what I am talking about.'"[58]

I also recommend Ward's book titled *Is Religion Dangerous?* I asked him over coffee how one could settle the dispute between Dawkins and myself about the real causes of violence in Ireland and other such conflicts. It was actually a rhetorical question, because I did not think it could be done. Keith, with his usual modesty and twinkling eye, told me that he had just done it—and recommended the book.[59]

Christians cannot (all) be dismissed as gullible, but neither can (all) Naturalists. Most Christian crises are in fact crises of Christians' own making. One grand theory explains the existence (or intractability) of the crises: There is no God. Notice, though, that what MacIntyre requires is that members of a rival tradition evaluate (in this case) Christianity—in terms of how it has or has not solved its own crises on its own terms. Simply to deny the existence of the Christian God is exactly what the relativist would expect. Are there Naturalists with the ability to enter sympathetically into the Christian worldview and help Christians to see, better than they can see for themselves, whether or to what extent they have solved their own crises, and whether there are potential crises that Christians have not recognized? I am sure that there are. So the part of this subsection that is beyond my ability to write is to find, read sympathetically, and evaluate the works of such desirable and essential critics.

4.3 Naturalist crises

In this subsection I propose three problems for Naturalists, and I believe (and hope) that I am being fair, in that many Naturalists themselves see these as

---

58 Keith Ward, *The Case for Religion* (Oxford: One World, 2004), 9.
59 Keith Ward, *Is Religion Dangerous?* (Grand Rapids, MI: Eerdmans, 2006).

problems. These are (1) the threat of self-referential incoherence, insofar as it is claimed that science (or something like it) is the only source of knowledge; (2) an *inadequate* account of the origins and persistence of religion; and (3) what I now simply call loss of the moral *ought*.

4.3.1 Self-referential incoherence

One of the shortest-lived philosophical positions was the verification theory of meaning: If a proposition is not a tautology, then it is meaningful only if there is some actual or imaginable way of showing it to be true. If not, it is not even false, but simply meaningless. Unfortunately, for the verificationists, the verification thesis itself is not verifiable.

If Naturalists make the bald claim that only science can provide genuine knowledge (e.g., Francis Crick [1916–2004], E. O. Wilson [b.1929]), then their positions face the same quick refutation as the verification theory of meaning. Scientism is a philosophical theory, an epistemological theory, and there seems to be no way to support it scientifically.

However, what about less bold (but perhaps vaguer) claims such as Post's: "acceptable methods of justification and explanation are *commensurable*, in some sense, with those in science" (see section 1.1 above; my italics)? We know generally what incommensurability means; we have versions from Kuhn, Feyerabend, and MacIntyre. But these have to do with scientific paradigms (Kuhn) or worldviews (Feyerabend and MacIntyre). I confess that I do not know what "commensurability" means with regard to methods. Does Clark's statement express it more clearly? I think it does: "Naturalism depends on taking rational, evidence-based empiricism, epitomized by science, as our way of knowing about what ultimately exists" (section 1.1 above).

The catch, though, is in the word "ultimately." Science does indeed give us our best empirical evidence regarding what exists in the natural world. But if science is understood in the current sense of discovering entities and natural causes, there is a bit of vicious circularity here. Science's job is to study the world naturalistically, and thus what it finds is—the natural world. If science cannot find anything else, should we be surprised? Existence claims regarding physical objects are often relatively easy to settle. There are exceptions: I read of a bird that was believed to be extinct, but then it was claimed that one was observed in a remote location. Teams of birdwatchers could be sent out to that area to try to confirm the report. However, non-existence claims are more difficult: search *the entire Earth* without finding the bird? The Russian cosmonaut Yuri Gagarin (1934–68) was (apparently) misquoted in saying during his 1961 spaceflight: "I don't see any God up here." Bluntly: there are questions, such as the non-existence of God, that science is specifically designed *not* to be able to address. One catch, though: An unobservable entity can be known by its causal effects. So without an adequate doctrine of special divine action, there is no *apparent* difference in the world whether one is an atheist, a Deist, or a theologian of the classical liberal sort.

Notice, though, that the sophisticated Naturalist, Flanagan, specifically rejects scientism and draws on a variety of resources, including philosophical and religious traditions, in constructing his Morally Naturalist ethic. I return to the issue of anti-scientistic methodology in section 5.

4.3.2 Explaining the persistence of religion

The new atheists have little to offer that goes beyond Hume's naturalistic account of the origin of religion, with the exception of Dennett's very readable presentation of a new discipline, called the cognitive science of religion (CSR), dating approximately from the beginning of this century.[60] Pascal Boyer (b.1964) and others hypothesize that we have inference systems that are turned on by different kinds of entities.[61] These are sometimes called cognitive modules. Some examples are: an agency-detection system, closely related to a system for detecting goal-directed movement; a system for keeping track of who's who; and systems dealing with the physics of solid objects, physical causation, and linking function to structure. To the extent that religious concepts have enough in common with ordinary concepts, they set off these inference systems, and this makes some sets of beliefs about the relevant entities natural, and therefore likely to be understood, remembered, elaborated in specific ways, and passed on to others.

Two questions need to be answered: First, is there sufficient *scientific* evidence for these theories? (The bibliographies I have seen so far are scant and tend to reference one another in a circular fashion).[62] Second, and this is much more difficult to answer: do the theories (Boyer's and his colleagues') really provide adequate explanations for the persistence of religion—especially after we have read their books?

I also have some scientific reservations about CSR. First, CSR so far provides no linkages between the "cognitive modules" listed above and neuroscience. For example, what regions or systems in the brain provide for "dealing with the physics of solid objects"? Second, many of the accounts given have the appearance of "just so" stories: our ancestors on the savannah needed to be able to distinguish quickly an agent from an inanimate object; religions result from an overactive

---

[60] Dennett, *Breaking the Spell.*

[61] Pascal Boyer, *Religion Explained: The Evolutionary Origins of Religious Thought* (New York: Basic Books, 2001).

[62] See Justin Barrett, "In the Empirical Mode: Evidence Needed for the Modes of Religiosity Theory," in Harvey Whitehouse and Robert M. McCauley, eds., *Minds and Religion: Psychological and Cognitive Foundations of Religiosity* (Lanham, MD: Rowman & Littlefield Publishers, 2005), ch. 6. Barrett says that "contributions from numerous scholars from many disciplines are desperately needed to move forward this . . . theoretical framework" (124–5).

agency-detection system that perceives agency where in fact there is none, but attributes it to spiritual beings. Third, it is cultural evolution, which happens at a much faster pace, that now accounts for the adaptation of beliefs to reality. The stocking of our brains with ideas is almost entirely the result of learning from our social environments.

I return to CSR below in section 5, regarding reciprocal gifts that Naturalism and Christianity might make to one another.

4.3.3 Loss of the moral "ought"

If the modern Naturalist Tradition began with Hume and his arguments against the necessity of postulating God to uphold morality, then we may be coming full circle. Two of the most respected philosophical ethicists of this generation have concluded that modern moral reasoning is in a state of disorder and that the disorder could be mended by returning to a theistic justification. In a thin volume with the modest title *Morality*, Bernard Williams (1929–2003) surveys the major approaches to ethics from antiquity to the present. He finds most of them defective in that they are not capable of answering the question why be moral (at all)? However, there is also a sort of theory that

> seeks to provide, in terms of the transcendental framework, something that man is for: if he understands properly his role in the basic scheme of things, he will see that there are some particular sorts of ends which are properly his and which he ought to realize. One archetypal form of such a view is the belief that man was created by a God who also has certain expectations of him.[63]

However, he says, it has been practically a philosopher's platitude that even if a God did exist, this would make no difference to the situation of morality. But Williams believes this platitude to be based on mistaken reasoning: "If God existed, there might well be special, and acceptable, reasons for subscribing to morality."[64] Unfortunately, concludes Williams the atheist, the very concept of God is incoherent; religion itself is incurably unintelligible.

MacIntyre has taken very seriously the challenge of Nietzsche's critique of traditional morality, but he finds little in modern thought with which to counter it. The development of theories in philosophical ethics from Thomas Hobbes at the beginning to the Bloomsbury group in the early twentieth century has been a failed attempt to provide a theoretical rationale for traditional morality. This has led him to conclude, as I noted above, that modern moral discourse is in a grave state of disorder—no one now knows the *point* of morality. In particular, we have

---

[63] Bernard Williams, *Morality: An Introduction to Ethics* (Cambridge: Cambridge University Press, 1972), 63.
[64] Williams, *Morality*, 72.

forgotten the context that once gave it its meaning: any notion of the ultimate purpose, *telos* of human life. I argued that Taylor's lengthy books, *Sources of the Self* and *A Secular Age*, were his attempt to recount the history of seeking a substitute for Christianity's theory of human purpose.

Modern philosophers have developed competing theories regarding the most basic moral claims: you ought to act so as to achieve the greatest good for the greatest number; versus: you ought to act so that the maxim of your action can be willed universally. But because morality is taken to be autonomous—that is, unrelated to other knowledge—there is no way to arbitrate between these most basic construals of the moral "ought." This impossibility results in the interminability of moral debates in our society. However, the interminability should not, says MacIntyre, be taken as the intrinsic nature of moral discourse, but ought rather to be seen as a sign that the entire Enlightenment project has taken a wrong turn.

I add to MacIntyre's diagnosis the claim that the moral ought-ness of morality has become a puzzle in modern thought because most moral theories have attempted to reduce morality to something else: pleasure, enlightened self-interest, sympathy, social convention. Of course, emotivism is the most radical reduction: moral judgments merely express one's attitudes or feelings toward an action or state of affairs. In light of this history, we should not be surprised that many contemporary attempts to account for ethics are attempts to reduce ethics to biology, since this is but further pursuit of the typical modern reductionist strategy.

The lack of moral objectivity may seem *not* to be a problem so long as we all agree on the basic outlines of morality, such as the idea that altruism is a good thing. But, so far, there has been no answer to Nietzsche, an atheist looking at the same Darwinian biology as the other naturalists. He regards other-regarding, benevolent, justice-seeking, self-sacrificial "morality" as "slave morality." Nietzsche writes: "From the beginning Christian faith has been sacrifice: sacrifice of all freedom, of all pride, of all self-confidence of the spirit; it is simultaneously enslavement and self-derision, self-mutilation." "For his part, the herd man of today's Europe gives himself the appearance of being the only permissible type of man and glorifies those characteristics that make him tame, easy-going and useful to the herd as the true human virtues, namely: public spirit, goodwill, consideration, industry, moderation, modesty, clemency, and pity."[65]

As already stated, MacIntyre sees Nietzsche's thought as the beginning of a Tradition of Moral Naturalism. While he sees Nietzsche as correctly having predicted the downfall of Enlightenment morality, he does not express great confidence that he himself has the resources to defeat this rival tradition. To this issue I also return in the next section.

---

[65] Friedrich Nietzsche, *Beyond Good and Evil*, ed. Rolf-Peter Horstmann and Judith Norman ([1886] Cambridge: Cambridge University Press, 2002), 44, 86–7.

5 Two Traditions and their gifts to one another

At great risk of oversimplification, I highlight two outstanding difficulties. One is the problem which has plagued Christian thought from the beginning of the modern age of empirical knowledge: how can one be justified in claiming to know of a God, especially if there are no obvious signs of divine action in the world? Second, if (for the Moral Naturalist) there is no God, then what is the source of moral knowledge? Is there any way to show that Nietzsche is not right after all?

I have two philosophical offerings to make. First, I suggested early in this chapter (section 1.1) that lacking a criterion for distinguishing science from any of its impostors—a criterion that could be suitably supported by science itself—the attempt to define Naturalism methodologically would fail. I offer here a way out of this epistemological crisis, if Naturalists are inclined to take it.

Second, what is the epistemological status of ethics? Neither (thoughtful) Naturalists nor Christians seem to know.[66] So my second contribution will be to offer a scheme showing a proper place for ethics in the hierarchy of science (Naturalists should appreciate this) and go on to argue that ethics, so placed, calls, most naturally, for a theological explanation (and Christians should like this). These two offerings should be useful for addressing several other outstanding issues.

5.1 The self-referential coherence of MacIntyrean methodology

I have already written a great deal about both Imre Lakatos's philosophy of science (Chapter 3, section 4.3) and his relation to MacIntyre's work on traditions. What I add here is what I call the "fractal structure"[67] of justification. What I mean is as follows: Lakatos has described the structure of science in terms of competing research programs. A research program consists of a temporal succession of theories, each of which is a relatively slight modification of its predecessor. In the case of a progressive program, each new theory is better than its predecessor (in that it at least has more empirical content than the predecessor, without simply tacking on *ad hoc* hypotheses, and occasionally some of this excess content is corroborated).

The labor Lakatos expended in showing his own methodology to be a minor modification of Karl Popper's (Popper's objections notwithstanding) can be explained by recognizing that he intended to cast his own methodology of scientific research programs not as a single theory, but as the most recent reformulation

---

[66] If you would like some instruction in confusion, try reading an encyclopedia article ·on "Moral Realism."

[67] Fractals are objects or sets with self-similar, non-trivial structure on all scales—for example, a snow-flake shape where successive enlargement of sections of its outline reveal the same pattern as the section itself only on smaller and smaller scales.

of a *research program* in the history and philosophy of science—as a progressive "problemshift" relative to Popper's. He later agreed to broaden the definition of "novel fact," thereby constituting a third version of the program.

So, in effect, Lakatos viewed the history of philosophy of science as *isomorphic* with the history of science itself. The justification of his methodology in this manner assumes a meta-philosophical methodology—a theory about the justification of philosophical theories, which is identical in structure to the theory it is used to justify. The importance of this move can be seen by contrasting Lakatos's work with his predecessors in philosophy of science. The Logical Positivists' verification criterion was rejected because of the recognition that when applied self-referentially, the criterion showed itself to be meaningless. Analogously, Lakatos argued that the major methodologies in philosophy of science, if considered as theories about scientific rationality, failed to measure up to their own standards. In particular, Popper's falsificationism is falsified by the history of science. Feyerabend suggests that Lakatos was the first to develop a theory of rationality "sly and sophisticated" enough to apply to science;[68] I claim that his real achievement was to develop a theory of rationality sly and sophisticated enough to apply to itself!

MacIntyre's recent work in ethics and epistemology reveals a similarly complex fractal structure. I had intended to describe this here in detail, but given the amount of MacIntyrean philosophy that readers have already had to take in and the fact that my account has been published elsewhere, [69] I shall be brief: The same self-referential twists can be found in MacIntyre's works. MacIntyre's reformulation of virtue theory is justified because it solves the problems its predecessors in the virtue tradition of moral reasoning could not solve, and, furthermore, explains why they *could not* solve them. But this approach to the justification of an ethical position is an instantiation of a broader theory of rationality, according to which a tradition is vindicated by the fact that it has managed to solve its own major problems, while its competitors have failed to do so, and by the fact that it can give a better account of its rival's failures than can the rival itself. But this theory itself needs to be justified by showing that it is a part of a large-scale epistemological tradition (the Aristotelian–Thomist tradition), and that this tradition is itself justified—by MacIntyre's narrative in which he recounts how it has overcome its problems, while its main contemporary competitor, modern Enlightenment reason, has not.

Why drag you, dear readers, through even this much more of MacIntyre? I explain below.

---

[68] Paul Feyerabend, "Imre Lakatos," *British Journal for the Philosophy of Science* 26 (1975): 1–18.

[69] Nancey Murphy, *Anglo-American Postmodernity: Philosophical Perspectives on Science, Religion, and Ethics* (Boulder, CO: Westview Press, 1997), ch. 3.

5.2 Ethics in the hierarchy of the sciences

A common model throughout the modern period has been the view that reality can be viewed as a hierarchy of levels of complexity, beginning with the smallest, simplest entities studied by physics, which form into the more complex entities of chemical compounds, and biochemical compounds. These in turn combine to form the various levels of complexity studied by biologists. The most complex of these biological organisms are humans, and their behavior is studied by psychology and the social sciences.

The late biochemist and theologian Arthur Peacocke has greatly influenced me. He provided two crucial kinds of inspiration.[70] He was the first to introduce me to resources for tempering the reductionism of the philosophy of science I had studied, by introducing me to accounts of downward causation in the hierarchy of complexity, or, in his preferred terminology, whole–part constraint. (See Chapter 9, section 4.2.3 for an update on this work.)

Second, he provided an account of the relation of theology to this hierarchy of sciences. Peacocke wrote that if it is the case that higher-level sciences study increasingly broad or complex systems, then the broadest, most complex system of all is that of God in relation to the entire created order. So theology belongs at the top of the hierarchy. (Compare this to Wolfhart Pannenberg's thesis that, if God is understood as the "all-determining-reality," then theology must be capable of incorporating all other knowledge.) Theology needs to be *conditioned* by what we know from below, but it cannot be reduced, for example, to our now (somewhat) familiar cognitive-science theories of religion. And recall (Chapter 4, section 3.1) that "theology" stands in here for the highly complex network of doctrines, each of which might be studied as a theological research program in its own right.

With my co-author George Ellis (b.1939), I have done further work on Peacocke's model. We argued that it is best to see the hierarchy above biology as forming two branches—one for the human sciences and one for the remainder of the natural sciences. One reason for this is that complexity and comprehensiveness do not always provide for an unambiguous ordering of the sciences.[71] In my current scheme, I have become convinced that the dividing point should be the science of ecology because it so closely ties the human world to the rest of the natural world.[72]

---

[70] See, for example, Arthur Peacocke, *Theology for a Scientific Age: Being and Becoming—Natural, Divine, and Human*, 2nd enlarged ed. (Minneapolis: Fortress Press, 1993).

[71] Nancey Murphy and George F. R. Ellis, *On the Moral Nature of the Universe: Theology, Cosmology, and Ethics* (Minneapolis: Fortress Press, 1996).

[72] See John Mustol, *Dusty Earthlings: Living as Eco-Physical Beings in God's Eco-Physical World* (Eugene, OR: Cascade Books, 2012).

Our second innovation was to argue that ethics should be placed in the hierarchy just below theology. So this gives the diagram in Figure 22.

Our general understanding of the relations among sciences in the hierarchy is that, first, the higher-level science must be consistent with the findings of the ones below. Second, the higher level is underdetermined by the lower. Third, lower-level sciences often raise what Ian Barbour calls "boundary questions": questions that can be formulated at one level but cannot be answered without insights from a higher-level science. For example, the number of elements on Earth, the remarkably large number of atoms in biochemicals, and the number of possibilities for their arrangement, allow for an *immense* number of compounds. How can we explain the relatively small number of compounds that actually exist? The answer comes from biology, the level above: only these few compounds are useful in living organisms.

Our insertion of ethics into the hierarchy is because the human sciences incorporate judgments of normativity: Take, for example, the sociological assumption that societies are based, ultimately, on coercion, and that coercion sometimes needs to be violent. What may appear as a simple statement about how human societies work can be seen, in reality, to be an ethical claim in that it may be put into direct

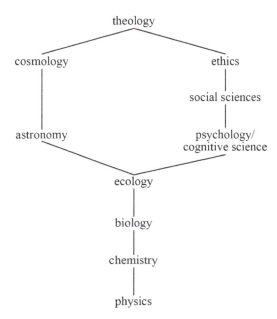

Figure 22 A branching hierarchy of the sciences, including ethics, which is intended to answer boundary questions arising from the human sciences. This hierarchy is topped by theology, which answers boundary questions arising from both ethics and the natural sciences

conversation with an ethic of nonviolence. Ethics is located in the hierarchy just below theology (or some other concept of Ultimate Reality). This is in response to MacIntyre's argument that without such a concept, moral disagreements often cannot be settled. The hierarchy comes together again at the top, since, at least in Christianity, boundary questions arising from cosmology (e.g., why is there a universe at all?) are subject to theological answers, just as are questions arising from ethics (e.g., is capital punishment moral?).

5.3 Gift exchanges

In this subsection I consider what the moves I made in the two previous subsections might, singly or together, provide in terms of insights into Naturalist and Christian Traditions, especially with regard to addressing the crises I identified for each. What we see in each case is that I have brought gifts that eliminate or ameliorate each, but in each case, there is also a downside for the rival. I begin with Naturalism.

5.3.1 A scientific methodology based on science

What Lakatos showed, in terms familiar to students of science, is that it is possible to use (roughly) empirical methods—histories of science and of scientific methodologies—to develop a non-self-defeating account of scientific methodology (along with a criterion of demarcation, something like that which Popper sought; see section 4.3.1). He, in his way, and MacIntyre's in his own, showed that Scientific Naturalists need to be neither scientistic nor vague in saying that they want only methodologies that are "commensurable, in some sense, with those in science" (Post, in section 4.3.1). That it is difficult in some cases to classify books as science or as history of science, and that a number of universities created departments in the history and philosophy of science, together suggest that the kinds of work Kuhn (the historian) and Lakatos (the philosopher) were doing were indeed commensurable with work in science itself.

Another advantage, as I see it, although a Scientific Naturalist might not, was Lakatos's emphasis on the fact that the hard core of a research program *in science* is often metaphysical.

There are two potential downsides to my "contribution" here. One is the fact that I and others have convinced fellow scholars, not just theologians, but also natural scientists and philosophers (with Naturalistic bents), that schools of theology could be considered, *at the meta-level*, to be theological research programs.

The much more significant downside is that, even with this immunization from scientism, it may prove difficult indeed for Naturalists to provide credible enough accounts of Ultimate Reality to validate a notion of the *telos* of life, and, in consequence, to provide moral guidance. For example, Dawkins has concluded that the feeling of awed wonder science gives is one of the highest experiences of which the human psyche is capable. He compares it with the finest passion that music and poetry can deliver.[73] But I fear that, just as with the theoretical reasoning that Aristotle saw as our highest good, it is available only to the "cream of the crop" in our world. (I was at a science and religion conference in South Africa and one of the participants asked why so much money was being spent on it, while so few schools in the country had money for enough science textbooks to go around.) More on this in my discussion of Flanagan's ethics in the following subsection.

5.3.2 Ethics in relation to science

If one adopts a model of the hierarchy of the sciences something like the one I present here, there is no need for a sharp distinction between ethics and the sciences, although there are (still) philosophers who would laugh Ellis and me out of the room: "had we never heard of the fact–value distinction?"

I am not sure whether those who think of themselves as Scientific Naturalists have much at stake in this issue. However, (insofar as I understand that pesky topic of moral realism) I would expect approval on the part of some Moral Naturalists and grave disapproval by others. In any case, be reminded that this model does not license the *reduction* of ethics to anything else. And, again, it means that there can be no contradiction of lower-level laws. James McClendon argues that no Christian ethics can be complete without taking into account what he calls three intertwined strands: the social strand, the strand that he calls the resurrection strand (what God has done and continues to do in the world), and, for our purposes here, the body strand (our physical needs, our delights and horrors, our feelings of shame, the comfort we take in the very bodily presence of others).[74]

The denial of any relation of ethics to nature, the "fact–value distinction," the "naturalistic fallacy" are aberrations, first, due to a (likely) misreading of Hume: he is merely stating the fact that authors of his day wrote long treatises on human nature or God, but then there is an "imperceptible" change to the language of "ought" or "ought not." This is not to say, as later readers have taken him to say, that it is impossible to argue from "is" statements to "ought" statements. Rather he says, in the text just below, that "as authors do not commonly [use caution here] he presumes to recommend it to the readers."[75]

The strongest argument for the detachment of morality from the natural world was G. E. Moore's (1873–1958) argument in his *Principia Ethica* (1903) that "good"

---

[73] Richard Dawkins, *Unweaving the Rainbow: Science, Delusion and the Appetite for Wonder* (Boston and New York: Houghton Mifflin Co., 1998), x.

[74] James Wm. McClendon, Jr., *Ethics: Systematic Theology, Volume 1*, 2nd rev. and enlarged ed. (Nashville, TN: Abingdon Press, [1986] 2002), ch. 3, *passim*.

[75] David Hume, *A Treatise of Human Nature*, Book III, Part I, Sec. I; ed. L. A. Selby-Bigge ([1739] Oxford: Clarendon Press, 1955), 469.

is a non-natural property entirely unrelated to any others, such as happiness or utility.

In contrast, MacIntyre makes the (Wittgensteinian) point that one cannot even know the *meaning* of an ethical system without knowing, or at least being able to imagine, how it is or could be socially embodied.

The downside of this placement of ethics in the hierarchy of the sciences is that an ethic needs to be related, as well, to a concept of Ultimate Reality. Consider a Christian critique of Flanagan's account of morality. His is strongly individualistic in that he focuses on *self*-development. It is true that he sees self-development to involve increasing one's capacity for compassion for others. But the question is whether he would countenance social practices that do much for those in need *and at the same time* require one to sacrifice one's own chance to flourish in the manner he describes. Clearly not: one of his examples of a person who is unable to pursue the talents and interests that constitute flourishing is a woman who devotes "all of her energies to . . . *caring for others*."[76] In Flanagan's account of the good life, there is no paradoxical twist such that she who pursues her own flourishing will lose it, and she who renounces her flourishing for Christ's sake will find it.

This last sentence, of course, is a paraphrase of Jesus. In our *Moral Nature of the Universe*, Ellis writes: "The paradoxical nature of an ethic of self-sacrifice or renunciation is captured in Jesus' saying that those who try to make their life secure will lose it, but those who lose their life will keep it (Lk. 17:33 NRSV)."[77]

So how do we adjudicate between an ethic that focuses exclusively on flourishing in this life and recommends exercising compassion for others *only so long as* it also contributes to one's own well-being, versus one that calls for self-sacrifice, even to the point of death, for those in need? The judgment will necessarily depend on whether one believes that this life is all there is, or not. And on whether there is a God who will cherish in the future those who sacrifice themselves in the present. Is there a divine reality beyond this physical world, or is the world itself the Ultimate Existent? There will come a point where ethical justification imports, either explicitly or implicitly, some account of Ultimate Reality.

5.3.3 Theology and/or the cognitive science of religion

As this young science develops, it may provide a more satisfying account of the origins and nature of religion, and it will surely garner more scientific support. Thus, it may turn out to be a means for Naturalists such as Boyer not only to explain religion, "but to explain religion away."[78]

---

[76] Flanagan, *Hard Problem*, 58; my emphasis.
[77] Murphy and Ellis, *Moral Nature*, 121.
[78] James A. Van Slyke, *The Cognitive Science of Religion* (Farnham, UK: Ashgate, 2011), 2.

However, there are two downsides here for Naturalists (or gifts to Theists). One is that it helps to solve the problem of religious pluralism for Christians. The second is that it can easily be incorporated into a theological program. A facile Christian response might be to say that insofar as CSR theories are correct, they explain other religions. Applying the theories to what Westerners often called "primitive religions," Christians may be saying: "yes, yes, this explains those strange beliefs and practices." Yet, if we apply CSR to Christianity, the naturalistic account is necessarily incomplete; it leaves God out of the picture. But this again is the relativist's sort of objection: "you say God is not needed to explain religion"; "I say that God is!"

Boyer's own contribution here is more legitimate. An important feature of his work is what he calls turning the question of the origin of religion upside down.[79] We tend to seek for one origin of the many religions. Instead, we need to recognize the *vast* number of *potential* religious concepts, beliefs, and practices and then explain why the ones that exist have survived. Is there something that religious concepts have in common that explains why they have been preserved and passed down to new generations? So, while I have attempted to avoid the language of competition, the best way I can think to put my conclusion to this paragraph is to say that Boyer and company have leveled the score. Christians have struggled to explain the great number and variety of religions; now CSR theorists are challenging themselves to explain the small number and uniformity of religions and religious concepts.[80]

The great gift that CSR brings to Christianity can be illustrated by showing how easily it can be grafted into a theological research program in a way that complements and confirms it. I was invited to speak to a CSR research group in Ireland, and the location led me to think of my favorite Irish theologian, Catholic Modernist George Tyrrell (1861–1909). Already a century ago, he had an elaborate theory about the *natural* development of religions: there are "natural laws of religious psychology," which tend to distort religious representations.[81] Points of overlap between Tyrrell's theory and current CSR are numerous. In other respects, they are complementary, and this is primarily in two ways. First, CSR fills in detail about the psychological laws and theological distortions that Tyrrell expected. Second, and much more important to anyone who is not a confirmed atheist, is that Tyrrell presents a plausible theory about how the divine operates

---

[79] Boyer, *Religion Explained*, 32.

[80] For a more detailed account, see Nancey Murphy, "Cognitive Science and the Evolution of Religion: A Philosophical and Theological Appraisal," in Jeffrey Schloss and Michael Murray, eds., *The Believing Primate: Scientific, Philosophical, and Theological Reflections on the Origin of Religion* (Oxford: Oxford University Press, 2009), ch. 13.

[81] George Tyrrell, *Through Scylla and Charybdis, or The Old Theology and the New* (London: Longmans, Green, and Co., 1907), 77.

within the process of the development of religion—it points to the top level of a Christian hierarchy of science.

By the end of his all-too-short career, Tyrrell had produced a sophisticated and humanly realistic account of the development of religion. His model had places for divine action and religious experience; for Scripture, narrative, and historical data; for morality, ritual, and sentiment; for metaphor and mystery; for dogma and theology; for first- and second-order language; and finally, for church authority and tradition.

He began with the problem of theological epistemology, rejecting both the medieval epistemology of authority and also the "conclusions theology" that attempted to deduce theology from Scripture. In its place, he offered what we could now call a hypothetico-deductive model of reasoning. Theology, like science, forms hypotheses, often regarding unseen realities; these hypotheses are tested by their ability to explain the data. The data comprise the actual life of the faithful, along with their more imaginative, anthropomorphic expressions of their experiences. Scripture is largely a collection of such first-order expressions.

Next, Tyrrell set out to account for how religious practices and first-order beliefs themselves come into being. He describes humans as having a sense that our lives are governed ultimately by some secret power (compare CSR's agent-detection module). Humans attempt to interact with and affect this unseen reality. Our faculties are well suited for acquiring knowledge of the physical world, but not suited for knowledge of this other reality, so we form dim images, necessarily imagining this "Infinite Subjectivity" in our own image and likeness. We think of it as a spirit whose knowledge and power far exceed our own[82] (one of Boyer's minimally counterintuitive concepts).

Humans seek a more detailed picture of this over-natural world, which develops by a kind of experiment. We find ourselves in situations that require some kind of action or some sort of emotional reaction. We act, and society records its observations of the consequences. This is the source of codes of morality and piety. But these codes raise the question of why *this* is the right way to act, the right set of attitudes. "[R]eflection sets the imaginative intelligence to work to construct some picture, idea, and history of the world to which this code strives to adjust our conduct."[83] These conceptions are communicated by tradition to each member of society.[84] CSR provides theories as to why certain ideas and codes are more easily remembered and passed on.

Tyrrell maintains that all first-order expressions of these experiences of the spiritual world and of attempts to visualize it are in poetic or "prophetic" language,

---

[82] Tyrrell, *Scylla*, 160–3.
[83] Tyrrell, *Scylla*, 207.
[84] Tyrrell, *Scylla*, 175.

which is symbolic, imaginative, imprecise.[85] His theory of religious language and that of CSR agree that the only language we have for religion is drawn from the natural world and has to be adapted. Tyrrell says that religious language is being used metaphorically; linguistic theorists point out that when a metaphor is used there are always ways in which what is being described is like the original application, but also in important ways *not* like it. So this is a more general theory of religious language than Boyer's, but Boyer's minimally counterintuitive concepts are notable instances that fit within Tyrrell's theory.

Tyrrell and CSR agree on the prevalence of "theological incorrectness," that is, theological formulations will not ordinarily match the ordinary believer's conceptions. However, while Jason Slone (b.1973) emphasizes what might be called the decay of theological concepts in the thinking of the ordinary believer, Tyrrell emphasizes that theology begins with these more natural concepts.[86]

I claimed above that from a theological point of view, CSR is necessarily incomplete because it leaves God's role in the development of religion out of account. Of course, this is the point, in the views of some, of engaging in naturalistic study of religion. So far, I have emphasized the convergence between Tyrrell's and CSR's theories of religious development, thus omitting his theory of divine action. Boyer and Tyrrell agree on the priority of codes of morality and piety to religious beliefs. A major point of difference, though, is between their accounts of the sources of moral codes. Boyer takes the sociobiologists' position and argues that our evolutionary past accounts for a universal set of moral intuitions. Tyrrell claims that we build moral codes slowly by trial and error, but this is just the beginning. In his later works, he wrote that our moral codes, as well as our religious practices and beliefs, are capable of being shaped by the action of the Holy Spirit. Either by deliberate reflection or spontaneously, an idea of God or of other spiritual realities, or of some course of action comes to mind. God's response is to provide, to those sensitive enough to notice, a feeling either *for* or *against* the idea. Tyrrell takes this to be the basis for revelation.

Note that if Tyrrell's anthropological dualism is replaced by physicalism, the (never explained) impulses from God *in the soul* need also to be replaced by a theory of divine action *in the brain*. So this is the point at which to turn to contributions, where available, to Christian epistemological crises.

5.3.4 A few brief remarks on Christian crises

Epistemology. I believe that providing a model of the hierarchy of the sciences helps to fill out the concept of a large-scale tradition of enquiry. It captures

---

[85] Tyrrell, *Scylla*, 178.
[86] Jason D. Slone, *Theological Incorrectness: Why Religious People Believe What They Shouldn't* (Oxford: Oxford University Press, 2004).

MacIntyre's contention that ethics is "parasitic" on social sciences by picturing ethics as the discipline that is needed to arbitrate among conflicting moral norms (now unintentionally) embedded in the human sciences. It emphasizes the necessity for more and better reflection by Naturalists on Ultimate Reality and the ultimate purpose of human life. Finally, it shows that the supposition that religious knowledge and scientific knowledge are essentially different is but an artifact of a particular stage in Western culture.

Suffering: It is clear that for the Naturalist there is no *logical* problem of evil. However, Christians have no monopoly on concern for the suffering of others. I have already used science (fine-tuning; Chapter 7, section 5.1) to partially address this issue. I add here that even a *scientistic* outlook provides a valuable ingredient to morality, whether Christian or Naturalist. Suppose that Flanagan's compassion could be universally extended; suppose that the kingdom of God *on earth* were to be pursued consistently. A significant problem in all cases is that we humans simply do not have the requisite knowledge of how to pursue the good of the world's neediest.

Stenmark, in pointing out that even politicians can be scientistic, quotes Jawaharlal Nehru (1889–1964):

> It is science alone that can solve the problems of hunger and poverty, of insanitation and illiteracy, of superstition and deadening custom and tradition, of vast resources running to waste, of a rich country inhabited by starving people . . . Who indeed could afford to ignore science today? At every turn we seek its aid . . . The future belongs to science and to those who make friends with science.[87]

Note that science, here, needs to be understood in both its pure and applied forms.

Divine action: As I noted above, the jury is still out on the plausibility of QDA. However, if Tyrrell is correct with regard to the minimal role of divine action in revelation, then all that would be needed to provide divine input into religious thought would be changes at the neuronal level. This, itself, is an open question. Some scientists say that quantum physics is irrelevant to brain processes, because neurons are so large compared to the scale of quantum events. However, the critical question is whether a nerve impulse stops or is transmitted to another neuron. This is not a deterministic event if the impulse is weak; it depends on the availability and positioning of neurotransmitter molecules in the fluid at the synapse. So, in my judgment, QDA could be relevant in the "yes/no" impulses that Tyrrell postulates as the exact source of divine action in human life.

---

[87] Stenmark, *Scientism*, vii.

There are two larger issues that deserve attention before concluding this chapter and the book. One is the extent of the relations between science itself and Scientific Naturalism versus the extent to which the Christian Tradition has been able to incorporate science. The final issue is, again, the question of Christianity's responsibility for the evils of the world.

5.4 Christianity's and Naturalism's relations to science

It is often assumed that Scientific Naturalism *qua* Tradition is backed by the whole of natural science—it incorporates it. In contrast, due to the influence of Kant and Schleiermacher, liberal-leaning theologians have pursued what Ian Barbour called a "two-worlds" approach to relating science to religion: they are such sharply contrasting enterprises that scientific knowledge is irrelevant to theology. Of course, Kant and Schleiermacher were intentionally immunizing theology from negative consequences of Newtonian science: in particular, the destructive deterministic conclusions regarding human free will and, thus, morality. However, with hindsight, we can see this as a Pyrrhic victory in two ways. First, the theology that Lindbeck has named experiential-expressivism evacuated theology of its *cognitive* content, as in Rudolph Bultmann's assertion that theology is only *about* one's existential relation to God. Second, the doctrine of the two-worlds relation between religion and science has resulted in a justifiable conclusion that the Christian Tradition has no place in it for science.

The purpose of this subsection is to consider, first, exactly *how* the Scientific Naturalist Tradition relates to science itself; and, second, to examine actual relations between science and Christian theology. In each case, I focus on one prominent figure: Carl Sagan and Robert John Russell, respectively.

5.4.1 Scientific Naturalism as experiential-expressivism?

The new atheists provide no help in relating their Naturalism to science itself, except, as already noted, Dennett's fine presentation of CSR. Therefore, I turn back to Carl Sagan, who, I believe, has been described as a high priest. His *Cosmos* does indeed inform the reader of much of the best of current science, as well as a great deal of its history. Ann Druyan (b.1949), who was Sagan's wife and co-author while filming the television series and writing the first edition of *Cosmos*, wrote a Foreword to that edition. In the first two pages she makes it clear that this was a "religious" project.

> The scenes we wrote and shot that [first] day became the opening of the show and the first words of the book: "The cosmos is all that is or ever was or ever will be." We were consciously going for a biblical cadence, words that would scope out the ambitious territorial range of our explorations in space and time . . .

Some religious fundamentalists found that first line offensive. To them it was a shot across the bow that Carl was out to steal their thunder. They were onto something . . .

The universe revealed by the relentless error-correcting mechanism of science was to him infinitely preferable to the untested assumptions of traditional belief. For Carl, the "spiritual" had to be rooted in natural reality . . . Scientific insights made him *feel* something, a soaring sensation, a recognition that he could only compare to falling in love.[88]

The author of the Foreword to the second edition, Neil deGrasse Tyson (b.1958), wrote that the book's treatment of scientific topics was persistently blended with other traditional fields of study, to reveal for the first time how and why readers should embrace all of the ways that science matters in our culture. "At the time, there was nothing fresher, more uplifting, or more empowering than the themes and messages of *Cosmos*."[89]

In his own introduction, Sagan wrote that "evolution has arranged that we take pleasure in understanding—those who understand are more likely to survive."[90] He also wrote that because science is inseparable from the rest of the human endeavor, "it cannot be discussed without making contact . . . with a number of social, political, religious, and philosophical issues." He therefore resolved to treat social issues whenever relevant.[91]

I believe it is clear that Sagan's book is meant not only as a science text, but also as a Naturalistic completion of the top of the hierarchy of the sciences, and in a remarkably MacIntyrean manner. At the top is his concept of Ultimate Reality, The Cosmos. The highest good for humankind is exploring its wonders. This calls for the virtues of truthfulness, social cooperation, and courage. But what are the epistemological relations among these levels? I have already given away my best guess in the title of this subsection: I believe that we have here an experiential-expressivist version of Naturalism. The concept of Ultimate Reality is not the product of an argument of any sort, but of feeling—the awe and wonder that humans can feel if they are willing to open themselves to it, to be uplifted and empowered by it.

5.4.2 One Christian scientist's analysis of the relations

I do not wish my quirky analysis of Sagan's brand of Naturalism to be taken to apply to all others. For example, Dawkins has an intriguing argument that God

---

[88] Ann Druyan, Foreword, in Carl Sagan, *Cosmos*, 2nd ed. (New York: Random House, [1980] 2013), xvii–xviii.
[89] Niel deGrasse Tyson, Foreword, in Sagan, *Cosmos*, xiv.
[90] Sagan, *Cosmos*, xxiv.
[91] Sagan, *Cosmos*, xxvi.

cannot be the Creator due to the theological claim that God is simple, and all creators that we know of are highly complex.

Several scientist-Christian scholars have written on how religion does or should (unfortunate mixing of categories here) relate to science. There have been a number of typologies; for example: (1) science–theology warfare; (2) science and theology in dialogue; (3) science and theology synthesized; (4) science and theology describing non-relating worldviews.

In contrast, several scholars have given a great deal of thought to the possible, actual, and desirable interactions between science and Christian theology. Peacocke's work has been important here, but I choose Robert Russell's analysis as the most sophisticated to date. He has set out a model for understanding the various ways in which science and theology can and have interacted positively. Russell accepts the possibility that theological and scientific rationality can have the same Lakatosian structure. He also accepts the value of the hierarchical structure of the sciences, with theology at the top.

Russell exploits the insight that the relations among the sciences in the hierarchy are asymmetrical. On the one hand, the characteristics of the lower-level entities and the laws governing their behavior constrain but usually do not determine higher-level phenomena. On the other hand, the higher-level phenomena tell us something about the lower level, namely that they must be such as to *permit* the development and behavior of the higher-level entities.

With this model in mind, Russell looks at various components of both scientific and theological research programs. All involve data and theories; both science and theology are imbued with philosophical assumptions such as the order of nature, the meaning of *time*. These are possible components in epistemological relations between theology and science. Another kind of relation is heuristic: theories are not deduced or induced from data, but are human inventions requiring imagination. So another possible benefit from cross-disciplinary dialogue is the provision of new conceptual resources for theory development.

Based on the above, Russell describes eight possible "paths" or ways of relating theology to a particular science.[92] The first five are legitimate ways for science to inform theology. The last three are ways in which theology may inform science:

1 Scientific theories may serve as data that place *constraints* on theology.
2 Scientific theories may serve as *supporting* data for theology insofar as they are explained theologically.
3 *Philosophical interpretations* of scientific theories may serve as data for theology.

---

[92] Robert John Russell, *Cosmology from Alpha to Omega: The Creative Mutual Interaction of Theology and Science* (Minneapolis: Fortress Press, 2008), ch. 10.

4 Scientific theories may serve as data for theology when they are incorporated into a *philosophy of nature.*

5 Scientific theories may function *heuristically* in theology by providing conceptual, experiential, practical/moral, or aesthetic inspiration.

6 Theology may provide some of the philosophical assumptions underlying science.

7 Theological theories may function heuristically in the construction of scientific theories.

8 Theological theories may lead to selection rules within the criteria of theory choice, that is, for choosing between existing scientific theories that all explain the available data, or for deciding what set of data the theory should seek to explain.

In summary, Russell says:

> The *asymmetry* between theology and science should now be quite apparent: Theological theories do *not* act as data for science in the same way that scientific theories do for theology. This reflects the methodological assumption that the academic disciplines are structured in an epistemic hierarchy of constraints and irreducibility. It also safeguards science from any normative claims by theology. It does, though, allow for the possibility that philosophical or theological commitments can stimulate the search for new theories and can function as a source of "criteria for theory choice" among existing competing theories in the natural and social sciences.[93]

5.5 Christianity, evil, and the Genealogical Tradition

I mentioned above that MacIntyre has severe doubts about the internal coherence of the Genealogical Tradition. I share his doubts, but I intend to take a different tack in responding to it, more theological than philosophical.

Following Nietzsche, Michel Foucault (1926–84) concentrates on practices of social control and aims to show how they distort human knowledge. It is striking that Foucault has developed a view of knowledge parallel to MacIntyre's in many respects. Both regard knowledge as originating from social practices, but whereas MacIntyre takes such practices to lead to truth, Foucault concentrates on practices of social control, and aims to show how they distort human knowledge. The critical Nietzschean point is that there is an essential connection between knowledge and power.

I take this conflict between MacIntyre (the Catholic) and the Genealogists (who might be seen as the negative image of Augustinian Protestants; that is, without

---

[93] Russell, *Cosmology,* 287.

concepts of grace or revelation) as a point of departure, a heuristic device, for asking what the Radical Reformation subtradition might have to offer to current discussions of epistemology.

Summing up the character of an entire Christian subtradition is impossible here. I therefore select four practices that (with exceptions) have characterized the Radicals through much of their history: (1) voluntary church membership (entailed by belief in the separation of church and state), (2) nonviolence, (3) revolutionary subordination, and (4) simple living.

I believe that John Yoder introduced the term "revolutionary subordination." In most cases, our culture sees only two options: either to meet an assertion of power with a counter-assertion or to wait passively to be run over by the aggressor. A number of Jesus' teachings have been interpreted as the passive option. A better interpretation is that Jesus, whose followers were mostly from the inferior classes, was suggesting unusual and striking behaviors to upset the social hierarchy, yet without violence to the attacker. Jesus' teaching can be seen as offering a third option: a way of living without worldly power, and yet retaining one's dignity and confining oppression and violence.

All four of these Radical Reformation distinctives can be seen as strategies for living in such a way as to curb the will to power. Nonviolence is the refusal to use physical force against another. Revolutionary subordination is a strategy for righting injustices without the use of any power other than that of the imagination. The separation of church and state is the rejection of institutional longing for alliance with the power of the state. Finally, learning to live with less reduces the need for power to defend one's economic privilege.

My proposal is that MacIntyre's epistemological account can be enhanced by two moves: The first is to acknowledge the (measure of) truth in the Genealogists' account of the epistemic distortions caused by the will to power. The second is to incorporate MacIntyre's epistemology into a tradition which has, from its beginning, recognized the dangers, both political *and epistemological*, of power, and has throughout its history sought to develop (from scriptural precedents) social practices that overcome those dangers. And this is a MacIntyrean move in itself— one of his finest examples of resolution of an epistemological crisis was Thomas's incorporation of Aristotelian epistemology into his theology.

A second reason for focusing on Radical Reformation theology is that historians have come to see that many of the cases of evil attributed to Christians were in fact due to their alliances with the political powers of their day.

6 Retrospect

Recall that this chapter has been included because one type of epistemological crisis is an encounter with a radically different rival. It is tempting, of course, to exclaim that I have just shown the Christian Tradition's complete superiority to Naturalism. Unfortunately, this has not been the case.

What I have accomplished, I believe, is an examination of the relative merits of the two Traditions regarding a variety of issues. Perhaps an equally important result is the following: MacIntyre is often accused of promoting an agonistic, conflictual approach to philosophy. In fact, he calls for sympathetic understanding of the rival, in particular so that one's own tradition (here, Christianity) can be tested against the strongest charges of the rival. Only by having done so can participants in that tradition make honest claims to have done their best to test the truths of their tradition. Criticisms from rivals are *gifts*.

Conclusion

My late husband, James Wm. McClendon, Jr., always told students, regarding their papers: "Tell 'em what you're going to tell 'em, then tell 'em, then tell 'em what you've told 'em." I think that I have done this so many times, in each chapter, that it would be tiresome to tell y'all again. Nonetheless, his advice was vital.

I have always told my own students that when they are writing long papers and, especially, dissertations, long sections and chapters all need "hooks" at both beginnings and endings to explain, in J. L. Austin's (1911–60) terminology, what each part is meant to *do*, to accomplish, toward the goal of the whole. I hope I have illustrated this task here, as well.

A third pedagogical note: I have spent nearly all of my adult life either as a graduate student or teaching graduate students. I believe that beginners in a field need to be treated as beginners, but, during a course of study, they should be gradually and thoughtfully brought to be junior colleagues in the field. Some readers may have noticed two types of progression in this text. Early chapters are short, and much of the terminology is explained. Later chapters are increasingly long, and explanatory material is kept to a minimum. This is because I expect that, over the course of your term, or even during the course of reading this book, you have become *my* junior colleagues, and I can write to you as my equals in the field.

I add only one concluding note about the overall plan and content of the book. I have argued throughout that, thanks to Alasdair MacIntyre, the concept of a text in philosophy of religion is what literary critic Stanley Fish (b.1938) has called a self-consuming artifact. I have argued (along with a number of other authors) that there is no such thing as religion in general; there are a number of traditions, some more "religious" in nature than others. In fact, there is no *separate field* of religion; the religious *aspects* of each tradition are bound up with all of the rest of the tradition. There is no religious epistemology as distinguished, for example, in our day, from epistemology or philosophy of science.

So while the entire text of this book is not what Fish calls a self-consuming artifact, its classification is. Jeffrey Stout writes of self-consuming artifacts that: "They announce a topic, and begin a refinement of reflection seemingly designed to produce an insight statable as a thesis about that topic [or standard list of topics, in this case]; but the refined turn of thoughts turns in upon itself, giving us not the expected thesis [or theses] but a new topic. The new topic is typically the inadequacy of the reader's assumptions, which the author at first seemed to share."[1] My purpose in so delimiting the title of this book—*A Philosophy of the Christian Religion for the Twenty-First Century*—was intended as a small warning of this turn.

Typically, when I point out to students the historical conditioning of concepts such as *philosophy, rationality, religion, truth,* a student asks: "But Prof. Murphy, doesn't this mean that your own work will be seen by later generations to be wrong?" I reply: "Certainly wrong in some respects; I only hope that it has been wrong in a *helpful* way."

I challenge readers to pursue issues that I have failed adequately to address here.

---

[1] Jeffrey Stout, *The Flight from Authority: Religion, Morality, and the Quest for Autonomy* (Notre Dame, IN and London: University of Notre Dame Press, 1981), 180.

Further reading

General

Philosophers and philosophical topics

- Audi, Robert, ed. *The Cambridge Dictionary of Philosophy*. 2nd ed. Cambridge: Cambridge University Press, [1995] 2007.

  Widely considered the best short reference; succinct but not oversimplified.
- Craig, Edward, ed. *Routledge Encyclopedia of Philosophy*. 10 vols. London and New York: Routledge, 1998.

  Wider than Macmillan both geographically and in terms of topics, including some religious figures and movements. Each entry begins with a brief and very useful summary.
- Edwards, Paul, ed. *The Encyclopedia of Philosophy*. 8 vols. New York and London: Macmillan, 1967.

  Reprinted in 1972 with two volumes per book. A *Supplement*, ed. Donald M. Borchert (1996) is essential for bringing it up to date.
- Zalta, Edward N., ed. *Stanford Encyclopedia of Philosophy*. Stanford, CA: Stanford University, 2016. Available at https://plato.stanford.edu/.

  Online, authoritative, updated regularly.

Histories of philosophy

- Matson, Wallace I. *A New History of Philosophy*. 2 vols. 2nd ed. Fort Worth, TX: Harcourt College Publishers, [1987] 2000.

  A very brief history of philosophers; a bit witty; written at the undergraduate level.
- Copleston, Frederick, sj. *A History of Philosophy*. 9 vols. Westminster, MD: Newman Press, 1946–74.

  Much longer and more detailed than Matson (e.g., in 1985 Image reprint, with three volumes in three books, each volume is about 500 pages. Has the advantage of drawing out connections with theological issues.

Theological references

This text presupposes that readers will already be familiar with some of the vast array of theological references available, so I list only the one I found myself using most often.

- Hastings, Adrian, et al., eds. *The Oxford Companion to Christian Thought.* Oxford: Oxford University Press, 2000.

  Wide ranging and only one large volume.

Philosophy of religion texts

- Anderson, Pamela Sue. *A Feminist Philosophy of Religion: The Rationality and Myths of Religious Belief.* Oxford: Blackwell, 1998.

  Intended to supplement rather than entirely replace philosophies of religion from a largely male perspective with reflections from a feminist perspective; includes Continental philosophical perspectives as well. Highly unusual, especially due to the representation of feminist insights in philosophy.
- Cheetham, David and Rolfe King, eds. *Contemporary Practice and Method in the Philosophy of Religion: New Essays.* London: Continuum International, 2008.

  In contrast to the majority of recent philosophy of religion texts, which turn out to be largely concerned with Christianity, this text intentionally provides perspectives from a number of major world religions, along with contrasting approaches to philosophical methods.
- Peterson, Michael, et al. *Reason and Religious Belief: An Introduction to the Philosophy of Religion.* 4th ed. New York and Oxford: Oxford University Press, [1991] 2009.

  Organized by chapters in such a way as to give an overview of topics usually covered in a philosophy of religion textbook. The authors provide an edited collection of original readings to be paired with chapters of the textbook: *Philosophy of Religion: Selected Readings.* 3rd ed. 2007. Focuses largely on Christianity, as does this text, but, in contrast, ignores historical transformations of problems.
- Pojman, Louis P. *Philosophy of Religion.* Mountainview, CA: Mayfield, 2001.

  A much shorter treatment than Peterson's; suited for a slightly more sophisticated reader.
- Thiselton, Anthony C. *A Concise Encyclopedia of the Philosophy of Religion.* Grand Rapids, MI: Eerdmans, 2002).

  Brief; quite readable.

References arranged by chapters

Note that these are not necessarily readings reflecting the sources used in the chapters (which will themselves provide guidance for further reading); but rather, in many cases, texts that parallel historical material and arguments made in this text.

1 Ancient and medieval ways of knowing the divine

- Allen, Diogenes and Eric O. Springsted. *Philosophy for Understanding Theology.* 2nd enlarged ed. Louisville, KY: Westminster John Knox Press, [1985] 2007.

Indeed, Allen's purpose was to present just enough philosophy to make theology more intelligible to students. This book is placed here rather than among general readings because of his particular attraction to and interpretation of Plato's philosophy.

- Brown, Peter. *Augustine of Hippo: A Biography*. Berkeley and Los Angeles: University of California Press, 1967.

  Considered one of the best treatments of Augustine's thought and particularly interesting for the ties between life events and intellectual developments.

- Cary, Phillip. *Augustine's Invention of the Inner Self: The Legacy of a Christian Platonist*. Oxford: Oxford University Press, 2000.

  More demanding reading than many others recommended here, but insightful treatments not only of Augustine, but also of Plato and the Neoplatonists, and Aristotle; relevant also to the inside-out epistemology of modernity treated in Chapters 2 and 3; and to Christian anthropology in Chapter 9.

- Kenny, Anthony. *A New History of Western Philosophy*. Oxford and New York: Oxford University Press [2007] 2010.

  Contains Kenny's four volumes from 2004 to 2007 in one book. Considered the best history since Copleston, it could also have been placed under general readings, but is placed here due to his particular expertise on Aristotle and Thomas.

- Wertheim, Margaret. *Pythagoras's Trousers: God, Physics, and the Gender Wars*. New York: Random House, 1995.

  Provides excellent insights into the influence of Pythagoras; incorporates a feminist perspective; and is just plain fun to read—Wertheim is a science writer rather than an academic.

2 Modern epistemology and the possibility of theology

- Livingston, Donald W. *Hume's Philosophy of Common Life*. Chicago and London: Chicago University Press, 1984.

  Of all the commentaries on Hume, this one has given me what I believe is the best interpretation of Hume's concerns and of the relations among his various writings.

- Schleiermacher, Friedrich. *On Religion: Speeches to its Cultured Despisers*. Trans. by John Oman. Intro. by Rudolf Otto. New York: Harper and Row, 1958.

  I don't think it is possible to appreciate the radical turn in modern theology without reading Schleiermacher himself. Originally published in 1799, revised several times, and translated later by Richard Crouter in 1988, I chose the 1958 edition because I have been told that it is a better translation of the German text, and because of my obvious appreciation for Otto's Introduction.

- Stout, Jeffrey. *The Flight from Authority: Religion, Morality, and the Quest for Autonomy*. Notre Dame, IN: University of Notre Dame Press, 1981.

A persuasive answer to the question of why modern philosophy came about when it did, and a depressing account of the effects of modern epistemology on theology (although I *suspect* that Stout may be more optimistic at this point).

- Toulmin, Stephen. *Cosmopolis: The Hidden Agenda of Modernity*. New York: Free Press, 1990.

    A complementary account of the origins of modernity, and brief remarks about the direction to be taken at its end.

- Wolterstorff, Nicholas. *Thomas Reid and the Story of Epistemology*. Cambridge: Cambridge University Press, 2001.

    Reid was a guiding light for conservative Christian theology in the USA, just as Kant and Schleiermacher were for classical liberal theology. Yet Reid is given scant attention in histories of philosophy, and he was a thinker ahead of his time in rejecting "the way of ideas."

3 Faith in late modern reasoning

- Bernstein, Richard J. *Beyond Objectivism and Relativism: Science, Hermeneutics, and Praxis*. Philadelphia: University of Pennsylvania Press, 1983.

    Bernstein devotes a section early in his book to "Cartesian anxiety"; that is, what if we follow Descartes in believing that there must be a universal, indubitable starting point for knowledge, and later philosophers convince us that there cannot be one? This book is one of the best antidotes to such anxiety.

- Brink, Gijsbert van den. *Philosophy of Science for Theologians: An Introduction*. Trans. by Chris Joby. Frankfurt am Main: Peter Lang, 2009.

    My chapter used philosophy of science to trace the development of post-foundationalism, and its consequences for understanding theological methodologies; van den Brink's book does the same, but at greater length. See my review in *Perspectives on Science and Christian Faith* (March 2011). It is also relevant to Chapter 8 on science and religion.

- Phillips, D. Z. *Faith after Foundationalism: Critiques and Alternatives*. Boulder, CO, San Francisco, and Oxford: Westview Press, 1995.

    Phillips and Plantinga are often seen as the most significant contestants for recent theological epistemology. My summary of Phillips could not do him justice, so here he speaks for himself, and addresses Plantinga, Richard Rorty, George Lindbeck, and Peter Berger.

- Placher, William C. *Unapologetic Theology: A Christian Voice in a Pluralistic Conversation*. Louisville, TN: Westminster John Knox Press, 1989.

    With the same goal as Bernstein's, this text is easier reading, and related specifically to Christian thought, but offers a *slightly* less confident antidote to relativism. Be sure to read the endnotes to each chapter that further develop Placher's thought.

- Plantinga, Alvin. *Knowledge and Christian Belief.* Oxford: Oxford University Press, 2015.

    This book, as with Phillips's, provides an opportunity for a much deeper and more recent understanding of his position. Shorter and more readable than his *Warrant and Christian Belief* (2000).

4 Faith and reason for the twenty-first century

- Chung, Paul Seungoh. *God at the Crossroads of Worldviews: Toward a Different Debate about the Existence of God.* Notre Dame, IN: University of Notre Dame Press, 2016.

    An excellent and readable account of MacIntyre's concept of tradition-constituted rationality. In addition, it supports the thesis of this entire text: that philosophical positions need to be understood within the context of the entire worldview (tradition) of which they are a part; it gives a more extended overview of recent developments in philosophy of religion, noting the relevance of twentieth-century changes in epistemology that were presented in Chapter 3; and spells out at length my brief comment regarding modern misunderstandings of Thomas's "five ways." Finally, it anticipates this text's argument (in Chapter 10) that Scientific Naturalism is now one of Christianity's most significant rivals.
- Knight, Kelvin, ed. *The MacIntyre Reader.* Notre Dame, IN: University of Notre Dame Press, 1998.

    I suggest that readers pay particular attention to Parts 3, 4, and 6; the interviews are remarkably enlightening.
- Lott, Micah. "*Reasonably Traditional:* Self-Contradictions and Self-Reference in Alasdair MacIntyre's Account of Tradition-Based Rationality." *Journal of Religious Ethics* 30, no. 3 (Fall 2002).

    A common criticism of MacIntyre is that he accepts the fact that standards of rationality and justification are relative to traditions, yet he claims to provide *a* method for rational adjudication among rival traditions. Lott provides a brief and readable refutation of this criticism of self-referential incoherence.
- MacIntyre, Alasdair. *The Tasks of Philosophy: Selected Essays, Volume 1.* Cambridge: Cambridge University Press, 2006.

    Pay particular attention to MacIntyre's first essay, "Epistemological Crises"; it provides the seminal insight to all of his later work on the nature of rationality and ties it to the stalemate in the philosophy of science of the 1970s. Also read carefully "Moral Relativism, Truth, and Justification."
- MacIntyre, Alasdair. *Whose Justice? Which Rationality?* Notre Dame, IN: University of Notre Dame Press, 1988.

    For a concentration on MacIntyre's understanding of how to adjudicate rationally among rival traditions, concentrate on chapters 10 and 18; for a much more insightful history of Plato and his predecessors, of Aristotle, Augustine, and Thomas than is presented in this text, read chapters 2, 4, 5, 6, 8, 9, and 11.

- Trenery, David. *Alasdair MacIntyre, George Lindbeck, and the Nature of Tradition.* Eugene, OR: Pickwick Publications, 2014.

    A fine account of the development of MacIntyre's thought, and additional justification for the claim of this text that his account of traditions and of their evaluation can be applied equally to religious traditions. Trenery helpfully chooses Lindbeck as a discussion partner for MacIntyre, thus adding valuable information about Lindbeck's position. He concludes that Lindbeck falls short in providing means of rationally comparing rival religious traditions, and therefore takes MacIntyre to provide an important complement to Lindbeck's work.

5 Three epistemological crises for Christianity in modernity

This chapter first considers epistemological problems facing the Christian Tradition throughout modernity and still lingering today. Because this section is largely a compilation of material covered in earlier chapters, I judge that no additional references need be added here. The second crisis is the role of higher biblical criticism in calling Christianity's truth into question, but it is treated briefly because an adequate treatment would require at least a whole text of its own. The third is the modern problem of religious pluralism, and again this is too vast a topic to be covered at chapter's length.

Biblical criticism

- Alter, Robert. *The Art of Biblical Narrative.* New York: Basic Books, 1981.

    Shows the value of reading biblical texts as literature in order to bring into sharper focus the Bible's most profound story.
- Frei, Hans W. *The Eclipse of Biblical Narrative: A Study in Eighteenth and Nineteenth Century Hermeneutics.* New Haven, CT and London: Yale University Press, 1974.

    Traces the change from taking the biblical worldview as that into which further developments in history were to be incorporated to treatment of the Bible as an object for scientific study. Along the way he illustrates the negative effects of the philosophy of language of the modern period, which took the meaning of language to be given by that to which it refers.
- Schüssler Fiorenza, Elisabeth. *In Memory of Her: A Feminist Theological Reconstruction of Christian Origins.* New York: Crossroad, 1984.

    Explains how to detect the surprisingly prominent role of women in the Bible, despite attempts by authors and later interpreters and translators who have minimized it.

- Thiselton, Anthony C. *New Horizons in Hermeneutics: The Theory and Practice of Transforming Biblical Reading.* Grand Rapids, MI: Zondervan Academic and Professional Books, 1992.

  Long and by no means easy reading, but it could be said to incorporate an encyclopedia's worth of knowledge about biblical criticism, and it relates it to trends in both philosophy and literary criticism.

Religious pluralism

- DiNoia, J. A., OP. *The Diversity of Religions: A Christian Perspective.* Washington, DC: Catholic University of America Press, 1992.

  Suggests changing the focus of discussions of religious pluralism away from the question of the salvation of adherents of other religions to focus more on the particular doctrines and aims of other religious communities.
- Kärkkäinen, Veli-Matti. *An Introduction to the Theology of Religions: Biblical, Historical and Contemporary Perspectives.* Downers Grove, IL: InterVarsity Press, 2003.

  Covers the history of the theology of religions from ancient to contemporary thinkers.
- Kärkkäinen, Veli-Matti. *Hope and Community*, Vol. 5 of *A Constructive Christian Theology for the Pluralistic World.* Grand Rapids, MI: Eerdmans, 2017, chapters 19 and 20.

  Having surveyed the history of Christian positions on religious plurality in his *Theology of Religions*, Kärkkäinen presents his own theological perspectives in these chapters. Chapter 19 argues that Christians themselves need not give up denominational distinctives, but they must come together in the fellowship of the Spirit before they will be able to engage in respectful dialogue with other religions (chapter 20). He bases his hope for such engagement on his theology of the Trinity.

6 The problem of special divine action

- Buckley, Michael J., SJ. *Denying and Disclosing God: The Ambiguous Progress of Modern Atheism.* New Haven, CT and London: Yale University Press, 2004.

  Valuable particularly for exhibiting the various strategies of the physico-theologians of what we call early modern science. The book is also relevant to Chapter 10, the development of a non-theistic culture in the West.
- Klaaren, Eugene M. *Religious Origins of Modern Science: Belief in Creation in Seventeenth-Century Thought.* Grand Rapids, MI: Eerdmans, 1977.

  The explanation I have relied on most in my account of the development of science stripped of divine action (in favor of natural laws) and, ironically, for theological reasons.

- Lewis, Geraint F. and Luke A. Barnes. *A Fortunate Universe: Life in a Finely Tuned Cosmos*. Cambridge: Cambridge University Press, 2016.

  A more readable exposition of fine-tuning than many others. Includes possible explanations apart from divine design; concentrate on chapters 1, 4, 7, and 8.
- Russell, Robert John, et al., eds. *Scientific Perspectives on Divine Action: Twenty Years of Challenge and Progress*. Vatican City State and Berkeley, CA: Vatican Observatory Press and Center for Theology and the Natural Sciences, 2008. Distributed by University of Notre Dame Press.

  The product of a conference sponsored by the Vatican Observatory to evaluate the progress made at five previous conferences that approached the problem of divine action from the point of view of six recent developments in the natural sciences. I particularly recommend the Introduction and chapters by Murphy and Peacocke.
- Thomas, Owen C., ed. *God's Activity in the World: The Contemporary Problem*. AAR Studies in Religion 31. Chico, CA: Scholars Press, 1983.

  Particularly useful for showing the difficulties in maintaining a doctrine of divine revelation without accepting the existence of special divine action in the world.

7 Modern problems of evil and suffering

- Allen, Diogenes. *The Traces of God in a Frequently Hostile World*. Cambridge, MA: Cowley Publications, 1981.

  Narrative in style, and more practical for *thinking about* pastoral applications than many other books in the field.
- Hick, John. *Evil and the God of Love*. London: Macmillan, 1966. 2nd revised ed. San Francisco: Harper & Row, 1977.

  Although this book has been criticized rather severely, no study of the modern problem of evil should begin without it. The contents of the two books are nearly identical; however, those who have had the patience to read both editions side by side see an evolution in Hick's thinking.
- Murphy, Nancey, et al., eds. *Physics and Cosmology: Scientific Perspectives on the Problem of Natural Evil*. Vatican City State and Berkeley, CA: Vatican Observatory Press and Center for Theology and the Natural Sciences, 2007. Distributed by University of Notre Dame Press.

  The product of a conference sponsored by the Vatican Observatory in order to bring up to date, in light of both biblical studies and current science, what had for centuries been the standard explanation for animal suffering and human suffering at the hands of nature (human or angelic Fall). It makes considerable use of the concept of fine-tuning, described in Lewis and Barnes, cited under Chapter 6.

- Tilley, Terrence W. *The Evils of Theodicy*. Washington, DC: Georgetown University Press, 1991.

  One of the best critiques of Hick's theodicies; uses contemporary philosophy of religion (speech-act theory) to reassess the contributions of Job, Augustine, Boethius, and Hume. The evil of theoretical theodicies is that they distract the reader's gaze from real evils, rather than encourage the countering of those evils.
- Wright, N. T. *Evil and the Justice of God*. Downers Grove, IL: InterVarsity Press, 2006.

  Leaning more heavily on the Bible, Wright makes points similar to Tilley's: evil is more serious than either our culture or theologies has supposed. He raises the question of how we can work toward the world we envision, in which we are delivered from evil.

8 Science and Christianity

- Brown, William P. *The Seven Pillars of Creation: Bible, Science, and the Ecology of Wonder*. Oxford: Oxford University Press, 2010.

  Brown demonstrates that most Christians fail to appreciate the diversity of perspectives on creation (at least seven) in the OT. (My favorite is chapter 5, his interpretation of Job.) This book is more imaginative—driven by a sense of wonder—than more argumentative treatments of science and Christian theology. He also draws out ecological concerns.
- Collins, Francis S. *The Language of God: A Scientist Presents Evidence for Belief*. New York: Free Press, 2006.

  Written by one of the greatest scientists of our age, this is delightful reading, in part because it incorporates so much of his own personal testimony.
- Dixon, Thomas. *Science and Religion: A Very Short Introduction*. Oxford: Oxford University Press, 2008.

  Students will appreciate the brevity of this book, but do not be fooled into thinking that it is in any way defective. Dixon claims that in the USA the broader topic of science and religion is commonly reduced to (often heated) arguments regarding Christianity versus evolutionary biology. This gives me an excuse to mention that there is now a plethora of books, written both by scientists and theologians, that manifest the compatibility of the two.
- Lindberg, David C. and Ronald L. Numbers, eds. *God and Nature: Historical Essays on the Encounter between Christianity and Science*. Berkeley, Los Angeles, and London: University of California Press, 1986.

  There have been a number of other fine histories of the relations between science and Christianity since this one was written; however, I include it in this short bibliography because, in my judgment, it single-handedly ("single-volumed-ly"?) put to rest what is now called the *myth* of the warfare between science and Christianity.

- Peacocke, Arthur R. *God and the New Biology.* London: Dent, 1986. Reprint ed. Gloucester, MA: Peter Smith, 1994.

  I would like to list all of Peacocke's works on science and Christianity here, but this was the first I read, and it has the advantage of presenting information available at that time on how to avoid reductionism in biology—a topic that is critical for the following chapter.

- Pennock, Robert T., ed. *Intelligent Design Creationism and its Critics: Philosophical, Theological, and Scientific Perspectives.* Cambridge, MA and London: MIT Press, 2001.

  It may seem to many that incorporating this book is an instance of beating a dead horse. Nonetheless, it is an impressive achievement, with 37 chapters presenting a wide variety of perspectives.

9 Christian anthropology, philosophy, and science

- Brown, Warren S. and Brad D. Strawn, *The Physical Nature of Christian Life: Neuroscience, Psychology, and the Church.* Cambridge: Cambridge University Press, 2012.

  Compact and easily readable; adds interest by incorporating brief biographical sketches. It is particularly important for current and future pastors because of the insights it presents regarding the implications for church life and spiritual formation of new discoveries in neuroscience that emphasize the bodily nature of humans.

- Juarrero, Alicia. *Dynamics in Action: Intentional Behavior as a Complex System.* Cambridge, MA and London: MIT Press, 1999.

  A critique of modern notions of causation and explanation that have, up to this point, interfered with a philosophical account of human action, along with an introduction to the "worldview changing" theory of complex systems. Not easy reading, but well worth the effort.

- Kerr, Fergus. *Theology after Wittgenstein.* Oxford: Basil Blackwell, 1986; Reprint ed. London: SPCK, 1997.

  At this point in the present text, it may seem that Descartes has now been left behind, but Kerr's witty arguments show that many significant theologians of our own day are still captured by the inside-out philosophy of the self that Descartes imported from the Catholic spiritual tradition into modern philosophy.

- Martin, Raymond and John Barresi. *The Rise and Fall of Soul and Self: An Intellectual History of Personal Identity.* New York: Columbia University Press, 2006.

  The most complete account I have yet to find of the development of concepts of human nature in the West, from ancient philosophy, through biblical times, and both theological and philosophical changes since, noting scientific influences.

- Murphy, Nancey and Warren S. Brown. *Did My Neurons Make Me Do It? Philosophical and Neurobiological Perspectives on Moral Responsibility and Free Will.* Oxford: Oxford University Press, 2007.

  Not easy reading, but in this distinguished author's judgment, one of the best arguments against neurobiological reductionism and in favor of a concept of mature humans as rational, morally responsible, and free, at least in the sense of not being determined by either biology or environment.

10 Naturalism and Christianity as competing large-scale traditions

- Barr, Stephen M. *Modern Physics and Ancient Faith.* Notre Dame, IN: University of Notre Dame Press, 2003.

  Barr's thesis, equally relevant to Chapter 8, is that recent discoveries in science are actually more consistent with Jewish and Christian doctrines than they are with the philosophy (or tradition) of Scientific Naturalism.

- Giberson, Karl and Mariano Artigas. *Oracles of Science: Celebrity Scientists versus God and Religion.* Oxford: Oxford University Press, 2007.

  A careful exposition of the views of six of the most accomplished anti-religious scientists, with a careful critique of the ways in which they present science as though it were philosophy and even alternative religion.

- Midgley, Mary. *Science as Salvation: A Modern Myth and its Meaning.* New York and London: Routledge, 1992.

  A clear, learned, and witty critique of the pretensions of scientists who extrapolate larger visions of the cosmos and humans' place in it from science itself.

- Stenmark, Mikael. *Scientism: Science, Ethics and Religion.* Aldershot, UK and Burlington, VT: Ashgate, 2001.

  Not only a clear exposition of Scientific Naturalism, but a critique of its claims to ground ethics and epistemology.

- Westphal, Merold. *Suspicion and Faith: The Religious Uses of Modern Atheism.* Grand Rapids, MI: Eerdmans, 1993.

  This is a perfect entry with which to end this bibliography. It presents the positions of earlier contributors to the Naturalist Tradition (Freud, Marx, and Nietzsche). More importantly for the purposes of this text: MacIntyre's method calls adherents of traditions to actively seek criticisms from their rivals and to evaluate them fairly. A book more for the church and seminarians than for the academy. The criticisms these three level against Christianity are all too true too much of the time. His first chapter is titled "Atheism for Lent."

Index

Achenbach, Joel (b.1960) 266

action, divine 3, 52–3, 78, 105–6, 115n14, 116, 123, 125–47, 183–4, 190–4, 206, 276–7, 281

aesthetics 21, 48

agency *see* human agency

agency-detection system 281–2

agnosticism 80, 119, 124

Albert the Great (1200–80) 30

Alexander, Archibald (1772–1831) 45

Allen, Diogenes (1932–2013) 9, 161, 164

altruism 244, 258, 283; *see also* pseudo-altruism

American Protestantism *see* Protestantism

Anabaptist(s) 170, 220, 250; thought 171; view of the soul 220–1; *see also* Radical Reformers

analytic philosophy 5, 55, 63, 66, 189, 239, 257; *see also* Anglo-American philosophical method

Anderson, Paula Sue (1955–2017) 4

angels, fallen 153; *see also* Fall

Anglo-American philosophical method: conceptual analysis 5, 54, 189, 239; *see also* Stout, Jeffrey

animals: Anabaptist views of 170; higher 28, 226–7, 250; suffering of 163–4, 168–72; *see also* Linzey, Andrew; Rolston, Holmes; Waal, Frans de

Anselm of Canterbury (1033–1109) 94–5, 98, 180

anthropic principle 173–4, 207

anthropocentrism 58, 161, 168, 171, 173, 179, 184, 292

anthropology: Christian 124, 181, 198, 209–50; and cognitive neurosciences 181, 198, 211, 241; theological 179

anti-reductionism 210, 240–1, 244–9; emergentist movement 245; role of context/environment in 246–8; *see also* physicalism, nonreductive

apologetics 12, 55, 90, 152; conservative 42; Lockean-style 43, 262; of Renaissance 114, 260; replacement for 117

Aquinas *see* Thomas Aquinas

Aristotelian–Thomist system 2, 36, 126, 285

Aristotle (348–322 BC) 12, 16, 20–2, 26–31, 190, 201, 266, 289; account of knowledge 97; influence of 13, 99; Islamic commentaries on 114; prime matter 16, 28; system of 97, 195; theory of motion 35, 47n25, 64, 82, 86, 96; *see also* hylomorphism

assumptions: Christian 202; endemic 152; logical 97; of modern science 183, 297–8; naturalist 272; patriarchal 92; theological 297

astronomy 19–20, 30, 74; of Galileo 129, 189–90, 195; heliocentric 36; of Kepler 129; new 84, 195–6; and theology 129–33

atheism 58, 61, 80, 100–1; anti-religion 279; anti-theism 261; and Deism 192; development of 106, 116, 124, 134–5, 190, 254–6; and liberal theology 141–2; methodological 272; rise of 252, 260–5; and science 147, 274; *see also* Naturalist Tradition

atheists *see* new atheists

atomism: ancient 127, 190; Epicurean 35; in epistemology 27; in human nature 238, 245; logical 66; in mathematics 36; modern 72, 82, 213; as philosophical system 195, 217; in physics 39n9, 127, 196, 213, 221, 241; and reductionism 249